BUBBLE BLOG

BUBBLE BLOG

*From Outsider to Insider in
Silicon Valley's Web 2.0 Revolution*

. . . . .

Richard MacManus

Typeset in 10.25/15 Mercury Text G1, designed by
Jonathan Hoefler and Tobias Frere-Jones.

Book design by Kevin Barrett Kane.

Paperback ISBN: 9798345973486

To Vic, Rosabelle, Harrison and James

CONTENTS

Innovation accelerates and compounds.
Each point in front of you is bigger than
anything that ever happened.
—Marc Andreessen

The Past is dead, and has no resurrection;
but the Future is endowed with such a life,
that it lives to us even in anticipation.
The Past is, in many things, the foe of mankind;
the Future is, in all things, our friend.
—Herman Melville, *White-Jacket*

Come, thou who makest such hot haste
To forge the future—weigh the past.
—Herman Melville, *Clarel*

BUBBLE BLOG

INTRODUCTION

■ ■ ■ ■ ■

MY SILICON VALLEY STORY began in September 2005, when I took my first trip to the valley—in fact it was my first trip to America. I'd just turned thirty-four, was born and raised in New Zealand, and had barely set foot out of my home country. I was running a tech blog that was beginning to make money, but only just.

Like anyone who works in tech but has never been to Silicon Valley, I had illusions about the place before I arrived. Some were formed by the books I'd read. I had thought all startup founders were crazy, mono-maniacal, and heroic, like Netscape cofounder Jim Clark, as portrayed by Michael Lewis in his book *The New New Thing*. But the founders I eventually met were strivers, like me. Many had been humbled by the dot-com boom and bust, so they were willing to listen to new ideas and new people—even ones from the other side of the world.

Some of my illusions proved correct on the surface, but I was ignorant of the deeper nuances. I'd imagined Palo Alto as an idyllic, tree-lined town with a main road full of cafés and burger joints—just like on the TV show *Happy Days*. That was largely true, but I hadn't envisaged the long, bumpy, busy, and dirty highways you must travel to get to Palo Alto, and which separate the rich and the poor of California.

I had also imagined Silicon Valley to be populated by a mix of rich old hippies and preppy MBA types. Again, this was true in broad strokes, but I had no conception of both how friendly these people would turn out to be (much friendlier than New Zealanders, I thought, or at least much more open), and how desperately much they wanted something from me. I didn't yet understand *what* it was they wanted from me; I just knew it had something to do with my blog.

To me, Silicon Valley was the modern embodiment of the American Dream in that it was a place outsiders could arrive at and begin their striving for a better life. And the thing is, everyone is an outsider when they first arrive in Silicon Valley; or at least, that was the accepted lore when I arrived in 2005.

Even Marc Andreessen, the guy who Jim Clark piggybacked off to launch Netscape in the 1990s, didn't come from the valley. Andreessen went on to become the internet's first rock star and the ultimate tech insider, but he was an outsider when he landed in the valley in 1993 (or so the story goes). He'd been raised in Iowa and went to the University of Illinois, so I imagined his journey west was not unlike that of W. Axl Rose a decade earlier, who famously—but possibly apocryphally—stepped off a Greyhound bus from Indiana and onto the hard but glamorous streets of LA.

Many years later, Andreessen would admit that he wasn't truly an outsider. "I used to think I'd traveled sort of this weird road from rural agricultural midwest all the way to high-tech Silicon Valley, and it was an unusual thing," he said in 2022[1]. But then he found out that Robert Noyce, the inventor of the microchip and one of the founding fathers of Silicon Valley, was also an "Iowa farm boy."

Some, like Andreessen and Noyce—would strike gold and set up camp in Silicon Valley for life. They would become the new insiders. Others, like me, would stumble into a version of the American Dream but ultimately go back home, to be outsiders once more.

As it happens, Andreessen is my exact contemporary (just over a month older than me). Like him, I completed college in 1993, in my case with a degree in English literature from my hometown university in

Wellington. I don't remember coming across the web, let alone Andreessen's Mosaic browser, during my studies. The closest I came to the internet was using Apple's HyperCard software for an information systems course.

Also like Andreessen, I took flight straight after college. But whereas he walked off the plane and into an engineering job in California, I arrived in Auckland, New Zealand, without a job and with dangerously low self-esteem.

A couple of years later—a personal dark ages of scrabbling for an identity or even a reason to live—I began tinkering with web technology through website builders such as Macromedia Dreamweaver and GeoCities. Several years after that, in 1999 (around the time Andreessen was starting his second company, Opsware), I finally got a job in the tech industry—if you can call technical writing and contract documentation a tech career. But I had at least turned a corner and found, in the web, something to strive for.

When the dot-com bubble burst in 2001, I was a web manager for Ericsson's NZ branch. Funnily enough, I was even an outsider in that company—they didn't know whether to put me in the IT team or the marketing team. I ended up in marketing, but I hung out with the IT guys at coffee and lunch breaks.

A couple of years later, in April 2003, I started a blog and called it Read/WriteWeb. Initially it was an outlet for me to explore the cutting edge of internet technology: things I didn't need to know to do my job but wanted to know because I was curious where web technology was headed. I didn't realize it at the time, but people in Silicon Valley were also curious about this because it was the depths of the post-dot-com winter.

By 2004, winter was thawing and Silicon Valley was experimenting with the web again. Blogs were one of the emerging technologies, along with wikis and primitive social networks like Friendster and MySpace. Because I was writing about these and other web trends, people from Silicon Valley began reading my blog, commenting on it, and linking to it from their own blogs. Amazingly, these people seemed interested in what an outsider—someone who lived seven thousand miles away, spoke funny, and had not gone to Stanford or Harvard—had to say about their industry.

It's almost impossible to believe now, but in 2005 not one of the top ten companies in the Fortune 500 was a technology company. The highest entry was Hewlett-Packard at number 11, but it had nothing to do with the web. Microsoft, which was coasting along at this point with its dominant Internet Explorer web browser, was number 41, and Intel was 50. It was a long drop then to Apple Computer at 263 and Amazon .com at 303. None of the other companies that would come to dominate our society were present on the 2005 list. Google had gone public in 2004, but it would not break the Fortune 500 until 2006. Facebook was a tiny startup working out of a rented Palo Alto office.

Today's list features three internet companies in the top 10 (at time of writing: Amazon at 2, Apple at 3, Alphabet/Google at 8) and a further two in the top 30 (Microsoft at 14 and Meta/Facebook at 27). These five companies led the way in creating the defining products of our current era—Facebook with social networking, Apple and Google with smartphones, Amazon and Microsoft with cloud computing.

This book starts in 2004, a time of transition for insiders and outsiders alike. Andreessen was searching for his next big thing after Netscape and Opsware. I was searching for myself and slowly making progress through blogging. The story runs until the end of 2011, when I sold my then full-blown media company and by which point Andreessen had become the most influential tech venture capitalist (VC) in Silicon Valley.

In those intervening years, several major tech trends happened that changed our society—and our culture. Hundreds of millions more people joined the internet in the first decade of the 2000s, thanks to a worldwide broadband rollout and PCs continuing their by-now-inevitable Moore's law advances. This allowed the social web to happen, with Facebook, Twitter, and other such companies becoming the centers of online conversation. Then the smartphone made it all portable, first with the iPhone in 2007 and then Android. Their respective app stores debuted in 2008.

A geekier revolution was also taking place in Silicon Valley—and indeed the entire tech industry—over this period. The World Wide Web became a full-fledged platform for startups. While web applications began as far back as 1993, with CGI scripting, it wasn't until the first decade of the 2000s that the computing environment became conducive to multimedia-driven, interactive websites. Browser technology settled after Microsoft was forced by the US government to compete in 2001 and, in 2008, took a leap forward when Google released its Chrome product. Online video wasn't really viable until 2005, when YouTube was created.

Meanwhile, Google and Amazon, among others, took advantage of "the wisdom of crowds"[2] to create powerful web products that increasingly seemed to predict what the user wanted—be it the right search result or the right consumer product to buy. Facebook and Twitter became platforms in their own right, allowing other startups to build on top of them. Also, data began moving to "the cloud" after Amazon launched its first cloud computing service in 2006.

All of this, which I chronicled on my tech blog, was bundled into a term that became a rallying cry for entrepreneurs in Silicon Valley: *Web 2.0*. It was coined in 2004 by O'Reilly Media, a technical books company led by Tim O'Reilly, a shrewd businessman who had built his career on watching carefully what computer programmers did and then documenting it before anyone else. *Web 2.0* was a clever term because it implied that this was a second generation of the internet. It was billed as a renaissance, a rebuilding of the startup scene after the dot-com boom and bust. The term meant nothing to the outside world, but it didn't need to—it was a term that startup founders could put in their PowerPoint presentations to angel investors and VCs, which in turn helped developers get jobs again in Silicon Valley.

As the Web 2.0 movement grew, in 2005 and beyond, O'Reilly and others attempted to retroactively define the term. But it resisted a firm definition, even after O'Reilly hired me and another blogger in August 2005 to write a book documenting it (that project was abandoned half a year later, just a few chapters in). Although O'Reilly Media went on to publish a one-hundred-page technical report on Web 2.0 at the end of 2006—written by a fellow tech blogger, John Musser—debate on the meaning of the term continued for several years after that. Over time, many developers positioned themselves against Web 2.0, disliking the hype that surrounded it and claiming it was empty of technical merits.

In any case, my blog—eventually ReadWriteWeb, aka RWW—became one of the defining Web 2.0 tech blogs. And, I must admit, I rode that hype wave for all it was worth.

I never got to meet Marc Andreessen—the ultimate insider—in person, but we did briefly communicate during my first trip to Silicon Valley. In 2004 Andreessen had begun working on his latest startup, the weirdly named 24 Hour Laundry. This company was building a DIY social network service that would eventually be called Ning. The premise was that anyone could create their own social network, similar to how GeoCities allowed anyone to create their own website in the 1990s.

The news about Ning's launch broke on Tuesday, October 4, 2005, on a relatively new tech blog called TechCrunch. It was the day before the start of the second annual Web 2.0 Conference, run by O'Reilly Media and held at the Argent Hotel in San Francisco. Andreessen wasn't on the event schedule that year (he had attended the inaugural Web 2.0 Conference in 2004), but he and his cofounder Gina Bianchini took advantage of the news cycle to launch their new company.

I was in town to attend the conference. The founder of TechCrunch, Michael Arrington, had kindly invited me to stay at his rented ranch house in Atherton, in the heart of Silicon Valley. (A couple of years later, Andreessen would purchase a $16.6 million Tuscan-style mansion in Atherton.) Mike had launched TechCrunch just a few months before my trip, and it had very quickly become the go-to blog for Web 2.0 news.

As soon as it launched, I'd reached out to Mike's cofounder, a British expat named Keith Teare, noting that TechCrunch "looks like a great resource about Web 2.0." Keith cc'd Mike, who immediately replied, "I am a big fan of your website and have been using it for leads on Techcrunch." We were similar ages—he was born the year before Andreessen and me—so we swapped emails and soon connected on Skype IM.

Since I was staying with Mike, I had noticed the TechCrunch post about Ning as soon as it went up in the early hours of Tuesday, about 1:00 a.m.—late-night blogging was all part of the adventure. The writer wasn't Mike, but Frederico (Fred) Oliveira, a young developer from Portugal who was also staying at the TechCrunch ranch. Both Fred and Mike were friendly to me, and I had felt an immediate camaraderie with them; we were "bloggers," and there was a lot of talk about Web 2.0 and the exciting startups emerging at that time, interspersed with rounds of Applewood pizza and episodes of *South Park*.

It had soon become clear to me that Mike was already an insider in this scene, by dint of his Atherton location and previous dot-com experience (he'd been a lawyer for startups). He had some kind of direct access to either Andreessen or Bianchini, or both, which I didn't yet have. Fred, too, had connected with at least one of Ning's founders, opening his own blog post about Ning by writing, "Gina from 24 Hour Laundry just IM'd me giving me the green light to talk about their project."[3]

I wrote a quick post that linked back to the TechCrunch post. I really had nothing to add, since I had not been given access to the product yet. But I wrote, "I can't wait to have a play." This initiated my first—and to this day only—direct contact with Marc Andreessen. Soon after my post was published, I received the following email from him: "Hi Richard—I read your blog—thanks for the kind words re Ning—if you haven't been activated for a beta developer account already, please send me the email address you used to sign up and I will turn you on!"

Marc Andreessen read my blog?! At this point, I knew I had found my calling. I emailed him back saying I'd signed up. A couple of hours later, he confirmed that my account was activated.

I felt like I'd just joined the ranks of Silicon Valley's insiders. And, as it turned out, tech bloggers were indeed the new nexus of Web 2.0.

PART 1

2004—2006

■ ■ ■ ■ ■

CHAPTER 1

AMATEUR JOURNO

■ ■ ■ ■ ■

I WAS A LONG WAY FROM SILICON VALLEY at the beginning of 2004, both geographically and in frame of mind. I'd recently turned thirty-two and had fine strawberry-blond hair that I obsessively brushed to keep neat, innocent-looking blue eyes covered by a pair of rectangular, semi-rimless glasses, and a ginger goatee with neatly trimmed sideburns. For my blogger profile photo I chose a selfie taken slightly from the side and cropped at my eyebrows, so that the top of my head was cut off. It accentuated my goatee and sideburns, giving me a kind of Max Headroom look. This was several years before selfies became a trend, so I was not looking directly into the camera. I was too awkwardly shy to do that anyway. Instead, I was self-consciously staring into the distance, as if dreaming about what life must be like in California.

"I'm a writer, web technology analyst and web producer," I described myself on my blog at the beginning of 2004. "The latter one pays the mortgage right now, but I'm working on increasing the influence of the first two in my career." And that, I wrote, was where my weblog came in. I worked for Contact Energy, one of New Zealand's leading power suppliers. As hinted at in my profile page, I found my day job rather dull—I managed the internal and external websites of the company, using a mix of off-the-shelf content management system software and whatever web publishing products Microsoft and Macromedia had at the time. The topics I wrote about in my blog were many years away from being a part of corporate websites.

Since I'd started it in April 2003, my weblog had mostly focused on analysis of the latest web technology trends—but it was also a learn-by-doing situation. I'd spent a good deal of time organizing the structure of the blog (creating the navigation, setting up subscription formats, deciding what to put in the sidebars, and so on), and I'd completed a full tableless CSS redesign in September. But I'd also veered off track at times, such as documenting my participation in NaNoWriMo—National Novel Writing Month—an annual challenge to write a fifty-thousand-word novel in thirty days, over the month of November 2003.

The "blogosphere" in 2003 and 2004 was largely made up of geeky people like me who treated the medium as a mix between an online journal and a tech-experiment log. I enjoyed testing new web technologies and applying them to my blog. At one point, I was "diving into XSLT to try and develop something interesting for my weblog's topic-based navigation"[4] (trust me, you don't need to know what XSLT stands for now). But blogs at that time were also personal, a reflection of the author's personality. I often referenced literature and music in my posts, such as comparing the Semantic Web to the hunt for the white whale in *Moby-Dick*, or starting a post about being a web generalist with a review of the Velvet Underground song "What Goes On" as performed on their *1969* live album.

Sometimes I look back on my early posts and cringe—did I have to write a post entitled "Liv Tyler waved at me" at 9:10 p.m. on December 1, 2003? No, I didn't, but earlier that day I'd attended a street parade for the world premiere of *The Lord of the Rings: The Return of the King*, a movie by fellow Wellingtonian Peter Jackson. It had been a beautiful sunny summer's day in Wellington, and I felt proud to be a kiwi—we were hosting a Hollywood party! In writing that post I was subconsciously connecting Jackson's Hollywood dream come true to my own Silicon Valley dream.

Silicon Valley felt very far away at the time, but at least I felt a sense of communion with it, thanks to blogging software and the World Wide Web.

During the first half of 2004, I was trying to figure out my role as a tech blogger and what topics I should focus on. I didn't know it, but several pivotal web-product launches of that time would help shape the future of Read/WriteWeb.

In February a young Harvard student named Mark Zuckerberg launched a new site called TheFacebook. Initially, its only users were his fellow undergraduates, but by the next month students from Columbia, Stanford, and Yale had joined the fledgling social network. Needless to say, all this was completely off my radar—I was halfway across the world and not a student at an elite American university.

Also in February 2004, a Canadian couple—Stewart Butterfield and Caterina Fake—launched Flickr, a photo-sharing website. While I wasn't immediately aware of Flickr, I was aware of the company that had launched it: Ludicorp. I had even written a couple of posts about it, or, more specifically, about its online game called *Game Neverending*, which I'd discovered at the end of 2003. I'd done one of those frivolous online questionnaires, this one entitled "What kind of Social Software Am I?" I could've been a wiki, a blog, the entire blogosphere, or other varieties of "social software" (the term we used at the time). Turns out I was *Game Neverending*, which I'd not heard of until that day. So I looked it up and discovered it was "a virtual world in which creativity and social interaction are the main drivers."

I never did get into the beta of the game, probably because by the time I discovered it Ludicorp had pivoted to Flickr, originally a mere feature of *Game Neverending*. I joined Flickr in August 2004, at the same time as I expressed an interest in exploring "multimedia blogging." By this time social software was well and truly in the air. I was also using a very geeky site called del.icio.us, which somehow made bookmarking a link a social activity. (The early success of del.icio.us in 2004 showed how nerdy the blogosphere was back then!)

But arguably the most impactful web product of 2004, certainly from a usage point of view, was Google's new web-based email service, Gmail. I joined it in July, a few months after the launch. Gmail was invite-only, but fortunately one of my blogger friends sent me an invitation code. Its most newsworthy feature was the one gigabyte of storage space, which was a hundred times more than what Yahoo and Microsoft offered. But what really stood out to new users was Gmail's use of DHTML (Dynamic HTML), a technique using JavaScript that enabled a web page to refresh itself in the background.

Funnily enough, Google hadn't invented this snazzy technique; it came from Microsoft in 1997. But Gmail was the first widely used consumer web product to base its user interface around DHTML. Later, in early 2005, a new term would be coined for this functionality: Ajax (Asynchronous JavaScript and XML). But regardless of the name, Gmail's interface seemed magical to many of us in 2004—for the first time, a major web product seemed as sophisticated as a desktop app on Windows PC or Apple Macintosh.

As if to prove that a new web era was beginning, Marc Andreessen quietly launched his third startup around the same time I joined Gmail. No doubt he'd heard all the buzzwords being bandied about within Silicon Valley and by bloggers like me—*social software, two-way web, user-generated content, tagging, microcontent,* and so on. The question for Andreessen, already a millionaire many times over, was what to do about it. He had dabbled in angel investing already and, indeed, would invest in his friend Reid Hoffman's social networking company, LinkedIn, later in the year. One option, then, was to use all his connections and capital and become a VC. But no, he decided it wasn't time for that yet. He still wanted to be "in the arena," as Theodore Roosevelt had once famously put it. (Roosevelt's full quote, "It is not the critic who counts. . . . The credit belongs to the man who is actually in the arena,"[5] has since become a rather obnoxious Silicon Valley maxim.)

Andreessen's third act would come to be called Ning. He later explained that at the time he started Ning, he was fascinated with Reed's Law, a form of network effects stating that a network becomes more valuable when people can easily form subgroups to collaborate.

The initial idea of Ning was to allow users to create "social apps" for groups. "Friendster hadn't worked, MySpace was just getting a little bit of traction, and Facebook was still at Harvard," he explained. "What we knew worked were focused applications: Craigslist, eBay, Monster. So our idea was to bring social into these domains, in the form of apps that groups could run for themselves: their own job boards, their own selling marketplaces, and so on."[6] It was this and similar theories of social software that fired the imaginations of entrepreneurs and bloggers alike in 2004.

Already, though, I had noticed a dark underside to the nascent social web. For all the geeky excitement and camaraderie that blogging and early social apps gave me, in my private notebooks I had started to complain about "the social pressures of the blogosphere—the need to be linked (loved), the quest for attention." Later, in a public post, I mused further on the emerging attention economy. "It may be a democracy of ideas, but sometimes it feels like a horserace,"[7] I wrote. These were early warning signs of what social media would turn into in the 2010s, on a mass scale.

But I put these premonitions of a darker side to Silicon Valley out of my mind. In 2004, as far as I was concerned, I was off to the races with my blog.

While trying to get linked to by an A-Lister, I inadvertently turned myself into a journalist. In March 2004 I interviewed Marc Canter, a Silicon Valley resident who was internet famous in the 1980s. Twenty years prior, he'd co-founded MacroMind—a company that created multimedia software for the Apple Macintosh. Through a series of corporate maneuvers I didn't understand at the time of the interview, by 1992 MacroMind had morphed into Macromedia. By that point, Canter had departed the company, but he'd be forever linked to Macromedia's subsequent success.

During our phone call, I was won over by Canter's loquacious charm. You can tell from my writeup that I was under his spell. I badly wanted to believe his tales of multimedia rock 'n' roll parties in the 1980s—the blaring music, huge video projectors, beer in the bathtub, smoke-filled hotel suites, and rented Cadillacs. His constant name-dropping and preposterous comparisons (he likened early MacroMind to the 1962 Beatles in Hamburg) only served to fire up my imagination even more about Silicon Valley.

I was also attracted to his talk about bootstrapping a cool startup and what it took to get such a company off the ground. "Every time I'd go do a demo or a speech somewhere," he told me about the first years of MacroMind, "I'd bring a couple of cases of software and I'd sell it at the back of the room."[8]

I was a nobody, living in a small country on the opposite side of the world, who was just interested in learning what was next in internet technology. Yet here I was talking to a Silicon Valley pioneer who had created and sold software products in the 1980s. I was a little star-struck, but also my fragile ego was boosted by this man's interest in me and my blog.

The resulting post was the first of mine to get a ton of traffic, after making the front pages of both Slashdot and Boing Boing, then two of the leading aggregators of tech news. It also resulted in my first article in a noted print publication. I sent it to the NZ version of *Computerworld*, and it turned up on page 16 of the April 19 edition. I was too excited to notice that my name wasn't even on the article! Nevertheless, I took it as a meaningful accomplishment in my young career as a tech blogger. "I'm an amateur journo (sometimes) and a professional web craftsman (all the time),"[9] I blogged after.

There's no getting around the fact that I was incredibly naive in 2004. It took me several years to understand what Canter was doing. Even though he was an outsider in Silicon Valley at that time—no longer in Andreessen's league as a startup success—he was striving to make himself relevant again. He was a professional insider, using his Silicon Valley history to lure in n00bs like me with his backstory. He exaggerated his past, making it more romantic than it probably was, and glossed over his mistakes.

The reality, as I discovered later, was that Canter had lost all his money in the 1990s. He took VC money for MacroMind in 1988, from the legendary venture capital firm Kleiner Perkins Caufield & Byers, and the plan was to do an IPO in 1991. But he was kicked out of the company in 1991, and the IPO plans were turned into convenient mergers. Canter had been handsomely paid off, but he blew it all over the rest of the 1990s on failed interactive TV startups and parties.

So at the time I interviewed him, Marc Canter was effectively starting from scratch in this new "social web" era and working hard to recapture his past success. His latest company, Broadband Mechanics, was building a product called PeopleAggregator, which Canter styled as a "digital lifestyle aggregator."[10] Naturally, he wanted attention for this new product, and he'd figured out that telling his story to bloggers was a way to get it in this new era.

The slashdotting was great for Canter, but it was also great for me. My blog was suddenly on the map with Slashdot readers, of which there were a large number back in 2004. So there was a symbiosis to our relationship as blogger and entrepreneur that I didn't fully realize until the slashdotting resulted in big page views and an increase in subscribers.

I met Canter in person the following year, during my first trip to the United States. He was forty-eight years old, a large man (over six feet and overweight), mostly bald and wearing a goatee and glasses. He favored bright Hawaiian shirts—daisy-chain yellows, electric purples, metallic pinks, tiger oranges—and was just as colorful in conversation. But for all his bluster and stories from the glory days of multimedia, he was also a family man—on his second marriage and with young kids. It made me wonder what it was like to have a meteoric rise in the startup industry when you're young, but then lose it all and have to scrabble to adapt when you're older. It was the flip side to the Andreessen story, which was the meteoric rise that just kept rising.

Only now, writing this book as a middle-aged man myself, can I truly empathize with what Canter was going through in 2004. His Web 2.0 story is just as much a part of Silicon Valley as the young rockstar founder story that he and Andreessen lived in the eighties and nineties, respectively. Nowadays, we'd say that Canter in middle age still had the hustle and was dedicated to the startup grind, but I don't think that quite captures what was going on when I met him. He was on the outer then, the same as me. But together, we could *maybe* get into the inner circle. He innately understood this, but I was just learning it.

In July 2004 the computer-book publisher Tim O'Reilly made a keynote speech at the Open Source Convention (Oscon), in Portland, Oregon. I listened to it while sitting at my desk in a Wellington city office building, via a podcast site called IT Conversations. O'Reilly had, starting in the 1980s, built up a successful publishing and conference business, which his own website described as "providing the picks and shovels of learning to the Silicon Valley gold rush."[11] As a tech analyst, he was someone I could relate to, and he too had an arts degree—although his was from Harvard, not Wellington.

O'Reilly, who had just turned fifty, had been doing talks like this for years. His modus operandi as an analyst was to closely track what developers were doing and build theories based on their activity. His favorite quote, which he repeated in every talk he did during the social-web era (or at least it seemed that way to me), was from the cyberpunk author William Gibson: "The future is already here, it's just not evenly distributed yet."[12] This was aspirational for O'Reilly, who had taken it upon himself to distribute—via books and conferences—the future that he saw developers building.

But even O'Reilly couldn't have known how right he would be when he told the Oscon 2004 audience, "Many of you are doing things that are going to be embraced by millions of people two or three years from now, or five years from now, or ten years from now."

The phrase *network effects* was repeated multiple times during his talk; he pointed to Amazon, Google, and eBay as companies that had already built large networks in their respective niches and thus had "opportunities for data lock-in." Even the newly launched Gmail was ripe for network effects. However, O'Reilly had a warning. "The real big issue about Gmail is who's going to own that data," he said. He knew damn well that centralization is the natural corollary to network effects, and that this could lead to the kind of monopoly behavior that Microsoft was infamous for during the first web era. So he laid down a challenge to the developers in the audience: create open-source peer-to-peer applications. "We have to Napsterize the address book and the calendar, we have to figure out how to make these things peer-to-peer applications, so that we own the data."[13]

Of course, it didn't turn out that way. We don't own our social network data nowadays, nor do we own "our data about who we communicate with and why," as O'Reilly had hoped for in 2004. Was he naive to think this was possible back then? Well, his job was to inspire developers and get them to buy his books. He could only lead them to the open-source P2P water well—it was up to them to drink from it.

There was no mention of the term *Web 2.0* during O'Reilly's Oscon keynote, but around June 2004 his company had begun to advertise its newest event, the Web 2.0 Conference, to be held in San Francisco in early October. The target audience for this was not developers, but businesspeople and investors. The theme would be "The Web as Platform," and the speaker list (which was overwhelmingly white and male) included Andreessen, Amazon founder Jeff Bezos, and a host of Silicon Valley VCs.

By the time October rolled around, there had been a marked shift in O'Reilly's attitude to network effects. The Web 2.0 Conference was, of course, where the term *Web 2.0* was introduced, and given the audience, it quickly became a capitalistic rallying cry for the internet industry. So, now, network effects were being *embraced*—not challenged, as at Oscon 2004. It was suddenly business time, not a time for open-source advocacy.

In the conference opening, cochair John Battelle (a media operator in his late thirties with whom I would later do business) talked about the opportunities in the new web era. He referenced one of O'Reilly's current theories, the "architecture of participation," explaining that it was "this idea of building your business by letting your customers build your business." This was another way of saying that a startup could build network effects with user-generated content, which formed what O'Reilly (who loved to dream up new terms) called "collective intelligence."[14] Battelle pointed to Amazon, Google and eBay—the same few companies O'Reilly had mentioned at Oscon, but this time flipped to become examples that entrepreneurs should strive to emulate.

It was striking how much the tone had changed in the two months between Oscon and the first Web 2.0 Conference in early October. Now it wasn't about challenging the network effects of companies like Amazon and Google, it was about "harnessing" network effects for your own business purposes. Perhaps the Google IPO, which took place in August—in-between Oscon and the Web 2.0 Conference—was the catalyst for this shift in emphasis, from Napsterizing the web to commercializing it instead.

Marc Andreessen's panel, held on the first day of the conference, was entitled "Lessons Learned, Future Predicted." This was just a couple of months after Andreessen had quietly founded Ning, which would be attempting to achieve network effects in the "social apps" market. In the session, Andreessen made no mention of having started something new; he was content to reminisce about the past, talk smack about Microsoft, and make generic predictions about the future (as he did regularly in media interviews). He was at this event to network with other entrepreneurs, perhaps raise some VC money, and pick up clues for success in this new web era. He wasn't here to talk his next book.

Nevertheless, it quickly became clear that Andreessen intended to get in on this new network-effects gold rush. He acknowledged that software was increasingly open source and that "the new lock-in is clearly data." He compared the new crop of data-oriented tech companies—Amazon, Google, eBay—to the "walled gardens" of the dot-com era, such as AOL and CompuServe.

Andreessen's assessment of the current internet business scene was that it was based on "eBay envy." It's easy to forget now, but in 2004 eBay was seen as a better business than both Amazon and Google. Its market cap was $77 billion, larger than Amazon ($18 billion) and Google ($23 billion) combined. Google, fresh off its IPO, was undoubtedly the sexier business, but eBay was the one everyone wanted to emulate.

"eBay built an enormous business around network effects by having the data lock-in," said Andreessen, explaining that you can't get your reputation data, purchase history, or store data out of eBay. "There are APIs and they let you do certain things, but it's all very carefully controlled and sort of a plantation owner / sharecropper kind of relationship,"[15] he concluded.

Even in 2004, many years before cancel culture, the plantation owner analogy was a risky one to use when talking to an audience of mostly white males. One of the other speakers, Dan Rosensweig of Yahoo, quipped that he couldn't be a plantation owner because he was a "northeastern liberal Jew," which elicited a round of laughter from the audience.

Dodgy analogies aside, it was clear Andreessen aspired to become a data plantation owner for this new era. "It makes total sense from a business standpoint," he said, before conceding that "it is a form of proprietary lock-in that is at least as strong as the form of lock-in that people used to have at the software layer."

He also sounded a warning that many people forgot about in the years to come, one that would prove fatefully accurate. He pointed out that a small startup with an open policy on data—he mentioned del.icio.us as an example—could easily change its terms and conditions later, or implement technical restrictions that make it difficult to move your data. So even a company founded on the idea of open data could lock it down at any time (as indeed happened with Twitter in the early 2010s).

Andreessen's final comment in the panel was an answer to a question from the audience, from none other than Marc Canter. He wanted to know if Andreessen would put his financial support behind open data standards such as FOAF (the friend-of-a-friend protocol). It's not about the money, replied Andreessen. "The day the major social networking sites actually start to support it," he said of FOAF, "it'll have some relevance." But, he added ominously, "there's nothing that can be done to coerce those companies into supporting it, other than end-user demand."[16]

I monitored the first Web 2.0 Conference from afar. I was intrigued by the potential start of a new movement on the web, so I reached out to Tim O'Reilly and asked to interview him for my blog. He agreed, and in November 2004 we did a Skype call.

I called him from my day job at the power company in Wellington. The office was open-plan, and I couldn't do the call at my desk when it had nothing to do with my job. So I hid myself away in a small conference room. I told a couple of the developers I was friendly with about the true nature of the call, but the IT and marketing project managers I interacted with daily knew nothing about it. If they had peeped into the conference room during that hour, they may've thought I was talking to a local web-design company about our company intranet.

I was nervous about the call and felt some impostor syndrome. At the start, O'Reilly was friendly but also a little sniffy. For my first question, I asked what key insights about Web 2.0 he had gotten from the conference that he didn't know beforehand. "When you work on putting together the program, you know what's in it, so I wasn't surprised terribly much by anything," he replied.

Oh Lord, I thought, *he already thinks my questions suck!*

I would later learn that this was what O'Reilly was like to everyone: outwardly friendly, but also somewhat arrogant. He was a self-important man and in love with his own theories, of which he had many. But at the time, fresh off the conference, I was fascinated by those theories and how they could potentially provide a framework for my tech blog. As the interview progressed, he warmed to me and seemed to appreciate the thought I had put into my observations about his Web 2.0 concept.

I asked him about one of his new catchphrases, "the commoditization of software," and how the nineties software giant Microsoft might adapt to the Web 2.0 era. "Microsoft remains committed to locking users in with their software," I said, citing the company's new operating system work-in-progress, code-named Longhorn (it was renamed Windows Vista the following year). In reply, he compared Microsoft to IBM in the 1980s, which had had to adapt its business in response to the changing tech environment. Microsoft would have to do the same, O'Reilly told me. "They can't keep up with the pace of a web-based offering, where you can roll out new products to all your users without even asking, and update products dynamically," he said. This turned out to be spot on; Microsoft morphed into a cloud computing giant in the

2010s, and its office software is now a successful meld of desktop application and online updates.

Other predictions from the interview were less accurate, in hindsight. One of my questions was about RSS (Really Simple Syndication), an open protocol that was fast evolving into the default method for syndicating content. Importantly, in 2004 it was the way people subscribed to blogs like mine, by copying and pasting an RSS address (a hyperlink) into an RSS reader, which was either a desktop or a browser application. RSS had a distinctive orange button that became a feature in the sidebar of all blogs. I also had separate buttons for My Yahoo! (Yahoo's latest portal, which, as of September, doubled as an RSS reader) and a product called Bloglines (my preferred RSS reader, as it was browser-based).

"RSS is clearly, far and away, the most successful web service to date," O'Reilly told me. He likened it to HTML and predicted that it would take over the internet just like HTML did. "We're basically dealing with a world of information overload and being able to tailor your personal portal is a pretty powerful idea." This was a highly attractive idea to web geeks like me. Unfortunately, RSS would eventually be usurped by social media feeds. As Andreessen had articulated at the Web 2.0 Conference, the fate of open standards ultimately depends on whether the big tech companies adopt them. As it grew popular, Facebook could've adopted RSS. But it didn't, because supporting an open standard for feeds would not provide data lock-in.

Like almost everyone else, I failed to see the downsides of network effects at the time. Perhaps because I was too distracted watching my RSS subscriber numbers going up.

The feedback I got from the O'Reilly interview, which I published in three separate posts over a one-week period that November, was really encouraging. For the first time, it seemed to me, it wasn't just fellow bloggers leaving comments on my blog, but people in the internet industry who were grateful for the insights.

Read/WriteWeb was far from being a full-time business, but I had been experimenting with monetization. At the start of December, I began participating in a sponsorship program that—in retrospect—now looks incredibly clumsy and naive. I announced on my blog that I'd be "paid US$800 per month for 3 months to write 1 blog post per week about a company called Marqui."[17] Canter had set this up, and a group of fifteen bloggers had signed up. We were being fed story ideas from Marqui, a product I knew nothing about at first and then discovered to be a rather unimpressive content management system for marketers.

A month into the program, I was having reservations. "I get emotionally attached to (and therefore write about) innovative Web 2.0 products and services like Flickr, del.icio.us, Bloglines, Feedburner, Pub-Sub, etc.," I wrote. "Marqui isn't one of those kinds of products."[18] The blogosphere was debating whether the Marqui bloggers were "shills," and there was also an email backchannel involving the sponsored bloggers, Marqui management, and various A-list bloggers of the time. But I found the discussions, including with my own readers, stimulating, and it was a learning curve for us all about what was—and wasn't—acceptable in trying to make money with blogging. Ultimately, I decided it was a failed experiment and so declined to renew the contract at the end of the three months.

Also at this time, I was setting up a new company with a fellow kiwi blogger, Phil Pearson. We may well have been the only two bloggers in New Zealand at that time, so we'd come up with the idea of starting our own services company for social software—principally blogs and wikis. We called it Weblog Solutions, and the company was registered in December 2004. The idea was to help NZ companies set up corporate blogs and advise them on how to use them, whether for marketing, project management, or "knowledge management" purposes.

It was a solid business idea, but unfortunately neither Phil nor I was adept at rustling up sales or promoting ourselves. We never did land a client, but we also didn't try very hard. Both of us had more than enough work on our plates already. He was an in-demand web programmer, while I was a web manager by day and a striving blogger by night (and sometimes during the day, hidden away in conference rooms).

At the end of the year, I did a post that would become an annual Christmas tradition on Read/WriteWeb. I titled it "Best Web 2.0 Companies of 2004" and named Google the best Web 2.0 BigCo, Flickr the best Web 2.0 LittleCo, and Feedburner (an RSS statistics app) most promising.

By this point, it was clear what the focus of my blog would be going forward: Web 2.0. I defined Web 2.0 as simply "using the Web as a platform," and this was a good enough guiding spirit for the new year.

CHAPTER 2

COMING TO AMERICA

■ ■ ■ ■ ■

ON A FRIDAY AFTERNOON at the end of September 2005, I set foot on American soil for the first time. I was greeted at San Francisco Airport by a big guy with tousled light brown hair, wearing a short-sleeved blue button-up shirt hanging loose over a pair of cargo shorts. He was tall—about six foot three, I guessed—so he towered over my five-foot-eight frame. I remembered that Marc Andreessen was six-three too, with the same large frame as this man, so I briefly wondered whether all Americans were this massive.

"Richard? Hi, I'm Mike," he said, and shook my hand. It had been a twelve-hour overnight flight and I hadn't slept, so my brain felt foggy. Plus, I was overwhelmed by finally being in the land of opportunity. I smiled and mumbled something like "great to meet you," and he led the way to his car.

Soon we were heading south down the famous 101 highway, in Mike Arrington's open-top sports car. It was so bright and hot that I was worried I'd get sunburned, so I took sun cream out of the laptop bag I was clutching and began applying it. Mike, who was tanned and relaxed in the driver's seat, looked over at me, bemused and perhaps wondering what kind of weirdo he'd taken in. "I have fair skin," I said, embarrassed and already feeling out of place in sunny California. We talked a bit about blogging and the startups we were both covering on our respective blogs, although I found it hard to hear amid the whirl of the motorway and the *thwack-thwack-thwack* sound of the tires on the road as we drove at speed down the 101. My ears were also still partially blocked after the flight.

We arrived at Mike's rented house in Atherton. It was set back from the street, with a large pine tree out front and the driveway sloping into the front entrance. The house, which was long and rectangular and had a flat roof, was painted sea green with white trim. I'd later learn that it was a 1950s Eichler-style house, also known as California Modern, and that there were more Eichler homes built in Palo Alto (a few miles further south, down the 101) than in any other city in the Bay Area. So this rented house in Atherton was the epitome of Silicon Valley—and indeed, a decade later, the main characters in the TV show *Silicon Valley* would occupy a house that reminded me a lot of Mike's.

It turned out that Mike had just moved into the house a few weeks ago, having shifted from LA to Silicon Valley to get back into the startup scene. He'd written about his new home on his personal blog, focusing especially on the backyard, which was on a one-acre section and featured a four-hundred-year-old oak tree. Socializing was clearly on his mind when he rented it. "The house is old but should be very nice for parties, with a large living room and huge patio," he'd noted. Indeed, almost as soon as he moved in, he held his first BBQ meetup, which would soon become a regular Silicon Valley fixture.

As Mike opened the front door of the house, we were ambushed by a large chocolate-brown Labrador retriever, who tumbled outside and began leaping up at me. "This is Laguna," Mike said, assuring me that she was enthusiastic but would soon calm down. Then out stepped a lean-looking guy with messy dark hair, a pale red top, and black jeans, who produced a tennis ball and proffered it to Laguna. This thankfully distracted the dog from me but got her even more excited. "Oh, this is Gabe," said Mike, as Laguna clamped down on the ball and tried to wrestle it away. "You know him from Memeorandum, of course." Mike then mock-admonished Gabe for riling up his dog again.

I had been testing an awkwardly named tech-news aggregator called tech.memeorandum over the past few months and had written my first review of the fledgling service a couple of weeks before. I'd been communicating with its American creator, Gabe Rivera, over email and Skype IM, so we nodded to each other as he continued to play with Laguna (who showed no signs of calming down). Gabe's site would later be renamed Techmeme and became the leading aggregator of tech news in the valley.

We walked inside and into the living room. It had seventies decor, with beige shag carpet and mahogany wood paneling adorning the walls. Mike pointed me to a small room at the top of the hallway to the left, empty except for a futon on the floor and a small dresser; this would be my room for the duration of my two-week stay. "Hey Fred," yelled Mike down the hallway, "come meet Richard."

Fred Oliveira, a Portuguese programmer and blogger in his early twenties, came out of one of the rooms to greet me. He was wearing a yellow designer T-shirt and slim blue jeans. Despite also being a Silicon Valley n00b like me, Fred looked self-assured and comfortable: the opposite of what I felt at that moment. He was working for edgeio, a company owned by Mike and Keith Teare, which at the time was the primary business venture of the pair. He'd also done the web design for TechCrunch, Mike's blog, which had started out a few months prior as the research vehicle for edgeio. As Mike had explained to me in his introductory email back in June, the idea for TechCrunch came about because his VC friends kept asking him what this or that company was all about and how it fit into the bigger Web 2.0 picture. "And since I am trying everything out anyway, why not write about it?" he'd said.

Fred warmly shook my hand, and we all joked around while Laguna bounced and barked at the newest member of this Silicon Valley blogger fraternity—me. I was relieved that everyone was so friendly, even this large dog nipping at my chin.

In later trips to the United States, I'd learn to stay awake as long as possible into the evening to make the jet lag more palatable the next day. But on this first trip, I was exhausted from culture shock and lack of sleep on the plane, so by the end of the afternoon I had passed out on the futon in my small room. I heard Mike knock on the door and say there was pizza and beer for dinner, but while I didn't want to appear rude to my host, I couldn't rouse myself again.

The next morning, a Saturday, I felt much better and immediately joined the others in the room at the end of the hallway, to the left. This was Mike's home office, and Fred worked from it too. Gabe had set up a temporary desk so that all of us could be together during my stay. Mike's desk was in one corner and held an elevated black MacBook, a bunch of books, notepads, piled-up cardboard software boxes, and various other bits (pens, stapler, and so forth). Random printouts and postal mail pieces were strewn on the floor beside his desk. On the window looking out to the front yard he'd pasted a TechCrunch sticker—the lowercase *tech* in red (resembling the Web 2.0 Conference logo), the *crunch* in a blocky black font, and a tiny vertical *.com* in black at the end.

I set up my laptop at my small borrowed desk and duly logged on to check the news on tech.memeorandum. "Google Confirms Free San Francisco WiFi Plans" was the top story, from an Indian American blogger named Om Malik. He was one of the rare early tech bloggers who was an actual journalist—he'd worked for *Forbes* and *Red Herring* during the 1990s. Om's blog was then rated number 96 on the Technorati Top 100, a new blog directory that was beginning to make waves among the blogger community. There were relatively few tech bloggers on the list at this point, although a couple of "gadget blogs" were among the highest ranked (Engadget at 2, Gizmodo at 4) and the cyberculture group blog Boing Boing was number 1. Otherwise it was political blogs, like Daily Kos and Instapundit, that made up much of the top 10. Neither Mike nor I was on the top-100 list at this point.

The conversation soon turned to my accent, especially how I pronounced *web*—Mike told me it sounded like "weeb." The name of my site, Read/WriteWeb, was already a tongue-twister, so I figured this just made my blog even more exotic. Mike also ribbed Gabe about how unwieldy Memeorandum was to say and spell, so I wasn't the only object of his good-natured teasing.

I had to admit, TechCrunch was a great name for a blog and also captured Mike's personality well. Not only was he physically imposing, but he sometimes adopted a no-nonsense tone in his blog too. He wasn't afraid to dismiss, and even insult, new web products that failed to impress him. When Google launched an eBay copycat called Google Base in November 2005, Mike called it "ugly" and "not a very interesting application in its current form."[19] But most of the time he was a curious and generous reviewer of new startups. His September 2005 review of Facebook, before it had opened up beyond US college students, was a good example. Since Mike wasn't a college student, he couldn't immediately access the site. But he contacted one of the early employees and was given a demo account, to which he gave a positive review.

In person, Mike was also frank in his opinions—he wasn't one of those tall people who slouched. He even said at one point during my stay, "I'm comfortable in my own skin." I remember it clearly because I felt the exact opposite at that time. As Mike became well-known in the tech industry over the next year or two, his self-confidence would often be mistaken for arrogance by other people. But I never had that impression of him. He was a confident man, for sure, but he also had a wry sense of humor that told me he didn't take himself too seriously.

I enjoyed my new surroundings, but I still felt overwhelmed by them and unsure of my status in Silicon Valley. One evening, while we were chatting alone in the backyard, Mike told me that he too was an introvert—it may not look like it, he said, but he often had to retreat to his bedroom to recharge his energy. I appreciated him telling me this because to me it looked like he was already the alpha tech blogger, even if Technorati hadn't yet recognized it.

The Web 2.0 Conference kicked off on Wednesday, October 5, at the Argent Hotel on Third Street in San Francisco. I'd gone into the city on the Caltrain earlier in the week, to take in the sights of Haight Street and familiarize myself with the Union Square area. But today would be my first experience of a tech event in America.

Since I wanted to arrive early on the first day of the conference, I'd arranged to catch a lift into the city with Keith Teare, Mike's business partner. Mike was more relaxed about the event, and he had posts to write, he told me, so he would arrive later.

Keith was a balding, fifty-one-year-old Englishman with a long history of running startups—he'd cofounded a London internet service provider and internet café in the 1990s, then moved his family to Palo Alto in 1997 and founded a domain-name service called RealNames. That company hired Mike, as a lawyer, in 1999.

During my stay at Mike's house, Keith dropped by regularly. He always seemed businesslike and even a little stern. He had firm opinions on startups and business strategy, which I took note of but didn't engage him in conversation about—perhaps I was intimidated by his industry experience. He usually dressed as how I imagined a VC would, in tan slacks and button-down shirt. I didn't get close to him, like I did with Mike, Gabe, and Fred, in part because I only saw him occasionally and in part due to the generation gap between us. (Ironically, I'm the same age now, as I write this, as he was in 2005, so I have more sympathy for his character now.)

A few months before I'd arrived, Keith and Mike had formed an incubator company called Archimedes Ventures. Although TechCrunch was technically a project of this company, Keith was much more focused on their nascent startup, edgeio, which aimed to be a classifieds site for the Web 2.0 era. As the senior partner and a self-described seasoned entrepreneur, Keith seemed concerned about how much time Mike was spending on TechCrunch. I would sometimes hear the two bickering over it. Even I could understand Keith's attitude toward blogging, though—it didn't seem like a proper business at that point. It was more like a hobby, allowing us to test new web products and meet like-minded people.

The Argent Hotel was a thirty-six-story building around the corner from Market Street, in the center of San Francisco. It was an impressive building with stone flooring, wooden panels, and gold-and-mustard-colored decor. The yellow-patterned carpet and wallpaper were beginning to fade, however, probably because they dated back to the mid-1980s when the building had been constructed. Alongside the gold-leaf domes and chandeliers of the main lounges, the overall impression was of a somewhat tired opulence. It seemed more like a space for investment bankers, rather than internet entrepreneurs, to convene.

But then I remembered that money was indeed top of mind for many of the conference participants. In July, MySpace—the biggest social network on the internet—had been acquired by News Corp for a reported $580 million. That event kickstarted the internet economy, making Web 2.0 not just a new web era, but a new speculative market too. The race was on to build social software applications across a range of different "verticals." YouTube had launched its beta in May, Reddit launched in June, and of course Andreessen's Ning launched the night before the conference. These startups, and many more, were reaching for the shiny new brass ring that O'Reilly had named "Web 2.0."

A couple of other acquisitions were announced the night before the conference started. First, Yahoo bought Upcoming.org, an events service created by a tech blogger named Andy Baio. There had also been action in the RSS reader market, with NewsGator acquiring one of its competitors, NetNewsWire (it had been an eventful year for RSS readers—my personal favorite, Bloglines, had been acquired by Ask Jeeves in February). The excitement generated by this business activity was palpable on day one of the conference. There was an audible buzz in the air as hundreds of entrepreneurs, VCs, and bloggers talked startups, network effects, mashups, and other Web 2.0 theories.

As soon as I claimed my press pass at the registration desk, I headed upstairs to the second floor for the morning workshops. It turned out that all the rooms were tiny, which meant it was standing room only no matter which workshop you attended. If, that is, you could even get in—there were guards posted at the entrances to bar people from entering if it was too full.

Somehow I squeezed into one of the workshops and stood at the back, my laptop bag pressed into my side as others jostled for position. I spotted the only other New Zealander I knew of at the event, Nat Torkington—who worked for the conference organizers, O'Reilly Media. Nat was about my age and had lived in the States since the late 1990s, after marrying an American. We had gone to the same university in Wellington, at around the same time, but I'd not met him in person until today. Nat was an outgoing guy and a natural in-person communicator, traits that I unfortunately lacked. He made me feel welcome—"Great to see another kiwi here!" he yelled at me over the hubbub of the crowded workshop.

I had several contacts I was keen to meet. One was Joshua Porter, with whom I'd recently signed a book deal with for O'Reilly Media. He was a twenty-seven-year-old web designer from Newburyport, Massachusetts, who wrote a blog called Bokardo. We'd begun corresponding in November 2004 and soon developed a good rapport over email and through reading each other's blogs. In May 2005 we coauthored an article for the web-design magazine *Digital Web*, entitled "Web 2.0 for Designers." Torkington read the article and linked to it in O'Reilly Radar, his company's blog. This attracted the attention of the man himself, Tim O'Reilly, which prompted O'Reilly Media executive Steve Weiss to email me and ask if Josh and I wanted to turn our article into a book. Excited by this development, Josh and I wrote a book proposal and eventually signed a contract at the end of August 2005, which included an advance of $10,000 between us (to be paid over four installments). We'd delivered the first two chapters of the book just before the conference and would be meeting Tim sometime during the event to discuss the project.

But first, I had to meet Josh himself. We'd Skyped during the first morning of the event and arranged to meet downstairs in between sessions. Josh was a few inches taller than me and had a nervous, innocent air. He had rimless glasses, close-cropped brown hair—probably a number 3 or 4 buzz cut—and wore a red sweatshirt with black trim, with sneakers and blue jeans.

We both looked uncomfortable in our surroundings at the Argent, but we drank the bland hotel coffee while chatting about how bustling the event was. I realized that while I was naive about the tech industry, in Josh I'd met someone who was even less experienced than me—perhaps because he was young and from the East Coast. Regardless, it became apparent that I'd have to take the lead in our upcoming discussions with Tim O'Reilly.

When we were called up to see Tim, we made our way upstairs through the crowd and were hustled into a makeshift meeting room by one of the O'Reilly Media PR people. Tim was talking to someone at the back of the room, so tentatively we walked over.

He was wearing a tailored silver-blue suit with the same sky-blue button-up shirt that all the VCs wore over here. At fifty-one years old, his brown hair was thinning and graying at the sides, and he had a long chin that accentuated his clean-shaven face. His eyes were the same pale blue color as mine—no doubt we shared a similar Irish ancestry. As Josh and I approached, the person he was chatting to (probably an employee) peeled away, and he focused his inquiring, slightly skeptical gaze upon us.

I think Tim was curious about who I was, this nobody from New Zealand who had become one of the most popular bloggers about his own theory—Web 2.0. He scanned me with his arched eyes, the sides of his mouth creasing into a familiar smirk. It was the expression of a self-made businessman, someone who was among the pioneers of the commercial web and knew it. He didn't seem impressed by me, and why would he be? I was dressed poorly, in a pair of blue jeans and a brown dress shirt (I didn't even own a proper jacket at that point). And I was nervous about meeting him. Even though I'd interviewed him over Skype last November, I didn't feel like I had established a meaningful rapport with him at that time.

The awkward pleasantries finished, Tim began talking about what he wanted the book to be. In his Southern California drawl, which always seemed to my ears to have an overlay of condescension, he went over the highlights of his preconference article, "What Is Web 2.0: Design Patterns and Business Models for the Next Generation of Software." The five-page article was his first attempt to define Web 2.0. (This was an era when long articles were spread over different pages, partly to get more page views.) He wanted our book to flesh out the "design patterns" that he had established. We simply nodded in response, as it had become clear that our input wasn't required during this meeting.

One of Tim's design patterns was "Data is the Next Intel Inside," a phrase he used in all his conference talks and during most interviews as well. Just as Intel's microchip was the core ingredient in almost all PCs during the 1990s and into the early 2000s—and was branded as such, with stickers on the front of each PC bearing the slogan *Intel Inside*—the key ingredient of a Web 2.0 service would be its database. Like the microchip, custom data would power services such as Google and Amazon—so Tim's theory went—and would form the foundation of what he called the "internet operating system."

It was heady stuff, and Tim clearly had set ideas on what Web 2.0 should mean and how our book would help explain it to web designers and developers. It didn't seem to matter to him what new ideas *we* might bring to the table, and before we knew it, he was talking about some online publishing experiments the company might try out with our project. The words *the long snout* came out of his mouth—a phrase he repeated several times—appearing to indicate a possible new wiki publishing arrangement to complement the actual book. A few months later, Tim would publish an article propounding on his long-snout theory, which had something to do with using the internet to publish early and often. (I'll be honest, to this day I still don't know what it means.)

Before we knew it, Josh and I had been shuffled out the door so that Tim could prepare for his next talk. Back outside, amid the hubbub of the conference hall, we looked at each other quizzically. If anything, we were now even less sure of what our book was about, but there would be plenty of time to sort through the details when we got back to our respective homes. For now, we each had a workshop we wanted to attend, so we parted ways.

When I walked into the conference the next morning, a Thursday, I poured myself a cup of hotel coffee and wandered over to one of the round high tables in the foyer, where I'd spotted a couple of people I recognized. It was two of a small contingent of Irish entrepreneurs, Fergus Burns and Jonathan Hill. Fergus ran an RSS startup called Nooked, which I had recently begun to provide advisory services to, and Jonathan ran an email and SMS marketing company called Infacta.

"I see one of your lot has been bought," Fergus said to me as I shuffled in beside them and slurped my coffee.

"What do you mean?" I asked. He nodded in the direction of a short man with blond hair, wearing a salmon-colored buttoned shirt and an oversized black jacket. He was perched on the side of a chair, surrounded by people—mostly men with glasses and tan slacks.

"That's Jason Calacanis, and he just sold Weblogs, Inc. to AOL."

I looked closer at the man, who was about my age, and saw that his smile was a mile wide and he was loving all the attention. He was talking and gesturing; even across the room, I could pick up bits of his New York patter and the odd squeal of delight from his audience. Every now and then, someone would walk up to the group and shake his hand.

It turned out that Calacanis and his cofounder Brian Alvey had sold their company to AOL for $25 million. It was an impressive sum for what amounted to a network of blogs. The deal wasn't far off what Yahoo had paid for Flickr, the trendy Web 2.0 photo-sharing service, back in March. If I wasn't sure whether blogging was a career before today, I was now converted.

Weblogs, Inc. was a collection of a few dozen topical blogs, many of which were a subdomain of WeblogsInc.com. The highest performer was a gadget blog called Engadget, which had its own domain and was run by a young tech journalist named Peter Rojas, whom Calacanis had poached from his archrival Gawker Media. Although Rojas was the talent who had turned Engadget into one of the top blogs (at the time, it was ranked number 2 in the world by Technorati), Calacanis had an even more enviable gift: getting attention. I didn't know him then, but I would regularly see him on the tech-conference circuit in the years to come, and I was always impressed by his networking skills.

At one such conference a few years later, a colleague and I were seated at a dinner table with around ten or twelve people. Everyone was picking at their starch-heavy plates of food while engaging in the usual conference chit-chat. This meant asking or answering two questions: "And what do you do?" closely followed by "What's been the highlight of the conference for you so far?" This typical, rather placid, scene was playing out when, out of nowhere, a grinning Calacanis approached the table. He immediately began to regale me and my colleague with funny stories, delivered rapid-fire one after the other in his broad Brooklyn accent. It was highly entertaining, but it wasn't a conversation as such . . . more of a comedy routine. Before we had a chance to get a word in, Calacanis had moved down the table to entertain another group of people. Soon he gravitated to the next table—and all we heard then was appreciative laughter from his new audience.

But back to 2005. I turned to Fergus and Jonathan and asked if they were going to the Web 2.0 party at Swig tonight.

"Wouldn't miss it," Fergus replied. I felt stupid asking, as of course both these foreign entrepreneurs would want to be at the biggest networking party of the conference. Not only were there sure to be VCs and other moneyed people there, but the party was being sponsored by several of the hottest Silicon Valley startups: Flock, del.icio.us, Flickr, Odeo, Technorati, wink, and WordPress. Even better, as I'd been informed in an email from a PR person a few days ago, it would be "free open bar and grub."

I felt more comfortable at the Web 2.0 Conference that day, which I spent watching keynotes and meeting entrepreneurs (and investors) keen to pitch me their startups. I noticed that people actually sought me out in the hallways—"You're the guy who writes Read/WriteWeb, aren't you?" Sometimes I'd be approached by a young lady with an awkward-looking guy in tow. The woman invariably worked for a PR firm and the man was a startup founder looking for some press.

At the end of the day, I had some time to kill before the Swig party so I headed to a nearby pub called House of Shields. The night before, it had been the location of the Web 1.0 Summit—a counterprogramming event pitched at entrepreneurs who couldn't afford the ticket price of the Web 2.0 Conference and bloggers who weren't on a Technorati list. As a still-young Generation Xer myself, I appreciated the irony and camaraderie of a bunch of outsiders poking fun at the new thing while playing drinking games based on a bygone era (the blink tag!). But I was also unironically enjoying the excitement of the main event, so I had not gone to the Web 1.0 Summit booze-up. Perhaps I was afraid I'd be called a sellout (a very Gen X concern).

The bar had a large, yellow-on-red neon sign above its entrance: *House of Shields, Live Music.* Inside, it was rectangular in shape, with the bar running across almost the entire downstairs floor. The room had a lot of wood paneling and basked in a dim orange glow produced by yellow interior lights mixed with the neon outside. There was an upstairs section too, with tables, but I was on my own for now—I'd be meeting Josh Porter and the Irish lads here soon—and so I headed straight to the bar and sat on one of the stools.

The experience of sitting in a strange bar by myself, nursing an IPA, reminded me of something that had happened nearly a decade earlier. In 1996 I was twenty-four years old and living by myself in Auckland, New Zealand, in a one-bedroom flat in a run-down converted house. I was disconnected from people at that time in my life. I didn't have internet—I could barely afford to feed myself—and nobody I knew owned a mobile phone. Even though I had little spending money, I was desperate to get out of my empty flat one Saturday night, so I caught a bus into the city. I didn't know what I planned to do, but I had to do something. I'd just sat down in the bus when I heard a voice behind me.

"Hey, how ya doing?"

I turned around, and a guy about my age leaned forward, his face open and friendly looking. He had curly brown hair and looked a little ragged— he had a few days' worth of beard on his face, and his grey eyes looked tired. He was dressed in blue jeans and a nondescript brown-patterned flannel shirt. I thought he looked familiar, but I couldn't place him.

"Hi, I'm doing all right thanks," I said, just to be polite.

"It's good to see you again, man," the guy said, smiling. He reached over the seat and proffered a hand, which I shook on instinct.

"I know you from somewhere, don't I?" I said, weakly. I just couldn't place him. Was he a guy I used to know in school—that one who left early to become a butcher? He *did* look like him, with the curly hair.

This guy also had a world-weariness about him, which brought back more recent memories—of a friend I'd made at my first job, in 1994, after I'd moved up to Auckland to look for work. That was Zak, from Liverpool, who was a couple of years younger than me but vastly more street-smart. I'd had an exciting nightlife (also a little dangerous at times) with Zak. He was an alcoholic and had disappeared from my life sometime in 1995. He'd been the first friend I'd made in Auckland, so I missed him—which was partly the reason I was on this bus and talking with a stranger.

By the end of the bus journey into the city—about a twenty-minute trip, with all the stops—I'd realized that I hadn't met the guy in the seat behind me before. I think he'd known that from the start. Regardless, we decided to go to some bars together, since we were both alone.

He bought the first drinks—mine was a beer, his a club soda and lime.

"I'm a recovering alcoholic," he said, noticing my surprised expression. He explained that even though he no longer drinks, he still liked to experience the social scene of bars. I probably shrugged and thought nothing more of it. Maybe it reminded me again of Zak, who I doubted would be a recovering anything, wherever he was now.

We went to the usual watering holes in the city that night, ending up in some dingy bar on K Road at two or three in the morning. I don't recall the exact details now, but it was a subdued night and we'd told each other our life stories. Eventually we parted and I got a taxi back to my one-bedroom flat. I never saw him again, and I don't remember his name now.

If that night out had happened in 2005, would we two strangers have kept in contact? Perhaps we would've sent each other a txt on our mobile phones or connected on MySpace the next day on our laptops. Fast forward another ten years—2015—and we both would've had smartphones, and I probably would've looked him up on Facebook that very evening—perhaps while he was up at the bar, getting the next round. But it was still the nineties; people came into and out of my life randomly, and such connections didn't stick.

Sitting there at House of Shields, in at least one way it was no different to my life in the nineties. On this, my first trip to the United States, I hadn't yet figured out how to get my mobile phone to work. (I discovered later that I just needed to buy a temporary SIM card.) But I'd noticed other people making calls on mobile phones. One popular model was the Motorola E815—a clamshell-style device that ran on Verizon's CDMA network. It had been released earlier that year and represented the state of the art in mobile-phone technology. If you flipped it open, it revealed a screen just over two inches tall. The other half had small, cushion-like numbered buttons and a circular navigation pad above.

Unbeknownst to me, a few months earlier, Google had acquired a tiny startup named Android. The news had received almost no press, and Google kept whatever they were building behind closed doors for a couple more years. Meanwhile, Steve Jobs had publicly unveiled an

Apple "iTunes phone" in partnership with Motorola just weeks before I arrived in Silicon Valley. It was called the Motorola ROKR, and Jobs hated it. Fueled by that disappointment, Apple would soon commit to building a smartphone in-house.

All of that was in the future, as I supped my beer at the House of Shields—phoneless and lost in my own thought—and waited for my friends to arrive.

The Colors of Web 2.0 party took over Swig later that evening, filling both floors of the modern bar on Geary Street, a few blocks up from Union Square. The event notice on Upcoming.org read, "While the big guys are giving away stress balls and business card holders, Flock, del. icio.us, Flickr, Odeo, Technorati, wink, and WordPress will be tending bar all night (read: free drinks!), tossing out t-shirts that were not made in sweatshops (seriously)."

The bar was heaving with people when we arrived. Many of the young and hip partygoers were employees of the startups mentioned in the promo, or friends of theirs. If they'd been at the conference earlier today, it was only to hang out in the hallways. The people who attended the conference keynotes, like me, were the other half of the party: less cool and slightly older—a mix of investors, founders, PR folks, and bloggers or journalists.

I mostly stuck with my new Irish friends, talking over the hubbub of an overcrowded bar about the Web 2.0 scene and our places in it. I told them that Read/WriteWeb and TechCrunch together probably had 70 percent of the conference attendees as readers—with me mostly focusing on Web 2.0 analysis and Mike covering the new startups.

I was also writing a blog for ZDNet, an established tech-news brand owned by CNET. It was called Web 2.0 Explorer—"Tales from the Web 2.0 frontier" was the tagline I'd come up with—and in it I covered much the same material as on RWW, although I tried to give it more of an enterprise slant. I blogged about the "web office," the business models of mashups, and the like. Fergus pointed out that there was still too much overlap in audience, which siphoned away juice from my RWW brand. He suggested I write about Web 2.0 for mainstream news websites like

BBC or the *Guardian,* or even the Silicon Valley magazine *Business 2.0.* It was a good suggestion, as mainstream media had yet to discover Web 2.0.

Since Mike and Keith weren't at the party, I had to make sure I caught a Caltrain back to Atherton later that night. The last one left around midnight. The Irish guys had hotel rooms near Geary Street, so sometime after 10:30 p.m. I found myself walking back down to Market Street with Josh Porter, who was staying near the conference venue. We reflected on our meeting with Tim O'Reilly and discussed learnings from the event that we might want to put into the book.

We came out on Market Street where it connected with Third Street and continued down toward Second and First and Josh's hotel—I still had some time to kill before my train. I don't recall specifically what we were talking about as we trudged along, lost in our own dialogue about Web 2.0, but perhaps it was "structured blogging," one of the hot topics of the conference. That was all about publishing different kinds of information—like events, reviews, and classified ads—using semantic markup, so that aggregators could pick up the data from all over the web. It was exciting in 2005 because it would be a way of extending blogging beyond navel-gazing, which was what it was primarily known for at the time (a little unfairly, given that some of us were becoming journalists).

Josh was telling me about a guy he'd met at the conference, who was building a tool to help people do things like movie reviews on blogs. "If they want to write a movie review," he explained, "they simply fill out a form with helpful fields for movie reviews: rating it, a brief synopsis, principal actors, etc." Josh was the more pragmatic of the two of us; he was a practicing web designer who focused on the usability of technology. For him, blogging was a tool that could be utilized by ordinary people in order to help others. As we discussed movie reviews, he remarked, "Don't you really appreciate it when someone tells you whether or not to waste your time going to a movie? They've added two hours to your life."

I was more interested in the higher-order patterns of web design, so I was prone to highfalutin theories like "design for data"—applying web-design principles to data. Talking about movie reviews with Josh, as we half-drunkenly wandered around San Francisco late on a Thursday night, I might've said something like, "Amazon is more a virtual agent than a website nowadays. The generation of the web we're in now is almost a living one, it's about movement and application of information."

We were still deep in conversation when I suddenly stopped and checked my watch. It was about twenty minutes till the last Caltrain! "Holy shit," I exclaimed, looking around me in confusion. I didn't know where we were, and the street now looked dark and empty. "Where are we, exactly?" I asked Josh, feeling my panic rising. Neither of us was carrying a mobile phone—and regardless, a mobile version of Google Maps did not yet exist—so it took us several minutes of looking at street signs to ascertain where we were. The Caltrain station was at the end of Fourth Street, but we were on one of the side streets off First. If I wanted to make that last train, I'd have to run.

Josh could see that I was full-on panicking now, so he asked if I was okay. I just told him I had to go. I ran down the street toward what I hoped was Second Street. After a couple of minutes I was out of breath, and then realized that I wasn't heading toward Second at all! By now I'd left Josh behind (he'd probably shrugged and walked back to his hotel) and was completely alone, lost in a strange, dark city, in danger of missing the last train back to my Silicon Valley lodgings. I composed myself just enough to figure out the direction of Fourth Street, then broke into a run again. I had fifteen minutes to get to the Caltrain station.

Eventually I arrived at Fourth Street and stopped a moment, hands on knees and gasping for air. I forced myself to stand up again, and after a few heart-pounding moments, I ascertained the correct direction to go. I sprinted as best I could toward the train station. I had maybe seven or eight minutes in which to make it, and I was still several blocks away. My laptop bag flapped at my side as I ran.

Tears formed in my eyes, and I was making anguished guttural noises. A small group of homeless people ahead watched me approach with bemused expressions. One of them stepped toward me. "Hey guy, do you need some help?" I swerved around her and kept running. By now I was in an unreasonable state of fear—what would I do if I missed this train?! Would I have to sleep on the streets like those people I'd just passed?

Finally, I saw the Caltrain station and ran into it, nearly out on my feet by now. With just a minute to go before the train left, I made one last stumbling push toward the tall silver train with red trim and leaped into the last carriage.

The overwhelming feeling I had as I slumped into my seat, wheezing for breath and soaked in sweat, was relief. I wouldn't be left behind—I wasn't alone.

CHAPTER 3

SPICY NOODLES

■ ■ ■ ■ ■

EARLIER IN 2005, I had made some contacts inside of Yahoo and had begun to think about trying for a job there. One of my contacts was a search engine executive named Elizabeth Osder, and I'd told her my dream gig on the internet would be web strategist/blogger, with input into product design. She replied that I "might find a gig in strategy for a web company" and promised to ask around inside Yahoo. She also wanted to know about my experiences with running ads in my RSS feeds, so there was some quid pro quo going on in these early emails.

Havi Hoffman, who worked in Yahoo's newly formed social media outreach team, was another helpful contact that year. After I told her and Elizabeth that I would be at the Web 2.0 Conference, Havi invited me to visit the Yahoo campus in Sunnyvale. We agreed on Monday, October 10, the week after the conference.

When the day arrived, Havi picked me up from Mike's house in Atherton just after 10:00 a.m., and we began the twenty-minute journey to Sunnyvale. She immediately apologized for being a bit under the weather. She'd been working a lot on getting the new Yahoo! Podcasts network up and running, she explained. I told her I was just grateful she was driving and that I was excited about my first trip to a Silicon Valley campus.

Havi was in her early fifties and had a ring of thick curly brown hair that framed a kind, inquisitive face. She had oval-shaped glasses, which she nervously adjusted as she asked me about my trip so far. Her voice had the tentative sound of a shy person, but I got the impression that she knew a great deal about how Silicon Valley worked. She told me that she'd lived and worked here since the dot-com era—her first job at Yahoo had involved cataloging web sites when it was still a directory.

When we arrived, I was immediately impressed by the beautiful, expansive setting of Yahoo's headquarters. The green lawns were immaculately maintained, with purple shrubs that matched the large purple logo on the side of the main building, and young trees dotted the perimeters. It was the middle of autumn, so what leaves remained were a mixture of green, yellow, and a mauve purple. I don't remember seeing a single dead leaf on the ground, so both the lawns and the paths bisecting them must've been meticulously tidied every day.

Yahoo's campus was still relatively new; it had opened in April 2001, in the middle of the dot-com crash. Its four buildings, each made of concrete and encased in glass with grey metal frames, were separated by large, manicured lawns and volleyball, bocce, and basketball courts. Inside, employees enjoyed game rooms and a fitness center as well as work spaces. Distinguishing this campus from others in Silicon Valley, including Google's and Apple's, was the bright yellow and purple branding around the grounds—yellow padding on the basketball poles, yellow umbrellas at the outdoor tables, purple EFT-POS machines. Especially notable was the large yellow entrance to the cafeteria, which looked like a giant Lego block with a chunk cut out of it. There were no signs on it, although in later years it would be repainted purple and a giant white Yahoo logo added.

We walked into the reception area, where a computer was set up for visitor check-in. On the desk were a small bowl of Yahoo-branded mints and a couple of bottles of water. After entering my details, a "Yahoo! Passport" visitor sticker emerged out of a little machine, and I put it on my polo shirt: "Richard MacManus, http://readwriteweb.com" it read, with the final *m* trailing onto the second line. Havi then led me upstairs and down some corridors, and we entered one of the office areas.

It was a familiar open-office setup—rows of cream-colored cubicle desks, each containing two people. Dividing boards painted bright yellow with a purple sash bisected the desks, and two yellow stars on the side of each divider listed the names of the people who worked there. On the desks were the usual things: open laptops, desktop computers with hardware towers (there was even the odd beige-colored 1990s monitor with a huge carcass), dark grey mice, and office telephones. The room itself looked new, but otherwise it was not that different from the office environment of New Zealand.

The people at their desks looked happy, chattering among themselves as we walked through. I spotted remnants of a recent Nerf-gun fight, with purple-and-yellow foam darts scattered around the office. Havi led me to the desk of a guy who looked about my age. He had well-cropped dark hair and was wearing a mid-blue button-down shirt and dark blue slacks. With his clean-shaven, tanned face and gleaming white teeth, he reminded me a little of Tom Cruise.

"Richard, this is Scott Gatz," said Havi. Scott stood up and shook my hand, smiling broadly. I probably said something like "Great to put a face to the name," since Scott was the first Yahoo employee I'd interacted with over email. He was responsible for the My Yahoo! portal, and in our early interactions he'd referred to himself as "the RSS guy at Yahoo."

Scott led me to a nearby meeting room, and we talked about a possible job for me at Yahoo. I had a tendency, common among New Zealanders, to downplay my previous work experience—before I was a blogger, I'd been a webmaster and then web manager at a couple of local corporations. An American doing the same work as a young professional would probably list their job title as vice president of web operations on their résumé, but I was incapable of talking myself up in that way. Scott seemed to understand this and assured me that it wasn't a matter of *will* I work here, but *what's* the right role for me.

Later in the morning, Havi introduced me to another Yahoo employee I'd encountered online, although we'd never emailed. Jeremy Zawodny was known in the blogosphere as Yahoo's resident tech blogger; he was a developer, perhaps a couple of years older than me, who had been at Yahoo for nearly six years and had written a tech book for O'Reilly Media entitled *High Performance MySQL*.

Jeremy had thinning dark brown hair and wore a pair of thin oval glasses over his clean-shaven face. He was dressed casually, in a charcoal shirt and blue jeans, but his gaze was sharp and his expression almost smug. Not in a bad way; he just had that air of effortless self-confidence that the best software engineers carry around with them—particularly, I was learning, if they work at a large Silicon Valley company.

He suggested we head over to the cafeteria opposite for coffee, so we made our way out of the office building. It was a lovely, cloudless autumn day and the sun was streaming down. As we walked across the clean concrete pathway toward the yellow cafeteria edifice, Jeremy explained that 25 to 33 percent of his job now was blogging. (I wouldn't have been surprised if he'd developed software to calculate that every week.) About a year or two ago, he continued, senior managers in the company—including Yahoo cofounder David Filo—had begun complimenting him on his blog and telling him to "keep doing what you're doing." Now, Yahoo was getting into blogging in a big way, he said, noting that Gatz had just started one.

We entered the cafeteria, which was called URL's, and I had another n00b moment as I cast my eyes around this large, modern eatery. It felt cavernous and new—the ceiling was very high and crisscrossed with silver lighting and ducts. Flags from around the world hung from it. Since it was before lunchtime, the cafeteria wasn't too busy and we walked right up to one of the baristas and ordered coffee. "It's all free here," Jeremy said, noticing my hesitant expression. I almost felt obliged to take advantage, so along with my cappuccino I got a Vitaminwater, a brand I'd been enjoying during my stay.

I followed Jeremy over to one of the grey rectangular tables and sat down in a yellow seat. We talked some more about the blogging and RSS scene. After a while, Jeremy took out his cell phone—a Motorola V710 flip phone with one-megapixel camera—and snapped a photo of me. It's a nice snapshot, still on Flickr today: I was wearing a striped blue polo shirt and thin oval glasses (not unlike Jeremy's), and my fine hair was carefully swept to one side. I'm overweight, so my face is somewhat puffy, but I look happy—if also a little overawed.

When he posted the photo later, Jeremy used my name as the title and added the caption, "Of ReadWriteWeb fame . . ." Although "fame" was overstating it, I did feel like I had a profile during that first trip to Silicon Valley—and that meeting people like Jeremy was helping to raise it even more.

During our conversation, Jeremy was a little dismissive of Yahoo's competitors. He claimed that Google "wants to be Yahoo 2.0" and that Microsoft was slow but had enough money to get away with it. He wasn't wrong that Yahoo had taken the early initiative in Web 2.0. As well as acquiring Flickr in March, it had quickly integrated RSS across its suite of products: news, mobile, email and podcasts. But he was underestimating the other big companies. Google had just released Google Reader that month (it would become the leading RSS reader the following year). That February it had also continued its run of impressive Ajax-based web products with Google Maps. Microsoft, unsurprisingly, was the slowest of the bigcos to embrace the new web revolution, but in November it went all-in on Web 2.0 with Microsoft Live, the brand name for its new software-as-a-service strategy.

We also talked about blogs becoming mainstream, which was part of Yahoo's strategy for Jeremy, Scott, Havi, and other employees. "The features that make blogs what they are (on-page discussion, chronological sorting, generous linking) will work themselves into 'non-blog' sites more and more in the coming months," Jeremy wrote in a post[20] the day after meeting me.

In hindsight, he was only partially right—blogs and RSS eventually gave way to social media and feeds. And, of course, Yahoo was soon eclipsed as a platform by both Google and Microsoft (as well as Apple, Facebook, and Amazon). But it was also true that, in 2005, bloggers were the standard-bearers of the new social web. We were, as Jeremy put it in the same post (albeit in sarcastic air quotes), "special." The fact I'd been invited to the Yahoo campus at all signaled that I was at the forefront of a movement—and perhaps on my way becoming a Silicon Valley insider.

During my stay at the TechCrunch ranch, Mike, Fred, and I had been discussing how to better team up. At the time, creating a network of blogs was a trend—in August, I'd joined the 9rules network, a community of web design–focused blogs. I'd joined it mainly because of their revenue-sharing advertising network, but also to help me connect with more of the design community. It turned out the 9rules network was more useful for swapping contacts (I was introduced to my next web host through them), but I earned very little income from it. Nevertheless, the idea had been planted in my head that blogs banding together could be useful. So Mike, Fred, and I decided to create our own network: the Web 2.0 Workgroup.

Fred created a new website and logo for the network, and RSS feeds for our three blogs displayed our latest posts on the site. In my launch post I noted that our blogs were all complementary: "Mike blogs on new products; Fred blogs on usability, design and dev; I blog about Web 2.0 trends and developments."[21] The idea, I wrote, was that someone who subscribes to one blog might also be interested in the other two. I also mentioned that we were looking to invite other bloggers into the network.

The first blogger we invited was Dave Winer, who had been publishing on the web since 1994 and had created one of the first web syndication feeds in December 1997. He then created RSS 2.0, which launched in 2003 and became the default syndication method for blogs like mine. I'd also started out as a blogger using his publishing software, Radio UserLand, and was an admirer of his essays about technology. I'd emailed him, as a fan, multiple times since starting my blog in 2003. He didn't always reply, but when he did, I sometimes got the impression that I'd accidentally insulted him. It was an early warning of his prickly personality.

Dave had recently sold Weblogs.com, a ping server used by blogs, to Verizon for a couple of million dollars. Mike and Keith had helped him broker the deal. A couple of days after my Yahoo visit, Dave invited the Web 2.0 Workgroup bloggers to dinner at a place called Jing Jing, in Palo Alto. He was a regular there, and he assured us that the spicy noodles there were fabulous.

Dave was fifty years old (again, roughly the same age as I am now), and in person he was a large, bearlike presence. He had thinning dark hair, thin rectangular glasses, and a full beard that had already gone grey. He did a lot of the talking at the dinner, but the rest of us were happy to let him take the lead, given his illustrious reputation. He was in a good mood, so there was no sign of the oversensitivity I'd sensed in our online and email communications to this point. Also, the spicy noodles were indeed spectacular!

Dave was not a fan of Web 2.0. While he recognized that the web had moved on from the dot-com era, he preferred to use his own term, "the two-way web." To be fair, he'd articulated his vision "for the Web as an easy writing and publishing environment"[22] back in January 2001, well before O'Reilly and Co. came up with the Web 2.0 moniker. That was when he launched TheTwoWayWeb.com, the website that became a part of our workgroup. I think he simply resented the Web 2.0 terminology and wanted people to recognize his prior art.

I was a fan of Dave's theories about the web in large part because he credited Tim Berners-Lee as its true progenitor. In the very first post I'd written on Read/WriteWeb, in April 2003, I mentioned both Berners-Lee and Winer as inspirations. I also admired Dave because, like Berners-Lee, he built tools to support his vision. He'd created weblog publishing software, syndication formats, developer scripting tools, and outliners (a form of word processing software that had an "expand and collapse" outline display). Not to mention his weblog Scripting News, which was a key influence on early tech bloggers like me. There was no doubting his credentials as both a visionary and a practical toolmaker.

Unlike Berners-Lee, however, Dave was neither humble nor self-effacing. Online, he had a curious mix of arrogance and sensitivity. He was opinionated, which was admittedly a good thing in blogging, but he was also quick to take offense. In one email exchange in May 2005 about advertising in RSS feeds, he was dismissive of my analysis of the situation ("I don't have an opinion on your thesis. Sorry.") and claimed that I'd misunderstood him. Perhaps I had, but what was striking about that email exchange is that he didn't once acknowledge that I might have made a good point.

We were never close, but many years later I finally got tired of Dave's attitude and stopped following him. It was a Twitter exchange in 2017 that did it. We were discussing RSS feed readers, and I had listed some of the features I was looking for at that time. I knew Dave was building a new feed reader product and added that I would be happy to be an early tester of it. His response: "Forget it. I do development for myself these days for this exact reason. Users feel like they don't have to do anything, just demand stuff." I replied, "I'm not demanding anything, I was simply stating my personal preferences in a feed reader."

It's a shame, in retrospect, because he had been friendly to me over spicy noodles in Palo Alto—and I think he may've paid for the meal, too. Mike also had his ups and downs with Dave, and he too fell out with him eventually. There's a saying that you shouldn't meet your heroes, but I am still glad I met Dave. He was generous to me in the early days, linking to a then-unknown blogger and occasionally replying to my emails, and he had built some of the most innovative web technology of that era, which I gratefully used.

But being nice to people is important, too. The two-way web is a miserable experience otherwise, as we all discovered a decade later.

As I neared the end of my first trip to Silicon Valley, I began to think more seriously about moving there. I'd enjoyed the camaraderie of Mike, Fred, and Gabe, and others I'd met in person for the first time, including Josh and Fergus. If I moved to Silicon Valley, I'd surely make many good friends: we were all around the same age and had lots in common—work, taste in music, sense of humor, and so on. And via that network we might reach the higher rungs of Silicon Valley—rungs that Mike had already reached.

I had become aware during my trip that the class system in the United States worked very differently from that in the Commonwealth. Everything here revolved around money. Mike clearly had money, but more importantly, he knew people with a lot more of it—and it was his ambition to join them. And yet, I thought I understood why the United States was the land of opportunity. It seemed to me that Silicon Valley was a meritocracy of talent. Everyone I'd met had been friendly and treated me like an equal. They wanted to know my opinions about their startups and who I'd met. They didn't care about my background or what I used to do for a job; they only cared about what—and who—I knew now. In New Zealand, in contrast, nobody had any interest in my blog (other than a couple of the developers at my previous day job). I soon realized, however, that the reason these Americans were so open and friendly was that they wanted something from me—some knowledge or networking connection that would help them make money.

While I wasn't on Mike's level in terms of wealth or personal network, Gabe and I were cut from the same cloth. Even literally, in that we both dressed badly! He usually wore black jeans and a long-sleeved T-shirt in a primary color. I wore striped blue polo shirts and cheap patterned T-shirts with blue jeans or tan slacks, and I had no dress jacket at all—or dress sense, for that matter.

Gabe drove me around a bit during my stay, since I didn't have a rental car. He liked to blast Van Morrison songs on his car's tape deck, so we would drive through Atherton and Palo Alto humming along to the likes of "Brown-Eyed Girl" and "Cyprus Avenue." We also chatted a couple of times over burgers at a local joint in Atherton or Menlo Park—one of those 1950s-style restaurants with cherry-red booths and an open kitchen. Tech.memeorandum was still less than a month old at this time, but at the TechCrunch ranch we had all been talking about whether to take venture capital to scale our respective sites. Gabe was certain, even then, that he wanted to grow his little company on his own steam (and that is exactly what he did over the next fifteen-plus years).

Mike had told me my blog was worth a million dollars, based on what Calacanis got for Weblogs, Inc. Blog valuations were a topic of discussion in the tech blogosphere at the time, and another blogger had also pegged the value of RWW at $1 million. Although I was starting to realize that my blog did have value, I was still thinking too small at that stage—I thought RWW was primarily useful to me as a networking tool, a way to meet people in Silicon Valley. But I knew that Mike was considering a VC infusion to expand TechCrunch, just because he was friends with a bunch of those people. In the back of my mind, I was slowly coming to terms with RWW potentially being more than just a part-time income stream.

Gabe used sarcasm to deflect serious conversations, but I could tell even at this very early stage that his only ambition was to build a self-sustaining business. Tech.memeorandum was fully automated at this point, so another thing we discussed was how he'd continue to iterate on the product. I was surprised when he said he was open to adding human curation—and that is what he ended up doing a year or two later.

I was already making a reasonable living from the web as a free-lancer. I'd quit my day job in August and was now earning income from various web consulting gigs, my ZDNet blog, and (a small portion) from Read/WriteWeb itself. But if I did move to Silicon Valley, I'd have to get a full-time job—I would need it in order to get a working visa.

Job opportunities at Yahoo and other startups I'd approached seemed plentiful. So, in the final days of my trip, I arranged some meetings with people who were currently employing me as a freelancer. I had decided to broach the topic of a full-time job with them.

The Wednesday before I left I had coffee with Chris Alden, a cofounder of *Red Herring*, a tech magazine from the dot-com era. He'd just started a new company to build an RSS aggregator called Rojo, and I discussed ongoing contract work with him. The plan was I'd help write a spec for a new feature in Rojo when I got back to New Zealand. After I mentioned I was considering moving here, Chris told me he would definitely hire me as a product manager *if* I lived here. That was good to hear, even though I knew he wasn't in a position to support my visa application.

On the day before I headed back to New Zealand, I met up with my ZDNet boss, Dan Farber, in his office at CNET headquarters on Second Street, between Howard and Folsom.

Dan was a longtime tech journalist; he'd worked for *PC World* and *Macworld* during the 1980s. I'd seen him at the Web 2.0 Conference—a short man with snow-white hair, white goatee, and rimless glasses, dressed in a suit. His lips always seemed to be pursed in a serious expression, but when I met him at the CNET office that day, I noticed that the corners would occasionally turn up and betray a wry sense of humor.

I also discovered that Dan had a way of peering at you that seemed to cut through any bullshit. I'd known from the start that I was dealing with a serious journalist, even in our email conversations. But meeting him in person—with his set mouth and no-nonsense gaze—I wondered what he really thought of bloggers like me. Did he think we were interlopers in his profession, or just another resource that established media organizations could utilize? In retrospect, I think it was the latter and that he was much more pragmatic than I gave him credit for in 2005. It said more about my own youthful insecurity that I felt like an impostor sitting in his office.

Dan told me he wanted to integrate the blogging format more into the newsroom. Along with his colleague David Berlind, he ran a tech blog called Between the Lines (tagline: "The blog for discriminating IT buyers"), which covered news from such large IT companies as Novell and IBM, as well as write-ups of tech conferences like JavaOne and PC Forum. They reported on web technology from the perspective of IT professionals ("What CEOs Should Know about the 'Recombinant Web'" was one headline from that time).

When he'd first approached me about the blog back in August, the plan was to add more in-depth coverage of the Web 2.0 trend to ZDNet's network. "I like blogs with lots of energy," Dan had told me over email. "Keeping track of what's going on, filtering for people what they need to know about the evolution of the Web and how it's changing user experiences, business models." In addition to "documenting that evolution," he added that "it would require some big thinking on occasion."

During that first in-person meeting, I jotted down some of the business metrics we discussed. I'd gotten 80,000 page views in September, my first full month of blogging on Web 2.0 Explorer. This was more than the monthly average for RWW at the time! Dan pointed out that Between the Lines got 800,000 that same month. He was politely putting me in my place, but point taken: I had much to learn about professional blogging. Dan also told me that ZDNet was giving bloggers like me 25 to 30 percent of the revenue it received. I would be earning between $1,000 and $1,500 from ZDNet every month, which was more than I was bringing in from RWW.

The metrics gave me pause. Sure, I could probably get a regular job at ZDNet if I asked. But couldn't I also apply the same formula for monetizing a blog to Read/WriteWeb? For Web 2.0 Explorer I was only getting a quarter of each month's advertising revenue; I could get 100 percent of it if I monetized RWW. Also, RWW was still only a part-time occupation for me. If I devoted all my time to it, then surely I'd be able to grow RWW page views to something akin to what Between the Lines was getting.

For the first time, I began to think seriously about turning RWW into a full-time business. There had to be some way, I mused, to set up RWW as a company and get a US work visa that way. Perhaps I wouldn't need a job at Yahoo or CNET.

The next day, a Friday, I headed home. Mike drove me to the airport, and Fred and Gabe came along for the ride. It felt like an emotional parting, and I didn't want to leave. *This could easily be home*, I thought as I waved goodbye to the guys and trudged into SFO departures.

On the plane, I reflected on where I was at with RWW as a business. I had only one steady sponsor at this time, Webmail.us, which was paying $800 per month for a banner on my "Web 2.0 Weekly Wrapup" post. I had started offering sponsorships in April, after an Atlanta-based startup called ThePort Network reached out with an offer to sponsor my weekly roundup of Web 2.0 news. I'd promised that their banner would display with the post both on my website and in my RSS feed. (Advertising within an RSS feed was a new thing—Yahoo had been fishing for my opinions on this all year.) When the three-month agreement with ThePort Network ended, I signed up another startup to take over: Onfolio. Between the three, I'd managed to get a regular sponsor for a single RWW feature for seven months in a row.

I jotted down in my notebook that I needed to expand where I placed advertising on Read/WriteWeb. There was no reason it should be limited to a single weekly post. It was time for me to pursue other ad and sponsor options for the site.

It would take time to ramp up revenue on RWW, though, so in the meantime I would continue to get by on my freelance income. In addition to my ZDNet blog, I had freelance contract work lined up with Marc Canter's company and with a media consultancy called 5ive (run by Susan Mernit, a dot-com veteran I'd met over coffee during my trip). I had other leads to pursue when I got home, including the RSS work that Alden had mentioned. Plus, I had the O'Reilly Media book—although it promised only a $10,000 royalty advance, to be paid over several installments, which I was splitting 50/50 with Josh Porter.

I was feeling optimistic about my ability to earn a living from Silicon Valley, and hopefully in time from Read/WriteWeb itself. But I also knew I'd have to continue doing everything from a distance, for now.

"It sure feels like a bubble, doesn't it?" So wrote Web 2.0 Conference coproducer John Battelle in a *New York Times* op-ed on Friday, November 18, 2005, about a month after I'd returned home from Silicon Valley. Without specifically mentioning the dot-com boom of the late 1990s and early 2000s, he noted that the internet "is exciting again, and once again folks are rushing in."

Then, a record scratch. "But regardless of all this déjà vu, we are not in a bubble," Battelle wrote. He spent the rest of the article arguing that claim, but of course he'd opened himself up to the accusation of protesting too much. The rest of the Web 2.0 era would be forever linked to the concept of a market bubble—and if or when it would burst.

The month before, two young engineers, Eran Globen and Ryan King, had started a satiric blog called supr.c.ilio.us—the name inspired by del.icio.us. The day after Battelle's article, Globen linked to it and noted that it was published on the same day as the latest TechCrunch BBQ, which he had attended. "Some 400 geeks munching on pizza and drinking free (as in beer) beer? I don't see no bubble here."[23]

I had already become a target of the mock blog's good-natured but anarchic humor. The week before, the pair had been interviewed by Irina Slutsky, a Silicon Valley reporter who was launching her own YouTube channel, Geek Entertainment TV. Slutsky introduced her debut show as "reporting from inside the bubble." She then asked Globen, "What is Web 2.0?"

"Web 2.0 is a conspiracy that was started by people deep inside the Illuminati," he deadpanned. Slutsky asked him to name names.

"Richard MacManus," King piped up. "Yeah, basically him," Globen affirmed, adding that "he's hiding in New Zealand right now."[24]

It was funny, and I immediately wrote a blog post in response, accepting and even encouraging the joke. But there was a serious side. Almost all the critics of Web 2.0—including actual journalists like Nicholas Carr, Andrew Keen, and every writer at The Register—objected to the trend because it implied there was a market bubble that would soon burst. But I sided with Battelle on this—I didn't think Web 2.0 was a bubble, because real value was being built in this new era. The startups I was reporting on weren't Pets.com 2.0.

However, I did think the term *Web 2.0* itself was increasingly problematic. The same week I'd been outed by supr.c.ilio.us, I reported in my weekly wrap-up that staff from the open-source browser Flock had banned the term from its office, and that del.icio.us creator Joshua Schachter was rebelling against being "the Web 2.0 poster child."[25]

By the end of 2005, even I was tired of all the arguments about the terminology. I wrote a regrettable post entitled "Web 2.0 is dead. R.I.P." Talk about biting the hand that fed me! A few days later, I tried to explain myself. "The term has become too overblown and nebulous—and is holding us all back." However, I promised that I would "continue to write about the technologies and impact of this current era of the Web."

And why wouldn't I? The bubble was only just beginning to expand

CHAPTER 4

BECOMING A BUSINESS

■ ■ ■ ■ ■

IN THE SECOND WEEK of January 2006 I got married to my partner of nine years, Maria. We had a four-year-old daughter, Rosabelle, who was one of the flower girls at the ceremony. The following week I was on a plane to the United States again—but not on my honeymoon. I'd been offered a place in Microsoft Search Champs, an invitation-only event held at Microsoft's headquarters in Redmond, Washington. Microsoft was paying for my travel and accommodation, so it was too good an opportunity to pass up. What web geek wouldn't want to visit the setting of *Microserfs*, Douglas Coupland's famous 1995 novel about Microsoft developers?

It'd also be my first trip to the grunge city of Seattle. Kurt Cobain had died there a decade ago, and I was kind of obsessed with him. One of the first nonfiction stories I'd written, during a writing course I took when I moved up to Auckland in 1994, was an homage to Cobain just after he'd killed himself. Later, I became interested in the conspiracy theories over Cobain's death peddled by the likes of Tom Grant, the private investigator who had been hired by Courtney Love and later turned on her. Part of the cultural fascination for me was the role the internet played in the after-story of Cobain. Grant made himself into a pseudo-celebrity based on his theories, which wouldn't have been possible without the web.

Search Champs was being hosted by the Microsoft Network (MSN) Search group, which had invited more than fifty bloggers, academics, and technologists. Microsoft had selected the group "based on who we are reading and we think would provide us great insight." I'd been recommended by Alex Barnett, a British expat about my age who worked for Microsoft in Redmond, and whom I'd gotten to know virtually as part of the tech blogger fraternity. Mike Arrington, Fred Oliveira, and Josh Porter had all been invited too, so I was looking forward to catching up with them.

The event would kick off on Tuesday evening with a reception at the Chapel Bar in downtown Seattle, near the W Hotel where we were all staying. I arrived in Seattle late on Monday evening, after a long series of flights from New Zealand. Fred had arrived earlier in the day and had emailed to let me know. By the time I had checked into the hotel and taken a shower, it was well after 10:00 p.m. and I was exhausted, so I gave up on any thoughts of meeting up with Fred. I looked over the email messages for the Search Champs and saw a welcome message from Brady Forrest, the organizer of the event. He'd listed the basic schedule and other FAQs and finished with this note: "There will be a small gift in your room when you arrive. It will include a Search Champs welcome packet with MSN Search team bios & pictures as well as a schedule. If you do not have one let us know."

I looked around and saw no gift. I checked outside the door of my room, but there was nothing. Anyone else would've left it to the next morning, but my jet-lagged brain was now obsessing about the missing gift basket. So I hit reply on Brady's email and wrote that I'd just arrived at the W Hotel, "but I didn't see a gift package in my room (with schedule etc)." To my horror, I noticed that this message had gone out to the entire mailing list. Mike Arrington, who would be arriving in the morning, was the first to reply: "Richard, No gift basket? Maybe that's a message. :-)." Dori Smith, a technical writer and the publisher of the Wise-Women community website, was next to reply. Sensibly, she suggested that "when you arrive" meant on Tuesday, which was when many of the Search Champs participants would be checking into the hotel. Then Rael Dornfest from O'Reilly Media chimed in and said there were three gift baskets in his room!

Embarrassed, I thought maybe I should just go to bed and sleep off the jetlag. Then I saw a message to the list from Emily Chang, who was part of the Web 2.0 Workgroup. She and her boyfriend, Max Kiesler, ran a web-design consultancy called Ideacodes, and both would be attending Search Champs. She wrote, "Richard—don't worry. Max and I sent you a gift basket from Ideacodes :)—champagne and cheese board arriving via room service shortly!" As soon as I read that, reception called to say that the gift basket was on its way.

An email from Kevin Briody, a marketing manager at Microsoft, followed a few minutes later: "I couldn't let a first time visitor to Seattle arrive without a proper welcome. So in addition to Emily and Max's champagne and cheese, you should expect a few of our fine local microbrews (we have some of the best) to arrive shortly, courtesy of the team at MSN."

I was now fully mortified and attempted to save face by replying once again to the list. "Looks like the party's in my room tonight," I wrote, adding that it was a "pity I'll be falling asleep very soon." Several gift baskets duly arrived in my room while the email thread continued. After an hour or so, when I was sure that no more hotel porters would be knocking on my door, I prepared myself for bed. I don't even remember now if I opened the champagne or any of the brews. But I'm certain I fell asleep as soon as my head hit the pillow.

The next day, while I was out exploring Seattle, an email arrived from Mike. He'd flown up from San Francisco and had evidently just arrived at the hotel. The email was addressed to Fred and me. "No fucking gift basket either," it read.

On Tuesday, a bunch of us—including Fred and Josh—went to explore the famed Seattle Central Library, designed by Rem Koolhaas and Joshua Prince-Ramus. It had opened in 2004, and we all had our digital cameras out, taking photos of the lime-green escalator, bright red corridors, and massive glass windows crisscrossed with steel netting. One of my Seattle-based blog buddies, Erik Benson, had recommended

I check out the "electronic bulletin board on the 5th floor that displays, in semi-real time, all the books that are being checked in and out, as well as searches, etc." That board was indeed a marvelous blend of two things that I loved: libraries and digital technology.

I'd arranged to meet Erik and his startup, the Robot Co-op, in the afternoon. Over the past few years we'd swapped emails now and then and commented on each other's blogs, but I hadn't yet met him in person. When I first began communicating with Erik, around 2003, he was working as a developer and product manager for Amazon. Now, he was building his own social software tools, with names like 43things .com and AllConsuming.net. These websites allowed you to track your daily activities online. It was an early form of social media, but focused on what you *did* rather than what you thought. If you had checked the home page on the week I visited, you'd have read that "210,751 people in 4,813 cities are doing 326,312 things including . . . see the aurora borealis, play strip poker, drink more alcohol, have better handwriting, own my own bar, read the Chronicles of Narnia," et cetera.

43 Things was well-intentioned in that it tried to help you set goals for your life. It was also a cool app for young urban types who were geeky enough to use the internet on a daily basis (still not true for most people in the world at that time). I tested out 43 Things in 2005, as I did many other Web 2.0 products. I only added seven "things" to my profile, one of which was "Visit Silicon Valley"—and I'd duly checked that off as "done." Erik's profile included day-to-day things that, frankly, I wished I could do too ("hang out at The Hideout every Wednesday"). I remember thinking that 43 Things was documenting a lifestyle that I aspired to but could only access online. Of course, this is exactly what social media turned into when it went mainstream over the next ten years.

Fred wanted to meet the Robot Co-op team too, so after lunch we both walked up the hill to the office at 1205 East Pike Street. It was a pleasant winter day and unseasonably sunny, or so I'd been told over email by the locals attending Search Champs. We walked past cafés— Starbucks, naturally, but there were other, more quirky ones too—and the odd hipster bar (including The Hideout, Erik's weekly place to be). We also walked past rows of nondescript but busy-looking office buildings, most of them no more than a few stories high. All of this gave me vibes of my hometown of Wellington, New Zealand—where the coffee was just as good and the weather just as bad! I could easily see myself living and working in Seattle.

When we arrived, Erik came downstairs to greet us. He was tall and lean, with a baby face and spiky black hair. He was about five years younger than me and looked as cool as I looked staid. I was wearing my usual blue-striped polo shirt and dark blue jeans with a cheap-looking brown winter jacket. I was still overweight, with my fine, straight hair combed unfashionably to the sides. I was the very picture of a newly married nerd with an unexciting social life. By contrast, Erik looked cool and youthful in his skinny black jeans, black T-shirt, and casual black blazer.

Upstairs in the Robot Co-op office, we met the other members of the team, including Erik's cofounders Daniel Spils and Josh Petersen. Daniel quizzed me about my stance on Web 2.0, which was an ongoing debate in the startup community—many developers and designers rejected the label, although just as many cashed in on it, too. I told him I was conflicted about the hype around the term, but I also believed there were significant changes happening in web development and design. I mentioned the book that Josh Porter and I were writing for O'Reilly Media, and that we were focusing on best practices for designing networked applications.

Before we left, I promised to try and make it to the Andy Warhol-themed party Erik was holding the following evening at The Hideout. In the meantime, Fred and I needed to get back to the hotel to prepare for the Search Champs welcome party, being held at the nearby Chapel Bar.

It was a cold but sunny Wednesday morning when our Microsoft charter bus pulled into a complex of redbrick office buildings, all no more than three stories high. This was Microsoft's Redmond campus, located about twenty minutes' drive from downtown Seattle.

The two days of Search Champs would be held in Building 31. I didn't know how this area of the campus compared to the others, but what I saw was an unexpected blend of office and nature. Green and red shrubbery lined the buildings, and evergreen Douglas fir trees dotted the exterior. It was the middle of winter, so the smaller deciduous trees inside the campus were bare, their reddish-brown branches blending in with the neatly patterned brick of the buildings.

Compared to the gleaming concrete-and-glass buildings and artificially neat lawns of the Yahoo campus, the Microsoft campus seemed calmer and more attuned to its natural setting. Perhaps that was simply because it was a decade or two older than the Yahoo offices, giving nature more time to come to terms with the encroachment of technology.

When I visited, in January 2006, Microsoft was on the cusp of another growth spurt. The company employed 28,000 people in the Seattle area, and its Redmond campus was about 8 million square feet. Just a month after I visited, the company announced plans to add another 3.1 million square feet onto the campus over the next three years—enough room for 12,000 more people.

Microsoft's corporate software was the main reason for its growth, but it was also keen to capitalize on the consumer web trend known as Web 2.0—especially since its Internet Explorer web browser still held around 90 percent market share. Just as Yahoo had begun to actively court tech bloggers like me (the reason for my campus visit several months earlier), Microsoft saw bloggers as a way to help promote its online services. It even had its own resident bloggers, most prominently Robert Scoble. I'd come across Scoble a few years prior—he was one of the first well-known bloggers to link to me. In July 2005 he would conduct a video interview with Steve Ballmer, then Microsoft CEO, who described blogs as "a great way to have customer communications."[26]

Of course, as with nearly every category of software, at first Microsoft thought it could conquer blogging. At the end of 2004 the company released its own blogging software, MSN Spaces, and interlinked it with its existing communications software, Messenger and Hotmail. However, Microsoft quickly discovered that bloggers were far too independent-minded to use its product. Even the political bloggers avoided MSN Spaces, preferring to stick with specialized blogging software such as Movable Type (which I used) and the emerging WordPress. Eventually, Microsoft realized that it could simply entice tech bloggers onto its actual turf—Redmond—and try to influence them that way.

We filed out of the bus and entered Building 31. The reception area had pale yellow walls with wood paneling and a brown-patterned carpet. There was a large potted tree in the middle of the room, and next to it was a foosball table with red and black players. The front of the table had the remains of a Windows.NET sticker on it; someone had tried, without success, to it peel off—perhaps a contractor or an overzealous manager had decided the sticker wasn't cool enough for a foosball table? Regardless, we continued upstairs and into a nondescript conference room.

Brady Forrest, a program manager at Microsoft, began talking about the agenda for our two-day visit. He was a confident-looking guy with styled brown hair and a goatee, dressed in a burgundy dress shirt and blue jeans. He explained that after opening presentations from a couple of vice presidents (I still didn't understand why American companies had so many vice presidents), we would go to breakout sessions with our assigned product groups. Fred, Mike, Josh, and I had been placed in the Live.com track of Search Champs.

Live.com was Microsoft's entry into an emerging product category known as a "start page." Part old-style web portal with news and interactive media (like MSN), part digital dashboard, and part RSS reader, the idea was to deliver a personalized home page when users started up their browsers. Indeed, Microsoft's version was originally called Start .com, evoking memories of the Rolling Stones singing "Start Me Up" in the famous Windows 95 TV commercial. Start.com was a better name than Live.com, but the latter was part of Microsoft's new Windows Live branding for all its internet software (where *live* indicated online).

The face of Live.com was Sanaz Ahari, a Persian American woman who had created it at age twenty-three. Perhaps because of her youth, she wasn't our track leader. But she was clearly the person who had the most knowledge about it. With her long black hair tied back, and wearing a straightforward black T-shirt and jacket over blue jeans,

Ahari was a focused presenter at Search Champs. She was nervous, but who wouldn't be at that age and, it must be said, presenting to a group of mostly male geeks. In our track of ten tech bloggers there were just two women: Dori Smith and Gina Trapani. It was about the same in the other tracks.

Ahari was most excited about the option for users to add interactive "gadgets" to Live.com—basically mini web applications that you could easily access on this one web page. It was common to have a weather-forecast app and a calendar app, as well as various email and note-taking apps. Start pages were seen as a greenfield environment for Web 2.0 because the hope was that the companies that hosted them would offer open access for web app developers.

One of the new things Ahari showed off to the assembled bloggers was a TV recommendations gadget, which she promised would be released soon. It enabled you to control your Windows Media Center box remotely, for example to record an upcoming TV show (remember, this was years before streaming TV). This kind of app was typically built using Ajax, the web development technique that had come to dominate Web 2.0 after the release of Gmail in 2004. Ajax allowed web apps to send and retrieve data from a server in the background, making web pages much more interactive than they'd been in the dot-com era. Sometimes start pages were referred to as "Ajax homepages" because of its influence.

Microsoft's overall Web 2.0 strategy was a familiar one: "embrace and extend" by integrating its web products into the Windows software environment. The company had been barred from integrating its dominant browser, Internet Explorer, into Windows after the US Justice Department won its famous antitrust trial against Microsoft in 2001. But they didn't face the same restrictions with browser-based applications. So Live.com was pitched to us that day as a "desktop on the web" where gadgets could be dragged and dropped between the user's browser and Windows desktop.

The emergence of smartphone apps a couple of years later put paid to the start-page concept—nowadays, the Live.com domain name redirects to the online version of Outlook. But in early 2006, start pages were one of the hottest areas of Web 2.0 development. So were APIs (application programming interfaces), which a new friend of mine had managed to turn into a compelling blog topic.

During the first day at Search Champs, I met fellow tech blogger John Musser for the first time. He was in the developer track, but we got a chance to chat in the breaks. Originally from New York City, John now lived in Seattle and ran a blog and online resource called Programmable Web. The site documented and commented on Web 2.0 APIs, which were fast becoming the default way developers integrated third-party web services into their applications. For instance, you could embed MSN Messenger into your website or blog using a Microsoft API. APIs also powered so-called "mashups," in which two web services were melded together to form a new application; the best example at the time was HousingMaps, which plotted Craigslist real estate listings onto Google Maps.

John had started his website the previous August, and in October he'd contacted me to ask if it could be included in the Web 2.0 Workgroup. He said he would contribute a "programmer's-eye-view of the Web 2.0 API landscape" to the group, along with "a very dry sense of humor." Mike, Fred, and I quickly agreed to add him, and soon we began swapping emails.

John was lean, with short-cropped black hair (slightly greying), and he wore a pair of small oval glasses. He was forty-four when I met him, so a decade older than me. He seemed more British than American, with his polite demeanor and the dry sense of humor he'd promised. We got on just as well in person as we did online.

Unbeknownst to either of us, we had become embroiled in an internal O'Reilly Media tug of war over a book about Web 2.0. In December, John had emailed me to say that he'd been contacted by O'Reilly Media to write an introductory book about the subject. He'd quickly whipped up a proposal, not knowing that Josh Porter and I were already working on a Web 2.0 book. When John's contact at O'Reilly Media discovered that our project would cover the same territory, his proposed book was put on ice. John was disappointed but graciously accepted that Josh and I were already well into our project. During the breaks at Search Champs, John and I chatted about the O'Reilly book situation. We agreed it was a case of crossed wires.

A few days later, midway through my journey back to New Zealand, I would discover that O'Reilly was still keen on bringing John on. On the stopover at Sydney, I opened my email and saw a message from our O'Reilly editor with the subject line *John Musser*. It was addressed to me and Josh and cc'd the editor who had approached John. Would we mind, the email asked, if John became a coauthor? I was about to board my connecting flight, but I quickly wrote back to Josh that I wanted to say no. We both liked and respected John a lot, but I didn't want to change our outline or writing plan. After I got back home, I found that Josh agreed with me and had spoken to our main contact at O'Reilly to nix the idea.

We thought that was the end of it, but over February communications with our assigned editor began to falter. We suspected something was up, so at the start of March we emailed to ask for a status update. The reply came later that day: our book had been canceled and O'Reilly was now "exploring other avenues toward completing this project." We were naturally very disappointed, as well as frustrated about the lack of communication or feedback from our editor.

I couldn't help but wonder if O'Reilly had asked John to take over our book. I emailed him about it straight away. He said that he was still in discussions with O'Reilly about doing something with them but didn't yet have a deal.

The O'Reilly Web 2.0 book eventually turned into a hundred-page report released later that year, in November 2006, entitled *Web 2.0: Principles and Best Practices*. It was written by John based on Tim O'Reilly's ideas. It was very different from the more design-focused book that Josh and I had been working on; in his announcement post, John noted that the report was being marketed to a business audience and "you won't find it sold in bookstores."[27]

I never had any hard feelings with John about this. We were both figuring out how to run a professional blog business, so we regularly swapped notes over 2006 and into the future. I put all the blame on our failed book project with O'Reilly Media. Even our main contact at O'Reilly had admitted, "We failed you, quite simply." It wasn't much consolation, but we both chalked it up as a learning experience.

Looking back on it now, the book project encapsulated something about Web 2.0 that I had an inkling of at the time, but had repeatedly tried to shrug off: Web 2.0, the trend everyone was so excited about and that was driving the new internet economy, was an amorphous concept. Nobody knew what it meant—even Tim O'Reilly, whose definition of it seemed to expand every month. In my blog I'd kicked back against the hype a few times, but the reality was I was riding the wave just as much as O'Reilly was.

As for Microsoft, it simply wanted to latch onto the new, new thing—whatever it was at any one time—and assimilate it into the Windows world. As part of this strategy, Microsoft had correctly identified tech bloggers, including John, Josh, Mike, and myself, as the carriers of the latest technocultural meme. We were happy to oblige because we understood that infecting Microsoft with our meme would help bring our niche blogs to a newer, more mainstream, audience.

On Friday, I headed back to New Zealand. My first layover was twelve hours at the San Francisco airport, so I'd arranged for Marc Canter to pick me up. I was helping him with a couple of reports as part of my ongoing work for his company, Broadband Mechanics, so he drove me to his house in Walnut Creek. There I met his wife, Lisa, and their two small daughters, and Marc and I discussed his latest project. It was for AOL, the dot-com company that was now trying to reinvent itself as a Web 2.0 company. Marc had been hired to spec out a new product, AIMSpace, which—like everything he did at that time—he envisioned as a "digital lifestyle aggregator," his term for a multimedia-laden social network.

Later, Marc took me and his family to a dinner at Max's Opera House in Burlingame. It was five minutes from SFO, so the plan was to eat and then drop me off at the airport for my flight home. I'd invited members of the Web 2.0 Workgroup to attend too, if they were in the area.

Mike Arrington and Gabe Rivera both came to the dinner, along with a bunch of other people I'd gotten to know over the past year—including ZDNet's Dan Farber, Rojo's Chris Alden, angel investor Jeff Clavier (a French man who now lived in the valley), and blogger Stowe Boyd. Mike also brought his girlfriend, Jenn, whom I'd first met back in October. I sat next to Chris, and we talked about the possibility of more consulting work for Rojo. The previous month I'd finished a market assessment and product analysis for him, and I was hoping to rustle up more work.

Freelance consulting was still my primary income source at this time. Although I'd had a few sponsors for Read/WriteWeb, it wasn't yet a dependable revenue stream. Around two-thirds of my income was coming from the freelance work I did for Marc, with the rest coming from ZDNet and irregular jobs like Rojo. In fact, I was hoping to bring other consulting clients on, to lessen my reliance on Marc.

Over the past year I had been exploring assistance in monetizing RWW, since sales and self-promotion weren't among my natural talents. In particular, I hoped to join an advertising network called FM Publishing. The company had been started in 2005 by John Battelle, the cochair of the Web 2.0 Conference. I'd emailed John to inquire about FM as early as April 2005, when he first began blogging about it and positioned it as akin to a book publisher (the FM stood for "Federated Media"). "I plan to partner with site authors, acting as a platform which provides important services to them—revenue (in the form of advertising), back end support, and the like,"[28] he'd written. He was already doing this for the popular tech-culture blog Boing Boing, in his self-described capacity as "band manager." So his plan was to turn that into a business.

I didn't think I needed help on the publishing side, but I knew I needed help getting revenue. "I'm a small tightly focused blog with high quality content," I'd written to John the previous April. "Writing is my strong point—not sales or promotion. Also I don't have the contacts to get good sponsorship deals. In short: I need help to monetize my blog."

It wasn't until nearly a year later that I finally joined FM Publishing. "I'm currently approaching 12,000 RSS subscribers and my traffic is very healthy these days," I wrote to John in early March 2006, cheekily adding that "I see you've added some sites recently which I'm sure have less traffic than me." John emailed me back: "As we tell all authors who join us, it'll be a while before real money flows in, but this looks good."

As John had warned, it was a slow start. In April 2006, I earned the grand sum of $153.94 from FM (rounded down to $150 for the check). For May it was $200 and in June $250. My agreement didn't preclude me from doing deals with sponsors with whom I had a direct relationship and who hadn't yet been in contact with FM. Mike was a member of FM Publishing too, but I'd noticed that he had begun to sell his own 125 x 125 pixel square adverts on TechCrunch sometime during May 2006. He had a web page setting out both his statistics ("over 3 million page views per month") and rates for the square ads ($7,500 per month). TechCrunch's traffic far outstripped Read/WriteWeb's—it was over ten times as much.

At first I had wanted to leave the revenue generation to FM Publishing. But after the first few months of disappointing payouts, I was finally ready to do some hustling myself. So, at the end of July, I wrote a post announcing that I was making RWW sponsor packages available. My plan was to copy Mike's business model and format of 125 x 125 square ads in the right sidebar.

When I didn't get any bites, about a week later I began emailing startups I knew—starting with the ones already sponsoring TechCrunch. One of these was Zoho, an Indian company that I'd written about since 2005 and was keeping tabs on for their emerging web office suite. They were now competing with the formidable Google, which had acquired a small online word processing startup called Writely in March. It was obvious Google was building a web office suite too, so it was imperative for Zoho to get as many users as possible before Google launched its full suite. Knowing this, in August 2006 I pitched them on sponsoring RWW.

"I noticed Zoho is a sponsor at TechCrunch and I wondered whether you'd consider sponsoring Read/WriteWeb too," I wrote. "There is obviously a strong correlation between our brands, particularly as I have a reputation for covering the 'Web Office' space." I added that, in terms of pricing, "I am obviously a whole lot less expensive than TC," with my rate for a 125 x 125 sponsor ad at $1,000 per month. That worked out at a $4 to $5 cost per thousand (CPM) advertisement impressions, which was nearly double that of TechCrunch ($2 to $3 CPM, based on the figures they'd quoted). I figured that RWW was a prestige publication, since I focused on Web 2.0 analysis rather than startup profiles. At least, that's what I told myself to justify raising my rate above that of TechCrunch. Also, my rate was FM Publishing's stated target figure.

Zoho's CEO, Sridhar Vembu, immediately emailed back. "Yes, absolutely, we will be happy to. Our Techcrunch sponsorship just ended too as of Aug 15, so this is perfect timing."

Emboldened, I reached out to Geoffrey Arone from Flock, a new web browser that was also a TechCrunch sponsor. "There is obviously a strong correlation between our brands," I said, copying and pasting my pitch to Zoho and adjusting it slightly. He emailed back to ask if I would "do a year for $10k." I realized that this was twelve months of exposure on RWW for not much more than he what paid TechCrunch for one month. This was too much of a hit to my ego, so I made a counteroffer of "$5k for now until end of Jan 07 (which is 5.5 months)" and he accepted that.

Thus, by the start of September 2006, I had four sponsor ads in my sidebar—Zoho, Flock, Pageflakes (a German start-page company I'd been talking to), and Text Link Ads (an advertising business from Cincinnati). In addition to these four sponsors that I'd gotten on my own, I had one sponsor via FM: the Australian software-as-a-service company Atlassian, which paid FM a higher CPM for a premium spot, the horizontal banner that ran in the site's header.

This was the real beginning of Read/WriteWeb as a business, and with both me and Mike now selling our own sponsor deals, it kicked FM Publishing into gear. In early October, FM's chief revenue officer, Chas Edwards, announced in an email to the FM publishers, "Our fax machine received insertion orders" of more than four times the amount in July ("hence those small checks for August"). The new advertising contracts were from a host of big American companies—Intel, Microsoft, WebEx, American Express, General Motors, Cisco, Hewlett-Packard, Symantec, and others—and he promised the ads would start running in November. "Keep in mind," he added, "Q4 and Q2 are the strongest months in the advertising business."

Revenue from FM did increase in that period, but it was still too inconsistent for my liking. By this point, FM was openly frustrated about the sponsor slots I was selling. At the end of November, Chas emailed to ask for a phone meeting. "We're having trouble keeping up with the units you're selling versus the ones we're selling, and on the ones we're selling, what the positioning will be," he wrote. "I'd like to get this ironed out asap! This confusion is preventing us from selling more skyscrapers and other units."

I wrote back to say that I was happy to get on the phone, but that "there's no confusion from my pov." I told him I was "simply selling units that you guys are not selling."

In fairness, FM was still a new business and so was busy ironing out its own scaling issues. But I was quickly learning that I wasn't a complete amateur in the online advertising business. Read/WriteWeb had some leverage now, and I was starting to use it.

CHAPTER 5

POWER LAWS

■ ■ ■ ■ ■

IN JUNE 2006 I flew to San Francisco for my third US trip. I arrived at SFO just after midday on Monday, June 19, after another sleepless twelve-hour flight. Mike Arrington was hosting me at his place in Atherton again, for which I was grateful. I'd also asked if he could pick me up from the airport, and he'd asked an assistant to calendar it. But when the time came, he wasn't there to greet me. I waited around with my luggage for about an hour and a half, every now and then ringing Mike's phone from an airport payphone. I kept getting his voice mail.

Eventually, I took matters into my own hands and hired a car from Budget Rent a Car. Despite the name, it was expensive. But I realized that I should've done this in the first place. I needed to be more independent and not rely on Mike or others, so hiring a car was a good start.

As I drove out of SFO, I was terrified of crashing. I kept reminding myself to drive on the opposite side of the road, while also trying to work out which exit to take. The Californian sun glared into my eyes, and I had to squint to concentrate. Fortunately, it wasn't peak-hour traffic, and somehow, I managed to get on the motorway heading to San Jose. Soon I was feeling comfortable behind the wheel, and the familiar *thwack-thwack-thawck* of the tires hitting the 101 calmed me down.

It was a gorgeous summer day, and it felt great to be in Silicon Valley again.

This time at the TechCrunch ranch, I noticed that Mike was busier than ever—his reason for not picking me up at the airport. I understood that I wasn't high on his list of priorities, so it didn't bother me. We both agreed it was better that I had a rental car to get around.

TechCrunch had exploded in popularity, and he was devoting a lot of time to it, in addition to the time he spent on edgeio, his startup with Keith Teare. Technorati now had TechCrunch ranked the eleventh most popular blog in the world, just a year after he'd started it, and the Feedburner RSS badge on Mike's site was nearly at one hundred thousand subscribers. I had yet to crack the Technorati Top 100 (although I would by the end of the year), and I had around thirty thousand RSS subscribers.

Despite Mike being so busy, we managed to collaborate on a story involving Digg, the trendy tech-news aggregator that had recently eclipsed Slashdot in popularity. Its founder, Kevin Rose, was in his late twenties and was one of the faces of Web 2.0—due in large part to his good looks. He had dark hair worn long at the front, full lips, and brown puppy-dog eyes. Add to that his lean profile and raffish stubble, and he looked like a cross between a young Steve Jobs and a singer in a boy band. He'd been on the cover of magazines, too; only instead of *Rolling Stone*, it was *BusinessWeek* and *Inc.*

Just before departing for California, I'd written about the relaunch of a famous internet brand: Netscape. AOL had put Jason Calacanis in charge of the brand, after acquiring his Weblogs, Inc. business the previous year. Calacanis had decided to turn Netscape into a user-voted news aggregator that bore a striking resemblance to Digg. Some bloggers—Mike included—thought this might be a "Digg killer" due to the considerable built-in audience the Netscape portal still enjoyed at the time. I noted in my piece that "Netscape gets a surprising 811 million monthly page views," compared to Digg's 200 million.

The key difference was that Digg was entirely controlled by the "wisdom of the crowd" (its users), whereas Calacanis had added editors (whom he called "anchors") to select which stories would feature at the top of the page. As Calacanis himself put it, he wanted "an editorial voice to balance the hive mind."[29] I'd written that this approach was "inherently less democratic, even if it ends up being more effective." I added, "I can't see any current Digg users defecting, but perhaps Digg should hurry up with those new features it's been promising!"[30]

In response to my post, Digg's CEO, Jay Adelson, emailed me. Naturally, he was skeptical about what AOL was trying to do with Netscape. "We will never have a small group of people provide oversight," he told me. Digg was about to launch its latest version, which they had nicknamed Digg 3.0. I suggested we record an interview with Jay and Kevin for Mike's new *TalkCrunch* podcast, meaning that RWW and TechCrunch would share the story. Digg's PR people readily agreed, so we arranged for them to call in to Mike's house via VoIP (Voice over Internet Protocol) on Wednesday evening.

The main story was that Digg was expanding beyond tech news. It was adding five new categories: Science, World & Business, Entertainment, Video, and Gaming. This seems unremarkable now, when Reddit (today's Digg) has thousands of categories. But in mid-2006, Digg was purely a tech-news aggregator, so this was an important move for them, and more generally, it was another signal that Web 2.0 was moving beyond its geeky origins. If ordinary people began to use Digg, then it could become a mainstream portal—just like Netscape. Reddit at this time was also focused on tech; it had just seven "subreddits," all of them very geeky. Reddit had been founded in 2005 and now, a year later, was much less popular than Digg, so it was Digg's game to win.

I remember being nervous during the Digg interview, since it was being recorded and I wasn't comfortable doing podcasts at that time. Mike was sitting at his desk during the call, and I'd pulled up a chair to sit beside him. My voice sounds small and shaky on the recording, partly because Mike and I were on speaker phone and the VoIP connection wasn't great. Rose, in contrast, was a natural. As well as looking like Steve Jobs, when he spoke he exuded a similar charm and confidence. According to Rose, they'd always had bigger plans than just competing with Slashdot. "We knew our game plan all along, and that we were going to be expanding outside of just technology news,"[31] he said during the call.

At the time of the interview, Digg was already a key driver of traffic to RWW. I would continue to obsess about Digg for my own business, while also writing articles examining its impact on the wider blogosphere. In particular, just how democratic was it, actually? That July I noted that "a page on digg.com called Top Diggers shows that a select group of digg users are highly influential."[32] Rose was right at the top of that list; of the 120 stories he'd submitted with his user profile, a staggering 119 made it to the home page—guaranteeing heavy traffic for those sites.

Later, I discovered that nearly 30 percent of front-page stories on Digg were contributed by just ten people. This wasn't too surprising, since many networks—internet or otherwise—have a similar "power law" dynamic. In my post about it, in early August 2006, I concluded that having an A-list of users was "no different to the blogging world [or] the Web in general."

The power-law dynamic didn't just apply to users—it also applied to content creators, in that a disproportionate amount of Digg front pages went to a select group of blogs. I knew of at least one tech blog that was able to charge high advertising rates thanks to the traffic Digg sent them. I was also aware that TechCrunch got dugg a lot more than RWW.

The power-law dynamic at Digg was much discussed in the blogosphere over 2006. Most of the controversy was based on the theory that the top users and the top sites must be gaming the system (and indeed, there was evidence supporting this). For a site that promoted "non-hierarchical editorial control"[33] by its users, this was a problem. In September, Rose announced an "algorithm update" aimed at improving "digging diversity." He added, "Users that follow a gaming pattern will have less promotion weight."[34] I reported soon after on RWW that Rose's post "caused an uproar amongst Digg's top users, who feel they have been accused of gaming."

I met Kevin Rose in person for the first time in February 2010, when he had been brought over to New Zealand to present at a local conference called Webstock. I took the opportunity to buy him and his friend Daniel Burka a lamb dinner at Pravda, a popular Wellington bistro.

Kevin was friendly during dinner, but also standoffish—in that self-assured way that popular kids usually have. He knew people wanted to get close to him, so his instinct was to keep them at bay. I made a few wisecracks about all the traffic Digg had sent our way over the years, but he didn't engage, and he also gave nothing away about the internal issues the company was facing at this time. My girlfriend sensibly steered the conversation back to vacation recommendations. Disappointed that I couldn't talk shop, I offered up some tourist advice instead: "You must try the Cloudy Bay oysters."

I followed up by email with Kevin later that week, wishing him well for the rest of his trip and that "we'll catch up perhaps at SXSW" the following month. He wrote back, "We tried the oysters the next day—soooo awesome, thanks for the tip! See you at SXSW, and thanks again for dinner!" Like any shy kid spoken to by the most popular boy in class, I was glad to be the recipient of his enthusiasm. But we never did meet at South by Southwest. In fact, we never had any communication again.

In the months following our dinner, Digg's relationship with its top users continued to fluctuate wildly. Eventually, after a disastrous 4.0 upgrade in August 2010, its power users migrated once and for all to Reddit.

For the rest of the week after the Digg podcast call, I attended the 2006 Supernova conference, run by a business academic named Kevin Werbach. It wasn't as good as the Web 2.0 Conference. In too many cases, panelists and speakers just talked about their own products or companies, and the event was targeted at businesspeople, not developers (the tagline was "Because technology is everyone's business"). That was true of the Web 2.0 Conference as well, but developers were at least hanging around the hallways there—which wasn't the case at Supernova.

The most interesting news from my perspective was Yahoo announcing more support for "microformats," a structured blogging initiative that had emerged the previous year. The theory was that making web content more structured through open-standard formats made it possible (or at least a lot easier) to create new aggregation services. The announcement was part of a larger story that Yahoo was pushing in the industry: that it was now an open platform and that developers were free to build things on its APIs and "mashup" its user data as they pleased.

Flickr was Yahoo's key product in these claims to be an open platform. It was popular among developers, and it was fun and relatively easy to experiment with photo-sharing data. At the time of the Supernova conference, Flickr supported two microformats on its user profile pages: hCard and XFN (XHTML Friends Network). This basically meant that your name and friend connections were in common data formats, so theoretically other social networks could use that data.

I was offered an interview with two Yahoo executives to discuss its ambitions to be an open platform. One was a Flickr founder, Caterina Fake, who was now leader of Yahoo's Technology Development Group. The other was Bradley Horowitz, a VP of product strategy.

I arranged to meet them on Friday afternoon in front of the Garden Court restaurant, next to the Supernova conference room at the Palace Hotel. Just before my interview, Bradley did a presentation entitled "Opening Up Yahoo." In it, he talked about some projects Yahoo had started to encourage third-party developers to build on its content, such as Yahoo! Hack Day and the Yahoo Developer Network. As one example, he mentioned that Flickr had "thousands of people" developing on its API, building everything from "frivolous toys and games" to "real valuable tools like Flickr uploaders and camera phone integrations."[35]

He also admitted that Stewart Butterfield, Fake's cofounder (and husband) was at first very resistant to opening Flickr to third-party developers. He said that Butterfield had been involved in a public debate about "opening up the Flickr API to would-be competitors that basically wanted to airlift users' content out of there." According to Horowitz, Butterfield eventually came around to the idea that "if it's done in a reciprocal way, such that we can get the data back into Flickr, that's actually a good thing for the user." He added that Yahoo intended to compete with companies that used Flickr data based on the merits of "the Flickr product and community."

Sure enough, the Flickr web services available in June 2006 allowed developers access to a wide range of data about user photos, including the "interestingness" algorithm. However, Yahoo had carefully ring-fenced commercial development. The Flickr API was "available for non-commercial use by outside developers," the company said, but commercial use was only possible "by prior arrangement."[36] That was Yahoo's way of making sure that other companies didn't build a better product or app than the Flickr.com website (although frankly, it's hard to imagine a better site being built, as Flickr was a joy to use).

After that talk, I sat down with Bradley and Caterina. Bradley, then in his early forties, was a neatly dressed man with dark curly hair and rectangular black-rimmed glasses. He regarded me with a mix of politeness and something I interpreted as condescension (or perhaps it was just the supreme confidence of an MIT-educated dot-com founder turned Silicon Valley executive). Caterina was a couple of years older than me. She had shoulder-length dark hair and was wearing an olive-green top over blue jeans. She too was polite but a little standoffish.

After doing my introductory spiel about why I was doing the interview, I realized that neither of them knew much about Read/WriteWeb. I had thought that Caterina, at least, would know who I was. I'd been a member of Flickr since its launch in 2004, and I had blogged about it multiple times since then.

I was a bit unsettled by the pair's reaction to me. Most of the other tech people I'd met in the United States—startup founders, developers, and product managers—were readers of my blog or had at least heard of it. I had the sense that people wanted to engage with me socially, that we were part of the same network. For whatever reason, I didn't feel that way in this meeting.

Bradley did most of the talking, and was an expert at keeping to his talking points. But it was something that Caterina said that stood out for me. We were talking about how the goal for Yahoo products was to achieve organic growth via social relationships. Caterina said that if Yahoo did a Superbowl commercial for Flickr, the mass of users that came via the TV ads probably wouldn't understand the product. But users who came to Flickr via their social network have a better understanding of the product and hence a better chance of using it.

It was an astute observation; sure enough, growth via social connections was the main reason Facebook would take off in the next year or two. It was also the reason why microformats never became popular—the social graph of people interested in them was just too small. Flickr users didn't care one bit about hCard and XFN. Portability of data wasn't why people joined Flickr—they just wanted to upload their photos to a cool website like their friends.

Third-party developers were also uninterested, and by and large they did not build Yahoo apps that used microformats. Instead, they preferred building the "frivolous" Flickr apps that Bradley had mentioned in his talk (part of the reason their attention would soon be diverted to Facebook and Twitter). Even early adopters of social software, such as tech bloggers, neglected to use the available microformat features to add semantic information to their profiles.

It was another key lesson for entrepreneurs and developers in the Web 2.0 era: keep things simple and frivolous, and hope users will come to your patch of the web and recommend it to their friends.

That Friday, I skipped the last day of Supernova to attend the first day of BloggerCon IV. It was an "unconference" jointly run by Dave Winer, the pioneering blogger and software developer, and Harvard Law School's Berkman Center. I later adopted the unconference format for my own RWW events, which began in 2009. But whereas we wanted to make money from our events, Winer liked to call his BloggerCon unconference "non-commercial" (although he sold blogging software for a living, so it was obviously a good promotional tool for him).

BloggerCon was held at CNET's office in San Francisco, so the location was familiar after my meeting with ZDNet editor Dan Farber back in October. Dan was at BloggerCon too, as were most of my blog buddies—Mike Arrington, Gabe Rivera, Susan Mernit, Marc Canter, Chris Pirillo, Anil Dash, and others. And yes, of the fewer than one hundred attendees, most were men—although the ratio was improved slightly by the presence of three founders from a conference called BlogHer.

BloggerCon was also deliberately low-key. When you walked into CNET, a hand-drawn sign to the left of reception pointed the way to the conference room. It was just a black marker pen on a large piece of paper, and it couldn't have contrasted more with the slick, neon-yellow signage of CNET at the reception desk. Another handwritten sign just outside the conference room prompted the attendees to sign in by filling out a name tag sticker.

The event got under way with Winer sitting at a desk facing the attendees. Sitting beside him was Doc Searls, another baby boomer blogger.

"This is sort of a different conference," Winer told the assembled bloggers in his opening remarks. "If you'll notice, there's, like, no audience—although it kind of looks like you're an audience, I guess, right? It's tempting, but if you hear somebody use the word *audience*, correct them and say, *participant*."[37]

In principle, there was a lot to like about this approach. As Winer went on to say, "There are plenty of commercial technology conferences where people pitch their products all the time. We don't need another one of those." Indeed, Supernova was just such a conference, so I was looking forward to seeing how different BloggerCon would actually be.

Unfortunately, being an introverted and shy person, I didn't participate much in the discussions that happened throughout the day. It turned out the "unconference" format tended to favor extroverted personalities, which meant the same old people—like Winer, Canter, and Pirillo—were doing all the talking. I blame myself for this; not having the gumption to speak up was another symptom of my long-running self-esteem issues. However, as I wrote in my summary of the event, I also felt the "discussion leaders" could've done more to encourage others to pitch in. I made sure that happened when we began running RWW unconference events a few years later.

Overall, though, it was a fun event over the two days, Friday and Saturday. The small turnout encouraged the sense of community that we all felt. Blogging was just starting to become commercial, but at the same time there was a determined effort—by Winer in particular—to make sure that bloggers held onto the "core values" of blogging. These values were ill-defined but emphasized things like authenticity, transparency, and a conversational manner of writing.

To close out the conference, Winer had asked Mike Arrington to talk on this topic. Mike started the session by joking about his previous career as a lawyer—the implication being that lawyers aren't known for their values. "Because of the support of people in this room, my blog got pretty big, pretty fast," he continued. "And so I went from the good times, when you start getting a couple of comments [and] 'oh there's a conversation taking place,' to the real hate stuff, that we all probably deal with every day." He added that he had "more hate comments today and more troll comments today, than actual real comments."[38]

This wasn't something I had experienced to the degree Mike had. Partly this was because his site was significantly bigger than mine, but also, Mike's blogging style was combative. He liked to poke and prod on issues in order to get reactions from people. My blogging style was more balanced—more journalistic, I suppose, although I didn't think about it that way at the time. The key difference between us was in who we wrote for. I approached topics from the perspective of a developer or an early adopter—trying to discover what can be built with a technology such as RSS and what a proactive user can do with it. Mike approached topics from a product or market perspective, which meant his posts were more attractive to a consumer or business audience—readers who were just beginning to discover tools like YouTube and Facebook and wanted to know more about them.

Because he now reached a broad audience, Mike experienced the downsides of the "wisdom of crowds" before me. Hate comments and trolling would, of course, become commonplace on social media in the years to come. It wasn't a new phenomenon, either; popular newsgroups and forums in the 1980s and 1990s had attracted plenty of shitposters and trolls. But the attacks did perhaps feel more personal, since blogs were so closely tied to the personality of an individual. Certainly Mike thought so.

He also thought bloggers themselves were beginning to leave nasty comments. "I think there's a trend toward people, non-anonymously, getting more vicious in their blogging and in their comments," he said, which brought the discussion back to what the "core values" for bloggers were. In the discussion that followed, various people told stories of their own experiences with trolls. But there was no resolution or answer to the question of whether the core values of bloggers were beginning to erode.

I didn't think this was a useful discussion, and even if I had been called upon (which I wasn't), I didn't have a good troll story to tell. So I began to tune out, checking my blog stats and tech.memeorandum while the debate raged on. I was also hanging out in the IRC backchannel, where many of my fellow introverts were chatting. In this way, BloggerCon was just the same as Supernova—if you lose interest in a session, there's always your laptop to look at.

Eventually, Mike changed the topic to something that was front and center for emerging pro bloggers like me: conflicts of interest. He wanted to explore the more subtle ways that this can influence a blogger. "What if I'm investing in a company, and I've disclosed that, but they have a competitor?" he said. "Or, you know, just the subtle ways that we can all push things we like and not push things we don't like—where's the line there?"

This was something I would grapple with in the coming months, as I landed new sponsors. Zoho was in the web office space and Pageflakes was in start pages—two product categories that I loved to write about. If anything, I ended up trying to avoid writing about my sponsors; over the following years, I wrote more often about Google Docs than Zoho, and Netvibes more than Pageflakes. In retrospect, I was perhaps a little unfair on my sponsors when it came to editorial.

The prevailing wisdom of the BloggerCon attendees was that bloggers should be very transparent: if you are writing about a topic where you might've been influenced by a sponsor, or even a friendship, then disclose it. But my ZDNet editor Dan Farber had an even deeper cut. "You have to know in your heart whether you're being honest, and [that] you're preserving your integrity, because that's all you have," Dan said. "You blow that away, you're done—you're finished." Om Malik, another longtime journalist turned blogger, had said a similar thing earlier in the session.

As RWW began turning into a media business over the rest of 2006, those words from "proper journalists" (a phrase I used a fair bit back then) were my guiding star. Integrity was the key—whether it was how you communicated on your blog and via comments on other blogs or how you dealt with conflicts of interest. We could talk about core values at an unconference until the cows came home, but ultimately a blogger only had one person to answer to: themself.

On the evening of Wednesday, June 28, 2006, I attended a party at Marc Canter's house in Walnut Creek. It was the public launch of PeopleAggregator, Marc's would-be MySpace competitor, which he was promoting as "a social network and blogging system in a box."[39] The following morning many of the party attendees would be on a plane to Seattle for Chris Pirillo's Gnomedex conference. I was staying the night at Marc's house and then going to the airport tomorrow morning with him, his family, and a couple of his Indian developers, Ashish and Gaurav.

Once again, I got lucky with the weather in Seattle—it was the middle of summer and gloriously sunny. I'd bought my own plane ticket from Oakland to Seattle, but to save money I was rooming with another of Marc's employees (also called Marc) at a hotel nearby the Gnomedex venue. The event was being held at the Bell Harbor Convention Center, right on the waterfront.

At the pre-party that evening, I caught up with fellow kiwi blogger Phil Pearson, who was one of the lead developers of PeopleAggregator. Coincidentally, we had both started blogging on the exact same day in 2002 and had communicated a lot by email and IM ever since. I'd met him in person for the first time in 2005, but this was our first meetup while in the States together. A good-looking guy with slick black hair, about seven or eight years younger than me, Phil was one of the rare kiwis who understood what I did for a living.

Gnomedex turned out to be the most fun conference I'd attended yet, mainly due to Pirillo's hosting skill. He was a human ball of energy, which rubbed off on everyone who attended. The content was eclectic and interesting, as were the party venues—at one point I found myself in a crowded hotel room at an after-hours party, singing "O Canada!" for reasons I don't recall. The other tech conferences I'd attended over the past year were straightlaced in comparison. For instance at

Gnomedex, Susan Mernit—for whom I'd done freelance work before she went full-time at Yahoo—did a talk about sex and relationships. If it had been any other conference, her talk would've been about widgets and microformats. There were some nice event touches, too; a room was set up for football fans to hang out and watch the World Cup quarter finals, which I did.

Another Gnomedex session that stood out for me was run by Ethan Kaplan, who worked in the technology division at Warner Bros. Records. Onstage with him was Dave Dederer, a founding member of the rock band the Presidents of the United States of America (most known for their 1995 hit single, "Lump"). The session opened with Dederer singing two songs from my favorite band, the Velvet Underground: "We're Gonna Have a Real Good Time Together" and "I'm Waiting for the Man." Then the pair discussed the music industry on the web. Dederer was in his early forties and had left his group a couple of years earlier, but he was clearly ahead of the curve—he said that online music was at 1 percent of its potential, but that it already made up half of the Presidents' revenue.

On Friday, I took a break from Gnomedex festivities to attend a dinner organized by the Yahoo! Publisher Network at Tulio on Fifth Avenue. It was pitched to me as "an intimate gathering of some fellow Yahoo's and industry thought leaders (like yourself) to break bread and discuss the state of technology and the Internet." It was, however, forgettable, in part because I no longer had any career ambitions with the company. Back in March, I'd flown to Sydney to interview for a job at Yahoo!7, a joint company formed by Yahoo and an Australian media network called Seven. The job title was Consumer Insights Manager, but it turned out they weren't very interested in the insights part. In the rejection email, I was told I had "a very strong background and incredible mind," but that two other candidates had "a better personality match for the role." Once again, my introversion and social awkwardness had killed off a career opportunity. Fortunately, those were two aspects of my personality that I could effectively hide—or overcome through the written word—on my blog and in the virtual consulting work I did. My meeting with Horowitz and Fake at Supernova had further disabused me of the notion that I had a special relationship with Yahoo. The company just wanted me to blog about their latest news. This helped me realize, once and for all, that Read/WriteWeb was my key asset going forward—and that I needed to spend more time on it, rather than try and land a nine-to-five job.

My notebooks from this time are full of plans for Read/WriteWeb—my goal now was to turn it into "a blog that makes me self-sufficient," which meant earning at least $6,000 per month. Once I'd achieved that, I noted, I would decrease or even drop my consulting work and other blogging jobs.

Part of my renewed strategy for RWW was to increase my daily content, "using shorter, more easily consumable posts," and to "build community" by interacting with readers in the comments. There was definitely momentum with RWW by this point, however I still wasn't all-in on it. I had one other external project on the go at this time, and it demanded a decent chunk of my time.

It was a comment left on my blog at the beginning of 2006 that led me to cofound a new company. It was from a guy named Michael Bayler, who was based in London and ran a blog called The Rights Marketing Company. It had post titles like "Media strategy predictions for 2006" and "Music Industry 2.0—read this and understand." The content piqued my interest, so I replied to the email notification, and soon Michael and I were chatting about business opportunities.

During a phone call a couple of weeks later, I learned that Michael was a marketing specialist who'd worked for the music industry in the 1980s. He was a confident and personable man who called me "mate" and peppered his conversation with phrases like "digital disruption," "brand strategy" and "consumer culture." He said he was keen to partner with me, given my status in the increasingly popular Web 2.0 world.

Michael was very persuasive, as all the best marketers are, and he quickly convinced me that his insider knowledge of the media and entertainment industries would be useful to me. He suggested we start something new that bridged our two worlds. I was looking for more income, and I also wanted to find a way into the traditional media

industry. Susan Mernit had been hiring me to write market analysis reports for the likes of Hearst and *TV Guide*. I enjoyed that work,
but it was irregular and I wanted to have more exposure to big media
companies.

What Michael had in mind was a new consultancy project called the
Media 2.0 Workgroup, an obvious copy of the Web 2.0 Workgroup I'd
founded with Mike and Fred. Michael had written a "draft mandate" for
this new group, which aimed to provide insights about the new internet
landscape to media owners, rights owners, and marketers. On our phone
call he talked about the group becoming "enablers for big companies
in advanced media" and said we would articulate the "new consumer
experience." He mentioned that British Telecom (BT) and Microsoft's
UK branch were already interested in signing up, adding that clients
like this need guidance on how to invest in technology-enabled media.

I was impressed that the Media 2.0 Workgroup was more formal
and structured than its Web 2.0 counterpart—indeed, it actually had a
business plan. I emailed Mike and Fred to let them know about it and
that I planned to join the new group. Neither was interested, so I continued the discussions with Michael on my own. He introduced me to
his business partner at Rights Marketing, Jonathan Lakin, who sent me
a proposed agreement at the end of March. The workgroup idea had
by now turned into a new UK company, the Micro Media Corporation,
which would be a sister company to Rights Marketing.

The draft agreement gave me 10 percent of the new business, with
Michael and Jonathan getting 30 percent each, 20 percent to be split
with contributors, and the remaining 10 percent "an allocation for other
execs that may be brought in at a later point to grow the business." I'd
also be paid a monthly retainer of $3,750 after the first few months
(I'd receive a discounted amount to start with). The remuneration was
attractive because I didn't yet have a regular income from RWW. Combined with payments from my other blogging and consultancy work, it
would take my freelance earnings well past the salary I'd been getting
the previous year as a web manager.

The draft contract stated that I was "expected to play a major role
in the development of the business," which I had already been doing

over February and March—primarily by being the point person for new contributors. I'd emailed a bunch of people I knew from the Web 2.0 world, including Josh Porter and John Musser. I'd also blogged about it, which led to people contacting me—one of whom was Pete Cashmore, who had recently started a blog called Mashable. Pete was a Scottish guy in his early twenties, and his blog would in time become a competitor to TechCrunch. But he was just starting out in early 2006, and in one of our emails at that time he said he was "working as a consultant right now, specializing in peer production and social software." Clearly, it was early days for him, too, in gaining advertisers for his blog.

Michael and Jonathan had initially called the product that we'd be producing IntraCast, a portmanteau of the words *intranet* (an internal company website) and *podcast*. But sometime during April that was changed to TransMission. Corporate subscriptions for this product, which was marketed in a PowerPoint presentation as "multi-channel leadership programs in Web and Media 2.0," would start at £2,500 per month. Other than that, I didn't know the specifics of how they were trying to sell this to companies like BT. I didn't need to know, as it was their job to sell this program; my responsibility was content and getting contributors.

During April I planned the schedule for the Breakfast Bulletin, a daily blog and podcast to be published early morning UK time (evening for me). We'd do three bulletins per week at first. I was already working every night, and this schedule would exacerbate that. Effectively I would be the managing editor for the bulletin, pulling in blog and podcast contributions about the day's theme. The freelancers were being paid $90 per contribution; not bad, bearing in mind that very few bloggers got paid for their work in that era. We launched the bulletin in late April.

Micro Media Corp ended up being a good source of monthly income for me over 2006, but it soon became clear that nobody other than BT was subscribing to it. Despite the talk of selling the product into various corporations, there was only ever that single client. I blogged about it on RWW in June, which brought in some leads. In September I posted an example of a bulletin on RWW and again put the call out:

"If your organization is looking for regular thought leadership in the Web 2.0 and New Media world, email me and I'll send you subscription details."[40]

But it wasn't my job to bring in corporate clients, so I was becoming frustrated with the lack of growth. Also, sometime in September 2006, I stopped hearing from Michael Bayler. My point person at Rights Marketing was now Jane Gough, who was a friendly and organized project manager. Michael had seemingly lost interest in Micro Media Corp, although I never found out why. Jane remained my main contact for the rest of the year.

BT's contract came up for renewal in March 2007, and so Micro Media Corp petered out with a whimper. It took me a further year to get my final payment from Rights Marketing—I was told finances had dried up. Ultimately, my 10 percent interest in Micro Media Corp led to nothing.

So, corporate blogging didn't work out for me. Fortunately, Read/WriteWeb was going from strength to strength.

CHAPTER 6

LOU REED

■ ■ ■ ■ ■

DURING THE SECOND HALF OF 2006, more and more of my focus was on building up Read/WriteWeb. In July 2006 I announced a major redesign of the site. The previous design had been a thin two-column layout on a white background, with red font for the headers and links. It featured a circular logo with the letters *R* and *W* inside, which I'd created in Photoshop using the yin-yang symbol as inspiration. Up till this point, I had done all the web design and development myself. This work was serviceable, but I needed a bit more design flair to keep up with TechCrunch, GigaOm, Mashable, and other Web 2.0 blogs. Also, the layout needed opening up to accommodate more advertisers and sponsors.

The new design, which went live in July, was certainly wider and more colorful. It had a red background with a cream-colored header and sidebar. It was now much roomier in the sidebar and header areas, with plenty of space for display ads. The main text area remained white, and I stuck with the red links. I had a new logo, too, although this was the weakest part of the new design. The yin-yang still anchored the top left of the page, but the letters had been removed, and the site name—Read/WriteWeb—appeared in a serif font in red and grey in the cream-colored header.

The design was a step up from my previous hacked-together designs, but it had clearly been a little rushed—there were glitches, especially with the latest Internet Explorer browser (version 7). The designer was Kevin Hale of Particletree, who was a member of the Web 2.0 Workgroup. I'd approached him in May, noting that I didn't have the money to pay him, but perhaps we could do a quid pro quo arrangement? Kevin was working on an online form builder called Wufoo. This wasn't a new idea, but his online form generator was powered by Ajax, the web development technique that had helped define Web 2.0. He agreed to design a new template for me in exchange for a review of Wufoo when it launched.

Kevin seemed to be very busy with Wufoo, so his communication was sporadic. I suspect he left my project till the last minute. Regardless, by July he'd delivered me a new template. Wufoo had recently gotten funding from Y Combinator, a now-famous Silicon Valley incubator that was then just over a year old. So he was onto bigger and better things, and we quickly lost contact.

Incidentally, the day after I announced my redesign, a new service called Twttr launched. It was a text-based application and only available in the United States. Users were prompted to share short status updates with a group of friends by sending a text message to a specific number (40404). Since Twttr was available only to those with a US phone number, I couldn't even test it out. Indeed, I probably found out about it only via a TechCrunch post—Mike had noted that "a few select insiders were playing with the service at the Valleyschwag party in San Francisco last night."[41] I did mention the new product in that week's RWW Weekly Wrapup, but since I couldn't use Twttr I promptly forgot about it.

Around this time I also began accepting offers from entrepreneurs and developers to write guest posts for RWW. The site had gained in popularity over 2006, so it was potentially a way for people to get attention for their own startup or passion project. I was happy to bring new writers on board, since it lifted some of the creative burden off me. The second regular contributor to RWW, as it turned out, became one of the site's enduring names.

Alex Iskold was a native Ukrainian whose family had moved to the United States in the early 1990s. He was about my age, but on arrival he didn't speak English, and so he attended a community college at first. He then studied computer science at New York University and became a software engineer for Goldman Sachs in mid-1994 (the exact same time I started my first job, in Auckland). Alex was onto his second startup by the time he contacted me in May 2006. His company was called AdaptiveBlue and had built a Firefox extension called Blueorganizer, which allowed people to "automatically collect, tag and share objects such as books, music albums and movies," as it was described to me in the first email pitch I received.

Alex emailed me several more times, requesting that I write a review of Blueorganizer. He was very persistent and kept following up on my empty promises to "look into it soon." During one of these email exchanges in August, he offered to write articles for me. One of his ideas was a post about the "new breed of smart client applications built on top of virtual web services like Amazon." I was intrigued with that idea, since Amazon had just released its first cloud computing product that March. Called Amazon S3, it was a cloud-storage solution and I'd blogged about it on ZDNet. But I hadn't yet found a way to discuss it on RWW, which had more of a consumer web focus. Also, given Alex's background as an engineer, I figured he'd be great at explaining the technical implications of what Amazon was up to with its new "web services" infrastructure products. The term *cloud computing* wasn't yet popular, so tech bloggers like me were still trying to figure out Amazon's strategy.

A couple of days later, Alex sent me his draft article, which he'd titled "The Emergence of the Web Services." The article was a very smart analysis of what Amazon, Google, Microsoft, and the like were building in the infrastructure layer of the web. He even had a graphic that neatly encapsulated the types of web services these companies were creating—"storage services" (such as S3), "messaging services," "compute services," and so on. Because English wasn't Alex's native tongue, there was a fair bit of editing to do—but it was clear to me that the content was top quality. I renamed the article "Web Platform Primer—What's Available via API?" and published it on August 22, 2006.

Because Alex was building a startup that utilized the new web platform services from Amazon and others, he was able to see the bigger trend emerging. As he put it in the article, "10 years of Amazon's expertise in large-scale distributed computing are suddenly available at a very reasonable cost to anyone who is paying attention." I immediately recognized that Alex's technical posts about the web platform would be the ideal complement to my own posts. Also, he was amenable to my edits. I had changed his opening to make it less abstract and more practical for web developers. Some people may have objected to this type of editing, but Alex wanted to fit in with the existing RWW style. "I see what you are looking for—clean, simple and factual style," he wrote back after seeing the published article. "I have no problems doing things this way."

Just a couple of days later, Amazon released the second product in its new cloud computing suite. Called Amazon Elastic Compute Cloud (EC2), it fit perfectly into the "compute services" section of Alex's post. Alex had written that there were "no generic examples of black-box compute services that are available today on the web via API," but Amazon's EC2 seemed like it had been released just to fill that void. I wrote up a quick post about the news, noting that the name "sounds like a Terry Gilliam movie" and then pointed readers to Alex's post: "he really captures the high level of why products like Amazon EC2 are increasingly important in today's Web landscape."[42]

This was the birth of what we now know as Amazon Web Services, which eventually got spun off by Amazon and became almost the most successful company to emerge out of Web 2.0—behind only Facebook. I'm proud that RWW was one of the first blogs to write about Amazon's web services, and one of the few to identify its massive potential. I have Alex to thank for that.

Alex's next post was a survey of the client apps using the new web platform, which gave him a chance to mention Blueorganizer and its use of the S3 storage service. I was okay with this type of subtle self-promotion, which became a common tactic used by future contributors to RWW. As long as it was disclosed in the post and didn't detract from the analysis of web technology—RWW's core focus—I didn't mind if a contributor slipped in the odd mention of their product.

RWW had several other regular contributors by the end of 2006, but the other one to have a significant impact in the years to come was Emre Sokullu, a young Turkish entrepreneur. Like Alex, Emre was a clever software engineer, and I valued his technical expertise when writing posts such as "GoogleOS: What To Expect" and "Search 2.0—What's Next?" Those posts generated a lot of discussion on the site, along with page views, and helped solidify RWW's growing reputation as the "thinking person's tech blog."

In early November I was back in Silicon Valley to attend the annual Web 2.0 Conference, now renamed Web 2.0 Summit, and with the theme of "Disruption & Opportunity." The name change was because the organizers, O'Reilly Media and John Battelle, were expanding and had added a companion trade show, Web 2.0 Expo, that was to launch the following year. It was a sign of the times: by November 2006 lots of business opportunities were opening up in the Web 2.0 ecosystem.

Several significant developments had emerged in Web 2.0 in the couple of months leading up to the summit. In September, Facebook introduced its "news feed" and opened sign-ups to anyone over age thirteen with an email address. I didn't sign up at that time, though; I was still more interested in RSS than social networks. In late September, a redesign of Google Reader was launched and I wrote an overexcited blog post about it. "It now has a look n' feel very much like Gmail,"[43] I gushed, adding that I thought Google Reader might soon be merged with Gmail.

Google was starting to piece together a lot of things by this point. In August it released "Google Apps for Your Domain," a set of apps for organizations that included Gmail, Google Talk, Google Calendar, and Google Page Creator. Then in early October it launched "Google Docs & Spreadsheets," an online word processor and spreadsheet. Slowly but surely it was creating an entire suite to compete with the mighty Microsoft Office.

At the same time, Google was further entrenching itself as the dominant consumer web company. In October it acquired the leading online video startup, YouTube. It was the first big acquisition of the

Web 2.0 era, since the $1.65 billion price tag was the first purely web M&A to go over a billion dollars since Netscape back in 1999. I remember feeling some shock over the amount Google paid for YouTube, but it turned out to be one of the deals of the century; in later years, the video platform would routinely earn revenue in the tens of billions of dollars per year.

Not to be outdone by Facebook or Google, a *BusinessWeek* cover story in early November outlined Amazon's bold new web services strategy. For the first time, it became clear that Amazon saw itself as much more than an e-commerce retailer. Now, at the height of Web 2.0, it was renting out its software infrastructure stack to startups and other companies as "web services." As Iskold put it in a RWW post, "Amazon is beginning to look more like an alternative Microsoft for the web computing era."[44]

There was so much to write about, so it's no coincidence that I was just about all-in on Read/WriteWeb when the Web 2.0 Summit rolled around. RWW had five sidebar sponsors by the end of October, and FM Publishing's ads were finally beginning to bring in half-decent money. The bulk of my income was now coming from RWW, so naturally that's where most of my energy was going.

By the time I arrived in San Francisco in early November, I'd basically ditched my ZDNet blog (although I gave them one final post later that month). I was still on a monthly retainer from Micro Media Corp, but I viewed that as a part-time endeavor. As for the consulting work that had helped keep me afloat over the past year, I was only doing a bit of that now. I'd dropped the technical writing work from Marc Canter and didn't have time to do research or analysis reports for others. I'd made an exception for my Irish friend Fergus Burns, who was giving me $1,000 per month to be a regular adviser to his RSS services company Nooked, along with the promise of a tiny bit of equity.

Fergus was also kindly putting me up during the first portion of my US trip. He'd booked a double room for us at the Hotel Nikko, so I would be rooming with him for five nights before heading to Mike's place at the end of the week for the last few nights of my trip. I'd told Fergus I was looking forward to staying in the city this time around so that I could attend the post-conference parties—"Traveling to and fro from the valley put a dampener on that last time," I said.

Aside from the increased opportunities for socializing, I was also beginning to get serious about the growing value of RWW. I planned to talk to my US contacts about expansion plans—maybe even talk with VCs about funding. In October I'd chatted to Mike about potentially selling my business to him, although the discussions didn't get very far. He'd offered to buy RWW for a 5 percent equity stake in TechCrunch, along with a $60,000 salary to work for him. I countered by asking for a 10 percent stake in TechCrunch and at least a $100,000 base salary. I wasn't sure if I wanted this, though, because I enjoyed being independent and I didn't want to subjugate myself to anyone—let alone Mike, whom I saw as my equal even though his blog was more successful than mine. But this halfhearted negotiation with Mike (he didn't even respond to my emailed counter) at least got me thinking about the value I was building with RWW.

Fergus made some interesting points when I told him about my stalled discussions with Mike. (Fergus and I were the same age, but he seemed to have a much better head for business than I did.) He suggested I commercialize the research work that I was doing for Nooked—and had been doing for a bunch of others before RWW got so busy. Why not set up an entity called RWW Research, he suggested, and then do a deal with Mike to sell the reports through TechCrunch as well as RWW? It was a good idea, and it would also get me back doing the type of product development and market research work that I had so enjoyed. But to pull this off, I would need help. I needed to speak to some investors to get my head around this expansion opportunity.

Fortunately, Iskold—now a regular guest blogger—introduced me via email to an investor he knew: Josh Kopelman of First Round Capital, one of the leading Web 2.0 VCs. Unfortunately, I accidentally blew off a meeting with him on Wednesday morning. I was to meet Josh for breakfast at 7:30 a.m. that morning, at Maxfield's in the Palace Hotel. But after a late night of boozing with Fergus and my other Irish entrepreneur friends, I slept through my alarm. Probably one too many pints at the Swig bar on Geary Street.

I didn't have a US phone, so it was only when Josh emailed that I realized my error. I replied that "for some reason I had thought our meeting was tomorrow morning" (a thin excuse) and asked if he was free later that day. He was very gracious in response. "My day today is pretty jammed," he wrote back, "but if you have time, feel free to head up to our meeting room (Sonoma room on the second floor) and we can try to grab 5 minutes."

It is a measure of my utter immaturity at this time that I continued to avoid meeting Josh, even when I had the opportunity to pop into the Sonoma room at the Palace Hotel. Later that day, on the way to another session or to an interview, I walked past the Sonoma room. However, I made the mistake of furtively looking in—only to see Josh looking directly back at me! My face reddened with embarrassment, and I quickly looked away. After I'd passed the room, I shook my head in frustration. It was now out of the question that I would meet him. Clearly, I did not respect the rules of Silicon Valley etiquette and no sane VC would ever invest in me.

Happily, I eventually connected with Josh at the end of the month, by phone, when I was back in New Zealand.

I had a busy Web 2.0 Summit, meeting with companies like Microsoft, About.com, Ask.com, and Automattic (which ran Wordpress.com). I asked for business advice from Toni Schneider, the CEO of Automattic, who had recently started up a VC firm called True Ventures. I knew that True Ventures had invested in GigaOm, the tech blog founded by longtime Silicon Valley journalist Om Malik. Even though GigaOm was a competitor to RWW, I was friendly with Om and had also talked to Toni before, so I knew Toni would be straight up with me.

His advice was to stick with my focus on quality, in-depth coverage of tech news. Nobody was doing analysis of the Web 2.0 space like I was, he said. He suggested I expand by writing about related topics like the mobile web (then still very much in its infancy; little did we know that in just two months, Steve Jobs would unveil the iPhone).

We discussed an idea that was thriving in the pro blogger community: running a network of blogs on niche topics related to the main blog. The idea was that if I started a mobile blog, for example, I'd hire someone to write the posts and then I would handle the business side of it. Both TechCrunch and GigaOm had networks, although each did it in a different way. Mike had started a couple of separately branded blogs, CrunchGear (a copy of Engadget) and MobileCrunch (about the mobile web), edited by hired bloggers. Om hired bloggers to cover niche topics, such as online games, under his main GigaOm brand. Toni said Mike's approach was the better strategy, since I'd be able to cross-link from RWW—this would drive my core audience to the new products and also build up Google juice for their domains. Most surprisingly, given his role as a True Ventures partner, Toni also advised me to bootstrap for as long as possible. VC funding changes everything, he warned.

As the Web 2.0 Summit drew to a close, I reflected that the vibe felt different this year. "Last year there were a lot more developers and designers running around, this year the crowd was overwhelmingly from the media and business worlds," I wrote, although I added that I still enjoyed the conference. While I felt that the Web 2.0 Summit "lacked in cutting edge new products,"[45] the networking made it all worthwhile—despite my failure to meet Kopelman.

I also noted that "undoubtedly my personal highlight was seeing Lou Reed play live (courtesy of AOL)." This had happened on Thursday evening, and I was in the second row when Lou ambled out onto the stage. He wore a brown sleeveless vest and dark blue jeans, and he looked lean and angry. With the bright blue-and-white logo of AOL illuminated behind him, Lou began playing alongside two band members. But he quickly brought the music to a halt, seemingly annoyed by the chatter in the crowd. "You got twenty minutes," he growled. "You wanna talk through it, you can talk through it. Or I can turn the sound up and hurt you." He then demanded that "Frank" turn up the sound, which Frank did—to an earsplitting volume, so that the music now sounded more like *Metal Machine Music* than *New York*.

"Who would have thought it would come to this—I'd be playing at a cyberspace conference, brought here by AOL, introduced by my kung-fu brother," he drawled, referring to the introduction to his set by CEO Jonathan Miller, with whom he apparently shared a tai chi mentor. He began playing "Dirty Boulevard," a song about the mean streets of New York—about as far removed as it can get from a sponsored stage at an upmarket hotel in San Francisco.

In a desperate attempt to keep the mood upbeat, Tim O'Reilly suddenly got up and started bouncing across the floor. He waved his arms around in a jerky motion, like a geeky facsimile of a sixties wild child. This act of madness or bravery inspired others to get up and dance too, and by the time Lou began strumming the familiar chords of "Sweet Jane," there was a nerd party happening right in front of me.

Lou glared at O'Reilly and his retinue, perhaps thinking about how much he hated hippies. But he continued his perfunctory performance of his most famous song, and there were no further stoppages. By the end, he was content to let his volume-distorted, East Coast–derived sound waves roll over these strange Silicon Valley cats.

Almost as snarky was the internet industry critic Nicholas Carr in his summary post about the Web 2.0 Summit. My own blog comments were cited by Carr as among "the tepid reviews of the third annual 2.0 boondoggle."[46] It was a fair cop, but overall I had enjoyed the event. To quote another Lou Reed song, I was "beginning to see the light" about the business opportunities Web 2.0 was presenting to me. Also like Reed, I was more than happy to pocket money from sponsors in return for my content.

On Friday I made my way to the TechCrunch ranch in Atherton, about forty-five minutes south down the 101. Mike was as busy as usual. I brought up the RWW Research idea that I'd chatted to Fergus about, but he was too absorbed in his own expansion plans for the TechCrunch network to care. Simply put, he was on a different level now. He was at the epicenter of the Silicon Valley startup scene, rather than skirting the periphery like me. A *Wall Street Journal* article dated November 3, 2006, had called Mike a "power broker" in the industry and quoted him as saying, "I want more page views than CNET in two years."

The article was written partly in response to Mike's recent post on CrunchNotes, his personal blog, in which he vigorously defended himself from accusations of conflicts of interest. "Techcrunch is all about insider information and conflicts of interest," he'd written. "The only way I get access to the information I do is because these entrepreneurs and venture capitalists are my friends."[47]

One of his friends was a twenty-six-year-old Australian entrepreneur, Nik Cubrilovic, who was staying with Mike when I arrived that Friday. Nik ran an online storage startup called Omnidrive and in his spare time wrote guest posts for TechCrunch. Nik was friendly and charismatic, although over the next couple of years Omnidrive would run into financial difficulties (and eventually fail altogether) and he would fall out with some of his fellow Australian entrepreneurs—one of whom said he invested $100,000 and lost it all. None of this was apparent in November 2006, though. He just seemed like a smart, ambitious young guy. I also noted that Mike relied on Nik to provide technical support and give him background information about the startups he wrote about—similar to what Fred Oliveira did for him the previous year.

After I arrived at Mike's place, Nik added me to an email thread with a bunch of Australian entrepreneurs about a gathering he was organizing for Saturday. Among the people on the thread were Mike Cannon-Brookes (a founder of Atlassian and future billionaire), Marty Wells (founder of Tangler, which I had done some analysis work for), Mick Liubinskas (a Sydney native who worked for Tangler), Chris Saad (a smart product guy who was also active in web standards work), and Cameron Reilly (a Brisbane native who ran a podcast network).

We all met up on Saturday afternoon, at Coupa Café on Ramona Street in Palo Alto. The shop talk about startups and the Web 2.0 Summit soon turned to planning a game of poker. Marty purchased four hundred candy poker chips, we stocked up on alcoholic refreshments, and we then drove back to Mike's house in Atherton.

It was a memorable night, at least for those of us who didn't drink bourbon straight from a tall glass; I'll refrain from mentioning who that was, but he apparently threw up in Marty's car on the way back to San Francisco. Throughout the night there was a lot of bad singing and terrible jokes, and even some dog wrestling (poor Laguna). The poker game itself was played mostly for laughs, although the two Mikes—Cannon-Brookes and Arrington—became increasingly competitive with each other as the evening progressed. I was content to have fun with the cards and enjoy the geek male bonding; most of the others were similarly inclined. Cameron, who was sat next to me, occasionally poked fun at me for being a New Zealander and was generally a hard-ass at the table.

I don't remember who won the poker game, or if there even was a winner, but we ended the night playing liar's dice—a game that involved trying to pick who is bluffing. This ended with a Mike vs. Mike duel. Despite his long, wavy hair and Aussie bloke persona (most sentences began with the word *mate*), it became clear that Cannon-Brookes had an ultracompetitive streak. He was still in his twenties at this point but was already building tremendous value with Atlassian. It would eventually IPO on the NASDAQ at the end of 2015, which made Cannon-Brookes and cofounder Scott Farquhar Australia's first tech-startup billionaires. He was pretty good at card and dice games too.

The games ended when Cannon-Brookes lost his last liar's dice on a technicality, which threw him into a tizzy. The other Mike laughed uproariously, having been declared the winner. I think Arrington left on that high note and went to bed, while the rest of us continued to empty his drinks cabinet. This may've been when the dog wrestling occurred, as I can't imagine Mike letting this happen to his beloved chocolate lab otherwise.

In many respects, 2006 was a breakthrough year for Read/WriteWeb. December revenue for the site was over $14,000, with most of it coming from the sponsor adverts in the right-hand sidebar. FM Publishing revenue was now about a quarter of the site's revenue. I had no employees yet and minimal costs, so it was nearly all gravy.

The site was growing every month in page views and subscribers. December exceeded 370,000 page views, continuing a pattern of steady growth of around 10 to 15 percent each month. I had around 40,000 RSS and email subscribers, which in the heyday of RSS readers was a regular and loyal readership. I was marketing RWW to potential sponsors as "the foremost Web 2.0 analysis blog" and noted that it was among Technorati's Top 100 blogs in the world (it was number 68 by the end of the year—still well behind TechCrunch at number 4 and even GigaOm at 35, but still I was pleased to be on the list).

Despite the rosy statistics for RWW, all the hard work I was putting into it was taking a toll on my personal life. By the end of the year I had moved out of my family home and was temporarily staying with my parents. I'd been having trouble communicating with my wife, and she had become intensely jealous of my overseas trips—with some justification, as we had still not gone on a honeymoon after our marriage back in January. It was all too much, and I moved into a two-bedroom rental early in the new year so that I could have some space to try and work through my issues. I was, of course, most worried about the impact the separation would have on our five-year-old daughter, but things had come to a head with my wife.

I also did not want to drop the ball with RWW, which had real momentum now; I was enjoying the thrill of building my own business and regular trips to Silicon Valley. Making a success out of tech blogging had changed me as a person, and mostly in a good way: I'd become more self-confident and felt that I'd finally discovered what I wanted to do with my life. RWW had started out as my online avatar, but it was much more than that now. It was a growing business—a media brand— and I knew that in 2007 I would be bringing other people in to help me write the articles and run the company. It was a dream come true, from a career perspective.

All that said, I was well aware that my work and life were completely unbalanced, with most of my time and energy going into work. I had a lot to figure out.

For all the problems in my personal life, things were looking ever more promising in the internet industry. In its December 25, 2006, issue, the venerable publication *Time* named the web-powered "You" as its Person of the Year. the accompanying article, written by Lev Grossman, used the term *Web 2.0* a few times (attributed to "Silicon Valley consultants"), and there was talk of an internet "revolution."

Reading the article now, with the benefit of hindsight, it did a great job of capturing both the hope and the concerns of the Web 2.0 era. Grossman acknowledged that tools such as blogs, YouTube, and social networks were "a massive social experiment" and perceptively noted that "Web 2.0 harnesses the stupidity of crowds as well as its wisdom." But he ended on a note of rose-tinted optimism common to that era: "This is an opportunity to build a new kind of international understanding, not politician to politician, great man to great man, but citizen to citizen, person to person."

Time's front-page coverage validated Web 2.0 as a cultural movement, which helped to bring RWW to the attention of even more mainstream people as the new year began.

PART 2

2007–2009

■ ■ ■ ■ ■

CHAPTER 7

RAPID GROWTH

■ ■ ■ ■ ■

THERE HAD BEEN RUMORS of a combined phone and iPod device coming from Apple, but what Steve Jobs announced at Macworld on January 9, 2007, blasted away all expectations. Using his trademark showmanship, Jobs calmly announced that Apple was "introducing three revolution-ary products," which he described as an iPod, a mobile phone, and an internet communicator. He repeated these three ingredients several times, slowly building the anticipation and eliciting whoops and anx-ious laughter from the audience. Then he delivered the punchline: "These are not three separate devices; this is one device—and we are calling it iPhone."[48]

Jobs claimed the iPhone would be both easy to use and "way smarter than any mobile device has ever been," taking shots at existing smart-phone products like the Motorola Q, Nokia E62, Palm Treo, and the BlackBerry. Unlike those other phones, which Jobs said were merely "a little smarter" than cell phones and too hard to use, the iPhone didn't have a QWERTY keyboard. Instead, Apple was introducing a patented touchscreen.

Jobs used the word *revolutionary* no less than ten times in the first fifteen minutes. But for once, the hyperbole about a new internet product was justified. Nobody had done a touchscreen smartphone before, and it would indeed change everything.

The one curious thing about the iPhone announcement, looking back on it sixteen years later, was that were was no mention of smartphone apps. Instead, Jobs pitched the Safari browser on iPhone as "the first fully usable HTML browser on a phone." It was certainly a vast improvement over the limited Wireless Application Protocol (WAP) versions of websites that many of us were used to at that point, but it also didn't quite live up to the "revolutionary" tag. We'd have to wait until the middle of 2008 for the launch of custom iPhone apps, via the App Store. For now, Jobs seemed to be promising that sites like Read/WriteWeb would become much more easily accessible via smartphone (he used the *New York Times* as his actual example).

Interestingly, just a week after the iPhone announcement, we saw a glimpse of the future of apps from a DVD rental service called Netflix. It launched a limited streaming service, with one thousand movies and TV series being made available to download on the internet over the next six months (it had seventy thousand titles on DVD). Up till this point, Netflix had helped popularize Web 2.0 via its website, which featured a slick user interface, algorithmic movie recommendations, ratings, and a "friends list" for sharing movie trivia. But now it was inching into the next era of Web 2.0, what we'd soon come to know as streaming and apps (although the word *streaming* wasn't yet being used—Netflix called it "electronic delivery").

The iPhone was released in the United States at the end of June 2007, but it wasn't available anywhere else in the world at that time. I had to wait till October, when I attended the Web 2.0 Summit, to buy one. I also had to "unlock" the iPhone before I could use it on my local mobile-phone network, which I did as soon as I got back to New Zealand. I needed tech help to do it, as it involved "jailbreaking" it, installing Secure Shell, resetting the root user's password, and all manner of other geekery.

Since the iPhone wasn't widely available outside the States until July 2008, with the global launch of the second-generation iPhone (as well as the App Store), 2007 was a transition year for the smartphone revolution. Apple had opened the door to a mobile future with its January 2007 announcement and mid-year US release, but Web 2.0 remained focused on desktop computer users for the remainder of that year.

Meanwhile, Read/WriteWeb continued to ramp up, with January 2007 my highest-traffic month ever. RWW got around six hundred thousand page views and had more than fifty thousand RSS and email subscribers by the end of the month. Soon after, I got my first newspaper writeup in my home country: the *New Zealand Herald* published a profile of me in early February 2007.

I was on a roll, but I also knew I needed more help on the writing side. In early March I published a guest post by a young freelance writer from Rhode Island named Josh Catone. He'd been a regular commenter on RWW articles and had initially reached out to offer a guest post about early TV streaming services, entitled "Internet Killed the Television Star: Reviews of Joost, Babelgum, Zattoo, and More." The post did well, and I asked if he'd like to become a regular contributor. He eventually became my first paid writer, which I announced on the site in mid-May.

I also began to get more organized by setting up a Basecamp project. Basecamp was project-management software by 37signals, a trendy software company from Chicago known for its Web 2.0 theorizing via blogging and conferences. (It had also developed Ruby on Rails, a popular open-source web application framework.) I pitched the new Basecamp to my writers as "a place where all the R/WW authors can discuss things and note down post ideas." In the beginning, we only used the Messages and To Do sections, so in effect it was a private forum rather than a full-blown intranet.

Shortly after announcing Josh as a daily news writer, I announced the first network blog to launch under the Read/WriteWeb banner: last100, a site about "digital lifestyle" services (what we now call streaming apps). It was to be written by a UK journalist around my age named Steve O'Hear. I'd decided to adopt Mike Arrington's blog-network formula and create separate sites; unlike him, however, I (stupidly) didn't tie the names into the main brand. Everything in Mike's network had *crunch* in the site title, and in hindsight I should've named each of my network sites ReadWrite*Something*. I later rectified this, but in May 2007 they had completely unrelated brand names.

Last100 was Steve's idea, and he had pitched me the concept at the end of March. I'd gotten to know him through Micro Media Corp, where he was one of the regular contributors. He'd also produced a documentary film about his visit to Silicon Valley, called *In Search of the Valley*, which he'd released independently last September. He had a lot of initiative, and I liked his pitch for last100. He explained that the name referenced the "last 100 feet" problem, the gap between the typical home's computer and its living room TV set (remember, this was before smartphones bridged that gap). The idea was to write about emerging areas like online video and digital music.

Steve and I went 50/50 on last100: he would be responsible for writing and editing it, and I would take care of the business side. As I say, I regret not tying the brand into RWW more, especially since it made it more difficult to land sponsors. But regardless, we launched the new site in May 2007.

The second RWW network site was AltSearchEngines, or ASE, as we called it, a 50/50 collaboration with Charles Knight. It launched in early June 2007. Charles, who was roughly ten years older than me, had been writing since January a monthly RWW post called "The Top 100 Alternative Search Engines" (the word *alternative* just meant search engines other than Google). It was a popular feature, so there was clearly reader demand for regular news about search engines. ASE was the first network blog idea—I'd broached it to Charles in March and suggested the domain AltSearchEngines.com. Again, what was I thinking? It should've been ReadWriteSearch.com!

Of the two new network blogs, ASE ended up doing far better. Right from the start, it had a clear agenda, potential sponsors, and a built-in audience in the form of hundreds of entrepreneurs who were trying to compete with Google. I wrote in my launch post that our goal was "to make it the definitive destination for everything related to alternative search engines—over 1,000 of them!"[49] The site motto, which came from Charles, was also a nice teaser for RWW readers: "The most wonderful search engines you've never seen."

I also collaborated more closely with Charles than I did with Steve. Partly that was a time-zone issue, as Steve was in the UK and so we only got to talk in the early mornings or evenings. Charles was from Charlottesville, Virginia—on the US East Coast—so we had more time to sync up. Steve was also more capable of setting his own agenda, whereas Charles needed some handholding in terms of how to write blog posts.

The key difference between the two sites was that ASE very quickly found its audience, and had six paying sponsors before the end of its first month. Charles's top-100 list was the main reason for the instant success of ASE, as he'd cultivated its loyal niche audience on RWW over the past six months. It turned out there was a big demand, relatively speaking, for a blog about search engine startups. He was also great at networking with these startups—he was genuinely passionate about the search community and made a big effort to understand and cultivate it.

Last100 was harder to monetize—we had just two or three sponsors at any one time during the first few months. Steve was writing excellent posts, and the content was more similar in style to RWW than what Charles wrote. In theory, it was a good idea to launch a RWW-style analysis blog about the early days of online streaming, but in practice it wasn't easy to rally a community behind this content in 2007. What people liked about RWW—that it explained the Web 2.0 revolution and put the technology in the context of societal shifts—didn't seem to translate to "digital lifestyle" products. In hindsight, it was probably just too early for last100: the streaming revolution wouldn't kick into gear until several years later.

In 2007 I traveled back to San Francisco for the first Web 2.0 Expo, which was being pitched as a trade show. I arrived on Friday, April 13. I planned to spend a week at the conference and doing other business, and then a week later my wife would join me for a holiday. We had recently reconciled, so I was back in the family home; one of my concessions was that I'd bring her to the United States for the much-delayed honeymoon. After San Francisco we would head to Las Vegas, where I would attend the Microsoft MIX event at the end of the month, and then we'd spend a couple of days in Los Angeles. So it was a mix of conferences and holiday time for me. Our daughter, Rosabelle, now five years old, would stay with her grandparents during this time.

For the first week I stayed at the Courtyard by Marriott on Second Street, mainly because CMP Technology (which cohosted the expo with O'Reilly Media) had given me a free room for the first few nights in exchange for me moderating a panel at the event. The panel, entitled "The New Hybrid Designer," would be a discussion of the modern web designer. I was the last appointment to the panel, so in order to get up to speed I suggested the panelists meet to discuss what exactly a "hybrid designer" is supposed to be. We arranged to have dinner on Friday evening at an Indian restaurant called Chaat Café on Third Street. I brought along Fergus Burns, who had also just gotten into San Francisco that day.

Also at the dinner were Emily Chang (who was in the Web 2.0 Workgroup, although that was basically defunct by this point), Kelly Goto, Chris Messina, and Jeremy Keith—all of us in our twenties or thirties. Other than Fergus, I knew Emily and Chris the best. I wasn't friends with them, but both were familiar faces on the Web 2.0 conference circuit. They were also representative (at least to me) of two different social groups in our little scene. Chris was at the center of a young, hip, developer-focused crowd that was attracted to Web 2.0 as a golden opportunity to create a more open, decentralized web than we'd had in the nineties and early aughts. Emily, a web designer by trade, seemed less interested in the "flower power" aspects of Web 2.0 and more focused on making a professional name for herself. Both had business interests in Web 2.0, of course, but they pursued them in different ways.

Chris and his then girlfriend, Tara Hunt, were the Brad and Angelina of Web 2.0. Together they'd started up a web consultancy called Citizen Agency, and they were popular, extroverted personalities in the internet industry. The pair also organized a kind of conference-within-a-conference at Web 2.0 Expo: called Web2Open, it was a free event where developers and designers discussed the tech issues of the day.

Although he was neither a startup founder nor a developer, Chris went to all the Silicon Valley events and parties. Ever since I'd met him, in around 2005, it felt like he was searching for his claim to internet fame. He would stumble onto it several months after that dinner. A "microblogging" app called Twitter had only just started to ramp up in 2007, so the design patterns for using it were still being worked out. In an August 2007 tweet, Chris suggested that Twitter use the pound sign to signify a keyword. This suggestion got picked up by other Twitter users and soon it became common practice, giving Chris the excuse to call himself "the inventor of the hashtag" for the rest of time.

Emily was also effortlessly cool, but in a more reserved way. She and her partner Max Kiesler ran a design agency in San Francisco called Ideacodes. If Chris and Tara were the partygoing popular couple of the Web 2.0 scene, Emily and Max were the quietly chic, gallery-hopping couple. They were ambitious, just like Chris and Tara, but they were less focused on opening up the world and more interested in capturing value in one part of it: the design profession.

The Web 2.0 Expo turned out to be an interesting mix of technologists and businesspeople. Both types turned up in spades. When the conference officially kicked off on Sunday, my first impression was of how large this event was. It was being held in the spacious Moscone Center, and there was no shortage of attendees to fill up those spaces. Even the press room was full from day one; at times journalists and bloggers were turned away. The signage inside the conference venue was also overwhelming—huge lime-green and azure-blue signs everywhere. Mostly they were banners with the Web 2.0 Expo branding on them, but giant session schedules also loomed over you as you walked the floors. Even the electronic Twitter board had a lime-green background.

Somehow, I got into the press room, which is where I bumped into Anil Dash. He worked at Six Apart, maker of the blogging platform I used: Movable Type. "This is the biggest Web conference I've been to since the late nineties," he remarked as we sat down for a chat.

An Indian American man with a goatee and close-cropped hair, Anil was wearing a pink button-down with a black blazer that day. This typified his relaxed yet self-assured style. Even though Anil was four years younger than me, it felt like I was talking to an older brother. He had been a blogger since 1999 and was a consummate insider in the valley, despite identifying as a New Yorker (he'd briefly moved to San Francisco in 2004 for his job, but by 2007 he and his wife were back in New York). He was not only an expert blogger, but an expert communicator too. He seemed to have an innate ability to form close connections to the people he met in the technology industry—an attribute that I sadly lacked.

I was still trying to figure out how to grow RWW, so I was keen to pick Anil's brain. He suggested that I differentiate from TechCrunch and defocus on startups. Explore the "categories of innovation," he said, adding that I should be thinking about how my blog can have longevity. He was one of the people at that time who thought Web 2.0 was a bubble that would inevitably burst, so he said it was important for me to continue with my analytical approach—to write quality content that stands the test of time. He also mentioned subscriptions as a possible alternate business model, citing John Gruber's Apple-focused blog Daring Fireball as an example. This was years before subscriptions became a widespread form of revenue for internet scribes, but it showed how forward-thinking Anil was: he wanted me to see past the shiny sponsored objects of Web 2.0. People whose time is valuable will pay for quality content, he assured me. It was sage advice, but I only had eyes for advertising revenue at that time.

Unsurprisingly, Anil had started using Twitter before me—his account started in December 2006, back when you had to know people in the valley to even know it existed. The first real wave of people joined Twitter in March 2007, after it became the trendy app at the annual SXSW conference in Austin, Texas. I joined as soon as I arrived in San Francisco that April. I don't recall who told me about it, but I signed up on Saturday, the day before Web 2.0 Expo started. My first tweet was a complaint about a squatter taking the "readwriteweb" username (I had signed up instead as @RWW). My second tweet was more descriptive: "checking out web 20 expo schedule. getting ready to join Fergus at Colibri Mexican Bistro—438 Geary St at 7.30. Then drinkies afterwards."

Those two tweets tell you all you need to know about Twitter in those days: you were either complaining about something or telling the world what you were eating. Twitter was so new back then, neither the technologists nor the businesspeople had any idea how to use it—or what its purpose was.

One of the things I was most looking forward to at Web 2.0 Expo was meeting some of my fellow ReadWriteWebers. Alex Iskold and Emre Sokullu would be there—though they'd been contributors since the second half of 2006, I hadn't yet met them in person. Several other new contributors were coming to the event, but the one I was most keen to meet was Sean Ammirati. Sean had begun posting on RWW while at SXSW in Austin the previous month, sending nine reports from the event and quickly proving the value of his work. Within a few years, Sean would be my chief operating officer, but at this stage he was working on biz dev for a startup called mSpoke.

Sean was about to turn twenty-seven years old—roughly nine years younger than me. He'd gotten into San Francisco, from his home in Pittsburgh, late on Sunday night. We met on Monday, sometime after my morning hybrid-designer panel. In person he looked the part of a young wannabe startup founder: short, tidy black hair, thin rectangular glasses, dark blue jeans, sky-blue button-down, and black suit jacket. He was lean and a bit taller than me, and had attentive dark brown eyes.

The email communications I'd had with Sean over March had suggested an eagerness in his character and a willingness to help and "learn by doing" (a common startup ethic). This all came through in person too, especially given his fresh-faced, youthful appearance. But I also noted a keen intelligence about him when it came to discussing the business of Web 2.0—almost an air of superiority. He'd been a research fellow at Carnegie Mellon University in Pittsburgh, one of the leading computer science colleges in the States. He told me in that first meeting that he wanted to become a venture capitalist, and I believed he would get there. For now, I was happy to listen to his theories about online advertising and scaling a startup, and he was just as curious to learn about my practical experience building a tech-blogging business.

Web 2.0 Expo was a hectic conference, and it was difficult to meet up with the other RWWers because we were all going to different sessions or having meetings. But I eventually caught up with Alex. In person he reminded me of a chess grandmaster, with his thick Ukrainian accent, sturdy frame, and large head with dark brown unibrow. He'd been in a lot of meetings at the event, drumming up interest in his startup, AdaptiveBlue. I admired Alex for both his prodigious intelligence (very much on display in his RWW articles) and his business hustle. I wished I was even half as effective as Alex at networking, but then again, he did live in New York and traveled regularly to the valley. Even though his accent suggested he was an outsider, I was much more so because I only visited the United States two or three times a year. Plus, I was still too shy and reticent to approach people at events. Fortunately, I had RWW to do my talking for me, so people generally approached me at these gatherings.

I saw Emre at the Ignite session at the end of the first day. Ignite was run by Brady Forrest, who had run the Microsoft Search Champs event I'd attended and now worked for O'Reilly Media. In this session, entrepreneurs and developers did short five-minute presentations about their startups or tech passions. It was entertaining. One of the presenters was Justin Kan, who wore a movie camera on his head as part of his ongoing mission to livestream his own life. The result was called Justin. tv, which in later years turned into a business called Twitch.

Emre was a thin, nervous young man in his early twenties, and he didn't speak a lot of English—a challenge at the time, though we would eventually develop a friendship that endured through the years. He'd immigrated from Turkey in mid-2005 and was trying to gain permanent residency. I knew him to be a smart, innovative programmer who was also passionate about open source—a great combination in Silicon Valley during Web 2.0—so I was sure he'd eventually get his green card. His startup, Grou.ps, seemed to be gaining a bit of traction too—it had launched in 2006 and claimed to have more than thirty-two thousand members by April 2007. Grou.ps was a DIY social networking tool, so it was in the same market as Marc Andreessen's Ning.

Later in the week, Brady organized and kindly invited me to a group dinner at Minako in San Francisco. The list of attendees was a who's who of Web 2.0 developers: Blaine Cook (Twitter founding engineer), Simon Willison (cocreator of a Python framework called Django), Cal Henderson of Flickr (who later cofounded Slack), Jane McGonigal (a game designer and later a successful author), David Recordon (then at Verisign, but he went on to become a senior engineer at Six Apart and then Facebook), and a whole bunch of other industry people whom I admired. I brought along Alex and Emre, as well as a new acquaintance, Taewoo Danny Kim from South Korea.

I don't recall having deep conversations with anyone outside of my core group of fellow international citizens, but just being at this dinner made me feel like I wasn't an outsider anymore. I still didn't feel like an insider, either, but I was at least insider adjacent.

The fact was, Web 2.0 was booming in mid-2007—and if there was a bust coming, it wasn't apparent to any of us. The hype of the new web was at an all-time high; this was cemented in my mind when I saw the IBM booth on the Web 2.0 Expo trade floor. It featured IBM staff milling around in red shirts—not IBM blue—and doing on-the-spot classroom sessions with microphones and videos. This was effective at pulling in the punters, I noted, as I watched people plop themselves into the IBM chairs to learn about Web 2.0 technologies.

As a fellow blogger quipped to me, "I don't go to Web 2.0 conferences to listen to IBM." Me neither, but it did confirm two things: one, we had the attention of enterprises and their IT departments; and two, Web 2.0 was now mainstream.

My wife arrived in San Francisco on the nineteenth, after the expo closed. We spent the next week doing the usual tourist things, like Alcatraz, Fisherman's Wharf, and Chinatown, and then hopped on a plane to Las Vegas. My portion of the Vegas trip, including accommodations at the Venetian on the Strip, was being paid for by Microsoft New Zealand.

I would be attending Microsoft's MIX conference, an event to promote the company's web technologies.

When we arrived at the Venetian, I was at first impressed by its sense of grandeur. The hotel had only opened in 1999, so it felt brand new with its polished stone floors, gleaming white granite columns, and golden roof with copies of old Italian art. Of course, I soon gathered that everything in the complex was copied from Venice, including a version of St. Mark's Square (with a large ice-cream shop at its center), replica sculptures, staff members dressed as statues, and gondola rides offered on canals within the walls of the hotel. At that time I had never visited Venice or anywhere else in continental Europe, so I had nothing to compare it to. Even so, it all felt like a giant fraud, which made my heart quietly sink during that first day. I realized that I wanted to see the real things, to feel what life was like in the real Venice. I resolved to make that happen one day.

The other thing that hit me about Las Vegas was the extreme heat. It wasn't even summer yet, but walking outside during the day was almost unbearable. Fortunately, I'd be spending most of my days in the air-conditioned Venetian conference center.

The focus for MIX this year was a new product called Silverlight, Microsoft's version of Adobe Flash. It would support what the industry called "rich internet applications" (usually shortened to RIA), which meant running high-definition video and other interactive media on the web. Just like Flash, Silverlight required a browser plug-in for users, which was provided for free for both PCs and Macs.

As part of the marketing push for Silverlight, I was invited to a blogger lunch with Microsoft executives Ray Ozzie and Scott Guthrie. Ozzie had taken over from Bill Gates as Microsoft's chief software architect the previous June, so he was still relatively new to his role—and, of course, replacing Gates at Microsoft was always going to be impossible. He was fifty-one and looked the part with his swept-back silver hair and Gates-like glasses. But in person, he came across as reserved and not entirely comfortable in the limelight. Whereas Gates always reveled in being the smartest person in the room—and made sure that you knew it—Ozzie seemed reluctant to accept that responsibility.

Mike Arrington was at MIX too, but he wasn't at the lunch. Mike had interviewed Ozzie and Guthrie onstage that morning, and it turned out he'd had extensive briefings with Microsoft already. I enjoyed the lunch, but I took a long time to get a question in to Ray. I had the same problem at corporate meetings: finding the appropriate time to pipe up and contribute to a group conversation wasn't a strong point of mine. While I was working up the courage to say something, Evan Williams—the CEO of Twitter, but also a pioneering blogger—noted that Silverlight was going to be great for his team because they could build a Silverlight application for Twitter using the same skillset used to build the web version of Twitter.

Right at the end of the lunch, I finally managed to get a question in for Ozzie about Microsoft's strategy for its Internet Explorer (IE) browser. IE still had between 75 percent and 85 percent market share (depending on which source you used), with only Mozilla Firefox in the double digits as a competitor. As had now become the norm, there was little sign of innovation in IE due to its dominance. What's more, the latest version, IE7, was the least standards-compliant browser of the time. When I asked my question, I noted that Firefox was on the road to becoming what Mozilla termed an "information broker"[50]—in other words, not just rendering HTML, but integrating with other applications (such as a calendar app). Other browsers were innovating, so I was fishing for a sign that Microsoft would use Silverlight as an excuse to start innovating again on browser technology.

Ozzie replied that Microsoft was creating a platform for developers to build componentized things, such as widgets and other web services. He didn't elaborate on IE's future role in this, saying only that the next version of IE was under wraps. His response didn't give me much to write about.

As the assembled bloggers were walking out of the lunchroom, I struck up a conversation with Williams. I mentioned that I'd joined Twitter the previous month and was enjoying it, but that someone was squatting on the @readwriteweb handle. He replied with a smile that the @rww username was actually better because it was shorter, which made it easier for other users to @ me. That was the last time I complained about the squatter.

When I was back in New Zealand, I emailed Emily Chang and Max Kiesler to ask if Ideacodes would be interested in doing the next Read/WriteWeb redesign. Among other things, I wanted to "find a better solution for the ads, lists, network links, etc." in the header and sidebar areas. I knew the redesign would have to scale with RWW's growth, including the new network blogs. Emily wrote back saying they were keen to take on the work.

The sponsor ads and the advertising supplied by FM Publishing, along with other bits and pieces such as a job board and Feedburner RSS ads, were now bringing in significant revenue. In June I'd made over $25,000 from RWW alone. My expenses were still low—I paid Josh an hourly rate for 12.5 hours per week (it later became 30 hours per week), hosting fees were reasonable, and the only other regular expenses were for things like banking and PayPal fees. Even the network costs were small. The ASE design had cost around $2,000, but that had paid for itself within a month or two due to a quick start with sponsors. By any measure, RWW was a very profitable small business.

The Web 2.0 industry was now big business. This was confirmed by the sale of two large advertising networks to tech companies in the first half of 2007. First, in April, Google acquired the online advertising platform DoubleClick for $3.1 billion. Microsoft quickly countered the following month by buying a digital marketing company called aQuantive for $6 billion. While I didn't use those platforms, RWW was—in its own small way—among the beneficiaries of record internet ad spending that year.

As if to emphasize that web business was expanding at great speed, Facebook announced a developer platform in May that enabled third-party companies to integrate their services inside the fast-growing social network. This was the news that finally impelled me to join Facebook! It's strange to think now, but at the time Facebook was not the most popular social network on the internet—particularly outside of the United States. Facebook had twenty-four million global users at its platform launch, but it was far behind MySpace at sixty-seven million. Indeed, in some countries, Facebook was the third biggest social network (in the UK, Bebo was more popular than MySpace).

But part of the new appeal of Facebook was that third-party developers could potentially make money from their apps, thanks to the developer platform. "You can build a real advertising business on Facebook,"[51] Mark Zuckerberg told developers and journalists. As I put it in my blog post about the launch, Facebook had "grown up"—it was obviously now much more than a social network for American college students.

RWW continued to grow rapidly in terms of page views and subscribers. By mid-2007 it was among the world's top 30 blogs, according to Technorati's list of "the biggest blogs in the blogosphere, as measured by unique links in the last six months."[52] Heading into the second half of 2007, RWW was at number 29—nestled just behind Gawker and in front of Instapundit. I was now ahead of GigaOm (33), although Mashable had overtaken me and, at number 17, was within range of competing with the mighty TechCrunch (4).

By August RWW was getting 775,000 page views per month—nearly double what it had been at the end of 2006. The RSS and email subscribers had also more than doubled, to nearly 90,000. It was heady stuff, and I was putting a lot of energy into figuring out how to sustain this growth rate. I jotted down in my notebook that I needed another daily writer and a webmaster to take over technical maintenance of the websites. In hindsight, I should've been thinking of staffing up more aggressively, but I was still learning how to be a media entrepreneur on the go.

I'd written up a three-page document for Emily and Max, outlining my goals for the site redesign. First and foremost, I wanted a "modern, sophisticated design that shows that RWW is a professional, high quality media property." I noted a lot of other technical and practical elements as well. For instance, I wanted to make sure that RWW continued to be a social hub for people interested in Web 2.0. One of my listed goals was to "encourage community and in particular comments." "It is crucial that we encourage discussions on the site and I regard this as #1 priority for the site overall," I added. Clearly, this was well before the time when social media began draining away conversations from blogs.

In mid-August Emily and Max sent me a proposal for the redesign work, including a generous "friends' rate" for the project. At the same time, I was having discussions with Six Apart (owners of Movable Type) and my web hosts Media Temple about upgrading our server setup. In addition, I was figuring out my taxes and investigating a business plan involving premium content.

With the business planning, redesign, publishing platform upgrade, sponsor management, SEO, and finalizing agreements with Steve and Charles on the network blogs—not to mention writing several RWW articles every day—I was now very stretched on the work front. I was trying to defocus other demands on my time. I'd been having informal discussions about a RWW China site with a guy named Gang Lu. But I hit pause on that. Among a list of things I wrote down in my notebook under the heading "Defocus" was this: "emails (do auto reply?)." But alas, generative AI software was still many years into the future.

One project I didn't put off was a new podcast site to be run by Sean Ammirati, called Read/WriteTalk. I'd learned my lesson about using the RWW branding for a new network blog. I set up a space on the server and handed over the design template, and Sean did most of the work to create the new site. It was his idea, and I was pleased to have a podcast site up and running under the RWW banner.

I announced Read/WriteTalk (tagline: "The people behind the web") at the end of August. We had quietly launched the site in mid-August, but I wanted to tidy up some of the design aspects before I publicized it on RWW. However, I was unexpectedly beaten to it by Valleywag, the notorious Silicon Valley gossip site operated by Gawker. Sean's first interview was with Jason Calacanis, the New York entrepreneur who had sold Weblogs, Inc. to AOL in 2005. Calacanis was on Valleywag's hitlist of tech personalities to snoop on (another was Mike Arrington), and they did a short post based on a quote from his *Read/WriteTalk* episode, in which Calacanis had compared entrepreneurs to samurai. It no doubt titillated the Valleywag readers, but also drew attention to our new podcast.

When I calculated my monthly revenue for August, it added up to nearly $34,000—a new record for RWW. FM Publishing had really come to the party that month, as $15,000 of it was from their CPM adverts. Given these increasingly big paydays and the still relatively low expense base for RWW, I knew it was high time to invest in more writer talent.

CHAPTER 8

NEW DESIGN

■ ■ ■ ■ ■

IN AUGUST, I began discussions with Marshall Kirkpatrick, a former TechCrunch lead blogger who was now working for a marketing company. Marshall was from Portland and working for a local company called SplashCast when I reached out to him by email. I asked if he knew of any freelance bloggers who might like to work for Read/Write-Web for around twenty hours per week. He emailed back, suggesting himself. It turned out he was thinking of leaving SplashCast to do consulting work, so he was open to another blogging gig. "If it's not me in particular that you're looking for, I've got a list of more than 30 bloggers now looking for blogging gigs, some of them very accomplished," he added.

Of course, I was looking for someone exactly like Marshall—he'd started out his tech blogging career in October 2005 working for AOL's social software blog (under Calacanis) and then went to TechCrunch for a six-month stint in mid-2006. Other than myself and other pioneering tech bloggers like Mike Arrington and Om Malik, no other freelance blogger had more experience in our fledgling industry.

I asked for the going rate for bloggers and for what he himself was looking for. He said that a half-time blogger would normally be in the price range of $2,000 to $4,000 per month, "depending on how much competition there is for the writer." He offered his part-time services for a monthly rate of $5,000, a 25 percent premium on the top rate he'd just quoted. Marshall was still in his twenties at this point, so I had to admire his self-confidence. I'd consistently undersold myself in the job market prior to starting RWW, and it had always bugged me (once I was old enough to realize that I'd been duped). So I wondered if this was a cultural difference—did Americans just naturally value themselves higher than average?

I counteroffered with $4,000 per month. Even that was more than I was paying Josh for thirty hours per week, but I was confident Marshall would make an immediate impact on RWW. At TechCrunch he'd been known for his breaking news coverage. Josh was more of a feature and profile writer, and I wasn't a natural newshound, so I realized that Marshall could be transformational for RWW. At the very least, it would make the site more competitive with the likes of TechCrunch and Mashable—both of which were covering the daily tech-news cycle.

I was impressed by Marshall's high rating of his own ability, but of course I didn't know him very well at this point. I needed to see if he'd live up to his own hype, so I suggested we do a trial run of three to four months, "to see if we work well together and we're both happy, etc." I also hinted that I'd consider offering him a small stake in RWW at the end of the trial period if he joined us full-time.

He agreed. "I'm an ambitious guy and am really excited to be a part of the RWW team—I'm damn proud, in fact," he said. "I think we'll work great together."

I didn't yet have a legal template to use for a freelance contributor—another thing I needed to sort out from a business perspective. Luckily, Alex Iskold gave me a consulting agreement template that he used for his company, so I filled in Marshall's details and sent that off. In mid-September I announced on the site that Marshall was joining RWW.

The site's focus would still be analysis of Web 2.0, but once Marshall joined, the amount of news and reviews on RWW naturally increased. My plan was for Marshall and Josh to provide all the news, while Alex, Emre, and some other regular contributors joined me in doing the analysis posts. All up, we were aiming for about seven posts per day—five news and reviews, the rest longer analysis posts. This was still a lower volume of daily posts than TechCrunch and Mashable, but I didn't want to go all-in on news like those sites. I was always aware that people came to RWW for explanation and analysis, so that had to be balanced with the need to cover the news cycle. We weren't as broad as our competitors in what we covered, but we went deeper.

One thing I hadn't considered when bringing Marshall on was the impact it might have on Josh. Marshall was several years older than Josh, plus he'd had prior experience as the lead blogger at the biggest tech blog. Many months later, Josh told me that he felt like a "second fiddle" once Marshall joined and that his work had, at times, become marginalized. I was largely unaware of this issue at the time, but it would be my first taste of the challenges of people management. Bloggers, I soon discovered, had egos—and it would take some deft leadership skills to keep a team of them in check. Marshall's blogger ego was particularly buoyant, but he also walked the talk. We had an immediate uptick in web traffic once he joined.

By the first week of October 2007, RWW had cracked the top 20 of Technorati's list of the world's most popular blogs. Of our direct competitors, only Mashable (8) and TechCrunch (4) were ahead of us. It was a milestone for our small but growing team. We'd also been ranked number 6 on a new "leaderboard" feature at Gabe Rivera's Techmeme site, the industry's leading aggregator of tech news. Unsurprisingly, TechCrunch was the top-ranked site. The *New York Times* and CNET were also among the top five, but RWW had been ranked ahead of many other mainstream media websites, including the BBC, *InfoWorld*, and *Wall Street Journal*.

This prompted a discussion on the blogosphere about "new media" versus traditional media. My take was that the top blogs on Techmeme's list had "evolved into media companies" (as I put it then). I claimed, somewhat tongue in cheek, that RWW "isn't a blog and hasn't been for some time—at least in the classic definition of a blog as a personal journal."[53] I added, however, that I was still a blogger.

We'd shortly experience one of the downsides of increasing popularity—web server strain and other technical issues associated with scaling—but for now I was busy preparing for another US trip. The Web 2.0 Summit was happening again in mid-October, and I was excited to attend for the third straight year.

I touched down at SFO on Sunday, October 14, and took a taxi to the Adante Hotel on Geary Street. It was a run-down establishment, but it was inexpensive and a nice ten-minute stroll to the Web 2.0 Summit venue—the much plusher Palace Hotel.

The summit would start on Wednesday, but I had a busy schedule at the start of the week. On Monday I attended a small event at the Grand Hyatt called Mobile 2.0, which an occasional RWW guest blogger named Rudy de Waele had helped organize. Much of the talk at the event was about mobile apps in Japan and South Korea, two countries that were years ahead of the Western world on mobile web technologies—although still prehistoric compared to what the iPhone App Store would soon unlock.

Rudy's presentation posed a question: "Is Web 2.0 going mobile?" To answer that, he showed a screenshot of the Facebook mobile web page on a 3G cellphone: an anemic-looking site with pitifully small photos and an awkward menu. So no, Web 2.0 hadn't yet gone mobile. Check back next year.

Later that day I met up with GigaOm's founder, Om Malik. I walked down to one of his local Starbucks, in the Embarcadero neighborhood on the eastern waterfront. It was the first time I'd sat down with him for a chat, but he greeted me like an old friend. Then in his early forties, Om had flecks of silver in his hair and cut a dapper figure in his button-down blue-checked shirt and tan slacks.

Om was a well-connected tech journalist and much liked in the tech industry by both entrepreneurs and other bloggers. Like Mike Arrington, Om was an insider in Silicon Valley—although he was much more relaxed and comfortable with this status than Mike ever was. At the time we met, RWW had only recently taken over from GigaOm as the third-most-popular tech blog covering Web 2.0, according to Technorati. Om showed no signs of this bothering him, even though his blog was the closest to mine in terms of its analytical focus on Web 2.0. In fact, he was generous in his praise of RWW and advice for me. He suggested I run a think-tank event on the future of the web, perhaps partnering with FM Publishing. He also made a feature request: provide topic and author feeds so that he could subscribe to certain topics and writers.

The Web 2.0 Summit began on Wednesday, and its theme was "The Web's edge." This was defined as "the places where the Web is just beginning to take root: the industries, geographies, and applications that have yet to be conquered by the Web's wide reach."[54] This seemed a perfect match for the type of content RWW did. We'd even done a series of posts the previous year that profiled the top web apps in many different countries—it helped solidify our reputation as the "outsider" tech blog that brought the rest of the world to Silicon Valley.

One of the young entrepreneurs I'd met back in New Zealand, Tim Norton, was also attending the summit. I'd begun chatting with him in 2006, and we'd met up in Wellington that year. He was currently building a software-as-a-service startup called PlanHQ and was in the valley drumming up interest from VCs and other influencers.

Tim was a barrel-chested guy in his late twenties, a bit shorter than me, with a beach-going tan and dark brown hair spiked up at the front. He tended to wear tight-fitting button-down shirts—open at the collar, chest hair visible—that showed off his muscular physique. His mental attitude mirrored the work he did on the physical side, in that he affected the kind of "hustle culture" bluster that would become increasingly common in the tech industry over the coming years. This was a bit unusual for a kiwi, but I couldn't help admiring his confidence. He had always been friendly to me and certainly wanted his startup to be covered on RWW.

When we met up at the Web 2.0 Summit, Tim had a camera crew following him around. This was for a planned reality TV series in New Zealand called *StartupTV*, he told me, adding that PlanHQ was one of five local startups being profiled for the show. He'd already managed to get an on-camera interview with Tim O'Reilly in the hallways, so he was buzzing when we met. We did a quick interview about RWW and my involvement in the Web 2.0 scene over the past several years.

The following year I was invited to join another TV show Tim was involved in: an elimination-type reality show simply called *Startup*, which was modeled on American Idol. I was one of three judges, and we taped the whole first series in Auckland throughout 2008. Unfortunately, the show never came out. Tim and I stayed in contact for several more years, but I lost touch with him after then. Later, he would finally get the startup success he so craved with a video-creation product called 90 Seconds.

Later that week I ran into another future master of hustle culture. Thirty-one-year-old Gary Vaynerchuk was a relatively new entrepreneur and video blogger with a wine e-commerce startup called Wine Library. He'd started a YouTube show called *Wine Library TV* the previous year and had reached out to me in April 2007 to inquire about a sponsor ad on RWW. "I am an outside the box thinker," he wrote in an email. "I am sure most wine video blogs wouldn't advertise on your site, but I am a little different." I finally managed to confirm the deal in late June, so his ad went up in July and ran until the end of September. When I met him in October, he was no longer a sponsor.

We were at the Ignite event on Tuesday evening, at the trendy DNA Lounge on Eleventh Street, when Gary sidled up to me. He was wearing blue jeans and a burgundy T-shirt with the *Wine Library TV* name and logo on it. He was about my height or just under, had short black hair, and was well tanned. That evening he looked tired, with rings around his eyes and a five o'clock shadow. But he was still as energetic as his reputation suggested. We talked about his sponsorship stint with RWW; he said it really helped establish him in the Web 2.0 scene. He effusively praised my blog for a couple more sentences, then he told me about his ambitions for his startup—he wanted to be a billionaire, and he wanted to buy the New York Jets! The only other person I'd met with this kind of blustery charisma was Jason Calacanis, also a New Yorker.

I didn't immediately understand why Gary wanted to make a name for himself in our little web scene. After all, he was already on his way to mainstream stardom, with profiles in the *Wall Street Journal* and *Time* magazine over the past year. He'd even appeared on *Late Night with Conan O'Brien* in August (he'd asked me to blog and tweet about it at the time). But hearing his broad New Jersey accent that evening at the nightclub, telling me about his outsized ambition, and then seeing him yuck it up later that night with Digg's Kevin Rose (the glamour boy of Web 2.0), I began to understand what he wanted. His goal was to be a Silicon Valley insider; it would become a part of the persona he was selling to mainstream media. The scrappy video blogger from New Jersey, the son of Russian-immigrant parents who went west to Silicon Valley and made his fortune. A Jay Gatsby success story for the internet age.

A decade later, when he was a big social media star and a poster boy for hustle culture, he wrote a blog post claiming that "30 was the year I decided that I was going to become GaryVee."[55] From that time on, he wrote, he was "going to live my life in the pursuit of my ambition." I'd met him early on in that story arc, when he was still ingratiating himself into the insider networks of Silicon Valley. That was why he'd advertised on Read/WriteWeb in 2007—it helped legitimize him in the tech industry.

I never managed to convince Gary to resume his sponsorship of RWW, but not for lack of trying—I sent a bunch of emails in the months following that meeting. But he'd already gotten what he wanted from me and was on to bigger things. Hustle culture would come to dominate Silicon Valley over the following years, most notoriously with the San Francisco and New York "tech bros" of the 2010s. Hustling wasn't in my nature, though, due to my congenital low self-esteem.

In any case, I was about to learn that there were more important things in life than money and power.

The first sign of health problems came before I went to the 2007 Web 2.0 Summit. Late that September, I was traveling by car to Kaikoura, a scenic coastal town near the top of the South Island of New Zealand. My wife and six-year-old daughter were with me; we intended to spend a few nights there and then visit my nana in Blenheim on the way back. But during that car trip I felt unwell and was frequently stopping to urinate. After we arrived in Kaikoura, my wife and I began arguing—partly due to my workload, but due also to my physical discomfort.

We ended up staying just two nights in Kaikoura instead of three. I was feeling both physically and emotionally frazzled, and my wife insisted I go and see my doctor when we got back. I put it off for a week or so but finally relented and saw him on Wednesday, October 10, just a few days before my scheduled US trip. He referred me for some blood tests, which I put off. I got on the plane to San Francisco instead—frankly relieved to be getting away from the stresses of home life.

When I got back from America about a week later, I put the blood tests to the back of my mind. I had a lot to catch up on with RWW, I told myself. But there were signs that I wasn't 100 percent—I felt very thirsty all the time, I was losing weight and having mood swings, and I generally felt tired and run-down. I put all this down to overwork and the continuing problems in my marriage. My way of coping was to knuckle down with RWW work.

Then Nana died, at age eighty-eight. The last time I'd seen her was at the end of September, on the holiday we'd cut short. Again, my family and I hopped on the Cook Strait ferry from the bottom of the North Island to the top of the South. Her funeral was in the second week of November.

On the ferry ride back home, I was extremely seasick. It was a rough journey, with large sea swells, but I had never felt as bad as that before. My body was telling me something, and this time I listened. I did the blood draw as soon as I got back. Then, finally, I went to see my doctor on Monday, November 19.

"I'm sorry to say this, old boy," my doctor told me that day, "but you have diabetes."

It took me a couple of weeks to understand that I'd gotten type 1 diabetes, an autoimmune disease where your body no longer produces insulin. Type 2 is far more common; it's when the body still produces insulin but doesn't process it correctly (it's typically associated with overweight people). What really shook me was finding out that type 1 is incurable, whereas you can recover from type 2. So I would have to inject insulin into my body every day of my life, from now on.

Not knowing how else to cope with this news, on November 26, 2007, I wrote a blog post about it. In my research I'd discovered many online resources for diabetics, including blogs and social networks. My best discovery was a niche social network called TuDiabetes, which had been created using Ning. Its founder, Manny Hernandez, had only just launched the site in March. He left a comment on my blog post: "It can be daunting at first, that is why TuDiabetes exists in part: to help you deal with it without feeling alone."

I realized that Manny was right: thanks to the web, I wouldn't have to go through this huge life change alone. It was some comfort to hear that, especially since I felt like I was dealing with other challenges in my life alone—the rapid growth of RWW and my topsy-turvy marriage chief among them. Part of my problem was that I was a poor communicator when it came to my personal life. I buried my work and home stresses deep inside so that my family and friends couldn't easily see that I was struggling.

I still had to meet the daily challenge of diabetes by myself, of course, but online I could ask questions on social networks and read about the experiences of other T1s. It was perhaps the first time I'd seen the true social power of the web in action.

A lot was happening in social networking in this period. Facebook was growing fast after its platform announcement in May, which seemed to prompt every other tech company—big and small—to jump aboard the social network hype train. A startup called FriendFeed launched in October and quickly gained a cult following among geeks like me—it was basically an aggregator of RSS and social media feeds. The same month, Google launched OpenSocial, a set of APIs that allowed developers to build an application once and install it across a variety of social networks.

OpenSocial was clearly aimed at kneecapping Facebook's proprietary developer platform. Basically every social network other than Facebook joined Google's initiative—even MySpace, still the leading social network. Ning also joined, so theoretically this meant a developer could build an app for diabetics that could be used across Ning,

MySpace, and Friendster. This idea pleased me, since I'd just discovered the value of the social web in managing a health condition.

Open standards for social networking seemed very promising, especially when Facebook waded into a privacy controversy in November. It had launched a new advertising system called Beacon that allowed its users to share things they do across the web to their Facebook news feeds—for example sharing an eBay listing with their friends. RWW described Beacon as "an attempt at conversational marketing, where users become product promoters"[56] The problem was, the system also allowed Facebook's advertising partners to gather user data—sometimes without a user's knowledge—for targeted advertising.

Beacon wouldn't be the first time Facebook tested the boundaries of user privacy, but somehow the company still managed to fend off its open standards competition and continue growing. As for Google's social networking project, well, I never did see an OpenSocial diabetic app get developed. But, fortunately for me, TuDiabetes continued as an independent community that I would visit as needed over the coming years.

It wasn't just me having health issues near the end of 2007. RWW's web server was also very sickly, with multiple outages on the site during this time. It was a mix of server-scaling issues and problems with the implementation of Movable Type 4 (MT4), the latest version of our publishing platform. It turned out, we were the first major site to upgrade from MT3.5 to MT4 on Media Temple, our web host. So we had unwittingly become the test bed for all the early bugs that typically reside in a new and complex piece of software.

The move to MT4 began in mid-August, about a month before the site redesign by Ideacodes started. The plan was for Media Temple to set up a new server for RWW, using MT4, so that Ideacodes could optimize the redesign for the new version of Movable Type. Things were complicated by the fact that Media Temple were moving us from a shared server environment to what they called a "dedicated virtual" server. In other words, this server would be ours exclusively—another sign that RWW had joined the big leagues.

Initial progress on the upgrade was positive, but toward the end of September we began to have problems with our existing live server, which we shared with other websites. We were still on MT3.5 on the live site, so we knew it wasn't an issue with the publishing platform. It may've been a simple scaling issue with RWW, since our page views were growing fast and we were getting regular Digg front pages (each of which brought a burst of traffic). But since it was a shared server, the problem may've also been with other sites on the server.

On Monday, October 1, while I was away from the office (having just returned from that fateful trip to Kaikoura and still feeling the first effects of the as-yet-undiagnosed diabetes), Marshall sent an email to our contact at Media Temple. "Wanted to let you know that RWW is taking a long, long time to load and I'm getting reports in some cases that it's never loading," he reported.

There was no immediate reply, so after logging in and seeing the latency issues for myself, I phoned Media Temple's helpline. It took a while, but eventually the issue was fixed. The server problems made me queasy—or perhaps that was my body's issues with elevated blood-glucose levels. Regardless, I wanted to get on our own dedicated server as soon as possible, and I told Media Temple this.

On Tuesday, October 9, Marshall sent me an exasperated email. "Are we moved to that dedicated server yet? The site was timing out when I woke up this morning, though it was back up in a bit. People keep telling me they love RWW but it's the worst loading blog they read (Mashable's pretty damn bad too though). TC [TechCrunch] used to have lots of issues like this but they sure don't anymore. Hope we can fix."

I replied to Marshall that I would chase up Media Temple yet again. "On the positive side, 2 digg frontpages today!" I added, knowing full well that this was a double-edged sword.

An executive from Media Temple replied to my latest despairing email and told me they were working closely with Six Apart to install MT4. He explained that there were still bugs that they were working through. It was slow going because this was Media Temple's first MT4 installation and so they were testing it extensively.

I began to question whether I'd made the right decision to do the upgrade to MT4. I had wanted the new design to take advantage of the new functionalities it promised, which was a perfectly reasonable business decision. What I hadn't counted on was the technical complications of being the first Media Temple customer to make this move. Add to that the unforeseen performance issues with the live site during October, and it was adding up to an almighty headache. I wished I had a COO to palm all this off on, but for now, it was up to me to sort it out with Media Temple and Six Apart—while keeping Ideacodes in the loop.

Shared-server issues continued throughout October, which pushed me to go live earlier than expected on the new dedicated server, running the still-buggy MT4. A site with a few bugs was better than a site that constantly went down, I reasoned, so I reluctantly gave the go-ahead.

The plan was to flick the switch sometime during the coming weekend and during off-hours. But a couple of days later, on a Thursday, we had yet another outage on the live site—and this time we couldn't even log in to Movable Type! After some frantic discussion with our various tech partners, I approved the domain-name switch to the dedicated server and MT4 that Thursday night.

"Ok, server upgrade was done," I reported nearly six hours later to Marshall, Josh, and Alex, adding that it was "very messy and there are a number of issues to fix." The post and comment publishing were now frustratingly slow, and we were seeing bugs in live that had not been picked up during testing. In addition, our RWW emails weren't getting through. The upgrade had, to put it mildly, not gone smoothly.

On Friday I got Six Apart involved again, now basically begging them to help. "The bottom line for me, as publisher, is that I have had a broken website (well, comments and entry creation at least, plus some other parts of the website such as Monthly Archives) for the past 24 hours and there's no sign of a resolution," I wrote, adjusting my email signature to "Editor & Exasperated Publisher, Read/WriteWeb."

Finally, after several stressful days, the tech issues were resolved. But it hadn't done my blood pressure any good—or my blood-glucose issues, for that matter.

In early November 2007 Mike Arrington and his TechCrunch CEO Heather Harde approached me about participating in a new awards competition they'd come up with, "the Crunchies." The idea (as far as I could tell) was to replicate the Webby Awards, which had been running since 1996. The Crunchies would focus specifically on Web 2.0 companies. TechCrunch would produce the show, with Read/WriteWeb, GigaOm, and VentureBeat as cohosts.

The night of the Crunchies was Friday, January 18, and the ceremony was held at the Herbst Theatre, an old-style auditorium in the Civic Center of San Francisco. Maria and Rosabelle had joined me on this trip, so I took them into the greenroom before the show started. Om was very friendly, but everyone else—including Mike—seemed standoffish, no doubt due to busyness and nerves. I guided my family to their seats in the upstairs section of the hall and made my way backstage.

I was presenting two categories: Best International Startup and Best Design. I had written short notes in my little red notebook for each. For the best international startup award, I said that the award "has special significance for me, as the only non-US blog hosting these awards." It went to Netvibes, the French start-page product that had become the trendiest in that category. I presented the award to Tariq Krim, its tall and handsome CEO. The best design award went to SmugMug, a photo-sharing website (which would eventually buy Flickr a decade later).

I wasn't yet used to being onstage, so I was nerve-racked when speaking and my face was conspicuously red from anxiety. I felt more comfortable when all four of the main bloggers were onstage together. Mike was a confident speaker, and he and Om had a good repartee on stage. Matt Marshall, the founder of VentureBeat, was a reserved man like me, but he looked the part in his business suit and white button-down shirt.

There was an awkward moment backstage when it was discovered that RWW had published the full list of winners at 7:30 p.m., when the event had started. But this was because Heather had sent out the winners list earlier in the day to all four blogs, giving an embargo time of 7:30 p.m. Turns out I had missed a follow-up email later in the day by Eric Eldon at VentureBeat: "Talked with Mike about the embargo time.

Please don't post before the awards start!" So our post went out, as originally instructed, when the show started. I thought nothing of it at the time, but Mike was angry at me backstage when he found out. I was just confused; I hadn't seen Eric's follow-up, so my only response was that I was given an embargo time and had complied with that.

Later, back at my hotel, I saw Eric's email and wrote back to everyone—my face now even redder than it was onstage. Erick Schonfeld, TechCrunch's lead blogger, replied and admitted it was their fault. Mike wrote back too and apologized for "tearing into you at the event." To be honest, I was so nerve-ridden during the show that I didn't recall being upset at whatever Mike had said.

I hadn't stayed for the Crunchies after-party, as it was late for my daughter. Truth be told, I was tired too. There were certain luminaries at the Crunchies that I didn't get to meet—Mark Zuckerberg was there (he won best startup founder, and Facebook won best overall), as were the Twitter founders (best mobile startup). In fact, I hadn't gotten the chance to speak with many people at all. So my feelings after the show were more of emptiness than elation.

The one person I do remember meeting that night, funnily enough, was Mashable's Pete Cashmore. He'd been in the foyer before the show, having bought himself a Crunchies ticket. We exchanged brief greetings, but then Mike spotted him and told him to leave. Mashable was competing fiercely with TechCrunch at this time, and its rise up the Technorati chart over 2007 had ruffled many blogger feathers—including mine. I thought Pete had somehow juiced Mashable's statistics, and I'd even lodged an "official complaint" with Feedburner's founders about it. Regardless, the competition between TechCrunch and Mashable had become almost ludicrous. Just a week before the Crunchies, Mashable held its own awards ceremony in San Francisco, the Open Web Awards, which cunningly implied that its community was everyone *but* the Crunchies participants.

By this point I had begun to ignore the rivalry, reasoning that it wasn't my battle. That said, one of my goals for RWW was to break into the Technorati Top 10. There was room enough there for all three of us, since RWW occupied a different space than the more news-driven

TechCrunch and Mashable. In my notebook, I wrote that I wanted RWW to be "The Economist of web tech blogs."

Despite the dueling awards shows, Pete had reached out to me by email suggesting that we meet up while we were both in San Francisco. He wanted to talk through whatever differences we had. I'd agreed, as I figured that we had more things in common than not as international outsiders. Also, I was curious to meet him in person—as far as I knew, this was his first business trip to the United States. His industry nickname was the Loch Ness Blogger because he was from Scotland and hadn't been spotted in Silicon Valley before.

I met Pete the night after the Crunchies, at the Borders bookstore café on Post Street. He was wearing a suit that seemed a little too big for his tall, thin frame. He was twenty-two and had closely cropped dark brown hair, with a light smattering of stubble on his face. It was the same look that footballer David Beckham was sporting at the time (he'd recently come over to play for the Los Angeles Galaxy). That probably wasn't a coincidence, I realized, because Pete was almost as handsome as Beckham—albeit with the sunken eyes and skinny frame of someone who spent too much time in front of a computer screen.

I had imagined the Loch Ness Blogger would be shy and awkward, but he turned out to be an overly caffeinated chatterbox. We talked about our shared interest in moving to Silicon Valley. I was thirty-six years old and married, with a school-age child, so there were many practical issues I'd have to sort through to make that move. But Pete was a twenty-two-year-old single man and seemingly had little to stop him. So I advised him to do it.

Silicon Valley was still a mecca for anyone who wanted to make it big in the tech industry. And sure enough, a few months after I'd met Pete in Borders, he emailed to say that he'd taken my advice and shifted to San Francisco. What neither of us fully realized was that the insider world of Silicon Valley was beginning to constrict around a set of five leading Web 2.0 companies.

Apple's iPhone was the talk of the town by the end of 2007, and in November Google had announced its competitor: an open-source mobile operating system called Android. Amazon had just announced its Kindle product, so it too was branching out into consumer devices, in addition to being the early leader in cloud computing. Meanwhile, Google Reader was now the dominant RSS reader and Facebook had all the momentum in social networking. Microsoft was perhaps the odd one out, since it was struggling to adapt to Web 2.0 with its awkwardly branded Windows Live project. But Microsoft still had dominant positions in PC, office, and browser software—which gave it the time and money to correct course.

While it would take another year or so to shake out, these five companies would soon be calling the shots in a few core Web 2.0 markets: social networking, smartphone apps, and cloud computing. It was the beginning of something new in the internet age—an oligopoly of companies exerting platform power. While small startups would, of course, continue to burst onto the scene in the coming years, often they did so knowing they'd have to compete for attention on the platforms of one of these big-five companies.

The end of 2007 also marked the end of an era for Read/WriteWeb. In December I announced our new design, which would become the iconic RWW look—lasting right up until I left the business nearly five years later. The new design immediately gave us a unique and modern identity in the tech blogosphere. The first thing that caught your eye was a plush red banner running across the top of the page, indicating the header area. Inside this banner were the logo, the site and network menus, the subscription buttons (RSS and email), and the search bar. The rest of the page was now entirely white, rather than the deep red-and-cream combo of the previous design.

I was blown away by that single slash of vibrant red in the header—it stood out like a beacon on the crisp white background. Overall, this design was much roomier and less boxy than its predecessor. The logo was much improved as well. We'd finally gotten rid of the '/' in the brand name, so it was now ReadWriteWeb instead of Read/WriteWeb. The *R*, *W*, and *W* were now emphasized in black type, while the rest of the letters were in an attractive silver; my Twitter handle was @RWW, and that acronym was now widely used as the shorthand to refer to our site—so it was nice to highlight that in the logo design. The yin-yang symbol had also been given a Web 2.0 makeover; it was now encased in a red box with rounded corners (everything had rounded corners in Web 2.0).

The redesign also added new sections to the home page, which would help drive traffic. There was now a Popular Posts list next to the lead story, a Featured Posts section directly below, and a Recent Comments section below that. There were other improvements, too, such as a new set of main categories.

Overall, I loved what Ideacodes had done—it had certainly met my goals for a "fresh and bold" new look for RWW. In the launch post, I noted that "this is the first RWW design where I haven't been involved in the coding myself."[57] It was yet more evidence that I needed expert help if I was to continue scaling RWW.

Feedback in the comments section, however, was mixed. I was surprised that many people didn't seem to like the new logo. Some of this was justified, as on closer inspection it had a few technical glitches—the two capital *W*s were not properly aligned, for example. Once I'd run it past some designer friends, I asked Emily and Max to do the necessary fixes.

While some of the criticism was constructive, we also got some nonsensical comments, like "I know the previous color palette was red but this seems bolder and red means stop to many of us." Hmmm, tell that to *The Economist,* or CNN, or Manchester United! I took the time to vigorously defend the new design in the comments, but honestly, I didn't care what other people thought. To me, it was fresh and distinctive. From this point on, RWW would always be—in my mind's eye—a website with this particular design and logo.

The same commenter who claimed that red means stop also said that the yin-yang symbol was "really trite." Some of our current and future RWW writers would've agreed with him—Marshall, for instance, was never shy in expressing his disdain for it. But this was one thing I would never change my mind on. Yin-yang had always signified to me the equal importance of the read and write functionalities of the web— the internet was for creation just as much as consumption. The concept of harmony was also important to me on a personal level; later I would explore it more by taking tai chi classes and reading up on the philoso-phy of Taoism.

Of course, the technical implementation of the design did not go as smoothly as I'd wanted. There were many bugs to sort through, and even a week after launch, a bunch of these bugs were still unresolved.

To make matters worse, at the end of December our site experi-enced outages once again. As usual, I tried to get answers from our web hosts and Six Apart. Media Temple's solution was to upsell me to more expensive hardware, while Six Apart demanded that RWW start pay-ing for their assistance. My frustration levels were boiling over. I would have to come up with a better way to manage the technical platform in 2008.

Despite the continuing site management strain, RWW was in a great place heading into the new year. We'd exceeded one million page views for the first time in December 2007, and we were growing strongly month over month. We'd risen to number 18 in the Technorati list of the world's most popular blogs, and our Feedburner RSS subscriber widget had now ticked over 200,000. As we entered the new year, I was feeling very positive about where RWW was headed.

CHAPTER 9

M&A

■ ■ ■ ■ ■

I HADN'T SERIOUSLY THOUGHT of selling RWW before 2008, but I knew I needed help to expand the business. Early in the new year Sean Ammirati put me in touch with Bob Evans, a senior executive at CMP Technology, a media company and coproducer of the Web 2.0 conferences. On a phone call while I was in San Francisco in January, Bob floated a potential acquisition. I didn't know what to think at this point, but I was curious to see where the discussions would lead.

CMP's main tech-media property was *Information Week*, which had been one of the leading industry magazines during the 1980s and 1990s. *Information Week* was still a print magazine in early 2008, and its accompanying website was part of something called the TechWeb Network. TechWeb.com itself was an IT news website, but it didn't have any of the personality that RWW, TechCrunch, and Mashable had. So I saw that RWW would be an attractive candidate for CMP's lineup of tech publications.

I signed a nondisclosure agreement, and during February I shared my latest business data with Bob and Fritz Nelson, one of CMP's business development people. I was still rather green on these matters, but I thought the figures for RWW looked good. Revenue had increased nearly twofold since April 2007, for example, and it was on track to double year over year. Likewise, the second half of 2007 had proven to be a boon in traffic growth.

At the end of February, CMP's owner—a public company called United Business Media plc (UBM)—announced a restructure of CMP into four separate, independent units. Bob and Fritz would now be working in the TechWeb division, whose CEO would be Tony Uphoff. I wasn't sure if this would impact our acquisition talks, but Fritz said it gave them "more focus and autonomy, including in pursuing our partnership."

By mid-March discussions had progressed well, but I still didn't have any idea of what their acquisition offer might be. I was promised "some early ballpark numbers" on March 21, ahead of my planned trip to the Web 2.0 Expo in mid-April. Fritz also floated the idea of announcing the acquisition at the conference. It was heady stuff, talking about being acquired by the company that coproduced the event. But I was already out of my depth, and I had no idea how to value RWW. So to help me with that, I reached out to one of RWW's regular contributors, Bernard Lunn.

I didn't know Bernard well at this time—only that he was a middle-aged guy who lived somewhere in the New York region, and for the past few decades he had worked for various B2B media companies I'd never heard of. But he seemed knowledgeable, and Alex Iskold had met and vouched for him. The consulting rate Bernard asked for seemed high to me, at $200 per hour, but I knew it would cost even more to go to a big accounting firm for a valuation. So I capped the hours at twenty and we went ahead.

I also asked Bernard to give me his advice on a "go it alone" plan. I already had a rough plan for this—Bernard, Alex, and Sean had helped me with that over the previous months—but I wanted to flesh it out more. Basically, if the acquisition didn't work out, I was looking to bring on someone to run the business and operations side while I focused on editorial and overall strategy. I also noted my thoughts on bringing Marshall and Josh on full-time, the former in an executive capacity—I suggested the title VP of content development, as I wanted to expand the premium-content side of RWW. I had questions regarding equity structure, salaries, and so on—all of which I asked Bernard to report back on.

Bernard started with the go-it-alone plan first, so I didn't yet know his thoughts on valuation by the time CMP finally made their first offer, on March 26, of $1 million upfront and a figure "in the range of about $2m" over an earn-out period of three years. I had no context for what a good offer looked like for a young business like RWW, but if this was a ballpark figure, then it felt like a ground ball to first base.

Fortunately, I now had another wooer! CMP's rival in IT news, Ziff Davis Enterprise Group (ZDE), also expressed an interest in acquiring RWW. Earlier in March I'd been introduced to Insight Partners, the private equity firm that had bought ZDE the year before. That came via a media industry veteran who had worked for CMP for twenty years but was now at ZDE as a consultant: Mike Azzara. Sean had introduced us in November; I was discovering that the American IT media world was a very small one.

I'd been discussing with Mike the possibility of him joining RWW on the business side, perhaps as my much-needed COO, but his salary demand was too steep. Instead, Mike introduced me by email to Kobi Levy, an employee at Insight Partners. I had no clue what a private equity firm might do with a small business like RWW, but I knew that having two companies competing to acquire it was a good thing. Especially since, between them, CMP and ZDE owned most of the popular IT publications of the 1990s into the early 2000s. CMP had *Information Week*; ZDE had *eWeek*. Both needed an injection of young tech-media blood, and RWW was a perfect fit.

When I ran CMP's proposed deal past Bernard, he agreed it was a lowball offer. He suggested I hold out for more and ask for 50 percent upfront. He added, "You don't need to sell—you are profitable and growing—and I believe there are many ways to build more value organically."

It was good advice, so that's what I took back to CMP. While they were considering their next move, Bernard and I attempted to get an offer on the table from ZDE. We did a call with Kobi, who I had since discovered was a junior "associate" at Insight, and Azzara, who had by now joined ZDE full-time as its senior VP of product management. As expected, on the phone they were vague about what the offer would be, but I got the impression they wanted me to run their fledgling blog network on salary.

A couple of days later I got a printed offer from ZDE. However, it was even worse than the CMP one: $1 million upfront and a vague profit-sharing arrangement for two years based on "an additional split of incremental EBITDA." I didn't understand the earn-out part, but I knew that this wasn't good enough. I said as much to ZDE in reply, and they asked how much I wanted for the business. Again, I consulted with Bernard, who suggested I go back with "a total valuation of $5m of which 50% would be due on closing." We'd previously discussed $4 million as a minimum, although Bernard had rightly noted that he could come up with figures to justify whatever amount I told him I wanted.

As I was about to reply to Kobi with my suggested offer, ZDE's CEO, Steve Weitzner, jumped into the email conversation. "As an ex-editor who has been through the transformation from a print to an online culture a few times now," he wrote, "I'm convinced it cannot be done without strong outside influences and I am anxious for ZDE to work with you." He asked me to hold tight for a couple of days "while I work to sweeten the offer."

I chatted with Alex on IM about the situation—I trusted his business instincts and I knew he was much savvier than me about these matters. He suggested I be upfront with both suitors about my $5 million expectations. Otherwise, he noted, they would likely continue to mess me around with variations on their lowball offers. Bernard agreed, so I gave ZDE the guidance.

ZDE promptly came back with a revised offer: $2 million upfront and an additional $2 million over two years based on "mutually agreed upon targets." The devil would surely be in the details of the earn-out, but I was pleased to get in the range of what I wanted. It also gave me the opportunity to go back to CMP and tell them I'd received a better offer. I gave them the same expectation note I'd given to ZDE.

CMP were slow to reply, but after I had held off ZDE for more than a week, Fritz emailed me: $2 million upfront plus "additional considerations payable over the next 2 years based on performance," with a maximum of $5 million in total. He warned that this wasn't an official offer, as the UBM head office would have to sign off on it. Regardless, the numbers sounded promising—although it did seem like the extra $3 million would be based on aggressive profit targets.

My main concern with both deals was how much control I would have in achieving the earn-out targets, but I figured we'd clarify that once I'd chosen between CMP and ZDE. The more straightforward offer, on paper, was ZDE's. But I was leaning toward CMP, based on the rapport I'd built up with Bob and Fritz and on CMP's involvement with the Web 2.0 conferences. I just needed more clarity from them, along with sign-off from their head office.

I was about to jump on a plane to San Francisco for the Web 2.0 Expo, so I suggested to Fritz, Bob, and Tony Uphoff (who I hadn't yet heard from) that we meet at the event.

On the opening morning of the Web 2.0 Expo, I met Marshall for the first time in the press room, on the third floor of the Moscone Center. He was a big-boned guy, a couple of inches taller than me, with brown hair and well-trimmed beard. He looked young, an impression further emphasized by the olive-green-and-white sweatshirt he wore over blue jeans and sneakers. As we shook hands, I noticed that his blue eyes looked nervous behind his small, red-rimmed rectangular glasses. But it wasn't the anxiety of someone who was uncomfortable in their own skin (which was generally the case with me); rather, it was about his surroundings. He didn't seem to enjoy the formal setting of a corporate press room.

As I got to know him more, I discovered that Marshall was very much a native of Oregon. He lived in Portland, a small city renowned for its *Keep Portland Weird* slogan. I'd not yet visited the "bridge city" (another term that suggested a city that wasn't your ordinary urban center), but it soon became clear that Marshall would never move to the big smoke of San Francisco. He was almost the polar opposite of, say, Mike Arrington or Om Malik, for whom the big city was a necessary conduit for their insider networking. Even Pete Cashmore had decided he needed to emulate Arrington and Malik, rather than stay put in the

UK. But Marshall, I knew shortly after I met him, would always live in Portland—not so much a Silicon Valley outsider as someone who wanted to deploy his talents on his own terms.

The self-assurance I'd noticed in Marshall from our first email interactions became even more evident as the conference progressed. On Wednesday he published an excellent report on APIs and developer platforms that quoted and summarized the thoughts of people he'd spoken to at the event. He appeared to be at ease wandering the conference venue and chatting to people about web technology. He also used quotes from people he'd surveyed on Twitter.

At the time I was using Twitter somewhat reluctantly—I'd had my first interaction with a troll the week before I flew to San Francisco, and I didn't like it. But Marshall had taken to Twitter like a duck to water; he used it effectively as both a professional research tool and a kind of ongoing diary ("I'm on 3rd floor in press room, trying to feed the hungry blog,"[58] he tweeted the day I met him). He told me during the conference that I needed to use Twitter more often and extolled its virtues as a journalistic tool. I knew he was right, and I did use it that trip to gather crowdsourced questions for an upcoming interview with Sun CEO Jonathan Schwartz. But I couldn't bring myself to use Twitter as an online diary. The fact that I was having secret discussions with two potential acquirers may've had something to do with that.

That afternoon at the conference, Bob Evans (whom I'd met for the first time the night before) took me to meet Tony Uphoff, now CEO of the newly formed TechWeb division of UBM, and Fritz, who had been the point person in our negotiations so far. Tony was a very tall man, with a long, clean-shaven face and reddish-blond hair. He was probably in his early fifties, but with his full head of hair and lean frame, he looked a bit younger. He wore a crisp-looking business suit, which was more formal than what I was used to in the valley—it made me feel underdressed in my ordinary dress shirt and jeans. Fritz was more in the Silicon Valley mold of blazer and slacks. He had a tanned, smiling face and looked to be in his early forties.

We found a private table. The first thing Tony said to me was that "London" (the UBM head office) had come back to him and wanted to lower the front end of the deal and put more on the earn-out. I didn't know how to respond, but I knew this would immediately make ZDE's offer more attractive, since they had offered $2 million upfront. I asked Tony what figures they now had in mind, but he said he didn't have any further details—the implication being that the terms of the deal were out of his hands.

Fritz jumped in and promised to get their head office to commit to an LOI (letter of intent) in the next day or two. Bob suggested he set up a lunch tomorrow for us to discuss more. Feeling a little deflated, I agreed, wondering if CMP was trying to back out of the deal.

I then rushed off for a press event at Microsoft's San Francisco office on Market Street. I'd be meeting Josh Catone there—another first chance to put a face to the name. Josh, it turned out, bore a physical resemblance to Marshall: brown hair, beard, thin rectangular glasses, around the same height, and even the same kind of casual clothing. But he didn't have Marshall's self-confidence and was quite reserved in person. This may've partly been an age thing. Josh was a few years younger than Marshall, and indeed, his awkwardness was familiar to me—I'd been more like him than Marshall in my early twenties.

I could also see that I would need to gently push and prod Josh to do the kind of networking at Web 2.0 Expo that obviously came naturally to Marshall. Regardless, Josh was happy to write up Microsoft's news (they were launching something called Live Mesh), so for once I didn't have to scramble back to the conference or hotel to quickly write up a news post. I was relieved to have both Josh and Marshall with me on this trip—the first time I'd had RWW colleagues sharing event duties with me.

Wednesday began with a 7:30 a.m. breakfast at Hotel Palomar, hosted by Web 2 Ireland, to which my friend Fergus Burns had invited me. The Irish government had paid for some of their local startups to travel to the valley, to promote themselves and meet the tech media. I was still doing monthly consulting for Fergus's company, Nooked, and I always liked Irish entrepreneurs whenever I met them, so I was happy to come along.

But my mind was elsewhere that morning, as I would be meeting both CMP and ZDE later that day. I'd be having lunch with CMP and then dinner with Azzara from ZDE. My main objective for the day was to try and get clarity from CMP on their offer—ideally, they'd give me a LOI, but Bernard had warned me that this might not happen. "They still seem a long way from a real deal," he'd told me. "I think there maybe internal turmoil getting in the way." As for ZDE, I just had to continue to hold them off while I waited on CMP.

After breakfast I went back to my room at the Mosser Hotel to psych myself up for the upcoming meetings. I messaged Bob, and after some back-and-forth, we arranged to meet at 11:30 a.m. at Momo's, at the corner of Second and King. He'd booked a table for three—himself, Fritz, and me—so apparently Tony would not be coming. I had a couple of hours to kill, so I wrote up a couple of blog posts in my hotel room, rather than go to the expo.

Momo's turned out to be right opposite the Giants baseball stadium. It served typical American grill fare, but I don't remember what I ate. As usual, we had good camaraderie—I felt like they understood the direction I wanted to take RWW under the TechWeb banner. They knew how media worked in the age of the blogosphere, and they saw me as a key part of the Web 2.0 conferences going forward. Fritz was also keen on adding multimedia to RWW—his main job at TechWeb was to run its video productions—and I liked that plan too. In short, I really wanted to sell to these guys.

Unfortunately, there was still no LOI, and I quickly ascertained that I would not get any further clarity on the terms of the deal during this meeting. Even worse, it was intimated that the $5 million figure Fritz had presented to me less than two weeks ago was unlikely to be approved by head office. So, despite being on the same page as TechWeb philosophically, the negotiations had actually gone backward since I'd arrived in San Francisco. Fritz promised again that the LOI would be forthcoming—by Friday at the earliest, he said, or Monday at the latest.

Frustrated, I walked back to the expo venue and tried to think things through. Even though my preference was to go with CMP, the only firm offer I had was with ZDE. All CMP had offered this week were promises and prevarication. Earlier in the day, I had talked with Sean Ammirati, who was also at Web 2.0 Expo. He'd been out to dinner with Azzara the night before and had warned me to expect a hard sell to sign the LOI with ZDE.

I would have to make a decision, one way or another, by the end of this week. ZDE had reserved the option to take its offer off the table by Friday, April 28, so any further delay would risk both deals falling through. ZDE's offer was reasonable, and despite not having the same warm fuzzies about ZDE as I had for CMP, I was almost certain I'd accept it on Friday if I hadn't gotten an LOI from CMP by then. I resolved to apply pressure to Fritz to get *something* to me in paper by Friday—Monday just wouldn't do.

Even though the situation was fluid and unsatisfactory, by the time of my dinner reservation with Mike Azzara I felt like I at least had a solid plan. As long as I got on with Mike and liked what I heard from him, and as long as he (a media industry veteran) didn't think I was a complete amateur, then most likely I'd be signing with ZDE on Friday.

Mike had arranged a dinner for three people—he'd be bringing along a new ZDE editor named Stephen Wellman, whom he'd just hired from (of course) CMP. The dinner reservation was at a restaurant called Two, in the trendy SoMa district of San Francisco, apparently in the original 1922 headquarters of the San Francisco Newspaper Company. Perhaps this was why, as I would soon discover, it was popular with media people.

The reservation was for 6:30 p.m., and I arrived a few minutes early. It was a brick building with a large maroon sign featuring a stylized orange T-shaped logo and the word *TWO* in white block letters. It was cold outside, so I went straight in. I explained to a waitress at the front desk that I had a reservation with Mike Azzara, but that I was a bit early. She checked the bookings, picked up a menu, and then beckoned me to follow her.

As we walked through the restaurant, my eyes adjusted to the dark brown wood surfaces and the warm golden glow provided by the coconut light fixtures. It felt like a cozy place for a business dinner, but I couldn't see clearly in the dim light, so I walked rather gingerly past all the tables. The waitress stopped at a table in the back, which was empty—Mike hadn't yet arrived. I was trailing several steps behind, so she waited for me to catch up.

Suddenly, I stopped in my tracks a foot or two away from the table. Sitting at one of the adjoining tables were none other than Tony Uphoff and Bob Evans! There was one other person in their party, but I didn't recognize them. Tony and Bob hadn't yet noticed me, so for a brief second, I considered turning around and speed-walking out. However, the waitress had spotted me looking at them. She went over to their table and asked if they were the Mike Azzara party.

I was mortified. There was no way I could escape now, so I reluctantly stepped forward to shake Tony and Bob's hands. They looked up at me with bemused expressions, wondering what I was doing here. My bright red face felt like a glowing beacon amid the murky lighting. I stammered an apology and turned to the waitress, explaining that this wasn't who I was meeting. Tony and Bob must've realized what was happening and began to smile broadly. Again I apologized, even though this mix-up clearly wasn't my fault. Grinning, Tony politely said it was no problem and that we'd catch up another time. The waitress led me to the front again.

Shaken, I told the waitress I'd just wait beside the front desk. Then Mike walked in, with Stephen following. Mike was a short, barrel-chested guy with dark hair and beard—he looked a bit like Steve Wozniak. After anxiously shaking hands, I explained to him what had happened. He was taken aback and saw that I was rattled. We'll find another restaurant, he said, and we made a hasty exit.

I don't recall what restaurant we went to, but the meal was pleasant enough. Mike was a good talker, and Stephen, a soft-spoken guy a few years younger than me, was friendly and curious about RWW. We talked about what ZDE was trying to do—basically, compete with CMP in the enterprise IT media market—and they also spoke about their experiences working for their prime competitor. (Mike had worked for CMP for nearly twenty years, Stephen for less than three years.)

Despite Mike's bluster about the prospects of ZDE, I didn't feel the same connection with him that I'd had with Bob and Fritz during our earlier lunch. He didn't seem as interested in RWW's future; the talk was more about what ZDE could turn into, with RWW somehow integrated.

Mind you, I don't think I fully understood ZDE either, at that point. I kept thinking of ZDNet—my old blogging gig. The confusion was natural, since both ZDE and ZDNet had been spun off from the Ziff Davis media empire. CNET had acquired ZDNet in 2000, and then in 2001 Ziff Davis created a new entity called Ziff Davis Media Inc., which bought back the content licensing rights from ZDNet to eleven publications, including *PC Magazine*, *CIO Insight*, and *eWeek*. In 2007 Ziff Davis Media sold off its B2B publications (including *eWeek*) to Insight Partners—the company I was actually negotiating with. To make matters even more confusing, Ziff Davis Media had declared bankruptcy the previous month.

Despite all these corporate maneuverings, I understood that ZDE expected RWW to link up with *eWeek*, which was known as a fairly bland enterprise IT publication, both paper and online. It had begun in 1984 as a business magazine named *PCWeek* and was renamed *eWeek* in 2000, during the era when nearly every new startup was said to be doing e-*something*.

Part of my reticence with the ZDE offer was my impression that Mike planned to fold RWW into *eWeek*. My preference was to keep the RWW brand separate. Weitzner, the chairman and CEO of ZDE, had told me their goal was to create a blog network—but he admitted he was unsure whether RWW would "complement or integrate" with *eWeek*. (Incidentally, he was also an ex-CMP executive and had been Uphoff's boss before the move to ZDE.)

It seemed likely that if the ZDE deal went through, RWW would be a secondary brand to *eWeek*. I was much more sure that CMP wanted RWW as a stand-alone brand, since the whole purpose of TechWeb was to be an umbrella network for different media brands. So that was another thing in CMP's favor as I weighed the two deals.

After dinner I had a conversation with Sean on the phone. He was surprised to hear that I saw Tony and Bob at the restaurant, but he said they probably already knew that ZDE was their competitor for RWW.

Sean must've sensed how shaken I felt, and he suggested we meet up for a drink to clear my head. I happily agreed.

We met at a bar near my hotel—I don't recall which one, but it was not the one Bob had invited us to a couple of days ago. I was, by this point, more than a little paranoid. We ordered beers and sat down at a table where I could keep an eye on the rest of the bar.

Sean looked excited to talk with me; I could tell he got a natural buzz from being in the middle of important business deals. His tanned young face couldn't help smiling, although he also had a look of concern about my anxious state.

We talked for a bit about the bizarre encounter with CMP. I'd previously learned, perhaps from Bernard, that CMP people have a mischievous sense of humor, so it was possible, I told Sean, that they'd somehow found out I was going to Two and had told the waitress they were expecting one more person and to send them through. But I knew this was unlikely; I was no doubt projecting my inner discomfort about not knowing what CMP was thinking. Why weren't they following through on their initial offer? It bugged me that I had even less clarity about CMP now than I'd had a week ago in New Zealand.

Sean had already told me over the last couple of days that he was willing to be a go-between for me and CMP, and he reiterated this as we supped our beers. He could have a private word to Bob in the morning, he said, and tell them they must get an LOI in front of me by first thing Friday morning. Would I like him to do that, he asked?

I demurred and said that perhaps I was being unfair to ZDE in all this. They'd made a decent offer in writing at the start of the week, and yet here I was stalling because of CMP's antics. Ultimately, I said, I could see past my feelings of unease about ZDE. I wasn't yet sure how they'd integrate RWW into *eWeek* (that hadn't been clarified at dinner), but I knew that whatever happened, RWW would have the organizational support to go to the next level—as my competitors, like TechCrunch and GigaOm, had done with their recent expansions into network blogs, events, and so on. The deal that ZDE had offered was good, I said, and was flexible enough with earn-out that I had a more than fair chance of achieving it.

Sean agreed it was life-changing money that ZDE was offering, especially considering that there was no capital gains tax in New Zealand. But, he asked which would I prefer to have as a partner, money aside?

I admitted that I much preferred CMP as a partner, as they seemed to "get" blogs. Also, I added, the Web 2.0 conference relationships could potentially make me a star player in the industry—maybe I'd even become Tim O'Reilly's sidekick in future events. Sean smiled and said he knew, from a couple of his sources, that CMP did indeed see me as a key part of the Web 2.0 conferences going forward.

But was that just a pipe dream? The reality of a CMP deal seemed to be slipping away, as I pointed out to Sean. He nodded but said it would be worthwhile to put one more squeeze on them for an offer on paper by Friday. I had noted Bernard's skepticism about whether Tony and his team even had the ability to set terms for a deal—that the problems stemmed from UBM red tape. But Sean thought that CMP could do a deal quickly if they really had to.

By the end of the night, I'd resolved to send an email to CMP first thing tomorrow, telling them I was going to sign with the other party on Friday morning unless they delivered a firm offer by then. I finished my beer and took a deep breath. Sean grinned and gave me an encouraging slap on the back.

Early on Thursday morning, after a phone call with Bernard on the East Coast, I sent my email ultimatum to Fritz and Bob. "I've given this *a lot* of thought over the past 12 hours or so," I wrote, "and it really is time for me to make a decision." I asked for "a firm, signed, LOI" before 9:00 a.m. on Friday, or I would "need to withdraw from these negotiations." I proposed a number equal to ZDE's in their LOI, with half on closing and the other half on a maximum two-year earn-out. I added, "It is simply not viable for me to follow the timetable we discussed yesterday" (in the end I opted for subtlety and did not mention the restaurant incident).

I forwarded the email to Sean and gave him my blessing to have a private word with Bob or Fritz if he wanted to, although I said there was "certainly no pressure from me to do it." I knew he enjoyed being a part of these negotiations, though, so I was pretty sure he would talk to Bob. He emailed back and confirmed my hunch. He also asked if I was intending to sign with ZDE if CMP didn't match. I confirmed that yes, I would sign with ZDE if CMP wouldn't "come to the party."

After I'd sent the email, I felt like a small part of the pressure had been relieved. I couldn't do any more. It was now CMP's move.

That evening there were a couple of parties to go to. The first, by invitation of CMP, was their "VIP party" at the trendy Temple nightclub in San Francisco, which was "exclusive to a select 200 people" (mostly Web 2.0 Expo speakers and sponsors). The other party, held at the same time, was hosted by Netvibes at Minna Gallery and would be attended by many of the conference attendees.

Sean and I went to the VIP party. Sean told me there was a good chance we'd talk to Bob and the CMP team privately tonight. Frankly, I didn't think there was any point in yet another meeting—I just needed a firm offer on paper the following morning. I wasn't in the mood for more feel-good discussions about the synergies of our partnership. However, I recognized the need to keep schmoozing for one more night.

When we entered Temple, a DJ was playing an up-tempo electron-ica set. It was, as advertised, a smaller, more intimate crowd than the usual Web 2.0 conference parties I'd attended to that point. We saw Tim O'Reilly talking with a group of his people near the bar, and Sean indi-cated we should go say hi.

It seemed to me that Tim was rather high. As we shook hands, he said that seeing me was like looking in a mirror. I wondered if he was referring to the ambition I'd voiced to Tony, Bob, and Fritz during the negotiations, to be Tim's sidekick in the Web 2.0 conferences. He was almost certainly aware that I was in talks with TechWeb. Otherwise, it could be a comment on my being a kind of poor man's O'Reilly in some of my blog posts—the theorizing about Web 2.0 and the trendspotting I was known for. Either way, I was flattered that Tim O'Reilly had com-pared me to himself, however obliquely.

We didn't stay chatting for long, as everyone around us was on a high and just wanted to party. Maybe it was simply Web 2.0 exuberance? In any case, we soon saw Tim and his friends on the dance floor. Tim had shown off his hippie dancing at the Lou Reed concert during the 2006 Web 2.0 Summit, and I recognized similar moves happening now.

Sean and I looked at each other with bemused expressions. The vibe at this VIP party was odd—it felt like we had missed out on a substance secretly handed out at the door or over the bar. Most of the people here seemed to be tripping out on something. I was beginning to think we didn't belong here, at this exclusive insider event in the heart of San Francisco. Yes, we were technically VIPs, but only because of the uncon-summated deal with CMP—we wouldn't have been invited otherwise. I felt like an impostor, a "straight" wallflower looking on while blissed-out Tim O'Reilly let loose on the dance floor.

We soon spotted Bob and Fritz, who steered us to a private booth so that we could chat. As expected, there was no news to report from UBM. The only new detail I gleaned from Fritz was that the upfront offer would definitely be no more than $1 million and they hadn't yet arrived at a figure for the earn-out. On hearing this, I couldn't help but let my exasperation show. I told them that my expectations coming into this week were that I'd have a decision by the end of the week, and yet we had made zero progress on numbers—in fact, it had gone backward! Fritz gave me a helpless look, but he promised to send an official offer by tomorrow morning, as per my request this morning. I just nodded. Inside, I knew this wasn't going to happen with TechWeb.

I didn't think there was any point hanging around at the VIP party any longer. Whatever drug the true insiders were on, it had put them on a different wavelength for the evening. Sean and I made our way to the Netvibes party. There would probably be RWW readers and sponsors there, I said to Sean, so it'd be good to show my face. Plus, I wanted to have a beer or two and relax a bit before the big decision day tomorrow.

Barring a miracle with CMP, I had decided I would sign with ZDE.

First thing Friday morning, I went to the Web 2.0 Expo and half-heartedly watched the keynotes. I was feeling like a zombie—the week had been long and (to this point) unfruitful on the business side. I had scheduled an interview with Sun Microsystems CEO Jonathan

Schwartz at 9:55 a.m., after his onstage Q&A with Tim O'Reilly. I had my crowdsourced questions, and I made note of what he said to Tim, so I was prepared in that sense. But, of course, I had other things on my mind. I had not received anything in writing from CMP by the time I made my way to the meeting room backstage, where I'd be meeting Jonathan. So I was mentally preparing to contact ZDE and tell them I'd be signing with them.

The interview was not one of my best. Sun was known for its computer servers and workstations, the Java programming language, and various pieces of infrastructure software. None of this was of particular interest to me, so I stumbled my way through the interview. Jonathan humored me on a few of my web-related questions, but fortunately he had his own talking points that he wanted to hit—the phrase "the network as a social utility" was deployed—and so we got through it. But I was relieved when it was over. (I would discover a few days later that I had somehow forgotten to save the audio recording, so I never did write it up as a post.)

I was heading to the press room when I bumped into Fritz in the hallways. By now, it was midmorning, so I wasn't expecting good news. But he said that CMP was going to email me an offer in the next ten or fifteen minutes. Their finance guy, Pat, was just checking the final details with Tony Uphoff. He patted me on the shoulder encouragingly and walked off.

I was a little dazed, but I went into the press room and immediately messaged Bernard. "It sounds like it could be a LOI, but we'll see," I wrote. I decided to go back to my hotel room so that I could focus on whatever CMP was sending me. I also needed to check out by midday.

The email arrived as I was packing. It was even more of a disappointment than I'd expected. The upfront was $1 million (half of what ZDE had offered) and the earn-out $2 million. So their $5 million email offer just a couple of weeks prior had turned into a $3 million email offer. To make matters worse, it still wasn't an LOI! "We realize you need to make a decision soon and we hope you consider the proposed framework and we will communicate a more formal position as soon as possible but no later than Monday," the email finished.

I messaged Bernard, expressing my disappointment with CMP. "I'm now going to move ahead with ZDE," I wrote. "That's a straightforward decision now. Can't delay any longer."

I had been keeping in touch by email with Kobi Levy from Insight Partners throughout the week. He hadn't put any pressure on me to sign—in fact, on Thursday he'd told me that "if you need a few extra days to think then that is ok too." However, now that CMP was out of the running, I just wanted to sign on the dotted line with ZDE.

I emailed Levy, Weitzner, and Azzara: "I'm very pleased to say that I'm now ready to sign the LOI and proceed to the due diligence stage! I am excited by the possibilities of our two companies working together and very much looking forward to closing this deal within the terms of the LOI." I added that I would go home to New Zealand first, and then prepare for a visit to New York within "the next 2-3 weeks."

But the drama for the week wasn't quite over yet. My hotel for some reason didn't have a printer, so I hadn't been able to get a paper copy of the LOI. This was in the era before e-signatures, so printing and faxing were still a thing. In my email, I asked if Mike was still in town—if so, could he print out the LOI and meet me that afternoon?

I followed up with a phone call to Levy. His first idea was to fax a copy of the document to the Mosser, but I told him I was about to check out. He then said he'd send someone to meet me in the afternoon. I had an evening flight back to New Zealand, so I had until the end of the afternoon to sign the LOI.

Once I'd checked out of my hotel, I went back to the Web 2.0 Expo and wandered around the exhibits for a while. All my RWW colleagues had left by this point, so I was on my own. I don't think I stopped at any of the stalls to talk to the startups. I just needed something to do while I waited for the ZDE document to turn up, so I walked around the expo hall and tried not to make eye contact with anyone.

Eventually, Levy called and told me he was sending a guy to a café in the Metreon, a nearby food and movie-theater complex. I made my way over there and nursed a coffee until the delivery man came. I don't remember anything about this person—whether he was a ZDE employee or someone connected to Insight Partners—but in any case, the transaction was quick. He handed me a folder with a printout of the LOI. I checked that it was the same as my electronic version, I saw the required signatures, and then I tiredly put pen to paper.

The deal was done.

CHAPTER 10

DUE DILIGENCE

■ ■ ■ ■ ■

AS SOON AS I GOT BACK HOME, RWW made it to the top 10 on Technorati. We were now one of the world's ten most popular blogs, based on how many websites had linked to us in the last six months. Alex had spotted it first, and Marshall confirmed it with a screenshot.

"I really am proud of us all and what RWW has become," I told the team. "Everybody I talked to at Expo had nothing but praise for RWW, especially compared to our competition."

To my mind, this also validated our 2007 redesign. That, together with the increase in our team members, was how we'd risen from number 18 to number 10 in Technorati in less than four months. We still had an issue with consistency of posting, something I nudged the writers about regularly. Compared to TechCrunch and Mashable, our two primary competitors, we were often slow to get posts up in the morning US time. But none of our writers were yet full-time on RWW (the closest was Josh at thirty hours per week), so there was only so much I could demand under these arrangements. I wanted to find a way to bring Marshall, in particular, on full-time—but obviously now wasn't the right time. I hadn't yet told any of the writers about the ZDE deal and didn't plan to until the forty-five-day due diligence was over.

I began preparing for my trip to New York. I planned to leave just two weeks after arriving home, which in retrospect seems insane. The flights to New York from my home in Wellington involved around twenty hours in the air, plus all the waiting around in airports. I also needed to organize a lot of paperwork before I left, so I'd made appointments to see my accountant and lawyer. As if that wasn't enough to deal with, FM Publishing was chasing me—and the rest of their authors—to sign an updated contract for our advertising relationship. Among other things, the new contract asked for a twelve-month commitment. I would need to find a way to delay signing that, since I didn't yet know what ZDE planned for RWW in terms of advertising revenue.

Meanwhile, while I was in San Francisco I'd received an invitation to attend New Zealand's annual media awards. I'd been told, in confidence, that I'd won Best Blog and they wanted to ensure I would accept the award in person. The ceremony was to be held in Auckland on Friday, May 9, at the Hyatt Regency hotel. I planned to combine that trip to Auckland with my New York journey. Maria and I would travel up to Auckland that Friday, and I would board my flight to the States on Saturday while she headed back home.

During those two weeks back in New Zealand, I had several phone calls with Insight Partners and ZDE and several more in-person meetings with my accountant and lawyers. If I had thought the due-diligence phase would be relatively straightforward, I was soon disabused of that idea. In one meeting involving my accountant, Bill, and my legal representatives, Gillespie Young Watson, we talked about how to structure the deal so that I wouldn't incur a big tax bill. ZDE had their own preferences on structure to avoid tax issues on their side. The lawyers recommended I get PricewaterhouseCoopers, one of the big global accounting firms, to advise on this. I should also get a US lawyer, they said, to make sure I was protected in that jurisdiction.

With all these accountants and lawyers getting involved, the complexity was quickly ratcheting up—not to mention the bills.

The New Zealand Media Awards were traditionally known as a knees-up for the local journalism industry—in particular its newspaper and television news shows. It was now in its thirty-fourth year, but the Best Blog category was only in its second year. It had been first awarded in 2007 to a political blogger, Russell Brown, whose weblog, Hard News, had been running since late 2002. Hard News was part of a community of New Zealand-centric blogs that ran on the domain PublicAddress. net, which Russell had set up.

I had met him back in 2005, when we were both on "the Imagineers," a government think tank about the internet and digital content. He was a likable man, about a decade older than me, who was passionate about the kiwi lifestyle and culture. He lived in Auckland and had done all the cool things an NZ journalist could've done—worked in student radio, written for a music magazine (*Rip It Up*, a free 'zine that I used to read regularly in the nineties), and gone to England for several years to write for their music mags. He seemed to know everyone in the NZ media industry, and his political leanings were liberal. He was, in short, the ultimate insider when it came to local media.

The NZ blogosphere, such as it was at that time, was dominated by political blogs. The two other finalists in 2008 were political blogs at opposite ends of the spectrum: David Farrar's right-wing Kiwiblog and Malcolm Harbrow's left-wing No Right Turn. This scene was completely alien to me; I didn't read any political blogs, let alone New Zealand ones. While RWW did have a profile in the local tech industry and had been written about by both of New Zealand's main newspapers, the *Dominion Post* and the *NZ Herald*, my focus had been global from the get-go. I often told people that only 1 percent of RWW's audience came from New Zealand.

When Maria and I arrived at the Hyatt Regency on Friday evening, May 9, I was a bundle of nerves. I wasn't used to being around people in the traditional media industry. I was definitely an outsider. That said, I was thrilled to be here because the award was a form of acceptance for me. It was something to be proud of, especially since my own father, Kevin, had been a journalist all his career. He'd worked for the daily newspapers of Dunedin and Timaru while I was a young child, and then in 1981, when I was nine, he and his wife Judy moved their four small children (I was the eldest) up to Wellington, where he worked for a farming magazine, *Dairy Exporter*, for the rest of his career. I never expected to follow in his footsteps; I hadn't trained to be a journalist, and when I started RWW in 2003, it wasn't intended to be a business. Yet here I was at the New Zealand Media Awards ceremony five years later.

As the ceremony began, I sat patiently with Maria. We were at one of the round group tables on the side and near the back—as far as I could tell, the big TV and newspaper companies had the tables nearest the front. I didn't know anyone else at the table, and I had to explain what blogging was more than once. I felt uncomfortable in my rented black suit and bowtie (the invitation had specified "black tie"). My face was clean-shaven but also tinged with pink due to the drink or two I'd downed to try and settle my anxiety.

I soon realized that I wasn't the only one feeling a bit tipsy—there was *a lot* of alcohol being consumed by the gathered media elite. The front tables, in particular, were becoming more raucous as the night went on. When my award was announced, I walked up to the stage and received a paper scroll announcing ReadWriteWeb.com as the winner of "Blog 2008." My category wasn't allowed to do a speech, so I was quickly ushered back to my seat.

When the show ended and people got up from their tables to mingle, Maria decided she wanted a selfie with New Zealand's most famous media celebrity, Paul Holmes. He was a former TV broadcaster whose heyday had been in the 1990s, when he'd had the highest-rating current affairs show. He was now fifty-eight and a popular breakfast radio host, as well as a newspaper columnist for the *NZ Herald* (in fact, he'd won the award for Best Columnist that night). Maria grabbed my iPhone and made her way to where Holmes was standing, talking and laughing with other local media luminaries—all of them looking completely plastered. I saw Maria tap him on the shoulder and indicate that she would like a photo of the two of them. She handed the iPhone to someone in the group while Holmes swung his arm around her. He grinned rakishly as a guy, who was clearly inebriated and struggling to operate my phone, took a photo.

We then made our way to the hotel bar to meet up with my good friend Dave, who was out on the town with a mate. I'd lived in Auckland a couple of different times during the 1990s, and I'd been out carousing with Dave and other friends on many a Friday night. Maria showed the guys her snapshot with Paul Holmes—it turned out the drunken photographer had only captured half of Holmes's head! I then bashfully showed them my award certificate. Dave invited me to come into the city and have some celebratory drinks in our old haunts, but I pointed to my black-tie getup and said I was overdressed for that. Besides, I said, I had to get on a plane to New York tomorrow.

It was late at night when I finally arrived at Hotel Chandler in New York City. It had been an epic journey, and I didn't know what to expect from this trip. Did I really want to sell my business to a company based literally on the other side of the world?

In our discussions, Insight and ZDE had made soothing noises about my role post-acquisition. In a call with Levy, Azzara, and an Insight bean counter named Jake Stein, we'd talked about me transitioning from all the business things I'd been doing at RWW—sales, operations, and so on—to focusing purely on editorial. They wanted me to extend the RWW brand with three or so new "verticals" (network blogs). What's more, they noted that ZDE was a legacy media business and so they'd like me to oversee its blogging business in general. This was all music to my ears, since it was the journalism side of RWW that I enjoyed the most.

However, in the back of my mind I was also aware that I needed to be in control of the revenue and expenses of RWW for at least two more years—since half the deal's value depended on hitting certain targets. What those targets were and how revenue and costs were defined would (I hoped) be clarified during this trip.

I spent my first full day, a Sunday, getting over my jet lag by wandering down Fifth Ave and the surrounding areas. It was springtime, but colder than I had expected. I checked out Central Park and went into the Apple Store at that location. I'd been instructed to buy an iPhone for my wife, but it was sold out. The second generation, the iPhone 3G, hadn't even been announced yet (that would happen in June). Still, I was surprised that there weren't *any* iPhones available in the New York Apple Store. Regardless, the store was very busy and people seemed to be buying iPods and computers. I spent some time fondling one of the MacBook Airs on display—it had only just come out in January and was said to be the "world's thinnest notebook."

I took some photos of Central Park and the city, but I had resolved to stay off social media during my trip. Only Bernard, Sean, and Alex from RWW were aware that I was here. I had told the rest of my writers that I was "traveling," but I didn't explain why. I was particularly uncomfortable with keeping Marshall in the dark. He was still only working half-time for RWW, so I wasn't under any obligation to bring him into business discussions. But for several months now I had been promising to discuss business expansion plans with him—he had ideas about premium content that I was interested in pursuing. I knew it made sense not to tell him about ZDE because he could decide to have no part in it and jump to a competitor. But I also didn't want to undermine the trust Marshall and I had built up since he'd joined RWW.

I planned to keep daily tabs on the site while I was in New York, but I hoped it would be business as usual for the week. I was happy with how RWW was going as a publication—we were hovering around the number 10 ranking in Technorati, and our page views and subscriber numbers were still growing. But I was worried about messing with a good thing by spending too much of my time focused on this ZDE deal. I just hoped the due diligence would be straightforward, so that the deal could be consummated in early June as planned. Also, I wanted to get back to blogging.

The due-diligence meetings would start at midday on Monday. But first, I had arranged to meet Bernard Lunn, who was based somewhere in greater New York.

Around 9:00 a.m. I finally put a face to the name, when Bernard met me in the lobby of Hotel Chandler. He was a guy in his fifties, clean-shaven and with a high forehead. His grey hair was a bit longer than it should've been and therefore unkempt, despite his obvious attempts to comb it back that morning. He was dressed in a mix of casual and business attire, with a buttoned shirt and sweater over blue jeans. When he greeted me, his accent was vaguely upper-class English—but one that had been diluted, perhaps after years of living abroad. The overall impression was of a professor of history who had gone into Manhattan to visit some bookshops.

It turned out, that wasn't far off. Over coffee, Bernard said that he'd studied history at Oxford University in England. His father had worked at MI6, the UK's Secret Intelligence Service, and as a boy he'd lived an itinerant lifestyle and was sent to boarding school in Britain. As he later relayed on his blog, "Wherever we lived, I always went to the Swiss Alps for 4 weeks every winter as my father was a fanatic skier." In his early career, he said, he'd been typecast as "the shy academic [who] had become a salesman." He later worked in a variety of IT sales roles and continued to travel extensively, including a job during the 1990s where he'd been "asked to run the Asian operations"[59] of some kind of banking software company.

I was never fully clear on what type of business software Bernard had spent his career to this date in, but it soon became apparent that it was quite different from the consumer web industry that RWW covered. Also, though he'd been feeding me useful information about the way CMP and ZDE did business, I discovered that morning that he didn't actually have experience in the IT media industry. Despite all this, he was a self-described salesman, and that was undeniably helpful to me at this point. He seemed to have the gift of finding the right buttons to push when negotiating business deals, something that I was a complete n00b at. So we hit it off, and at the café he gave me more useful tips about how to deal with ZDE and Insight Partners.

One thing we discussed that morning was how to approach RWW's sales targets. I needed to have control over sales for at least the next two years because of the earn-out. Bernard said I should have a point of view on this going into today's meetings. In his view, the options were twofold: go all-in with FM Publishing (which currently sold roughly half of RWW's advertising) or hire a RWW "sales guy" and use the ZDE sales team as a lead generator. I pointed out that I currently sold the other half of RWW's ads myself, to the sponsors. Since FM had already proven it couldn't manage my sponsors, maybe I'd need to pursue both options.

In any case, I needed to get more clarity on what support ZDE would offer regarding sales. Because RWW was currently a New Zealand business, there were international tax implications to hiring people. That was a big part of why I wanted to sell RWW—to clean up its legal structure and make it a purely US business, or a part of one. But I wasn't yet clear on how ZDE planned to incorporate RWW into its current structure, which was complicated by the fact it was owned by a private equity firm.

After coffee with Bernard, I went back to my hotel room to mull over my tactics going into the first in-person ZDE meeting. I knew hardly anything about how the IT media business worked here on the East Coast, and I was also nervous about meeting the big-city financial analysts from Insight. I wished Bernard could attend the first meeting with me, as I could use a wingman who had business nous. But I knew I was on my own from here on out.

The ZDE office was located at 28 East Twenty-Eighth Street, in the Midtown South area of Manhattan. I'd quickly learned that the best way to get to an address in New York City was to note the connecting streets, and I was amused to see that one of them was Lexington Avenue. I knew this name from "I'm Waiting for the Man," a Velvet Underground song about buying heroin at the intersection of Lexington and 125—way uptown. ZDE was a block from Lexington, but downtown. And judging by all the grey and brown high-rise buildings, there wasn't much rock 'n' roll romanticism at this location.

I entered the nondescript fifteen-story building that ZDE occupied and asked for Mike Azzara at reception. He came down to greet me, and we rode the elevator to ZDE's office, which was on one of the middle floors. If I was expecting a modern office like Yahoo in Silicon Valley (or, for that matter, ZDNet in San Francisco), I was disappointed. ZDE's office looked like it was from the 1980s, with its beige walls and tatty brown carpet.

As we walked into a conference room, a tall young guy—smiling from ear to ear—reached out to shake my hand. It was Kobi Levy, the Insight Partners associate who had started the deal process. He looked to be in his late twenties or early thirties and was stylishly dressed in a suit. He was a handsome, clean-shaven guy with short-cropped dark hair, and he looked eager to get down to business. The other person in the room was Steve Weitzner, ZDE's chairman and CEO. He was an amiable-looking man in his mid-to-late fifties, I guessed. He had a full head of grey hair and a matching grey beard, and wore a light brown button-down shirt and camel suit.

A lunch was brought into the room as we chitchatted about my long plane journey and my first impressions of the Big Apple. Soon enough we took seats at the conference table and talked through how RWW would be integrated into ZDE, including—crucially—how the blog would maintain its autonomy. I was told that we would become a wholly owned subsidiary, but ZDE would take some of the business burden off my shoulders—accounting, sales, HR, and so on.

We made some tentative plans around the working relationship, establishing that I would report to Mike, but I would continue to run the day-to-day business of RWW. We didn't make any specific plans around accounting or sales, but the general agreement was that ZDE would provide resources for this, which would be internally charged to RWW's expenses. I would manage the RWW budget, which Steve and Mike assured me would give me control over the earn-out targets. I didn't fully understand how that would work, since I had never run a wholly owned subsidiary inside of a larger company. But in the interest of moving the discussions forward, I accepted that ZDE would put in the appropriate structure.

After the formal discussions, Steve and Mike took me out to dinner. I was pleased to have the opportunity to get to know Steve more. He seemed genuine about admiring what RWW had achieved so far in its young life, and he clearly wanted some of our blog mojo to be injected into ZDE. Over dinner he told me that he saw RWW as one of the best examples of where B2B journalism must rapidly evolve to, adding that traditional B2B media companies—like ZDE—needed to adapt quickly.

Also, both he and Mike admired my recent redesign of RWW. The new design captured the blogger spirit, Steve told me, but placed it in a context that was more expansive than a typical blog—it was more like a media company approach.

I was thrilled to hear all this, and I felt like Steve understood both what RWW was at present and what it could become with a bit more structure in place. I didn't quite warm to Mike in the same way, despite this being our second dinner together. Perhaps it would take more time to get us on the same wavelength. But, ultimately, Steve was the guy in charge, and so having his support was vitally important to me.

The only jarring note of the day came right at the end, when we were finishing up dinner. Tuesday's due diligence would be focused on RWW's finances. I think Steve wanted to give me a friendly warning that discussing financial statements with a private equity firm would not be straightforward. He noted that the revenue I'd entered into a spreadsheet for February and March was slightly below what I'd previously projected, which could result in Insight pushing for a decrease in the final sale price. Insight, he explained, would want to close with the exact same EBITDA multiple as in the original projections.

EBITDA was an accounting acronym I'd quickly come up to speed with once I'd begun talking to both CMP and ZDE; it meant "earnings before interest, taxes, depreciation, and amortization." That is, earnings after expenses but before tax and other accounting adjustments. The "multiple" was just that, the EBITDA figure times a specified number—in our case, twelve. So if EBITDA for the 2008 tax year, which ended March 31, was slightly less than what I'd projected, then multiplying that revised figure by twelve would result in a reduced sale price.

Perhaps noticing my shocked expression, Steve quickly followed up with a few suggestions to adjust the spreadsheet so that it more closely matched the original projections—for example, removing the redesign costs, which should be capitalized. This was the kind of practical accounting knowledge that I lacked, since I didn't have a background in business. I also didn't have a COO or other business partner to lean on (although this wasn't Bernard's area of expertise, either). So I felt a bit vulnerable now, knowing that the bean counters at Insight Partners were looking for financial gotchas to spring on me. However, I could also see that Steve really wanted to get this deal done and was trying to help me.

After the dinner I went back to my hotel to look again at the spreadsheets. I made the adjustments Steve had recommended and sent it off to ZDE and Insight. I emailed Bernard, too, and he wrote back with his moral support. We arranged to meet again at nine the next morning for a pep talk before I faced off with the financial analysts from Insight.

Tuesday's financial discussions were with Kobi Levy and Jake Stein. Jake was in his mid-twenties; it looked like he'd just come out of business school (which I soon found out that he had). Despite his fresh-faced youth, he had a confident look in his eye that unsettled me. Maybe it was my imagination after Steve's warning last night, but I felt that Jake looked at me as if he were the keeper of arcane accounting knowledge that he knew I didn't have.

Like Kobi, Jake wore a stylish suit and was clean-shaven, with an efficient haircut. As usual, I had tufts of hair that refused to be tamed by whatever styling cream I'd used that morning, and I was wearing slacks and a dress shirt, along with a warm but not very trendy jacket. I'd become aware during the last couple of days that my attire was not as suitable in Manhattan as it was in Silicon Valley—men who worked in offices seemed to wear suits, which was (in my experience, at least) rare in the valley.

My discomfort worsened as we got down to brass tacks with the spreadsheets and financial projections. I did, however, let my feelings be known regarding any potential change to the sale price. I told them straight up that it could be a deal breaker if they tried to cut the price specified in the LOI. Kobi said it was one of his bosses who wanted to stick to the exact EBITDA multiple. He wouldn't promise not to change the price, as it wasn't up to him. But he said that he could see I was unhappy about it and would relay my position to his boss.

At this point, it did occur to me that I'd likely never meet these higher-ups at Insight Partners. Just as unknown head-office bureaucrats had torpedoed any chance of a decent offer from CMP, these faceless private equity honchos could do the same for ZDE. Insight had sent a couple of relatively junior people to do the due diligence with me. Which was fine, I suppose, but I would've preferred to know who was really making the decisions—especially if they wanted to nickel and dime me on the sale price.

We went through my spreadsheets in some detail, but Jake had a list of things he wanted me to send once I was back in New Zealand. These included a copy of the accounting software I used, the annual accounts for 2006 and 2007 from my accountant, and the Google Docs spreadsheet I used for sponsors. I promised to send those through as soon as possible.

I didn't see Steve at all that day, but he sent me an email later expressing his support. He wanted to let me know that it was his intent to go forward with the deal as originally offered. This might require "some debate with Insight over the next day," he said, but he didn't want me to worry that a small miss on my February and March projections would impact the purchase price. Everything was headed in the right direction with my business, he assured me.

The agenda for the week included a dinner on Tuesday evening with Mike and Stephen Wellman, the ZDE journalist I'd met in San Francisco. At some point during the day, Mike told me that he wouldn't be able to make it. However, he said Stephen would take me out as planned.

I'd never been to a jazz club before, let alone one in the heart of New York City. So I was thrilled when Stephen and I entered the Jazz Standard, a club on Twenty-Seventh Street. It was one of his favorites, he said as we walked down some stairs to the basement venue. Our table was close to the stage, and we had a beer while we waited for the evening's entertainment to begin.

Stephen was a big guy about my age, with a kind, fleshy face and receding hairline. (I would find out later that he was struggling with his weight; in later years I would see pictures of him much slimmed down.) He was a quiet character, and I saw hints of depression in his facial expressions. His official title at ZDNet was senior vice president of community & content, which seemed to imply that he was the most attuned in ZDE to blogging culture. He was certainly knowledgeable about blogs and social software, and we chatted about this for a bit. But I was most interested to know about the band we'd be seeing tonight.

I must've seemed like a total tourist to him, wide-eyed and excited about being in this Manhattan jazz club. But he indulged my curiosity. We'd be watching a band called John Ellis and Double-Wide, Stephen told me, and tonight happened to be the launch of their new album, *Dance Like There's No Tomorrow*. I asked if he got to see live jazz bands regularly, and he nodded with a smile. I was suitably jealous and chuckled that it must be like living in a Woody Allen movie.

Upstairs was a barbecue restaurant called Blue Smoke, owned by the same people who ran the Jazz Standard. I ordered a steak dinner, and as it was brought to our table, Ellis and his band started playing songs from their new album. It was a five-piece (three white guys, including Ellis, and two Black guys). I had gone through a jazz phase when I was younger, reading up on it and borrowing CDs from Wellington Library, so I knew the history of jazz and its conventions. I wasn't sophisticated enough to judge how good Ellis was as a saxophonist, but I enjoyed the laid-back and at times meandering tunes. As expected, there was a lot of saxophone noodling from the leader, and the band members traded off on their respective solos.

The lighting in the club was perfect: suitably dim, with the band highlighted on a backdrop of what looked to be red-cushioned walls. The ambience of the place—the mood lighting, live jazz playing a foot or so from me, a light smattering of dinner conversation and clinking of wine glasses around us—gave me a buzz that I hadn't expected from this evening. So this was life in the big city, huh.

At the end of the set, I bought a CD of the new album as a memento. As Stephen and I walked back out into the hubbub of a New York City night, I thanked him profusely for a wonderful experience. I'd had a taste of the real Big Apple, or at least the version of it I'd consumed in movies and on scratchy old CDs from my local library. I knew this was just a break from my current reality. But for a couple of hours at least, I'd been able to relax and not think about spreadsheets and EBITDA multiples.

Wednesday morning at ZDE was less stressful, with no talk of RWW finances. In fact, it was more about getting my opinions on various ZDE initiatives—their multimedia efforts, what it meant to be a blogger in 2008 (the words *passion* and *authenticity* were listed on the agenda as a guidepost to that discussion), and how to grow ZDE's developer community, DevShed.

By lunchtime the official due diligence appeared to be over. I was on my own for the rest of the day, and there would be no need for me to come into the office again tomorrow. I'd already cut short my trip by a day and booked a Friday-morning flight home, after realizing that the meetings with ZDE and Insight wouldn't take the whole week.

I didn't know what to do with myself for the remainder of my time in New York City. Kobi wanted to do lunch with me before I left, and I was also planning a dinner with Bernard and Alex. But both appointments would have to wait till Thursday, due to everyone's busy calendars. The only thing I wanted to do before I left was see the Empire State Building. I figured I would do that between lunch with Kobi and dinner with my colleagues.

It wasn't as if I lacked things to do in New York. I could've gone to MOMA or the art galleries in Chelsea that Wednesday afternoon, but it had been an intense week and I was feeling worn out. I felt like I couldn't relax and enjoy the city—the jazz dinner seemed to have been an exception. So I ended up doing some tourist shopping (T-shirts, fridge magnets, and the like) and then going back to my hotel room to catch up on RWW business.

I decided to finally write the detailed email I had promised to Marshall about our editorial operations. "Firstly I have to apologize for not spending more time talking to you in recent weeks," I began. "I have been very busy on the biz side of things." That was certainly true but obviously avoided the whole truth! I went on to note that I didn't think our content was "as good as it could be right now," adding that one reason was that I hadn't been as involved in editorial as I needed to be. I was the site's editor, so any content issues were ultimately on me.

Marshall was our "senior blogger," I said, and we'd originally agreed for him to do two to three posts per day during his twenty paid hours per week with RWW. He was in fact averaging about two a day, or ten to eleven per week. Some were detailed and had a lot of thought put into them, so I wasn't *too* concerned about quantity. However, I did want to see at least one post per day from him in the morning, West Coast time, on a consistent basis—which had been a bugbear of mine for all the US writers.

I then commented on the blogging output of our small team of daily writers. Two were doing well, but I wasn't entirely happy with the third's writing. I wanted Marshall's feedback on that, and I added a few suggestions for helping the writer with story selection. However, I reserved the harshest comments for my own output: "I'll be honest, my posts have sucked recently! Being so much focused on biz has affected my ability to keep up with the latest web apps and blog about them. So I hope to solve this by removing some admin burden from myself, incl sales." I finished by promising (again) to forward the premium-content discussion, and asked if he'd like to increase his hours at RWW.

I skirted the real issue—that I had spent the last four months trying to sell the business. I had, in fact, spent more time talking to Bernard about M&A than with Marshall talking about content. All going well, the ZDE deal would be finalized by early June, but even then I would have to spend a lot more time integrating our business into ZDE. So I was worried about how this would impact editorial going forward.

I was also feeling guilty about not bringing Marshall into the ZDE discussions. However, he claimed he made more money consulting than he did with RWW, so it was the right business decision not to involve him. He could easily find another blogging home, and I couldn't risk that. As I'd implied in my email to him, his content was currently the best of the crop (I'd somehow squeezed out two posts while in New York, but they were both poor by my own high standards). I resolved to do my best to keep Marshall happy and involved on the editorial side, and then bring him up to speed as soon as the ZDE deal was finalized.

Thursday was my last full day in New York City. Over email that morning, Kobi had asked if I had a preference for lunch. I'd replied, "anything 'New York-ish' is fine with me."

"This is kind of touristy," Kobi wrote back in response, "but how about the famous Carnegie Deli?"

Touristy was where I was at—especially with a visit to the Empire State Building that afternoon—so I readily agreed. Kobi mentioned a few business details to be tidied up as well, so we would hold our final meeting over lunch.

Carnegie Deli was at the intersection of Seventh Avenue and Fifty-Fifth Street, about a thirty-minute walk from my hotel on Twenty-Eighth Street. For some odd reason, I decided to take a taxi. Perhaps I just wanted to add to my touristy experience that day and go crosstown in a Manhattan Yellow Taxi, as if I were a character in *Sex in the City*. Needless to say, it was rush hour when I jumped into a taxi fifteen minutes before our 1:00 p.m. meeting. The taxi crawled its way uptown and I soon realized I'd made a mistake in not walking—especially since it was a sunny spring day.

I arrived about fifteen minutes late; the taxi had taken the exact same amount of time as if I'd walked it. Kobi was sitting in a booth when I stumbled in, and he looked confused as I explained about the taxi. "Why didn't you walk?" he asked, incredulous. I had never felt so much like a tourist.

The deli was famous for sandwiches with at least one pound of meat, so I ordered a pastrami and corned beef sandwich. Sure enough, an open-faced sandwich piled with a massive amount of thinly sliced meat soon arrived. The restaurant's motto was "If you can finish your meal, we've done something wrong." I determined to give it a good go, but there was no question I would be walking it off afterward. No more taxis for me that day!

Kobi was very friendly and enjoyed seeing me tackle the ridiculous sandwich, but there wasn't much more to say about the business deal. I just had to send them more financial documents when I got back home and hope they wouldn't try any more tricks to reduce the sale price. In between mouthfuls of meat washed down with Diet Coke, I told Kobi that I had enjoyed meeting Steve and his ZDE team, and I felt that Steve understood what RWW needed in order to take the next step as a tech-media business. (Steve himself had slipped into the background again that week while Insight Partners finished due diligence.) We seemed to be aligned on the plan to fold RWW into ZDE's operations, although I reiterated that I would be trusting them to set up a suitable structure for sales and admin. Kobi assured me that ZDE would do the right thing on the operations side—they all wanted me focused on editorial and on expanding the RWW brand.

I nodded, gulped down another forkful of pastrami, and told Kobi that I was comfortable moving forward with the deal. Insight and ZDE were keen to get it done too, he said, grinning as I started to show signs of meat fatigue—not even halfway through the sandwich. It was just a matter of working through the final few weeks of paperwork, he added, handing me a napkin for the soon-to-arrive meat sweats.

After lunch, I walked back downtown to the Empire State Building—or maybe I should say I waddled. The view from the top quickly cleared my head, though. It was a fine, cloudy day and I could feel the hum of the city as I gazed out on the mass of high-rise buildings. It sounded like millions of people were chattering all at once, continuously inter-rupted by honking cars. Even though I couldn't see anyone eighty-six floors below, the density of people on the ground and inside the build-ings pulsed through me. I could feel the vibrations of America in my bones, like Walt Whitman's "body electric" come to life.

There was a cliché in the tech industry at the time that "Web 2.0 is made of people." It went through my brain at that moment that New York City is really about the people, too. *This is what a real human city looks and feels like*, I marveled. To think I would soon become a part of this energetic, throbbing scene—a hopeful blogger from the other side of the world, married off to an eligible American suitor from Manhattan.

In a way, it legitimized what I was doing with my life and fulfilled a destiny I'd only peeked at when I was younger. One of my favorite courses at university had been American Literature, which I'd taken as a part of my English literature degree. I'd loved *The Great Gatsby*, *Moby-Dick*, and *Catch-22*. I identified as a seeker of the American Dream—although more like Nick Carraway, in my quiet determination, than Jay Gatsby with his overt striving. I was also Captain Ahab, pursuing something deep inside of me that I didn't fully understand yet—would I ever? But at least, I told myself, I recognized the absurdity of it all, like Yossarian.

Fanciful yearnings aside, I had a real life to go back to tomorrow—and that included a still independent blogging business. When I got back to New Zealand, I would need to focus back on RWW's editorial operations; my team needed me to guide them. I also wanted to get back to writing at least one post per day, the blogging rhythm that had gotten me this far. I needed to take care of business—bring home the bacon, as Andy Warhol used to say (according to Lou Reed). I had sponsors to email, FM Publishing revenue to monitor, stats to check, budgets to review, expenses to keep a tight rein on.

Suddenly I felt exhausted, so I made my way back to the elevators. I just wanted this business deal to be consummated. But to get that done—to drive it over the line—I would have to rejoin the masses on the streets below.

CHAPTER 11

BACK TO BUSINESS

■ ■ ■ ■ ■

THE DAY I LEFT NEW YORK, I saw on Techmeme that Condé Nast had acquired the technology blog Ars Technica for an estimated $25 million. Condé Nast also owned Wired.com and Reddit, so Ars would be joining an enviable roster. I did some back-of-the-envelope calculations and figured that it must've had revenue of around $2 million per year to be worth that much; that is, if it had sold for the same EBITDA multiple that I was negotiating for. RWW was on track for around $335,000 in revenue, but we were also younger and less established as a business.

When I got back to New Zealand, I was still thinking about the Ars deal and what it meant for my proposed deal with ZDE. I wasn't too worried about the difference in sale price—Ars was a ten-year-old website that claimed to have more than five million readers and thirty million page views per month. Much of that traffic would've been generated by its forums, which were very popular with IT people. Nevertheless, it was an established media business and, at the time, significantly bigger than RWW.

What really caught my eye was cofounder Ken Fisher's comment that they'd chosen to sell because they realized "an acquisition would be the quickest way to accelerate the growth of Ars." He went on to say that "we looked positively on what Condé Nast has done with WIRED.com and reddit.com (both acquired in 2006): left their leadership alone to grow their sites, while helping them with tools and resources along the way."[60]

As I noted to Bernard over email, I had the same reason for selling as Ars did: taking RWW to the next level and scaling its operations. However, it bugged me that I wasn't as sure about ZDE's ongoing support as Fisher seemed to be about Condé Nast's. "It occurred to me that we really haven't gotten much assurance from ZDE that they'll be putting resources into RWW to 'accelerate the growth' of RWW," I wrote to Bernard. "Should I push more for that? As of now the only assurances I have is that ZDE will attempt to take some of the admin burden off my shoulders (accounting, etc.), but other than that we're on our own."

The first week I was back home, Kobi set up a phone meeting with Larry Handen, the managing partner at Insight who oversaw the ZDE business. "Larry and the rest of the team here want to move aggressively to close this deal asap, so Larry wanted to spearhead the conversation himself," Kobi said. I was asked to have my lawyer on the call too.

The call focused on the legal structure of the acquisition, which was complicated a little by the fact that RWW was an NZ company. After the meeting, Insight sent me a document with a list of due-diligence requests, many of which duplicated what we had covered in New York. I was beginning to feel uneasy about all the paperwork and associated costs—my legal bills were stacking up. I was also desperate to get back to focusing on RWW business and editorial. But what did I know—perhaps this was just how M&As worked?

Soon after, Larry wrote to suggest that we extend the "period of exclusivity" around the deal from June 6 to June 15. Since I had no intention of opening negotiations to other companies at this point, in practice this just meant extending the target closing date. While the delay was annoying, again I didn't feel like I knew enough about the process to object.

Insight's lawyers and accountants duly sent my lawyer and accountant requests for information over the next few weeks—some of which I wasn't even cc'd on. But by June 20, there was still no end in sight for the due diligence. I especially wanted to see the final sale agreement document. I asked for an update, and Larry replied, "We are quite close."

Finally, a few days later, I received a draft of the share sale agreement. However, there was an issue with the formal definition of *trading profit*, on which the earn-out half of the deal depended. To my mind, the definition was too complicated and included potential gotchas. Rather than have my lawyer swap PDFs with their lawyer about this crucial definition, I emailed Jake Stein, the twentysomething financial analyst at Insight I had met in New York. I hoped he would clarify matters by using the 2007 spreadsheet I'd supplied months ago as an example. "Frankly, the legalese here has me totally confused," I wrote. "So that I can understand this definition better, Jake would you mind sending me an example of what 2007 fiscal year looks like using the above definition?"

In response, Jake promised to "create a new, simpler definition of Trading Profit."

Another week of emails and phone calls passed, putting us a couple of days into July, so I sent an exasperated email—this time cc'ing Steve Weitzner from ZDE. "I have become a bit concerned in recent days that we are getting bogged down in legal minutiae," I wrote. "We are now well past the date envisaged in the LOI (9 June) and these delays with the legal drafting are costing me a lot of time and money." I added that the key remaining issue for me was the trading profit definition, "which I am not yet satisfied we have clarity on."

Steve replied and promised to step in, but that was the last I heard from him for over a week. I had the uncomfortable feeling that Insight and ZDE were stalling—but why?

By this point Larry was only sending terse replies to my emails; most of the back-and-forth was happening with Jake. I had no issue dealing with Jake, but he was a relatively junior employee at Insight. It concerned me that I had little direct contact with the actual decision makers at Insight, or anyone senior at ZDE for that matter.

A bunch more emails full of legalese and accounting data flew back and forth between myself and Insight (and our respective lawyers), edging us toward a definition of trading profit that I could live with. But by July 11, I was fed up with the whole process. There was too much fine print on what did or did not constitute revenue and expenses, and I continued to get requests for information that I had thought we'd covered during my trip to New York City.

I wrote to Bernard that it felt like I would only achieve the earn-out "if I'm lucky and somehow squeeze my accounts into all kinds of restrictions." It certainly *didn't* feel like the kind of deal Ars Technica had agreed to with Condé Nast.

My gut feeling was that this wasn't right. Why should I sell something I'd created and worked so hard to build up if the company acquiring it wasn't willing to help it grow further? Perhaps, I reflected, RWW was still too young to sell—after all, Ars had taken a full decade to get to this point. I told Bernard that I'd "think more over the weekend about whether I'm comfortable proceeding."

Over the next couple of days, there was an attempt on both sides to set up yet another phone call for the following week. But I knew that it would only kick the can further down the road, with the lawyers scuttling after to kick it some more. Enough was enough.

First thing on Monday, July 14, I sent an email to Insight and ZDE to advise that I was withdrawing from the negotiations. "It is now 5 weeks past the original deadline for closing in the LOI, and I have become increasingly frustrated over the delay and how complicated the deal structure has become," I wrote. "This in turn has made me concerned about whether this will be an environment where RWW can work effectively to build real value." I also no longer believed I would hit the earn-out targets. "It has become apparent that there will be too many restrictions on my ability to grow the business, and no real support," I told them.

I noted that I had spent approximately $50,000 of my own money to get this deal done. These included legal and accounting fees, the costs of my trip to New York, and Bernard's ongoing fees. I added that this didn't include "the opportunity cost of trying to close this deal, when I could have been focusing on expanding the business."

There was some back-and-forth by email and phone after that, with Steve and Kobi (the only Insight representative to respond) trying to get me to reconsider. It emerged that Insight and ZDE were pursuing another deal at the same time—although it wasn't specified with whom. So they had been stalling! I wondered out loud to Bernard and Alex whether it was TechCrunch. Bernard suggested FM Publishing. This was all speculation, and it didn't matter anymore.

I was ready to move on, but Kobi really wanted me to come back to the table. On Alex and Bernard's advice, I decided to play a little hardball—I figured, what the hell? I upped the sale price by 50 percent, citing the Ars Technica deal and the even more recent $30 million sale of PaidContent.org as evidence that blog businesses had increased in value since our initial discussions. The *Guardian* had announced its acquisition of PaidContent that very weekend, for what was likely a high EBITDA multiple, so I'd taken this as yet more evidence that ZDE was getting a bargain with RWW.

My heart wasn't in the negotiations anymore, and I knew it wasn't going to happen. I just wanted to get back to writing blog posts for RWW and reconnecting with my editorial team. I'd wasted almost half a year trying to sell my business, with zero result. It was high time to get back to doing what I loved. If RWW was going to scale up, it would be as an indie media business.

One of the first things I did after pulling out of the ZDE deal was to tell Marshall what had happened. I had penciled in a closing bonus and incentives over two years for him and the other writers, so he wouldn't have been left out financially had the ZDE deal closed. But I apologized for not telling him about the potential sale until now. I'd been afraid he would walk, I said, given he was technically a part-time contractor during the negotiations. But now I wanted to focus on building up the business with Marshall on board full-time—if he agreed.

He seemed to accept the situation. I'd felt uncomfortable telling him, and he was obviously taken aback. But there were no hard feelings, which was a relief. With my confession out of the way, Marshall told me about his plan for developing content systems that would improve

RWW as a tech-news destination. His main idea was to use RSS feed aggregation to discover news stories before our competitors, which sounded intriguing to me.

We were still in the Technorati Top 10 list at this stage—hovering between spots 9 and 10. We were also ranked number 4 on the Techmeme Leaderboard. Our page views were running at around 1.5 million per month, and we had more than 220,000 RSS and email subscribers. So, despite my months of distraction, we were still doing well. But I was aware that our momentum was in danger of stalling if I didn't push new content initiatives and improve our editorial systems.

I'd known for many months that I needed help to grow the business—after all, that was the main reason I'd wanted to sell to a larger media company. So now, after all the delays and eventual collapse of the acquisition deal, I felt I had to move quickly and bring on at least two executive-level people. I'd mapped out two different roles to be filled: VP of content development and VP of business development. The former was for Marshall, and the latter was tailored for Bernard (who was unsure whether he wanted it). Whoever filled the biz dev role, I envisioned the three of us forming a leadership team for RWW. I'd be a hybrid CEO and editor; overseeing the business and content strategies but focusing my daily efforts on leading the editorial team.

By the end of July, with Bernard's help, I came to an agreement with Marshall for the VP of content dev role. I announced it on the site on July 31, noting that he "will be responsible for driving a lot of our upcoming content developments," including "premium content, publishing system enhancements, and more magic things."

Also in July, I hired my mum Judy as a part-time accounts manager for the company. When I was a boy, she had worked part-time for an accountant—in addition to being the full-time caregiver for four children—so she knew how to deal with company accounts. I certainly needed help with the growing paperwork of RWW, and I was grateful to be able to hand over the invoices—both from writers and to sponsors.

Next, I wanted to firm up the business development role. First and foremost, I wanted someone to take over sponsorships and advertising.

However, this wasn't something that seemed to interest Bernard. I was still paying him a generous hourly rate for twenty hours of business advisory services per month, plus we'd made an agreement for him to build an enterprise channel for RWW. For the latter he was getting a good monthly retainer, a revenue share of the channel's main sponsor, and a small equity stake in the company. So he was doing rather well out of RWW. He wasn't working full-time for us, yet he had a monthly income equivalent to a senior employee's full-time salary. Also, the revenue-share arrangement wasn't ideal for RWW going forward—although it had been capped at twelve months.

Hiring hesitation aside, Bernard thought we could be doing better with FM Publishing. One of the many reasons I'd pulled out of the ZDE deal was that I wasn't confident I could hit the earn-out targets—mostly due to the restrictions Insight Partners proposed, but also due to the variability of revenue from FM Publishing. Some months it was great, and other months it dipped markedly. Bernard suggested I introduce him to FM as "our new Biz Dev guy" and he would talk to them. This I duly did.

Meanwhile, I turned my attention back to editorial matters.

Even though over half of 2008 had now disappeared in a blur of unconsummated business dealings, I had still managed to expand our writing team. I'd hired Sarah Perez as a freelancer in early January, after subscribing to her personal blog the previous year. She had a full-time IT job in Tampa, Florida, and did blogging for Microsoft on the side. She told me she'd be able to quit her IT job and go full-time on blogging if I could offer her twelve posts per week on RWW. I'd readily agreed, and Sarah officially joined RWW and quit her day job. Marshall and I both loved her posts, and by the middle of 2008 she was an established part of our daily writing team.

Another new writer started in May: a twenty-year-old Black woman from Atlanta named Corvida Raven. She ran her own blog, SheGeeks, and described herself as "an avid follower of ReadWriteWeb." After a successful trial post, I hired her as a regular blogger at the same per-post rate as Sarah. Corvida made an immediate impact—one of her first paid posts made it to the top of Techmeme while I was in New York.

During the due-diligence hubbub in June I hired another promising writer. Frederic Lardinois was a thirty-two-year-old graduate student from Portland who had a tech blog called The Last Podcast ("opinionated web 2.0 news and commentary"). He'd responded to a short blog post I'd put up on June 15, 2008, advertising for a new blogger to "cover breaking web tech news and product reviews" at RWW. I wrote, "Ideally we're after a blogger based in Silicon Valley, who can attend the local events on our behalf and meet with startups," but I was open to "non-Valley bloggers too." (How could I, of all people, discriminate on geography?)

One of the first news stories Frederic covered for us was the launch of the Apple App Store on July 10, 2008, the same day that the second-generation iPhone 3G launched. There were 552 apps in the store at launch, Frederic noted, of which about a quarter were free. That same day, I posted a bunch of screenshots of the iPhone 3G. Because New Zealand was a day ahead in time zones, I'd received my iPhone 3G before many US tech bloggers had gotten their hands on it—for once, I had an advantage over my American blogger friends.

None of us realized it at the time, but that day marked the beginning of a big societal shift from the desktop web to smartphone apps. There were hints that online content was morphing into something new as well. In January, Netflix had announced that its rental-disc subscribers were now entitled to unlimited streaming at no additional cost. A couple of months later, Hulu launched publicly. So video streaming was starting to become a part of the culture, too.

Despite the launch of the App Store, along with the Android market in September, it wasn't immediately clear that apps would be the right format for the likes of Netflix and Hulu. A radically new version of the web's markup language had been released in January: HTML5. It was thought that HTML5 would, among other things, encourage multimedia services in browsers. That seemed viable, because over 2008 we saw long-overdue innovation on the browser engine front—Firefox 3 was released in June, and in September Google launched a groundbreaking new browser called Chrome.

Ultimately, of course, smartphone apps won out. But in mid-2008 it was an open question how streaming—and other multimedia—would evolve on the internet.

Trends of this type were the focus of my small but growing team in 2008. Despite not knowing how things would settle, it was clear that Web 2.0 was expanding beyond the desktop and beyond text-based applications. So it felt natural that RWW would expand too.

Amid the excitement of hiring new writers, I lost one of my regulars that year. Josh Catone had decided to leave RWW and was finishing up the same week that I hired Frederic. Josh had been my first blogger hire at RWW, back in March 2007. However, I'd had issues with some of his articles for a while now and had sent him a recent final-warning type email about it. Despite his problems with consistency, Josh had written several of our most popular articles during his time at RWW. I also liked Josh a lot as a person. So when I broke the news to the team via Basecamp, in a message entitled "Welcome Frederic, a Fond Farewell to Josh," I emphasized that it was sad to see him go. "Once a RWW writer, always," I noted.

After the acquisition debacle, I was determined to put more structure around the RWW business. If I couldn't get an established US media company to provide support for RWW's growth, I thought, then I'd have to make RWW itself into an established US media company.

The usual startup route for creating a US business was the Delaware C corp. In order to do this, I would need a US lawyer. The same week I ditched Insight and ZDE, Alex had introduced me to his corporate lawyer, Camille Linson, who lived just outside of New York. I told Camille that I wanted to set up a US business with "a solid equity structure" for key employees. Also I asked for her help in drafting the contract for Marshall, who would be my first full-time hire.

Unfortunately, over the next several months I discovered the many accounting and legal complications for a New Zealander running a US business. The process turned into a palaver almost as frustrating as the acquisition negotiations.

Camille was very helpful in sorting through these issues, though. In particular, she helped me make sense of a report I commissioned from the NZ branch of Pricewaterhouse Coopers. The report, which arrived in September, cost me a decent chunk of change. But I was disappointed in it because it didn't make a decision to incorporate in America any easier—in fact it made it harder and more complex.

Given all the accounting grey areas, and the lack of a clear direction from PWC, I had little choice but to continue as an NZ business. I was annoyed that I couldn't do as seemingly every other global entrepreneur had done before me and create a Delaware C corp. The only silver lining was that I had made an excellent business contact in Camille.

In the end, my NZ lawyer had to draft Marshall's contract. Sticking with being an NZ company also allowed me to bring Bernard on board as my new COO. In my announcement of that on December 1, I wrote that "Bernard will assume responsibility for most of the non-editorial functions of our business—sales, business development and other operational matters."

It had taken nearly a year of extensive (and expensive) discussions with various lawyers and accountants to establish a decent structure for my business—albeit one that wasn't ideal, since it was still an NZ company. But at least I now had my leadership group: me, Bernard, and Marshall. This gave RWW a certain level of validation as a media business. But it was nothing compared to the validation I felt when, on September 23, the *New York Times* announced that it was expanding its technology section and promised "a steady stream of content from three of the most respected tech blogs on the Web: VentureBeat, GigaOm and ReadWriteWeb."

We'd been fishing for a mainstream-media syndication partner ever since the ZDE deal went south. As usual, it was partly inspired by what our tech-blog competition was doing. TechCrunch had inked a syndication deal with the *Washington Post* in May, and GigaOm had a similar deal with *BusinessWeek*. We'd first tried the *Wall Street Journal* but got nowhere. Fortunately, Alex Iskold had a contact at the *New York Times* and reached out in July. His contact responded positively, and Alex handed the conversation to Bernard to follow up.

At first, we didn't know whether a syndication deal would generate revenue or was just a way to get more exposure for our niche publication. We soon found out that it would be the latter—the *Times* wouldn't be paying for our content. Our contact explained, "Our standard deal is hosting 50% of your feed in exchange for a clickable logo on our tech section front as well as links back to stories/posts on your site from each hosted story/post." Bernard followed up with a phone call, in which he learned how the syndication would work from a practical perspective: we would tag the *Times* on any article we thought should go to them. The 50 percent figure was approximate; it was our call which content to send, and it would be automated at their end.

I signed off on the deal in early August; and yes, the contract specified that RWW still owned the copyright for the content. We'd been told that VentureBeat and GigaOm had already inked their deals and would debut on the *New York Times* website before us. That was slightly annoying, as there didn't seem to be much of a technical reason for the delay, but we didn't want to complain too much. We'd already begun to appreciate that being featured in the digital pages of the world's most prestigious newspaper was great marketing for RWW.

When our feed was finally added to the mix in October, it was a thrill to see the RWW logo on the *New York Times* website. I excitedly messaged my family: "This is pretty cool, mostly because now when people stare at me with bemusement when I say I blog for a living, I can say 'we're on the NYT—heard of them?'"

As well as giving me something to brag about, the syndication partnership was now front and center on our media kit for sponsors. It was one thing to be in Technorati's Top 10, but what really solidified our reputation in the tech industry was being in the *New York Times*. Indeed, it was great for the reputation of blogs in general. As I noted in my launch post on September 23, 2008, it was "further vindication that blogs are increasingly being accepted as mainstream news and analysis providers."

The traffic we got from syndication ended up being negligible—in December there were around 5,500 click-throughs to our site from the *Times*. But I didn't care about that at all. The added value to our brand was much more significant. Plus, as I said to Bernard and Marshall in an email, it was "nice to be buddies with the NYT."

That validation also made my decision to withdraw from the ZDE deal much more palatable. It gave me confidence that we would make it as an indie media business.

In late October 2008, Maria and I traveled over to the United States again on my annual pilgrimage to the Web 2.0 Summit in San Francisco. Before that, however, I had a few days in Los Angeles courtesy of Microsoft.

The Microsoft Professional Developers Conference was being held at the Los Angeles Convention Center. I soon discovered that downtown LA was the opposite of downtown Manhattan in terms of excitement and glamour. It was completely charmless and devoid of interesting shops or restaurants. It didn't help that our hotel was in the so-called financial district (the San Francisco financial district was equally dull). Even the Staples Center—less than a decade old and home to the LA Lakers—was just a large concrete bowl as I walked past it on my way to the convention center every morning. It would've been different if I'd made it to a game—as it happened, the Lakers played their crosstown rivals, the LA Clippers, on the Wednesday I was there. But alas, I was otherwise engaged.

The 2008 conference was notable for hosting the announcement of Windows Azure, Microsoft's cloud computing platform. Within a decade, Azure would become arguably Microsoft's most important product—it's certainly the straw that stirs the drink at Redmond as I'm writing this book. Ray Ozzie, who in 2008 was more than two years into his role as Microsoft's chief software architect, announced Windows Azure in his opening keynote. He called it "Windows in the cloud" and positioned the new product as an operating system for cloud computing. He claimed that Microsoft had begun to build it in 2006, just a few months before Amazon released its groundbreaking EC2 platform.

Later that day, I was among a small group of bloggers and analysts on a roundtable about Azure with Ozzie and a couple of other Microsoft executives. I asked Ozzie about the relationship between Azure and

Windows, the desktop computer OS that was Microsoft's core product. He explained that both operating systems would develop alongside each other and that there would be a "bi-directional innovation transfer" between the two (whatever that meant). He claimed that Azure was not designed to replace the desktop OS any time soon, although he said later in the meeting that eventually people "will commonly think of this cloud thing as being just another computer." He was right about that.

While I was in LA, I got to meet one of my longtime blog buddies, Lucas Gonze. He'd been one of my very first interview subjects on RWW when, in October 2004, I'd published an email interview about his P2P music-sharing website startup, Webjay. In retrospect, Webjay can be seen as a bridge between the Napster era of online music and the streaming era that would soon emerge, led by Spotify—which launched that very month, October 2008, although it would take a few more years to reach the US. Like Napster, Webjay didn't license music; it just offered links to music files on external websites and a way to create shareable playlists. A couple of years later, Gonze sold it to Yahoo. Even in 2004 I could see that the line between Webjay and the ultimately illegal Napster was a fine one, and perhaps that's why Yahoo shut Webjay down in 2007.

In any case, it was great to finally meet Lucas in person, over dinner at a downtown Japanese restaurant called Honda Ya Izakaya. His movie-industry girlfriend, Karen, joined us, and she and Maria talked while Lucas and I traded web gossip. Among other things, we discussed the global financial crisis and its impact on the internet industry. There was a lot of talk in the tech blogosphere about "belt tightening" and "battening down the hatches" for a possible recession. *Wired* magazine, the bastion of internet optimism, even theorized that the crisis would burst the Web 2.0 bubble.

I was mostly interested in how the global financial crisis would impact web innovation, since economic downturns were known to be a time of opportunity for new startups. *Perhaps there will be a new web era*, I thought. Lucas didn't think the financial crash would cause a generational turnover, as had happened with the dot-com crash. In response to a blog post I'd written earlier that month, "What's Next

After Web 2.0," Lucas had floated his latest theory, "located computing."
He was referring to devices like Boxee, which at the time was a promising media player for your living room TV. Although box-top sets never
panned out as a product category, in later years we did indeed get such
devices as Amazon Echo and Sonos speakers.

I liked talking to Lucas because he always focused on technology
innovation, rather than on the business aspects of the startup economy.
Due in large part to the financial crisis, the tech blogosphere had gotten
very business-oriented—especially in blogs like TechCrunch, Venture-
Beat, and GigaOm. A sample Techmeme page from earlier in October
was dominated by business stories: Twitter's search for a business
model, Bloglines being usurped by Google Reader, Google monetizing
its start-page product, startup layoffs, a fall in VC funding. At RWW we
often had things to say on these stories—one of the links on Techmeme
that day was to Corvida's post "Revenue Model for Twitter Coming
Soon"—but it was never our forte. Partly this was because none of our
reporters were in Silicon Valley, so we weren't necessarily getting those
business tales firsthand. But it was also because I just wasn't that interested in business stories.

Chatting with Lucas reminded me of why I'd gotten into blogging
in the first place—to network with forward-thinking technologists and
discuss what was next in web technology. I was determined to keep that
the modus operandi of RWW as the web industry continued to expand,
financial headwinds or no, into the cloud and beyond.

My wife and I were in San Francisco on the night Barack Obama was
elected president of the United States. After watching Obama's victory
speech on TV, we decided to walk down to Union Square to see how the
locals were taking the news. Well, it was a carnival atmosphere: throngs
of people smiling and cheering in the streets, whoops and honking
horns piercing the air, the cable cars inching their way through the
crowds on Post Street, amid shouts of "Yes, we can!" (Obama's slogan).

By the time we got back to our hotel around 11:00 p.m., I was so
buzzed that I had to write a blog post. "Whatever your political per-
suasion, I hope you agree that this is a significant turning point for the

US—and the world," I wrote, rather naively. This was years before the great divide of American politics that eventually resulted in the election of Donald Trump in 2016. But I got a taste of that future in the comments section of my blog post and in my Gmail inbox. "If I want political comment, I know of many places to get that," wrote one grumpy emailer. He'd happened to arrive at RWW via the *New York Times* but declared that he'd never visit again after seeing the Obama post.

Sentiment was very different in my tech bubble. Most of the attendees at the Web 2.0 Summit seemed just as happy as I was at the election result. However, there was also a lot of trepidation about the economy. The theme of the conference was "Web Meets World," but if you read most mainstream tech media, you'd think *world* was a synonym for *global financial crisis*. The *Wall Street Journal*'s Kara Swisher saw Mary Meeker's annual PowerPoint presentation of internet economy trends as "depressing content" and an "entire bummer,"[61] whereas my post on the same presentation had "there is hope" in the headline.

Perhaps it was my naivete at play once again, for Meeker had focused on the recession, which she claimed had been "a long time coming." She even explicitly compared the current tech market to "early 2001." But I heard notes of optimism for entrepreneurs and developers, too, when she pointed to "under monetized" social networks, video, VoIP and payments companies—all of which she said are "driving powerful usage growth" among consumers. Meeker was also very bullish on the mobile market, noting that the iPhone 3G had sold a million units in its first three days and ten million apps were downloaded in that same period. Those rays of light on the tech side were what I wanted to focus on, not the doom and gloom of the general economy.

While roaming the Palace Hotel hallways during the event, I was pulled into a video interview with Alison McNeill from Bub.blicio. us—the only tech blog with a name even more difficult to say than Read-WriteWeb. I was clean-shaven and still wearing a rather cheap-looking thin black jacket (why I hadn't bought a blazer by this point, I don't know!), along with a grey-patterned button-down and blue jeans. I tried to steer the conversation away from the economy and into the technology aspects, but those weren't the talking points Alison was looking for.

When she asked if I was enjoying the conference, I diplomatically said that it had "a different focus this year—more of a mainstream focus."

Despite the roiling economy, RWW was riding high at this time. We'd nearly reached two million page views per month, including almost a million unique visitors. After the personal turmoil of the failed acquisition earlier in 2008, I was just happy to be back at the helm of a fast-growing blog business. The Web 2.0 Summit was also a great opportunity for the key members of RWW to meet in person and plot our further expansion.

On Thursday, Team RWW had dinner at Katsuko, a local Japanese restaurant. Present were the new leadership group—me, Bernard, and Marshall—along with our two most loyal and helpful unpaid contributors, Alex Iskold and Sean Ammirati. It felt unusual to be all in the same room together, but there was also an undeniable camaraderie between us. Even Alex and Sean, who had their own separate business interests, were fully invested in our continued growth. We all felt that RWW was unique among the leading Web 2.0 blogs, with our focus on technology over business.

The internet was indeed becoming more and more mainstream. Over sushi, we discussed how RWW would help this wider audience of people understand the importance of the internet in our world—and show them the opportunities. All of us were aware of the problems in the economy, but we were determined not to be the skeptics in the room (I was content to leave that to Swisher).

I'd always been a techno-optimist, and all of us around the table shared that trait. We had our political differences: Marshall had socialist leanings, while Sean was on the conservative side of the spectrum. I was in the middle—a liberal, but also a pragmatist when it came to business and politics. Regardless, we could all rally around the optimism we felt about technological progress. "What's next on the web" was our motto, and our team goal was to widen our community of readers over the coming year. The web water is good, we would proclaim, so come on in!

CHAPTER 12

SEPARATION

■ ■ ■ ■ ■

AS THE NEW YEAR DAWNED, I wrote up some goals for 2009 in the red 3B1 Warwick notebook I habitually carried with me. As a business goal I wrote, "Solidify, then expand." The RWW leadership team was busy dividing up the workload and new projects for the year. The goal was to continue growing. That's what Silicon Valley startups did, after all.

But I also wanted to expand my personal life. I was thirty-seven, restless, and starting to think that my youth was disappearing. These are, of course, classic symptoms of a midlife crisis, so let's call it that. Despite the surprising business success of the past several years, and despite my marriage and the love and pride I felt in raising my seven-year-old daughter—despite all that, I thought there were things missing from my life. As in all nascent midlife crises, those missing things were difficult to pinpoint. Creative fulfillment, perhaps? A vibrant social life? Maybe it was just a sense of regret that I'd wasted my youth—certainly that was true of my teen years and early twenties, a period stifled by depression.

Having a young family and running a thriving, exciting media business should be enough for any man of my age, I reasoned. Yet here I was, still searching for something more.

The RWW expansion picked up steam over January. After hitting two million monthly page views in December, we were on track to surpass that in January. On a single day in mid-January we got 150,000 page views (our highest-ever daily number). That said, we were also currently running at a slight loss for the first time since we'd absorbed the M&A expenses last year, mainly due to the increased expenses of three executive salaries and more freelance writer invoices. Our sponsor and advertising revenue was still solid, despite the economic headwinds, but I told Bernard that getting the monthly trading profit back into the black by Q2 was a priority.

In order to further focus on our business, we'd decided not to participate in the Crunchies awards show in early January. We felt the branding was too TechCrunch-centric, but also the previous year's profit of less than $10,000 had proven it wasn't a big revenue generator. Another factor was that relations between Mike Arrington and me had soured a little during 2008. We were both under pressure that year, and what little communication we managed was brusque and unfriendly on both sides. I felt bad about it and had emailed an apology, hoping to reestablish the friendship, but had not received a reply.

The night before the Crunchies, I received an email from Mike: "I'm sorry you won't be part of the Crunchies tomorrow evening Richard. It isn't the same without you. Hope we can work together again this year." I appreciated the note and the willingness to mend fences. I wrote back wishing him luck for the event, adding, "I kind of miss the 'good old days' of blogging, so hope we can work together in the future."

As part of the renewed focus on core RWW business during the first quarter of 2009, we planned to increase revenue by launching several new "channels," each of which would have its own sponsor. These would be subsites of RWW, but closely connected to the brand and part of the same domain. We'd already launched an enterprise channel back in August, which Bernard was running. However, we didn't have a sponsor for it and it wasn't yet a subsite (technically, it was just a category of RWW). So there was much work to do on both operations and the sales side.

As part of the channels strategy, we'd announced in November that we were disbanding our network—meaning the two separately branded network blogs, AltSearchEngines and last100. I gave my share of each blog to its author, Charles Knight and Steve O'Hear respectively. Neither site had gained enough traction, in either page views or revenue, although Charles had developed a cult audience for ASE that I couldn't help but enjoy.

Soon after that announcement, Bernard came up with the idea to use the format "ReadWrite[channel]" for the naming of our channels. The enterprise channel became ReadWriteEnterprise, but it took us several more months to overcome the design, server, and other technical challenges in implementing it.

Finally, in early April, the RWW menu had three channels listed in it: ReadWriteTalk (Sean's podcast), ReadWriteEnterprise, and ReadWriteHire (Marshall's job-board project, formally called "JobWire"). But it took even longer to get our first sponsored channel up and running. In the end, the first channel to land a sponsor was not ReadWriteEnterprise, but rather a new channel called ReadWriteStart. It focused on "profiling startups and entrepreneurs" and was exclusively sponsored by a Microsoft program called BizSpark, which provided software support to startups.

FM Publishing had brought the ReadWriteStart sponsorship to us, on the condition that the channel's content strategy be aligned closely with Microsoft's marketing objectives. Since what Microsoft wanted already fit within our wider content remit ("Web Technology news, reviews and analysis"), I was okay with it. Even better, we already had two writers who were passionate about the business of startups, Sean and Bernard. So, by the end of April, ReadWriteStart was launched.

In truth, I was frustrated at how long it was taking for the channel strategy to get off the ground. Even by the end of April, the design was messy and we hadn't done a good job with the URLs. For some reason we'd chosen to go with ReadWriteWeb.com/ReadWriteStart, which was too long and unwieldy. Why didn't we just make it ReadWriteWeb .com/Start? (Eventually that change was made.) I was also disappointed that we hadn't yet gotten a sponsor for ReadWriteEnterprise.

March 2009 marked the end of my streak in attending the official Web 2.0 Summit and Expo conferences. Instead, I went to the smaller, lesser-known Emerging Technology Conference (ETech), hosted by O'Reilly Media in San Jose. Partly this was to push myself out of the Web 2.0 bubble and explore emerging topics like the internet of things (IoT), mobile web, and open platforms. Indeed, the conference helped kick-start my interest in IoT, which I defined as "the Web in real-world objects." Over 2009, I became the first professional tech blogger to write regularly about IoT, which put RWW ahead of the curve on that subject. It was only when hardware such as Raspberry Pi (first released in 2012) and startups such as Nest (which launched its first product in 2011) came along that it became a widespread trend.

After ETech, I took the Caltrain up to Mountain View to visit the Googleplex for the first time. My intention was to talk to Google about its nascent open platforms. More than any other big tech company, Google relied heavily on the web for its profits. Google's search property and its increasingly profitable advertising business, AdWords, were web-based businesses. Google saw both Apple (on mobile) and Facebook (social networking) as threats to its revenue stream, so it had launched two open-standards-based projects to compete: Android and OpenSocial.

It was a glorious, blue-skied day in Mountain View when I arrived. I was met by a member of Google's core PR team, who led me to lunch at one of the cafés inside Building 43. There I met a few other members of the comms team, and we chatted about how blogs like RWW preferred to work with companies like Google. I'd found most PR firms in Silicon Valley to be very savvy in dealing with bloggers—they knew how to buddy up to us and find out our topical interests before pitching things. Nowadays, PR and online media are full of noise and the kind of impersonal communication that social media encourages. But back in 2009, before social media took over everything, PR and blogs tended to have a symbiotic relationship—we needed them as much as they needed us.

After lunch I met David Glazer, a director of engineering who oversaw OpenSocial, an open standard for social networking. This initiative would allow Google sites to interconnect with the likes of MySpace and

Ning. The idea was clearly to compete with Facebook, and at RWW, we were generally supportive of it. Unfortunately, the project would be hampered over the next few years by Google's confused social network product strategy. At the time of my trip, Google was promoting something called Google Friend Connect, which would turn into a variety of products over the next two years: Google Wave, Google Buzz, and finally Google+. All of them failed to make inroads into Facebook's ever-increasing popularity, and so OpenSocial eventually faded into the background.

Google had much more success with its open-source platform for smartphones, Android. But this future success was far from obvious on that sunny day in March 2009, when I met Eric Chu from Google's Android team. At this time, there was only one Android phone on the market: the T-Mobile G1. Unlike the iPhone, the G1 didn't have a touchscreen; instead it had a weird-looking "swing-out keyboard." The G1 was a Neanderthal compared to Apple's *Homo sapiens* device. It was hard to envision how it could ever compete with what Apple had produced.

But Chu told me that Google intended to build a platform, not a handset. The goal for Android, he said, was to build an ecosystem that embraced many different handsets and OEMs (original equipment manufacturers). Even that seemed like a long shot in March 2009, though. The top smartphone OS on the market that year was Nokia's Symbian, which had nearly 39 percent market share, with the Blackberry maker Research In Motion second (20 percent). Apple iOS was third (16 percent), and Android's market share was negligible.

However, the bet that both Apple and Google made—that smartphone operating systems should be app-based and not device-based—turned out to be the correct one. The app revolution was already underway in 2009, even if most people didn't know it.

After I returned from that trip, Maria and I separated. Unlike our separation at the end of 2006, this was permanent. I drove eight hours or so to Auckland, where my aunt Mary kindly agreed to let me stay while I sorted my life out.

I got myself set up with a mobile internet account with Vodafone (at this time in New Zealand, public Wi-Fi wasn't common), and I visited various cafés every day to work. I began seeing a therapist to work through my emotions and try to find ways to cope with this personal crisis. Communications with my wife were fractured and difficult, and divorce attorneys came into the picture. I worried about my daughter and knew I had to return to Wellington soon, to find a nearby place to live.

This turmoil affected my ability to run my business. One of the missteps we made with the channel strategy during this time is directly attributed to me having other things on my mind. In early April we hired a senior IT journalist to become our VP enterprise content and programs. The idea was that this person would assume responsibility for the ReadWriteEnterprise channel (still unsponsored). I'd been hesitant about hiring another VP-level person. This would be the third full-time hire, after Marshall and Bernard, and I wasn't sure it was necessary. Quite apart from the extra cost to the business at a time when we were not profitable, I thought the primary need for the ReadWriteEnterprise channel was someone to write daily posts for it. I questioned whether this person would be willing to do that with a VP title to their name. Despite my misgivings, we went ahead and filled the role. But I made it a clear requirement in the contract that we expected two to three posts per day.

After the first week, our new hire had written five posts. At this point I should've been more patient—it takes time to get settled into a new position, get used to the content management system and editorial processes, and so on. But I was already in a frazzled state of mind due to the difficulties in my personal life. So instead of waiting for a bit, I wrote an email on Friday reiterating my expectations for at least two posts per day. I added that "This isn't optional, it's a requirement of this job."

Our new VP resigned over the weekend. It was, in the end, an amicable parting of ways. But I was annoyed with myself for hiring another VP when my intuition had told me it was the wrong decision. What Enterprise needed was a blogger who would knuckle down with the daily writing.

These mistakes were the least of my worries at this time, but I knew it was yet another reason I needed a home base again. Later in April, I went down to Wellington to visit my daughter and find a rental property. Fortunately, I quickly found a little semi-detached two-bedroom house in the suburb of Petone, Lower Hutt. It was about a ten-minute drive to see my daughter, and I could set up one of the rooms as a home office. The place was a bit run-down, and I had hardly any furniture to put in it, but I was pleased to find an affordable home to start the process of getting my life back together.

I moved into the rental in early May. I had a lot to organize with the move, in addition to dealing with lawyers and my angry wife about the separation. But it was also time for me to get down to business.

On Monday, May 11, the first week in my new abode, I wrote an email to Bernard and Marshall. "I was looking at RWW finances tonight and I'm afraid it's not overly positive. So far this year we've made a trading loss every month." I asked for updates on the premium report Marshall was working on, the loss-making ReadWriteHire job board, and ReadWriteEnterprise (which I labeled "a continuing problem"). I said I would be looking at potential writers for Enterprise that week, "but they will need to be at the low end of the writer pay scale."

There were a lot of problems to solve—both personal and business— but at least I was at my desk in front of my iMac computer once more, albeit in a smaller home office and one I didn't own.

We released our first premium report in May, on the topic of online community management. This had been Marshall's baby, and he'd worked hard on it for four months. It was a hefty report, at seventy-five pages, and included case studies and analysis of how to run online communities in the Web 2.0 era. It had advice on blogging, RSS readers, Facebook, Twitter, and more. In addition, Marshall had set up "a companion online aggregator that delivers the most-discussed articles each day written by experts on community management from around the web."[62] It was impressive work from Marshall, even if it did take longer to produce than we'd have liked.

We were selling the report for $299 and hoped it would generate revenue quickly; the first four months of the year had been disappointing from an advertising revenue perspective. We were holding steady with our own sponsor revenue—the sidebar square ads sold out every month—but we were very concerned at FM Publishing's performance. Both March and April numbers from FM came in lower than expected. We did have a $60,000 advance from FM to build up the enterprise channel while we continued to search for a sponsor, but we'd have to pay that back eventually. I told Bernard, "We simply can't go on like this, we're going to have to cut costs if this keeps up."

We'd also gotten word from FM that TechCrunch was dropping them and going on their own with ad sales. GigaOm had already announced they were leaving FM last November. So RWW was now one of FM's premier tech blogs, along with Mashable and VentureBeat. We hoped this would help our cause, since there would theoretically be more advertising units for us now. But it was also a sign that FM's business model was perhaps shakier than they were letting on.

On the technical front, we had some big decisions to make. At the end of May I wrote an email to the leadership team and our tech crew—Mark Carey (a Movable Type expert) and Jared Smith (our webmaster, who had joined RWW a couple of months prior). Mark and Jared were part-time workers, but they were both solid and knowledgeable. We'd cycled through a couple of webmasters before Jared, but he had proven himself much more reliable than his predecessors; later in the year, we hired him full-time.

Under consideration were changing web hosts and a shift from Movable Type to WordPress. Both would be huge moves, but changing the content management system would be an especially heavy lift. Movable Type was becoming increasingly unstable as a content management system (CMS)—the continual run of bugs and server problems it caused were driving me nuts—and WordPress was now the default choice for professional blogs. Most, if not all, of our direct competitors used WordPress, so RWW was an outlier in this respect.

Regardless of the revenue and technical problems, RWW continued to grow in traffic and popularity. We'd gotten 2.58 million page views in May, and our average time on site had increased as well. This was partly a reflection of the growing prominence of Web 2.0 technologies in mainstream culture—perhaps typified by Twitter CEO Evan Williams's appearance on the *Oprah Winfrey Show* in April. That same month saw a race between Ashton Kutcher and CNN to become the first Twitter account to reach a million followers (Kutcher won).

As our traffic grew, so did our writing team. Jolie O'Dell, a smart young woman who dyed her hair bright red and had a personality to match, joined us at the end of April—our first writer based in Silicon Valley. (She described herself as "bicoastal," but when I approached her she was based in Palo Alto.) I'd seen on Twitter and on her blog that she was a talented writer and passionate about social media. She was also keen to do some video for us, and I told her we were open to it, "for example at conferences, and interviews with startups."

We further shored up our Silicon Valley base with the hire of Dana Oshiro, a Canadian now living in San Francisco. She'd had some tech-blogging experience with Mashable and Bub.blicio.us, and did marketing work in the tech industry, too. She was active with all the requisite social media tools and seemed a good fit for our ReadWriteStart channel, so she joined us at the start of June.

Starting at the same time as Dana was Steven Walling, who was younger than Jolie and Dana and hailed from Portland. He seemed to fit my description of what I'd wanted for ReadWriteEnterprise from the beginning: young, enthusiastic, and willing to write multiple posts per day. However, he didn't have any tech-blogging experience, and I wondered if he was perhaps too young (in his early twenties, I guessed). But in the end his enthusiasm won me over, especially after he expressed an interest in the enterprise space. "For some time now I've been keeping up with the Enterprise 2.0 scene," he told me, "and currently have about 100+ feeds I read directly related to the field."

So by the middle of the year, we had an excellent roster of daily bloggers (Sarah, Frederic, Jolie on the main site, in addition to me, Marshall, Bernard and our various other contributors), Dana on ReadWriteStart, and Steven on ReadWriteEnterprise. It took the pressure off me to write every day and gave me an opportunity to write more on topics that were a little removed from the daily tech-news cycle—like IoT.

Something curious had also happened with our Twitter account, @rww, during this time. Technically it was still my personal account, but increasingly I was using it to promote RWW articles. On or about May 20, @rww was added to Twitter's "suggested user list" (which everyone abbreviated to SUL). This meant that when a new user joined Twitter and expressed an interest in technology, RWW was now among the suggested users to follow. Just ten or so days on the SUL had resulted in a surge in traffic, making Twitter now a clear second in social referrers behind the still-popular tech-news aggregator Digg.

Marshall and I discussed the merits (or otherwise) of being on the Twitter SUL. He had misgivings about it, quoting a prominent blogger who had suggested that those on the SUL were "afraid to speak truth to power." Marshall noted that we'd been "unafraid to criticize Twitter" so far, but it was now an ethical issue how we covered the company, since we were on its SUL. He suggested we add a disclosure to posts we did about Twitter.

I thought the "truth to power" claim was nonsense and that it was common knowledge the top blogs were on the SUL. I told Marshall that, in fact, we had some catching up to do with our competitors. "RWW was last to get on there by a long way," I said, pointing to TechCrunch's 654,000 followers and Mashable's 742,000. At this stage, early June, RWW had 79,000 followers.

Marshall said he respectfully disagreed with my stance, but that as editor I had the final say. So we didn't add a disclosure to posts about Twitter. But it illustrated one of the differences in our styles. Marshall was, to his great credit, always very interested in the ethics of the big internet companies—he was one of the first bloggers to highlight Facebook's privacy issues, for example. Sometimes he was overly enthusiastic about criticizing these companies. His first post about Facebook's privacy changes in June was a long rant based on a misunderstanding on his part. But I was glad he was passionate about these issues because

I was more focused on the broader tech trends and making sure that RWW lived up to its tagline, "What's next on the Web."

When it came to the business of running a professional blog, I tended to be the pragmatic one and kept a constant eye on what our competitors were doing. To me, it was great news that RWW had finally made it onto Twitter's SUL. Indeed, it eventually became one of RWW's key business assets as social media continued its steady takeover of the world.

Another of my passion projects as a tech reporter was the Semantic Web (it was always capitalized at the time). In May I'd done a presentation to a Wellington tech gathering about web trends. I'd made the case that open, structured data (the so-called Semantic Web), real-time web apps such as Twitter, and "beyond the PC" things like mobile and IoT were all new or noticeably different trends in 2009.

The Semantic Web was a vision for the internet that the web's inventor, Tim Berners-Lee, and the World Wide Web Consortium (W3C) that he led were pushing hard. I thought it was an admirable goal—to make the web more structured and based on open data. This was important because despite the talk of "open platforms" by big companies, including Facebook and Google, there was a growing suspicion that they weren't quite as open as they claimed.

In an April 2009 interview with Wired, Mark Zuckerberg used the word open nearly thirty times! The media—including RWW—was guilty of indulging Zuckerberg and other tech CEOs when they talked about openness. On the other hand, supporting open standards was a core part of RWW's mission—the web, after all, is the ultimate open internet platform. To provide an alternative to the version of "open" being promoted by platform companies, I thought it was important to put some focus on the W3C's Semantic Web efforts. So I wrote several articles about it over 2009.

The middle of the year brought another overseas trip. First, I went to a Semantic Web conference in San Jose called SemTech. Next was Lift, a conference in Marseille, France, that focused on IoT, augmented reality, and other "hands-on" internet technologies. On the way back from Europe, I stopped over in Boston. I had always wanted to visit MIT in Cambridge, so I scheduled a bunch of interviews there. The one I was most looking forward to was with Tim Berners-Lee—and specifically, I wanted to talk to him about the Semantic Web.

Tim's assistant, Amy van der Hiel, had emailed me his office location beforehand: 32 Vassar Street, at the corner of Vassar and Main Streets in Cambridge. "We're in the big, crooked Frank Gehry building—you can't miss it."

As I approached the Stata Center on the day of our meeting, I saw a set of buildings that looked like a mashup of 1930s futurism and modern commercialism. It was a hodgepodge of brick, mirror-surface steel, brushed aluminum, and corrugated metal. One of the buildings, which looked like an upside-down bucket, was painted bright yellow. Several others jutted out at odd angles. Windows protruded like eyes on stalks. The complex had opened just over five years earlier, and it must've felt like a UFO landing in the middle of Cambridge.

For all the strangeness of the Stata Center, I warmed to it immediately. It seemed like a real-world mirror of what the web was at this time: lots of jagged edges and shiny silver futurism; a sense that the structure wasn't entirely stable, but with sections of redbrick solidity. I knew the web still seemed alien to many people, just like these headquarters of the W3C, but the growing success of technologies like blogs, Facebook, and Twitter proved that it was here to stay.

As instructed, I entered the Gates Tower (named after the Microsoft founder) and took the elevator to the fifth floor. Amy came out to greet me and quickly ushered me into Tim's office. Before I knew it, I was shaking hands with the inventor of the World Wide Web.

Tim, who had turned fifty-four earlier that month, was wearing a teal-green short-sleeved shirt and light blue slacks. He was a bundle of nervous energy with a receding hairline. His apparently habitual twitchiness came through in his speech; he stuttered slightly, and words flowed out of his mouth a little too quickly. Despite his nervy demeanor, he was relaxed and friendly. He politely invited me to sit down and only followed suit when I did.

Tim peered at me with what, at first, I took to be an innate curiosity. This, I guessed, was a big part of why he was a celebrated inventor. He looked and acted like a normal middle-aged man, and yet this was someone who had invented one of the most important mass-communication mediums in history.

Then it occurred to me that he was looking at me expectantly, waiting for me to start the interview. I cleared my throat and told him that my blog's name was inspired by the first browser, which he had developed in the early nineties and called (rather confusingly) World-WideWeb. It was a read/write browser, meaning you could not only browse and read content, but also create and edit it. The web browser that popularized the web a few years later—Andreessen's Mosaic—was read-only; it had only half the functionality of Tim's original browser. Anyway, I told Tim—and I was stuttering myself by this point—that his read/write philosophy had been a huge inspiration to me.

We then got down to business with the interview. He talked at length about the topics he was passionate about—the Semantic Web and something called "Linked Data" (a subset of the former). My main goal was to connect these rather academic topics to the wider tech industry, so I asked about search engines, e-commerce, and a new natural-language processing engine called Wolfram|Alpha, which had been released the month prior. He diligently steered all my questions back to his vision for the Semantic Web, but (in retrospect) I can see that he was also very prescient about the future of internet technology. Wolfram|Alpha would later be seen as an early precursor to the AI chatbot that now dominates the internet, ChatGPT. This was almost impossible to envisage back in 2009, yet Tim clearly understood that conversational interfaces would be key in the future.

"It's possible that as compute power goes up, we'll see a proliferation of machines capable of doing voice," he told me. "It'll move from the mainframe to being able to run on a laptop or your phone. As that happens, we'll get actual voice recognition and pattern natural language at the front end. That will perhaps be an important part of the Semantic Web." While the Semantic Web itself never took off, he was exactly right about the increasing power of what came to be called "machine learning."

After the interview concluded, we stood up and shook hands again. Up till this point, I hadn't even thought of asking for his autograph or for a selfie, but fortunately his assistant Amy was much more aware of the situation. She gestured to my iPhone and asked if I'd like a photo of me and Tim. "Oh! Absolutely," I said, a little too enthusiastically.

It had been a long trip—in a trying year, personally—and I was physically and emotionally drained. But in the resulting photos with Tim, I am beaming and flushed with pride. Here I was, a nobody from New Zealand who less than a decade ago was a mere "Web Knowledge Coordinator," standing beside the modern equivalent of Johannes Gutenberg. If it hadn't been for Tim, I wouldn't have a successful blogging business. Indeed, I might never have found my way in life at all.

Amy gave my phone back and then took a hardback copy of Tim's book, *Weaving the Web*, off one of the shelves. She handed it to Tim along with a black marker pen. He opened it up and wrote on the title page: "Richard, Thank you for ReadWriteWeb. KUTGW." I didn't know what the acronym meant until I looked it up back at my hotel: "keep up the good work." That gave me the boost of adrenaline I sorely needed as I embarked on the long plane journey back home.

In July, RWW had 2,650,000 page views, of which nearly 1.3 million were unique visitors. Nearly half (49 percent) of visits were from Firefox users, with 25 percent using IE. Safari (12.5 percent) and Chrome (8.5 percent) were the next most popular.

That Firefox dominated our statistics in 2009 indicated that our readers were tech-savvy and likely to be open-source supporters. In the much wider home and office market, Microsoft still had nearly 70 percent web-browser market share with IE; Firefox was second, at just over 20 percent. But Firefox users were *our people*, and our people were the early adopters who pointed to where the market was heading. It was obvious IE was toast, if you looked at our stats and read our posts about browsers—which highlighted the innovations in Chrome and Firefox, and the lack thereof in IE.

The real question was, would Firefox be the next mainstream browser of choice, or would it be Google's Chrome (released last

September)? But the answer to that question was becoming more obvious in 2009.

Back in March, when I had visited the Googleplex, I'd also walked over to the adjacent Mozilla headquarters—a rather drab mud-brown building that stood in stark contrast to Google's shiny, colorful new complex. At this time, around 85 percent of Mozilla's revenue came from Google, in exchange for Google being the default home page and search engine of Firefox. Frankly, Mozilla was under Google's thumb, and now it had to compete against Google's impressive new Chrome browser too. If I had to pinpoint one sign that the rose-tinted view of Web 2.0 as an open-platform paradise was about to come to an end, the emergence of Google Chrome would be it.

In a sit-down interview that day, Chris Beard, Mozilla's chief innovation officer, visibly bristled when I suggested that Chrome performed better with heavy-duty web apps. When I cited Google's claim that Chrome's isolated tab processes meant a more stable browser, Beard replied that Firefox too was very stable and that it didn't crash much these days. That he even had to mention the crashes was a giveaway, though: it was an all-too-familiar problem for Firefox users, although it had improved recently. Regardless, for those in the know (that is, RWW readers), it was clear that Chrome was already technically superior to Firefox. Not only that, but Google had market muscle and was starting to flex it. One of our readers perceptively commented, "At the bottom of your Google-distributed RSS feed, which I read in Google Reader, this article had a huge Google AdSense ad for 'Install Google Chrome.'"

By mid-2009 it was noticeable, at least to RWW readers, that the internet winds were shifting. The big internet companies were encroaching more and more into Web 2.0—and Google in particular was positioning itself well; it was poised to take major steps in the desktop-browser market and also building an open-source smartphone OS. Apple iOS was only third in the latter market at this point, but everyone knew it had the most advanced smartphone and mobile-app marketplace on the planet.

It wasn't just at the browser or device level that internet bigcos were making their presence felt. Amazon was the early leader in the nascent cloud computing market, while Facebook was now the leading social network (it had surpassed MySpace in number of unique US visitors in May 2009). Microsoft remained a late adopter in Web 2.0—for example, it launched a search engine called Bing in May. While taking on Google in search was almost impossible by this point, Microsoft's war chest of Windows revenue ensured that it would continue to be a major web player. Together, these five companies—Google, Apple, Facebook, Amazon, Microsoft—would come to dominate the internet within a decade. And it all started to coalesce for them in 2009.

I'd argue it was Facebook's purchase of the trendy geek app Friend-Feed in August 2009 that illustrated once and for all that big companies were in control of Web 2.0 now. It was Facebook's first major acquisition. In 2007 Zuckerberg's company had acquired a "WebOS" system called Parakey, which had been developed by two Firefox engineers, and it had bought out ConnectU in 2008, but neither was a strategic product acquisition. FriendFeed had a small but avid user base along with a couple of significant product innovations that Zuckerberg coveted for his own product.

One was the Like button. While FriendFeed didn't invent it (Flickr had a Favorite button and Digg had a Digg It button, for instance), it had much more of a social twist than the others. FriendFeed's implementation more widely shared Likes, which helped to expand connections between users, which helped to increase "engagement"—quickly becoming the key metric of the social web. Facebook had already copied the Like button earlier in 2009, but it didn't immediately have the subtleties of FriendFeed's implementation. The second innovation FriendFeed had was real-time updating, which Facebook would soon incorporate into its News Feed—allowing users to see updates from their friends in real time, as they were posted.

While the acquisition would undoubtedly improve Facebook, many early adopters of FriendFeed were dismayed at the news. Bloggers especially loved FriendFeed, as it was a place on the web where they could aggregate all their blog feeds and social software activity. It also allowed them to monitor which trendy services others were using and talking about. My own FriendFeed page automatically updated whenever I posted something on RWW, "dug" a story on Digg, uploaded a photo to Flickr, added a bookmark on del.icio.us, posted a message on Twitter, loved a song on Last.fm, and so on. I had around twenty Web 2.0 services plugged into FriendFeed, and at the time it was acquired, it was sharing fifteen posts per day (although mostly from Twitter).

But, in truth, FriendFeed wasn't a product that was "sticky" in and of itself. I maybe visited my FriendFeed home page once or twice a day and spent a few spare minutes to like or comment on stuff. All the RWW bloggers used the product in a similar way. We had also been one of the first tech blogs to profile FriendFeed; Sean interviewed the founders in early 2008 for our *ReadWriteTalk* podcast. So we loved the product, and it was a fan favorite among our readers too. However, you couldn't deny that the real action was increasingly on the likes of Facebook, Twitter, and Digg.

The sentiment among FriendFeed users about the acquisition was overwhelmingly negative. When cofounder Bret Taylor's feed updated with the news, scores of people left comments. Many of them disliked Facebook and were angry that their beloved indie service was being gobbled up. One of the first to comment summed it up nicely: "Uh. Well, that's the end of that."

I don't think that commenter meant it was the end of Web 2.0 entirely, but—to me, at least—it signaled the end of a certain innocence. It was unavoidable now that some companies were getting more and more powerful, at the expense of both open-source projects (like Firefox) and niche products (like FriendFeed).

CHAPTER 13

UNCONFERENCE

■ ■ ■ ■ ■

IN JULY 2009, we began planning our first RWW event. It would be in the "unconference" format, which had been suggested to us by Kaliya Hamlin, an expert on digital identity. The key aspect of an unconference was that it wasn't based around presenters with PowerPoints talking to a mute audience; instead, a discussion facilitator would get everyone in the room talking. It was a very "read/write" concept, since the audience would be actively involved in the sessions. Obviously, this would mean a much smaller event than, say, the Web 2.0 Summit. But it was a perfect fit for our RWW brand and we immediately jumped on the idea.

Kaliya had emailed us about this on July 10, while attending a Tech-Crunch event at a local VC firm, the "Real-Time Stream CrunchUp." The format was typical for tech conferences: presentations and panels. One session featured TechCrunch editor Erick Schonfeld moderating a panel with Jack Dorsey of Twitter, Chris Cox of Facebook and Bret Taylor of FriendFeed. TechCrunch certainly had no problem getting high-quality panelists, given that it was the ultimate insider tech blog. But Kaliya didn't like being "lectured at." "The unconference facilita-tor in me is going nuts," she wrote, "seeing this missed opportunity to support real conversations about the cutting edge of the web. The inno-vators are still just at the beginning and conversation is important."

She suggested RWW run an unconference on the same theme, the real-time web, to get a proper discussion going. "We all make a small amount of money, but actually move the field forward," she said, adding that she didn't want another "alpha male talk fest." She suggested the Computer History Museum in Mountain View as the venue and August or September as the timeframe.

I immediately wrote back and said it was a great idea. I suggested we time it for October, near the upcoming Web 2.0 Summit, when we would all be in San Francisco. Marshall and Bernard also loved the idea: "Pontificating pundits is so 1.0," quipped Bernard.

Over August, we solidified our plans and chose a date: October 15, the week before the Web 2.0 Summit. We decided to call it the Read-Write Real-Time Web Summit, thus continuing the RWW tradition of hard-to-pronounce names. Marshall worked with Kaliya on the event programming, and we hired a very organized woman named Chloe Caviness to project manage it—working with the venue, caterers, signage company, and so on. Marshall also had the idea of creating our second premium report to coincide with the event and focusing our daily blog coverage on the real-time web in the month leading up to the big day. So there was a lot to do.

By September the event was our primary focus. I could see we were getting stretched on resources, though, so I decided to put a hold on several ongoing projects—including a third channel, any further country channels, and an e-book idea that Bernard had floated. I also suggested putting a hold on our discussions with Automattic, the leading Word-Press vendor, to move our web operations to its VIP hosting platform.

I'd initiated the WordPress project in August, after getting fed up with Movable Type bugs and ongoing issues with our existing web host. I'd seen Automattic CEO and WordPress cocreator Matt Mullenweg in Wellington that month (he was on holiday and we met up for coffee), and I'd griped to him about our publishing problems. He explained the WordPress VIP setup, and I was intrigued—they already hosted GigaOm and some other big media properties. So by early September we'd begun doing tests on their servers.

Bernard rightly pointed out that our tech staff weren't very involved in the event, so we should continue the tests with WordPress. I agreed, and Mark Carey, our Movable Type consultant, carried on with that work. It's just as well we did, because the fact we were in discussions with Automattic was enough to rouse Movable Type owners Six Apart out of their slumber. During September they'd gotten word that Automattic was wooing us, so one of their executives reached out to me on Skype and proposed that "we try to not just fix your site, but take it to a new level." Since moving publishing platforms would be a massive undertaking, I wanted to keep the option open of staying on Movable Type. But I was somewhat skeptical. As I noted to my team after, "My lingering concern with them is stability/performance, as that is one thing WP has built a solid rep for but 6A hasn't."

While the event preparation and projects such as the CMS review were going on, my personal life received a boost—but once again, I managed to make it complicated. I'd begun dating someone I'd met through advertising for a RWW "editorial assistant."

We already had an editorial assistant, but he was only part-time and wasn't picking up on a lot of the grammar issues we were having. After yet another complaint from a reader, I sent a frustrated message to the writing team. "We really need to take care with grammar," I wrote. "I've said about a million times to carefully read your own articles after you publish, so please get into that habit."

But clearly, we needed more editorial resources, so I put the word out on the site and through social media. Several people emailed me about it in early September. One was Elyssa Timmer, an American who had lived in Wellington for the past eight years. She described herself as a web strategist, so at first glance she didn't seem suitable for the editorial-assistant role. I wrote back and politely explained, "It seems like this job may be too junior for you." I didn't expect to hear back, but she replied and admitted that she was probably overqualified. "But my current personal circumstances leave me looking for lower stress work in an interesting area," she added, and suggested we meet up for coffee to discuss.

I looked once more at her résumé. There was one intriguing thing in it that could be useful to RWW, since we were in the middle of planning for our first event. She'd written that she "co-founded Webstock, New Zealand's premier web conference." I'd been to Webstock a couple of times and thought it was one of the best-produced tech conferences I'd ever attended. On that basis alone, I thought it was worth meeting Elyssa to talk. Perhaps she could help project manage our upcoming summit.

"I think it's worth meeting for a coffee to discuss," I wrote back. "The main requirement is editing tasks, but there may be other areas of the business where you could help too (we could do with some project mgmt help, for example). And I do like your background."

We met a couple of days later, on a Friday morning at a café in Wellington. It was soon clear to me that Elyssa wasn't suitable for an editing role, but I thought she'd be helpful in a project-management role. The upcoming event was foremost in my mind, but I was also thinking about the operations side (the CMS and server issues) and our internal communications systems (in particular, improving how we used Basecamp).

After thinking about it over the weekend, I offered her a twenty-hour-per-week role as a project manager. We'd do a trial month to see if it worked out for us both. Since our budget had been for a junior editorial assistant, I noted, "The rate I'm sure is less than what you get consulting, however this will be ongoing work and it's in an exciting industry." She was indeed shocked about the pay rate (I countered that we'd review it after the trial month), but she readily agreed to work for us. We arranged to meet again to debrief, this time at a café near my home suburb of Petone, in Lower Hutt.

During that meeting, we made a list of things for her to work on, and afterward I introduced her to the team. Elyssa immediately began to make improvements in how we used Basecamp. I also added her to the event mailing list, which included Kaliya and Chloe. "I think we need someone from RWW to keep track of progress, on details such as venue hire, website progress, etc," I'd written. "So please look at Elyssa as being RWW's rep in the daily project mgmt, thus allowing Marshall to focus on [the premium] report and Bernard on sales."

Over the next two weeks, Elyssa and I were in daily contact as she got up to speed. We also met on consecutive Mondays at the same Petone café, Caffiend. It was nice to meet with a RWW colleague face-to-face every week—something I wasn't used to. But, of course, it also allowed us to get to know each other more on a personal basis. I discovered, for example, that she had recently separated from her kiwi husband—since May, in fact. I'd been separated since March, so we were in similar circumstances. She had a five-year-old son and was devoted to him—part of the reason she had wanted flexible working hours. I had my eight-year-old daughter, so again we had something in common.

It was after the second Monday meeting at Caffiend (our fourth café meeting overall) that I decided to suggest a dinner. I think I was rather vague as to the purpose of the dinner, so when she got back to her home that Monday morning, she emailed and asked, "Is this dinner or dinner?" She meant, was this a working dinner or was I asking her out on a date? I hadn't thought that through, so Elyssa was right to prod me on it. Over Skype messaging, we eventually established that it would be a date dinner.

It wasn't a great idea to start a relationship with an employee, but nevertheless that's what I did. And to be fair, we were good for each other over the coming months.

It was the morning of October 15, 2009, and I was at the Hotel Avante in Mountain View, California, for the unconference. I was nervous and apprehensive about how the day would go—this was RWW's first event, and the team had put in a huge amount of work. In truth, I hadn't had to do much in terms of organizing. Chloe had taken care of operations, Bernard the costs and sponsor sales, and Marshall and Kaliya had done most of the preparation for the schedule. Elyssa had kept an eye on the project management. It hadn't all gone smoothly: there was a lack of order in the event communications and finances that bothered me and prompted several emails to Bernard. I planned to sit down with him after the event to talk it through.

Bernard and Marshall were here at the Avante with me, as was Frederic, who had made the short trip from Portland. Dana and Jolie were already in San Francisco and would be attending the event. Our newest writer, Alex Williams, had also come down from Portland. So most of the key editorial members of the RWW team were here—the exception was Sarah, who was heavily pregnant with her first child.

Unfortunately, neither Sean nor Alex could make it; both were busy with their own businesses. However, I'd made plans to meet up with Sean at the Web 2.0 Summit the week after. Among other things, he would be a good sounding board for the growing concerns I had about Bernard.

The team and I arrived at the Computer History Museum by shuttle at around 7:30 a.m. The day was already promising glorious sunshine, and that helped to settle my nerves as I sipped my takeaway hotel coffee and admired the view from outside. It really was a delightful venue, with a swath of green grass laid out in front of a shiny white-and-silver building. It had previously been the HQ of Silicon Graphics, a famous 1980s computer company, before being converted into the museum in 2002. So the venue felt modern and yet classic Silicon Valley at the same time.

Inside the building, I inspected the check-in table and the signage in the hallway and then the setup inside the main room. It was a cavernous space, with plenty of natural light coming in through the windows. Giant silver air-conditioning ducts ran across the ceiling, which made me think of an aircraft hangar. Rows of white and black chairs were laid out in front, along with a projector and screen, and multiple round tables were dotted throughout the rest of the room. Even the tall sponsor boards looked great—very professionally designed.

Everything looked high-tech and new except for the large pieces of white paper that had been pasted together on the front wall. But that was on purpose—the schedule would be filled in on the fly by the attendees, using red, blue, and black marker pens and colorful letter-sized pieces of paper. Kaliya and Marshall would be organizing that after my introductory speech.

Ah yes, the speech—now I was nervous all over again, so I walked back out of the main room and over to the coffee cart we'd hired for the day. Another cup of joe was unlikely to calm me, but I didn't have any specific setup duties and so I had to do something to take my mind off the speech. Also, this gave me a chance to greet some of the attendees, who were just beginning to file in. Many of them hadn't met me in person before, so I didn't quite know what to say as they walked past me. But several of my blogosphere buddies also arrived—including Chris Saad and Ben Metcalfe—and they stopped to say hi and wish me luck.

When the time came to open the conference, I gulped down the last of my coffee and made my way to the front of the room. It was now filled with people—we had sold out the event and were expecting around three hundred attendees. The large room was buzzing, and it occurred to me that this was the sound of hundreds of happy RWW readers gathered under one roof. That was unusual in itself, since RWW was a completely virtual community every other day of the year. It gave me a jolt of pride to realize that the little website I'd created just over six years ago was now hosting a real-life event in the heart of Silicon Valley.

When I reached the projection unit, I turned and faced the rows of seated techies. I waited for the hubbub of conversation to settle down as I tugged nervously at my navy-blue blazer. I suddenly began panicking about how I looked, but I reassured myself that my hair was well combed and my beard meticulously trimmed. I fidgeted with my glasses as Kaliya shouted out for everyone to hush. Slowly, rows of expectant eyes trained themselves on me. Okay, then, this was it!

"Welcome, everyone, to the ReadWrite Real-Time Web Summit. I'm Richard MacManus, the founder and editor of ReadWriteWeb. This is a one-day event in which we'll explore the technology and business of the real-time web, which has been one of the biggest and most disruptive trends of 2009."

I'd somehow got those words out without my voice cracking too much, and I soon settled down and methodically went through my list of people to thank. I daresay it wasn't the most charismatic speech the attendees had ever heard (many of them would've seen Steve Jobs in action!), but I did my awkward best. I finished up by introducing Marshall, who would give a keynote presentation about the real-time web. I also noted that we'd have a premium report coming out on this topic "in early November" (unfortunately, we'd missed the deadline to finish the report by the time of the conference). I handed the mic to Marshall and, with no small measure of relief, took a seat at the front.

Marshall's presentation was the only one of the day, and it was a good primer for the topics that we hoped would define the agenda. But we weren't in control of that—it was up to the attendees to fill in the schedule with suggested breakout groups.

To get that started, Kaliya instructed everyone to form a big circle with their chairs. At the same time, she began handing out colorful sheets of paper and marker pens. There was a buzz of excitement in the air as everyone noisily shifted their chairs and then sat down again—or milled around in small groups—to make their suggestions. Already, this was better than silently listening to the second presenter at a traditional conference. Normally you're struggling to suppress a yawn and craving a third cup of coffee by this point, but at our event people were moving around and chattering about their passion topics.

After fifteen or twenty minutes, Kaliya—who was stationed in the center of the circle—began calling up people to add their sessions to the agenda board. One by one, she proffered a microphone to each person carrying a filled-in piece of paper, and they explained the topic before going over to the agenda board to tape it up.

This process alone proved that the unconference format was perfectly suited to RWW and our readers. Most of the people at the event had opinions about technology—the smart, informed opinions of practicing technologists and hardworking entrepreneurs—so they had unique insights on what topics or issues were top of mind in the still emergent business of "the real-time web." Monica Keller, who was responsible for activity streams and openness at MySpace, had an orange sheet of paper with the following words in red marker: *Real time privacy / Unforgettable mistakes / Brainstorm on fix*. Erik Sundelöf, cofounder of a citizen-journalism startup called AllVoices, wrote on his sheet, *Real-time ranking of news/content*. Jason Hoyt, the chief scientist at a website for academics called Mendeley, proposed a session about real-time science.

Within thirty minutes the entire mass of white paper was covered with giant Post-it notes like this and everyone was itching to get started with the breakout sessions. Kaliya wrapped up the agenda-setting part of the day, and we all dispersed to different parts of the main room— or to smaller designated rooms on the same floor—to participate in the first groups.

I hadn't proposed to lead any of the sessions myself. Our job at RWW was to report on what the industry was doing and thinking, so I was mostly just curious about what the attendees wanted to discuss. Throughout the day I cruised in and out of sessions—rarely staying for an entire breakout. Partly this was just to show my face in as many sessions as possible, as the founder of the company hosting this event. But also, I wanted to take the temperature of all the discussions— which ones were full of ideas and enthusiasm, which were contentious, which were dull (there were only a couple). This would help me decide which topics were worth exploring more and potentially writing up later as RWW articles.

One of the sessions I stayed in for a while was run by Jason Shellen from Google. He'd been one of the creators of Google Reader and was running a discussion entitled "What Do We Hate About the Real Time Web." The common theme was that users didn't have enough control over feed consumption and other management tools for the real-time web. (Interestingly, Twitter had released a new product that very day to help with this—lists. But it was too soon to say how well lists would work or how much Twitter would promote them.)

It was noted at Jason's session that "openness with other companies and agreed upon standards are needed." This was a constant theme at tech conferences and meetups during the Web 2.0 era, but sadly, all too often the proposed open standards never took off. What happened with Twitter is a classic example. Despite all its talk of being an open platform in the first decade of the 2000s, Twitter's protocol was proprietary—and was destined to remain so. One of the other sessions at our event in 2009 was run by the creators of PubSubHubbub, an open protocol for distributed publish–subscribe communication. Although Google was actively supporting it, it was never used by the likes of Twitter or

Facebook. That isn't to say that this and similar sessions didn't eventually make their mark on the industry: years later, Mastodon would be among a new generation of decentralized social media projects to adopt the protocol.

Another big discussion point in Jason's session was how to filter the information "firehose," as it used to be called. What is the source authority? Who are the experts? Can we filter out boring stuff? Again, with the benefit of hindsight, we can see that such discussions didn't lead anywhere fast. Filtering was not solved by the likes of Twitter or Facebook during the Web 2.0 era. Quite the opposite, in fact; as the 2010s unfolded, both of those companies became notorious as hotbeds of misinformation and hotheaded opinions. Still, a bunch of startups tried valiantly to solve filtering during 2009 and beyond—one of them being Jason's latest venture, Thing Labs.

Many of the sessions were just as stimulating. By the end of the day, the RWW team was a mix of exhausted and elated with how the event had gone. As the attendees made their way out after the final wrap-up, some of them came up to me and said they had loved the summit. "It was the best event I've been to in years, and I mean it," the blogger and author Violet Blue said later. She reported that she felt "completely energized" and had "so many new ideas about what I want to do next." John Borthwick, the founder of the New York City incubator Beta-works, said "it was excellent—friggin' great in fact." [63] He had brought a handful of his team members across the country for it and wished he'd brought more. These comments were a good representation of the responses we received at the Computer History Museum late that afternoon.

Of course, as CEO of RWW, I couldn't help but wonder if we'd made a profit on the event—I was worried about this, but I'd find out the answer in the coming days. That aside, I felt like we had just made a valuable contribution to a fast-growing part of the Silicon Valley economy, the real-time web. I had a feeling that at least some of the ideas discussed at our event—not to mention the relationships forged—would lead to new web products, new protocols, or new features in existing products. So, after all the preparation and focus that had gone into the event, and despite the unknown factor of whether it was all worth it financially, I felt confident that we'd do more events of this kind.

The following day, a Friday, the RWW team met up at the Red Rock café in Mountain View to work and debrief. I also took the opportunity to have one-on-one meetings with each of our bloggers present: Frederic, Jolie, Dana, and Alex. I'd be doing the same with Bernard and Marshall tomorrow, as well as having other management meetings. But the Friday was about getting to know my writers better and setting goals for them.

Frederic and Jolie had both impressed me in the lead-up to the event, and I wanted to hire them both full-time. Frederic was a relatively quiet person, but he was hardworking and probably our best daily blogger at that point. Jolie was more inconsistent in terms of post quality, but she had a terrific personality and was clearly very smart. Dana was still a bit of a mystery to me in terms of her fit with RWW. She wasn't getting the page views that the likes of Frederic and Jolie regularly got, and she seemed to have bigger plans for her career than simply being a blogger. But everyone liked her, and I told her we might be able to expand her role a bit with RWStart, as she was keen to engage with the startup community more. (In later years, Dana moved into venture capital and eventually became a partner at one of these firms—so she was destined for bigger things.)

As for Alex Williams, our newest team member, he was already a solid performer. I'd hired him at the end of September to take over ReadWriteEnterprise. It turned out he was Marshall's best friend, although I hadn't realized that until Alex was on the shortlist with one other person. Marshall hadn't wanted to influence the decision, and indeed he didn't: Alex was the preferred candidate by that point, given his journalism background and experience writing about enterprise topics. I also saw that he had a lot of initiative and seemed very involved in the emerging cloud computing community. This would stand him in good stead—five years later he founded a cloud news and analysis site called The New Stack, which I ended up working for in 2020.

When I first met him, in October 2009, I didn't know much about Alex. He was about seven years older than me and was balding, with a big-boned stature. He seemed friendly enough but often wore a serious expression—sometimes even dour—and so I didn't quite know what to make of his personality. In our one-on-one at Red Rock, he opened up and we got to talking about things like baseball (which he followed with a passion) and our respective kids.

At some point during our meeting, Alex brought up his background in podcasting. Sean's *ReadWriteTalk* podcast had been on pause for the past six months, since he was so focused on his own startup, but Alex was keen to resurrect it. He told me he'd coproduced the first Gnomedex podcasts with Doug Kaye in 2005 and then ran an event called Podcast Hotel that same year. I was interested in the podcast idea, but I told him my main priority was to ensure that the troublesome Enterprise channel got some momentum at long last. The previous writer for the channel, Steven Walling, had ultimately been a disappointment, so I was hoping that Alex would turn it around—and certainly I'd been impressed by his posts so far.

Later that afternoon, the team and I took the Caltrain from Mountain View to Palo Alto. It was only three stops away, but somehow we got off at the wrong stop, so it actually took us two Caltrain rides to make the short journey. Perhaps our brains were all fried by this point in the busy week, but we eventually found our way to University Avenue. We stopped at University Café, which a couple of us knew was an iconic Silicon Valley spot—it was where Mark Zuckerberg had first met the legendary angel investor Ron Conway about five years earlier. It was a clear day, so we took one of the tables outside and talked more about Silicon Valley lore.

After that, we walked to a local sports bar and played some pool. We stayed there into the evening and at one point recorded a video to send to Sarah, who was about to have a baby in her home city of Tampa, Florida. I don't recall whose idea it was, but we passed around Alex's phone and each of us recorded a message for Sarah. "We're having a good time," I said during my portion of the video, "and it'd be great if you were here as well, to complete the editorial team." But obviously, I added, she was somewhat occupied right now. I hadn't yet met Sarah in person, so I finished with, "I'm sure we'll get to meet face-to-face at some point in the near future, so take care and we'll catch up with you online pretty soon."

The camaraderie of the team at this moment was something special. We were missing Sarah, but otherwise it was great to spend time, in the physical world for once, with my fellow bloggers. I wasn't yet worried about losing any of them to competing blogs, although that would happen in the not-too-distant future. For now, though, we were Team RWW, hanging out at a Palo Alto bar with Facebook employees and other local techies. We were part of the Silicon Valley scene, for that one night at least.

The next day was another clear, sunny California day. In the morning, Bernard, Marshall, and I met up in downtown Mountain View for our scheduled management meeting—and also my one-on-ones with each of my lieutenants. I knew the one with Bernard might get awkward, and I was anxious about that.

I liked Bernard personally, and from a strategy perspective he was always full of good ideas. He'd also been a sage business adviser to me during the acquisition negotiations with ZDE and TechWeb last year. But since he'd come on as COO about ten months earlier, a continuing lack of structure in the business had been bugging me. As COO, his role was to make sure that our daily operations were well-planned and finances kept in order. But it still felt too chaotic for my liking: the amount of time it took for us to get ReadWriteEnterprise off the ground, the ongoing issues with our publishing platform and web hosts, the unpredictable revenue flow from FM Publishing and our sponsors, the lack of a budget, and now the event planning.

The unconference had undoubtedly been a success from a content and community perspective, but there had been several communication breakdowns while planning it and I didn't yet have a clear idea of how it had done financially. While that wasn't all on Bernard, it was (I thought) the COO's job to put structure around a big project like this—to have a solid budget and documentation around the action items. But that hadn't been the case.

Elyssa had been my sounding board for the past month on what to do about all this. After discussing it with her before the unconference, back in New Zealand—usually, it must be said, over dinner, wine, and the odd cigarette on the back porch of her house—I had decided to write up a set of KPIs (key performance indicators) and business processes to present to Bernard. I came up with five KPIs, the first three of which were revenue-based. The other two were about achieving "operational efficiency," by which I simply meant making a plan for everything—budgets, resources, a process for report sales, and so on. To give but one example, I wanted our financials to be better managed, with the KPI "ensure that ReadWriteWeb has a fully fleshed out and regularly tracked budget in place (including revenue lines and projections) and that the company is using Xero [our accounting software] in a complete and efficient manner."

During our one-to-one meeting, Bernard dismissed the KPIs as "micromanaging." I pointed out that annual revenue goals aren't exactly "micro." I also said that I wanted to be regularly updated on operations, so I asked him to start sending me a weekly report—I added that I'd be asking the same of Marshall in his role. Not surprisingly, he bristled at this too.

The meeting was tense, but I held firm that the business operations needed more structure—which was the COO's job to implement. At the same time, I tried to stay positive about his personal strengths. I said that while systems and processes didn't appear to be his forte, I knew he was strong in business development and sales. I politely suggested that business development might be a better role for him at RWW.

Bernard was having none of that. He didn't want a demotion—in fact, he then began angling to become CEO! (I had to admire his commitment to the bluster.) He talked about the need for RWW to raise money in order to compete and that this would mean forming a board of governors. I told him I was open to that, but I didn't want *him* as CEO—especially when we couldn't even agree on the role of COO. In reply, he said that if we raised money, "the board" would choose the CEO, not me. By this point I was exasperated, and we didn't come to an agreement over the KPIs for his current role.

I emailed Elyssa later that day. "I honestly think the next step is a 'take it or leave it' type meeting," I wrote. "Either he agrees to the KPIs and doing weekly reports etc.... or he finds another job."

My next port of call was San Francisco, for the Web 2.0 Summit. I was keen to meet up with Sean, who would be there for a couple of days. I wanted to get his opinion on the Bernard situation, but also, I was curious how his own startup, mSpoke, was doing. He'd obviously been busy on it, since *ReadWriteTalk* had been off the air for the past six months. I wasn't worried about the podcast, since I didn't see that as a big focus for RWW at this time. Also, it was part of the deal of unpaid partnerships with entrepreneurs like Sean and Alex Iskold that some periods would be relatively inactive. But I knew I could always talk through business decisions with either of them, any time we happened to be in the same place at the same time.

Sean and I met up on Tuesday, October 20, after the first day at the summit, which was being held at the Westin Hotel in San Francisco. I was still buzzing after Mary Meeker's latest internet trends presentation, which I'd quickly posted about on RWW. Meeker had told the entrepreneur-heavy audience that financial markets had rebounded from the financial crisis of 2008 to 2009. She was particularly bullish on the mobile internet market and noted the impact of "powerful new publishing / distribution platforms"[64] like YouTube, Facebook, and Twitter. It seemed like boom times again for Web 2.0, and I felt that RWW was being carried along on this swell.

When we sat down for dinner that evening, I told Sean about how well the unconference had gone and that it had been a wonderful to spend time with the team. I also told him about my tense meetings with Bernard and that I thought I'd probably end up letting him go. To my surprise, Sean responded that there was a chance he might be available to take over as COO, if I was open to that. This I hadn't expected to hear, so I asked what was up with his own business.

It turned out that Sean and his cofounders were having financial issues and looking for more funding. If that didn't come through, they would probably have to wind down the business. He was in Silicon

Valley not for the summit, but rather for an important funding meeting with their VC firm that would determine the company's fate. I asked him to keep me posted, as I would absolutely love to have him as COO if he was available.

A few days later, as I was on my way back to New Zealand, Sean informed me that they would indeed be winding down mSpoke, so there was a decent chance he'd be available to work for RWW by the end of November. I replied that I'd like to continue that discussion.

Just as Sean still had some things to work through with mSpoke, I still had some things to work through with Bernard. While I was in San Francisco, I'd sent him a long email setting out my expectations for the COO role. I'd reiterated that I would be implementing KPIs and that I expected a weekly report from him going forward. He hadn't yet responded in full, so I wanted to give him a chance to do that.

After I got back, Sean and I spoke again via Skype. He still had some negotiation to do with his mSpoke board about how to wrap things up there, but he was confident that he'd shortly be available to work for RWW—which he was keen to do. For my part, the decision was looking more and more clear cut. I'd given Bernard a chance to get his act together since my email ultimatum on October 20, but by the end of October he still hadn't responded about his KPIs. Also, I'd just begun the weekly report process for all the management team, and his first report was unacceptable. I'd told everyone that I wanted a project-by-project breakdown, progress on timeframes, and similar detail. Bernard's first report had none of this and hadn't addressed most of the items that were in his high-priority list.

Enough was enough! But before I notified Bernard of my decision, I needed to be 100 percent sure that Sean would take the job. I made the offer to Sean on Wednesday, November 4. It included a small slice of equity and a generous salary, so he was happy with it. He just had to confirm that the mSpoke board would let him take the RWW job. Since they were no longer able to pay him, I figured it was the least they could do—but of course that was up to Sean to confirm. He duly gave the all-clear on Thursday evening.

On Friday, I gave Bernard his notice. "This is one of the hardest business decisions I've had to make and it saddens me to deliver this news to you," I wrote. Firing people is never easy, I had learned over the past several years, and this was by far the biggest such decision I'd had to make. I'd let go of a few writers for not performing, but it wasn't the same as parting ways with a member of your management team.

While I was upset that it had come to this with Bernard, I was confident that Sean was the right person to move things forward for RWW. As part of our informal interview process, Sean had sent me a couple of the spreadsheets he'd created in previous jobs. They were financial and resource planning models, and I was very impressed by their level of detail, particularly the way he'd done financial projections. As soon as I saw those spreadsheets, I knew this was exactly what RWW needed.

Not wanting a repeat of the acquisition communications failure, I'd told Marshall about the COO situation several days before giving Bernard his notice. He was sad that Bernard would have to go, but he understood my decision.

Sean wanted to keep things quiet for the first several weeks, as part of his agreement with the mSpoke board. That was fine by me, as I needed to make sure the handover from Bernard to Sean went smoothly. I'd need to introduce Sean to all our sponsors, as well as FM Publishing and our various suppliers (our web hosts and so on). It also gave me a few weeks to liaise with Bernard over the terms of his final payout and the public messaging of the news.

Bernard and I had some vigorous back-and-forth, and I had to consult my NZ lawyer a few times, but by mid-November we'd come to an agreement. Bernard could've made things more difficult, but he accepted the decision and told me he had his own startup plans brewing. So, in the end, it was an amicable split.

On December 1, I made the announcement about our new COO on RWW. By the end of that month, I was feeling great about the decision. As expected, Sean made an immediate impact on the business: we had a solid financial plan going into 2010, and he hit the ground running with FM Publishing and all our sponsors. He'd also confirmed by the end of November that our first event had made a profit of a bit under $40,000.

This clearer financial picture gave us the confidence to hire a few more people before the end of the year. We added two more writers, Mike Melanson and Chris Cameron, and a new production editor, Abraham Hyatt (another Portlander). I was particularly pleased to have Abraham on board, as it would enable me to focus more on the overall content strategy for RWW, as well as on writing my own posts.

We also, finally, made the decision to move off our current web hosts. We decided to stick with Movable Type, since Six Apart had stepped up and agreed to give us more assistance, but we'd be moving to one of their preferred web hosts, Contegix. Elyssa had gotten that deal over the line.

By the end of 2009, things were lining up well. It had been a crazy year for me, with the breakup of my marriage and the business wobbles. But our first RWW conference in October had been a turning point—it gave both me and the company a much-needed boost.

To cap the year off, RWW hit three million page views per month for the first time in December. We were on a roll again. *I* was on a roll again.

PART 3

2010–2011

■ ■ ■ ■ ■

CHAPTER 14

MEETING WEIWEI

■ ■ ■ ■ ■

FOR THE FIRST TIME, in March 2010, I was headed to Austin for South by Southwest (SXSW), the popular internet conference I'd heard so much about. It was going to be an epic trip because, in addition to stops in New York and San Francisco, I'd also be visiting Colorado and Portland for the first time.

Eight of us from RWW attended SXSW that year: myself and Elyssa, Sean, Marshall, Frederic, Jolie, Mike Melanson, and our webmaster, Jared Smith. Sean was a regular at SXSW, so he would've gone regardless, but I also needed him there to help organize a party we were cohosting at Austin City Limits Studio with PBS, NPR, and *Frontline*. The headlining act was Band of Skulls, an up-and-coming rock group.

PBS had approached us about the City Limits party in January. We'd have to pay $3,000 to be named a cohost, but we jumped at the opportunity. Clearly, RWW was the fourth wheel among the hosts—they'd likely chosen us to get some internet street cred among the SXSW Interactive geeks. But we couldn't pass up having our name associated with three prestigious American media brands.

I'd also gotten another, more unusual, offer, this time from New York City. Lou Sagar, a business agent based in the Big Apple, emailed us in early February. "I am working very closely with Ai Weiwei, the leading

Chinese contemporary artist, and unquestionably, the most prominent blogger in China," he'd written. "I am extremely interested in exploring whether Richard would be receptive to participating in a 'conversation' with Weiwei at the prestigious Paley Center at the Museum of Television and Radio, on the topic of Art, Social Networks, and the impact it's having on art, culture, and on social activism." The visit was scheduled for March.

This checked all the right boxes for me, as I was very interested in art at this time and I was familiar with Ai Weiwei's work. He was a controversial figure in China and known to the international community for his constant needling of the Chinese government. He was famous worldwide as an artist and activist, and it would be an honor to share the stage with him. I asked for further details, and Lou replied saying that Jack Dorsey (former CEO and now chairman of Twitter) would be participating too, but from San Francisco on a "live feed." At this time, Dorsey was a popular figure in the tech industry, although not widely known by the public. Still, he was a name that would help sell tickets to the New York cultural establishment. I'd be the odd one out, being totally unknown outside of the Web 2.0 complex. But I was keen to meet both Weiwei and Jack, and I was sure this would raise my public profile, so I readily agreed to participate.

Lou said he'd cover flights and hotel for Elyssa and me, so we booked it in. The only problem was the timing—the PBS event was on Sunday, March 14, and the Paley Center event was the following night in New York City. I'd have to get the earliest cross-country flight possible on Monday. But again, this was an opportunity I couldn't turn down.

All of this was ahead of me when Elyssa and I touched down in Austin on Thursday, March 11. We'd already had several days in Colorado by this point, staying with her parents in Aurora. Elyssa had brought her five-year-old son, Josh, across from New Zealand; he was staying with his grandparents while Elyssa and I went to Austin.

In truth, it had felt a little strange to travel as a family group from New Zealand to Colorado—I'd been dating Elyssa for less than six months, and yet here I was meeting her parents in America. I liked

Elyssa a lot, but she was pushing for things I just wasn't ready for. She'd recently brought up moving in together, moving to Colorado (if she could get approval from her ex for Josh, which seemed unlikely), and even having a baby together.

Elyssa was also emotionally demanding, which contrasted with my need to be alone at times. She would regularly tease me for living in a small rental unit—which she called my "hovel"—and for driving a little Volkswagen Polo (she drove a sturdy Volvo station wagon). The implication was that I should step up and be a family man again in her large Island Bay house. But I didn't want that, although at some point (when I had time) I did want to buy a proper house in Petone so that my daughter could stay with me more often.

Thus, I was feeling a little on edge as we arrived in Austin that Thursday. However, I was looking forward to my SXSW experience and spending time with the RWW team. Perhaps spending time together at the so-called geek Mardi Gras would also be good for my relationship with Elyssa.

As expected, SXSW was a whirlwind of socializing. The business meetings in Sixth Street cafés and the twenty-four-seven carousing were everything—the keynote presentations and daytime panels turned out to be beside the point.

Elyssa and I met up with most of the RWW team on Friday evening, and we all ended up at a random bar late that night. It was relatively low-key, and I was paying for the beer, since none of us knew where the insider parties were happening. If there was a member of our team who would've known, it was Jolie. Unfortunately, we didn't see her.

We had made Jolie our community manager the previous November—the first time RWW officially had someone doing this role. A vivacious and intelligent woman in her twenties, she had flame-red hair and a charismatic personality. She was popular within Web 2.0 circles and helped raise our profile in certain online communities—Digg, especially. I'd given Elyssa the responsibility of managing Jolie, but that relationship was bumpy. In truth, over the past three months we'd had a number of issues with Jolie's performance. She was inconsistent, and we never quite knew what she was up to. I'd even heard on the grapevine that she was looking for another job.

All that said, I liked Jolie, and she had one quality that the rest of us lacked: she was cool. I was rather hoping she would help RWW raise our profile at this trendy tech event, so it was disappointing not to see her that first night out.

While we didn't manage to find the right party on Friday night, I had an enviable invitation to attend a dinner on Saturday evening at the Oasis restaurant, on Lake Travis just outside of Austin. John Pozadzides, a Dallas-based founder of a web statistics app called Woopra (of which RWW was an early user), had invited me and Elyssa. The Oasis was usually packed at this time of year, he told me, but he "had a hook-up there" and promised a table overlooking the lake, where we'd see "the most beautiful sunset in Austin."

Poz, as he wanted me to call him, had an ulterior motive for the invitation. He requested an interview with me for the podcast he and Cali Lewis (from GeekBrief.TV) did together, *Wealth Nation*. I was happy to do it, as Poz was fun to chat to and I really did appreciate his dinner offer. He left it open for me to invite other members of the RWW team to the dinner, so I invited Sean and Marshall. In the end, only Sean came along with us.

The view was indeed breathtaking. Our table was on a balcony looking out onto the lake, and it was a clear, blue-skied evening. Right above us was a bronze statue of a woman diving into the picturesque scenery.

Poz's partner, Vi, took a photo of all of us on the balcony just as the sun was about to disappear. The sky was orange and pink, and for once I looked relaxed and assured. I was wearing a navy-blue dress shirt and blue jeans, and my hair and beard looked almost golden set against this pretty backdrop. Elyssa was leaning into me, looking lovely in a white-patterned dress. Sean was on the other side of Elyssa, and he, too, was smiling and relaxed.

A professional photographer named Trey Ratcliff also joined us that evening. Trey ran a popular travel photography website called Stuck in Customs, and over dinner he told us of his plans to move to New Zealand.

It bemused Elyssa and me because both of us wanted to eventually make the opposite migration: from New Zealand to America. Of course, I wasn't yet sure if I wanted Colorado to be my destination, whereas Elyssa dearly wanted to settle back in her home state. Trey also told me he'd gone to our Real-Time Web Summit last October, which I was surprised to hear.

After a very pleasant dinner, John dropped us back in downtown Austin. I told Elyssa I wanted to go straight to a Digg-sponsored event at the outdoor Stubb's Bar-B-Q venue. We got there just after 9:30 p.m., after Digg's Kevin Rose and Alex Albrecht had done a live taping of their podcast (I'd had dinner with Kevin the previous month, while he was in Wellington). But we were in time to catch an alternative rock band called the Walkmen, who put on an excellent show. Stubb's was heaving with people, most of them younger than me. It was an incredible atmosphere.

While at the Digg show, I bumped into Mashable founder Pete Cashmore, whom I hadn't seen since January 2008. A lot had changed for both of us during the past couple of years; certainly, our respective blogs were much more popular now. But Mashable had grown the most—it had even overtaken TechCrunch in the Technorati list (Mashable was now third and TechCrunch seventh; RWW was ninth). This was perhaps peak Mashable, as it was hip and attracted the type of young audience packed into Stubb's that night. Generation Y, the youth of the day, were flocking in droves to Facebook and the other social networks that Mashable covered.

Although we attracted our fair share of Gen Y readers, RWW's audience was on the whole a bit older and geekier; Twitter was more our kind of social network. Our readers also appreciated the wider and deeper coverage of tech trends that RWW offered.

There was more than enough room in the growing social web for both of our sites, of course, and Pete and I smiled warmly as Elyssa snapped a photo of us. These were good times; we had nothing to complain about.

Sunday evening was our party at the legendary Austin City Limits Studio. It was a PBS production, really, and they had organized the event and the onstage musical talent: Nicole Atkins as the opener and Band of

Skulls as the main act. We had an allocation of tickets and thus thought all we had to do was shepherd the people on our list (mostly our sponsors) through the door. But this turned out to be easier said than done.

The PBS security staff at the event insisted that there were no lists for the event, so we were having trouble getting our people in—including ourselves. Having ascertained that there wasn't a special cohost entry into the venue, Elyssa and I joined a long line with lots of other people. At the rate it was moving, it didn't look like we'd even get in at all. I messaged Sean to ask what was happening, and he came out to meet us. There had been a pre-party, he said, and it turned out that was the only time our list would be honored. Clearly there had been a miscommunication because I'd not even considered that we had to turn up super-early to get in. Elyssa and I continued to stand in line while Sean went back to the front of the queue to plead our case.

Meanwhile, a few of our sponsors had spotted me in the line, and one by one they came over to ask when they were getting in. I tried to explain about the list mix-up and that it didn't seem like we would get our people in. The looks I got back were part mystified and part angry—these were people whose companies sponsored several industry blogs, and they were clearly unaccustomed to standing in line for events cohosted by those blogs. Fortunately, Sean came over while I was talking to one of the sponsors and assured them they'd get in. I didn't know how Sean planned to do this, but I recognized that his assurances were better than my "there's nothing we can do" shrugs. We had to at least make a show of doing our best to get them into the venue. Once again, Sean went back to talk to security.

Eventually we got both ourselves and our sponsors in, but it had seemed unnecessarily stressful—and quite embarrassing for us, in terms of our sponsors' expectations. We'd learned the hard way that even though we were cohosts of the event, the reality was that we had little control over it. Next time at SXSW, we'd make sure to organize our own event.

I was already rather anxious that night, since tomorrow morning Elyssa and I were flying out to New York City for the Ai Weiwei event. We had to be at the airport at 5:00 a.m., but it was 11:00 p.m. by the time the main act came onstage. I supped a beer and distractedly watched the three-piece Band of Skulls play. They were admittedly awesome—the front man was a short, skinny dude with shoulder-length blond hair and an electric guitar who resembled Kurt Cobain. Also like Cobain, he was shorter than his bass player, a tall, lean woman who looked like a member of the Ramones.

Partway through their blistering set we saw Sean again. He looked pretty stressed out, and I asked if he was okay. He said he'd had an issue with Jolie at the door. She had brought along a bunch of bloggers and had tried to get them into the venue but had been turned back by PBS security. Rather than accept this, Jolie had argued with the security team. "We were just going in circles, and frankly I didn't feel she was helping," Sean said, wiping his brow. The situation apparently escalated when Jolie overheard someone from PBS say that Band of Skulls had given them a list and that those people would be getting in. She began yelling at the security staff, which meant Sean had to step in and sternly tell her to move on. At that point, she finally left.

For all the trouble the evening had been for RWW, we were happy that at least our sponsors had gotten in to enjoy the show. But it was nearly midnight by this time and I was anxious to get back to our hotel for a few hours' kip before heading to the airport. Sean said he'd stick around for the rest of the night to schmooze with the sponsors. Elyssa was buzzing from the show and wanted to stay for the rest of the Band of Skulls set. But she could see I was a bundle of nerves and needed some rest, and so we left as the band played on.

I didn't know much about the Paley Center for Media before I entered its impressive white stone building on Fifty-Second Street. But I knew it was about as "old media" as it could get in New York City—and I mean that in a good way. Formerly the Museum of Television and Radio, it was a cultural institution, but also one that aspired to lead "today's media conversation" (as the website tagline put it). The organization's bread and butter were television and radio—two mediums that America helped define in the twentieth century—but it was also interested in what it termed "emerging platforms." This is why a little-known tech blogger from New Zealand was invited onstage with Ai Weiwei and Jack Dorsey.

Elyssa and I arrived around 4:30 p.m. to meet with Lou Sagar, the agent who had booked me for this evening. He was a smartly dressed, well-tanned man who looked to be in his early sixties. With his thinning grey hair, active eyes, and a broad smile reminiscent of Jack Nicholson, he struck me as the kind of guy who knew a lot about New York culture. He also took an immediate liking to Elyssa, but I was too distracted by the thought of meeting Ai Weiwei to worry about it.

After an hour or two of meeting production people and discussing the evening's format, I left Elyssa at the front of the building and was taken to the backstage area. I was shown the TV studio, which was well stocked with TV screens and broadcasting equipment, and then guided into the green room, a small waiting area where I'd be until the show started.

There Emily Parker, the MC for the evening, greeted me warmly. She was a tall, striking brunette woman in her mid-twenties. Like others I'd met that day at the Paley Center, she seemed steeped in New York old media—despite her youth, she'd already worked for the *Wall Street Journal* and the *New York Times* and was now a fellow at the Asia Society's Center on US-China Relations. As we chatted, I also learned that she was working on her first book, about democracy on the internet.

As if to complement her almost perfect career progression, Emily was wearing a stylish purple-print dress for the evening. She was the picture of urban sophistication, and I felt shabby in comparison. I was wearing stonewashed blue jeans, a purple-and-lime-green-striped shirt, and a black blazer. But I quickly reminded myself that Steve Jobs always wore jeans, so I'd be fine. Also, the purple stripes on my shirt were kind of a match for what Emily was wearing, so I didn't feel so bad after all.

After a short while, Lou brought in Ai Weiwei. He was fifty-two at this time and had close-cropped black hair and a well-groomed beard with flecks of grey in it. He wore a bright white shirt, dark linen pants, and a black blazer. We were roughly the same height, but he was quite a lot broader. He had a presence about him—like he knew he was famous, but he was comfortable enough in his own skin to not care about that. He also displayed no sign of nerves about going onstage.

Lou introduced me to Weiwei (his first name), who shook my hand and gave me a friendly smile. He told me he was a fan of RWW and was very interested in what we wrote about. I was stunned he even knew what RWW was, so I think I just mumbled something like, "It's an honor to meet you."

Weiwei's demeanor reminded me a bit of Tim Berners-Lee—there was a kindness and humility to him that I immediately respected. It even seemed like he was trying to put me at ease before we went onstage. However, unlike with Tim, I sensed a rebellious streak in Weiwei. There was a playful gleam in his eye, and it was also evident in the way he wore his shirt—the top button was conspicuously undone, leaving the collar splayed wide open, and the bottom hem was not tucked in. Perhaps I was reading too much into it, but from what I knew about him, Weiwei liked to do things his way.

I recalled a conversation I'd had a couple of years ago in Australia, when I'd met a Chinese entrepreneur at a tech event we were both speaking at. I'd asked him about Ai Weiwei (I knew about him even then), and the entrepreneur had chuckled knowingly. "Ai Weiwei's untouchable," he told me. "He can get away with things that other Chinese people can't." The implication was that Weiwei's fame protected him from the Hu Jintao government; that they wouldn't crack down on him for fear of causing an international uproar.

With Weiwei now here, we were ready for the night to begin. We were all led to the wings of the stage, where we watched Paley Center president and CEO Pat Mitchell give her introduction. Eventually, she introduced Weiwei. He calmly walked out and acknowledged the crowd's enthusiastic applause with a bemused smile. If he was hated by his own government, then it was the complete opposite among this audience of liberal elites. I was introduced next, and the audience politely clapped as I nervously took my chair next to Weiwei. Very few among this East Coast crowd would've known who I was. Jack Dorsey's clean-shaven digital avatar was already waiting in a monitor to my right, and Pat formally introduced him. Like Weiwei, he wore a white shirt and black blazer—although the top of his shirt was neatly buttoned up.

Pat then handed it over to Emily, who immediately made it clear that the discussion for the evening would be focused on Weiwei's political activism and the grander theme of democracy on the internet. Emily told the audience that this was a major event in China: "I think Ai Weiwei has been sent here as a messenger for the Chinese netizens, so I know they will be watching avidly to see what comes out of this meeting."

Surprisingly, she asked me the first question. She wanted me to give a general overview of the differences between internet culture in the US and China, adding, "If you have any questions, we can always turn it to Ai Weiwei." I would certainly have questions about what the internet was like in China, but I started by giving my usual spiel about the emergence of the Read/WriteWeb at around the time I started my blog. I noted the rise of social networks, including Twitter, and said, "In the Western world, it's very much been about getting everybody to contribute to the web, to talk on the web and network on the web—and there's been a real, you know, freedom of expression around that content." (Of course, the West would get its comeuppance about "freedom of expression" in later years, in the form of misinformation and other hateful content, but at this time we all wore rose-tinted glasses.)

I knew only from secondhand reports what the internet was like in China, although in preparation for this event I had researched and written several posts about the topic—including one entitled "China's Twitter Clones." We also had ReadWriteWeb China, a Chinese-language version of our site hosted by Sohu (a Chinese web portal, similar to Yahoo) and run by Lei Zhang from the translation service Yeeyan. Zhang had started this in late 2006 by translating our articles—initially without my permission, but when he contacted me in early 2007, I was happy to hear about it and encouraged him to continue. In early 2009 it became an official RWW international channel.

I told the Paley Center audience that since China had clones of all the Western social-web tools, the main difference I saw between internet culture in the West and in China was "only in the degree of freedom of expression." The first Chinese Twitter clone, Fanfou, had been shut down by the Chinese government in 2009; since then others, notably

Sina Weibo, had emerged to take its place. Given that Jack was on the panel, I specifically mentioned that Twitter was also currently banned in China, but that there were "a number of Twitter clones in China that are being used by a great number of Chinese people." I then passed the discussion over to Ai Weiwei to tell the audience about his experience.

Weiwei noted that they could not use Twitter, YouTube, or Facebook in China, and that Google might soon be added to that list. (It was an active debate at the time—I'd gone to a SXSW panel a few days before that had discussed Google's prospects in China.) "Basically, it's a society which forbids any flow of information and of freedom of speech," Weiwei remarked. He explained that even though the Chinese internet had lots of clones of Western apps, their usage was closely monitored and censored by the government—users weren't allowed to mention his name, for example.

He went on to say that he'd started out in 2005 by blogging to promote his work as an artist, but that had been shut down by the Chinese government in 2009, after his blog had gotten popular. So he began using Twitter and quickly got hooked on it. He added, however, that only a small proportion of Chinese netizens had access to his Twitter because of the great firewall.

Emily then brought Jack into the discussion, and he told the story of how he created Twitter. Things got more interesting when Weiwei asked Jack why they hadn't provided a Chinese-language version of Twitter. Jack's response was that technical constraints had prevented that so far (Twitter was known to have outages in its early years—many early users will remember seeing the "fail whale" on a regular basis). Another reason for the delay, he added, was technical difficulties in supporting the character sets in Chinese languages.

I tried to do my journalist bit and press Jack on whether Twitter would officially enter the China market, and if so, would it stand up to the government and resist censorship, as Google had recently started to do? It turned out that Jack hadn't even realized Twitter was banned in Twitter until a few weeks before, and he clearly wasn't interested in trying to compete in the Chinese market. So my questions were unfortunately moot. The rest of the evening passed by in a similar manner—there were no real-world implications for anything that was said, so it was all rather academic. However, Weiwei did get feisty during the audience Q&A, when a woman who identified herself as a Chinese American businesswoman suggested that China's growing middle class was happy.

"I don't think you should give credit to a nation that deprives people of human rights," Weiwei snapped back. "You say they're happy? I'm sure, because they made money so easily."[65]

In the years to come, I followed Weiwei's life and career closely—although I had little direct contact with him, other than the odd message via Twitter DM. Less than a year after we shared a stage in New York, Weiwei was arrested by the Chinese government. That was in early 2011, and he wasn't allowed to travel overseas again until mid-2015. I read later in his memoir that he had been detained for nearly three months in an anonymous building in Beijing. So, he hadn't been untouchable after all.

To his great credit, Ai Weiwei has never once wavered on his democratic beliefs and continues to use Twitter for digital activism to this day. Also, as Jack promised, Twitter did eventually come to support the Chinese language. The service is still officially banned in China, but so is every other major Western internet product (including Google).

So was this an "historic conversation" about the future of democracy on the internet, as the Paley Center—and RWW itself—promoted back in 2010? In the end, no "positive social change" came out of it, so in that sense history will view it as little more than a good night out for some liberal New Yorkers. But on the other hand, I did get to meet Ai Weiwei, who I'm certain will be remembered as one of the great artists of the early twenty-first century. Turns out, he was a fan of the Read/WriteWeb too.

The Ai Weiwei event was a big deal for RWW; we thought it could potentially bring us to the attention of thousands of influential people across the media and technology industries. Maybe we'd even get some serious mainstream attention, since Weiwei was being interviewed by CNN and other big media companies during his stay in New York.

In addition, we'd gotten the rights to exclusively livestream the event and had set up a special page on our site for it. Prior to the event, it included a bunch of our articles on digital activism and a video documentary telling Ai Weiwei's story.

In support of all this, the rest of the RWW team had arranged to meet up late afternoon on Monday at an Austin coworking space called Conjunctured. Our webmaster, Jared, would handle all the technical matters regarding livestreaming on our website. Mike and Frederic would write up articles on the day. The rest of our writers, including Marshall, would monitor Twitter and other social media while the event was running. Sean would be managing the whole operation and had also set up a Google Talk chat line with Elyssa in New York, to relay any necessary messages to me.

With one exception, the entire team in Austin showed up to Conjunctured. Even Dana Oshiro, who no longer worked for us, was there. The conspicuous absence was Jolie, our community manager. In the group email she'd made an excuse about having prior interview commitments and added, "I didn't know the coworking space was going to be so far away!" In reply, Sean pointed out that it was just a three-minute taxi ride, which she could charge to the company.

When I discovered the next day that Jolie was the only one who hadn't been with the team that evening, I was furious about it—especially since she'd also caused trouble at the door of the PBS event on Sunday night. "I've only seen you for 10 minutes through all of SXSW," I emailed on Tuesday. "You're our full-time community manager, there is really no excuse for missing either of our events." After a bit of back-and-forth, I arranged to have a sit-down with Jolie when I arrived back in Austin on Wednesday afternoon.

The Interactive part of SXSW would be over before I got back, but I had bought a ticket for the SXSW Music event. Elyssa would be traveling back to Colorado to spend more time with her parents and son. My plan was to unwind in Austin over the following five nights and enjoy a bunch of live music. I didn't know of anyone else going to SXSW Music, but I figured there would be a few Interactive refugees there. In any case, I wanted time to myself to think through personal and business goals.

While I was on the way back to Austin on Wednesday, Jolie published a post to her personal blog entitled "Why SXSW Sucks." The gist of it was that there were too many people, which prevented her from having "a wonderful time meeting up with my friends."[66] The post got a lot of attention on the social web that day. She'd made some good points about the lack of good technology content at the event and about the increased danger to women because of what she termed "swarms of douchebags." But still, I couldn't get past the fact that she was more focused on wanting to meet up with her friends than on the job that was paying her to work the event.

I met up with Jolie late on Thursday morning, on Sixth Street outside one of the popular diners. As ever, she stood out in the crowd—her bright orange hair was tied back into pigtails, and she was carrying a pair of roller skates. But I could see in her eyes that she was apprehensive about the meeting and that something was weighing on her. Since it was around lunchtime, I suggested we go into the restaurant to eat and talk properly.

After we'd ordered, I repeated my concerns about the team not seeing her during Interactive. We'd had two important team events over the past several days, I said, and our community manager hadn't contributed to either of them. She was apologetic and began talking about her bad experiences. Pretty soon tears welled up in her eyes and her voice faltered. This caught me off guard. I assured her that I was no longer angry; I was just disappointed she hadn't done her job. She'd talked in prior months about her periods of depression, so I tried to be sensitive to this as we continued talking.

Over the course of the lunch, it became clear that neither of us wanted her to continue as RWW's community manager. I honestly hadn't known how this meeting would turn out—whether I'd have to let her go or whether Jolie would convince me to give her another chance with RWW. I was open to the latter, but evidently, she wanted out. She told me of her plans to branch out from tech blogging, maybe do some product-management work for startups. I said I understood, and so we mutually agreed that she would leave RWW. I told her we'd be flexible about the timing and asked her to let me know later by email what (if any) work she wanted to do for us before she moved on.

The rest of the lunch was more relaxed, and at the end of it we parted on good terms. Back out on Sixth Street, we hugged and I sincerely wished her all the best. "I'm sure we'll see you around," I said.

Soon after, I messaged the management team to tell them Jolie was leaving and began preparing a note for the rest of the team in Basecamp. Of course, there was one more twist in the tale—after our lunch, Jolie promptly posted to her blog that she had "quit" RWW. I immediately emailed and asked her to please not message it that way. "It was a mutual decision that you should go, and that is best way to message this publicly," I said. To her credit, she quickly removed that language.

Less than two weeks later, we found out via Jolie's blog that she had joined Mashable. Since it was posted on April 1st, I emailed her and rather ungraciously asked if this was an April Fool's joke. But soon I recognized that this made sense for Jolie—she was still young and was a talented blogger, when she put her mind to it. Mashable was lucky to have her.

This left RWW without a community manager and short one daily blogger. With our next event slated for May, we needed to move quickly to fill the vacant position.

During SXSW Music I stayed at the Hyatt Regency, which was a little further uptown and over a bridge. Even though it was still walking distance from all the action downtown, it was far enough away to make me feel isolated. I had thought I'd see at least a few people from Interactive at the music event or around the hotel lobby, but after I'd parted ways with Jolie on Thursday at midday, I didn't see a single geek in the remaining four nights in Austin.

Starting on Thursday afternoon, I wandered Sixth Street and all the satellite streets to check out the music. I was a fan of the NPR podcast *All Songs Considered* and had noted down some SXSW acts I'd heard on their show and liked. One was a band called Cymbals Eat Guitars, who were playing a 2:00 p.m. set at the open-air Mexican American Cultural Center stage. But I was forced to leave after just a few songs because of the earsplitting volume at the venue. I soon discovered this was a common theme at SXSW Music: extreme amplification, to the point where all I was hearing was screech and noise. It wasn't the relaxing vibe I was hoping for. Or perhaps, at thirty-eight, I was simply feeling my age.

Since I had no one to talk to and was too shy to strike up a conversation with anyone standing next to me at a concert or bar, I spent a lot of time thinking about RWW and where I was at in my personal life. On the business front, I was feeling overwhelmed with all the typical things a startup CEO has to deal with—finances, managing people (and finding new people when required, which seemed to be a never-ending cycle), legal (complicated by being an NZ company), resource allocation, and the various wanted and unwanted requests on my time that came with running a media company.

It was a productive time for RWW, but that meant it was super busy. We'd just released our second major premium report, although it was already clear that it wouldn't be as profitable as we'd hoped. Our second Silicon Valley event was coming up in early May, and we continued to churn out new channels. We'd launched ReadWriteCloud at the end of January and had another couple in the works—one for developers, called ReadWriteHack, and a smartphone apps one called ReadWrite-Mobile. The international channels were ramping up as well.

Through all this, my personal life was far from settled. Even a year after I'd separated from my wife, I was still trying to hash out a financial settlement. At issue was the value of my business, which our two sets of lawyers and accountants were busy racking up large bills arguing about. I was also acutely aware that my daughter was growing up fast (she would be nine later this year) and that I needed to spend more time with her.

On Saturday, the weather suddenly turned cold and windy. I went to one party in the afternoon dressed in a light jacket but had to return to my hotel afterward to put on my winter jacket. That evening there was going to be a tribute concert at Antone's nightclub for Alex Chilton, from the seventies band Big Star. The band had been scheduled to play at SXSW that week, but Chilton had died suddenly on Wednesday, aged fifty-nine. I'd heard that at least one member of REM—a longtime favorite band—would be at the tribute night.

I knew I'd have to turn up early to even get into Antone's, so I made sure I was there before the first warm-up act had started. The famous Austin blues club had been one of the first music venues on Sixth Street (although its present location was on West Fifth Street). I was expecting a grand-looking establishment, and the signage and billboard above the front door did nothing to dissuade me from this—underneath the Antone's logo, the billboard improbably read *Free Day Show / Sweden Goes SXSW*. However, when I got inside, I was surprised by how small the venue was.

While I was sipping a beer at the bar, I overheard a conversation between the barman and another punter about the extreme volume at SXSW shows. The barman nodded in agreement but said that going deaf was an occupational hazard he'd had to accept as part of his job. That seemed crazy to me, but what did I know about being young and free in a music city like Austin?

Halfway through my beer, the first act got onstage. To my dismay, it soon became evident that the amplifiers had been turned up way too loud again. The act was a bad version of the young David Bowie, strumming an acoustic guitar at deafening volume in a song that somewhat resembled "Space Oddity"—or, at least, I heard snippets of that kind of song between the squarks of tinny feedback. I quickly decided I couldn't take it anymore, so I gulped down the remainder of my beer and left. The growing line of people outside Antone's gave me strange looks as a I scurried out the front door and back "down the street," as the Big Star song went.

I soon discovered that every bar on Sixth Street was hosting an aggressive guitar-rock band, so I looked at my SXSW Music map to see what other options there were. The Central Presbyterian Church venue on East Eighth Street seemed like a good bet for a more relaxing vibe, so I walked in that direction. It turned out to be an actual church, and there I saw an act called the Watson Twins. A pair of beautiful brunette women from Louisville, Kentucky, they sang sweet harmonies above the melodic organ and relaxed guitar of their male backing band. Included in the set was a cover version of Sade's "Sweetest Taboo," a song I remembered fondly from the eighties.

After the show, I bought the band's latest CD, *Talking to You, Talking to Me*—an ironic title, given how alone I felt at SXSW Music—and complimented one of the ladies about the Sade cover. I think these were the only words I'd spoken to anyone in over forty-eight hours, other than ordering a chili dog at a Sixth Street cart or a beer at a venue. Ms. Watson politely thanked me for the compliment and duly signed the CD.

I continued on my way, and for the next hour or so I checked out the bars in and around Sixth Street, but no matter where I went the music was uncomfortably loud. I eventually circled back to East Eighth Street, but by then even the church had turned the amps up!

Now armed with earplugs, I decided to walk down to Antone's again—it was now about 11:30 p.m. Maybe I'd be in time to catch the Big Star tribute. But, as expected, the line was extremely long. So I called it a night and began the lonely trek back to my hotel uptown, where at least it would be quiet and warm.

CHAPTER 15

COEDITORS

■ ■ ■ ■ ■

IN MID-APRIL 2010, I decided to make a change in our management duties. Marshall would become coeditor, alongside me. After seven years of RWW, this was the first time someone other than me would share the title of editor.

There were several reasons for this decision. First and foremost was to strengthen our news business. Following the Web 2.0 news cycle had never been my main interest, whereas it was something that competitors like Mike Arrington and Pete Cashmore reveled in. Marshall was much more of a newshound than me, so I wanted him to take over that aspect of our daily coverage. It would allow me to focus on leading the feature and channel writers and to double down on RWW's reputation as the thinking person's tech blog.

Another reason for the change was to take some of the editorial workload off me, allowing me more time to work with Sean on business growth and strategy. By this point, RWW had a team of around twenty; in particular, our writing team had grown significantly over the past year. So it made sense to share at least some of the editorial responsibilities, especially if I wanted to continue attending to business matters.

Finally, I wanted to de-emphasize the premium reports, which had been Marshall's project. We'd done two reports over the past year, but neither had earned enough revenue. I felt it was better to put the resources we'd been devoting to reports (mostly Marshall's time) back into the blog. I also thought it would allow Marshall to focus his other role, as VP content development, into initiatives for the website—for example, I had always been keen to develop topic pages.

The goal driving all this, as ever, was to increase page views. While we still wanted to diversify our revenue—we hoped to make money from our next event, for example—the bulk of the company's revenue came from CPM advertising, a combination of our monthly sponsors and the display advertisements provided by FM Publishing. More page views meant the ability to nudge up the price of the monthly sponsor packages (the CPM rate would remain the same). Meanwhile, FM Publishing told us they had no shortage of ads to supply us—and the more of their ads we ran, the more we earned.

Our tax year ran till the end of March, and for the 2010 financial year just ended, we'd hit the $1 million revenue mark for the first time. I still had ambitions to eventually sell the business, and in order to do that we'd need to continue growing in revenue. Some of our competitors had to demonstrate strong annual revenue growth to satisfy their VC shareholders. I didn't have that kind of pressure, since RWW was entirely bootstrapped, but even so I wanted to be able to go back to the likes of TechWeb and ZDE in a year or two and show off an impressive EBITDA growth rate.

Looking back on it as I write this, I regret not giving more consideration to the option of treating RWW as a lifestyle business. I was making an excellent personal income from the blog and providing employment to around twenty other people; there was no immediate danger of this changing. I recall discussing the lifestyle-business scenario with Sean several times back then—I think he felt a moral responsibility to remind me of it on occasion. But every time, I dismissed the option. Something was driving me to continue growing the business every year, and I couldn't see past that as a goal.

I'm a quietly competitive person, and so I enjoyed measuring our success and influence against big hitters like TechCrunch, Mashable, and GigaOm. The prestige of running one of the top ten or fifteen blogs in the world was another driver—I didn't want us to slip back down the Technorati charts. And growing by a factor of two or five every year was just what was expected of tech or media startups at this time. Related to that was my wish to hold onto Sean and Marshall, my two key employees. Both were ambitious people—Sean's career goal was to become a VC, while Marshall keenly wanted to be part of a startup success story. I felt that neither would want to work for a lifestyle blog, so I'd most likely lose their services if I chose to go that route.

I had my own personal reasons to chase growth, too. To reach a divorce settlement with my ex-wife, I'd either need to sell the business or raise VC money to pay her out—and both relied on revenue growth. Her lawyers had specifically rejected the option of me giving her an ongoing equity stake in the business. It had been made clear that, one way or another, I'd have to give her a large sum of money.

So for all the above reasons, I didn't view RWW as a lifestyle business. More's the pity, as running a tech blog was a life I enjoyed. Despite the daily business pressures, I felt I was born to be a tech blogger, and I wanted to continue doing it.

In early May I flew over to San Francisco once again. My plan was to attend the Web 2.0 Expo during the first week, followed by our own event on Friday, May 7—the ReadWriteWeb Mobile Summit. We were basically repeating the formula of October's Real-Time Web unconference—same Mountain View venue and similar audience numbers, just a different topic. The following week, Sean and I would fly to New York to attend something called Creative Week, in which RWW was a media partner.

I arrived in San Francisco on Sunday, May 2, and the following evening attended the latest Ignite meetup, held at the Mezzanine on Jessie Street. Brady Forrest had come up with the format several years ago: each speaker had five minutes to talk on a subject accompanied by twenty slides, automatically advanced every fifteen seconds. I always found them fast-moving and fun, and on this evening, it was also a good excuse to catch up with my old kiwi blogger friend Phil Pearson.

By this point, Phil was doing what I had so far failed to achieve— he was living and working in America. He was a developer for Ning,

Marc Andreessen's social networking product, and seemed to be having fun as a single man on the Silicon Valley dating circuit. I didn't necessarily think I could emulate Phil in the latter department, since he was younger than me and looked like Don Draper from the TV show *Mad Men*. But I enjoyed hearing all about his social life in San Francisco and wished, once again, that I could live here too.

After Ignite, Phil and I met up with another industry friend of mine, David "Lenny" Lenehan, from Sligo in Ireland. I'd gotten to know Lenny on previous trips to the States via his friendship with Fergus Burns—the Irish entrepreneur I'd met back in 2005 on my first US trip. Lenny was the developer of an online-poll product called PollDaddy, which we'd been using on RWW for several years, and had also written some articles for us. He was in some ways the opposite example to Phil of how I might live my life going forward: he was in a long-term relationship in Ireland but was able to travel regularly to the States for work.

I was torn between wanting to emulate Lenny's lifestyle, except from New Zealand, or following Phil's lead and trying to get a US working visa. Perhaps I could find a middle ground and live in Silicon Valley for a year, I reasoned, so that I'd still be available for my daughter after that year concluded. I didn't come to any decisions that night, but I enjoyed catching up with Phil and Lenny over drinks.

I wasn't especially looking forward to the Web 2.0 Expo that week. The schedule was uninspiring, and it was unlikely I'd discover any cool new startups on the trade-show floor, since the only startups that could afford it now were already well established and written about. I felt that the official Web 2.0 conferences had become too corporate, focusing less on startup innovation and more on the ever-increasing power of the big tech companies. Indeed, the very theme of the Web 2.0 Expo this year was the "Power of Platforms," which was being positioned as "Helping business choose and leverage the right Web platforms for success."

There was no doubt that platforms were in charge of Web 2.0 by this point. Facebook in social, Google in search, Amazon in cloud, Apple in smartphone apps, and a few other perennial contenders like Microsoft and Adobe—these were the companies bringing the web to the mass-consumer and enterprise markets. The latter was the audience that

O'Reilly Media and TechWeb targeted now for their Web 2.0 events. Whereas at RWW, we still prided ourselves on focusing on entrepreneurs and developers—indeed, this was our audience for the upcoming unconference.

Even so, we sometimes got caught in the crosshairs of internet culture going mainstream. In February our website had been hilariously mistaken for the Facebook login page by thousands of people. We'd published a post entitled "Facebook Wants to Be Your One True Login." It was a news analysis piece written by Mike Melanson about a partnership between Facebook and AOL. In typical RWW fashion, Mike had placed this news into the context of a broader, more important trend: Facebook's API being increasingly used as a login on third-party websites (such as AOL or RWW). The article was a compelling read for our core audience of techies, but it quickly began getting an unusual number of comments from what looked like ordinary, non-technical people.

Hundreds of comments poured in over the first day. "ok cool now can I get to facebook," wrote one of the first of them. "The new facebook sucks> NOW LET ME IN," wrote another "when can we log in?," "just want to get on facebook," "Just let me in please," "I WANT THE OLD FAFEBOOK BACK THIS SHIT IS WACK!!!!!"—on and on these types of comments rolled in.

At first, we were perplexed by this, until we realized that people were trying to log in to Facebook on our site! Like other blogs, we'd recently introduced the option of leaving a comment on RWW by using your Facebook ID to verify yourself. The people who were commenting on this post were doing just that, except they were expecting to be taken to their Facebook news feeds. Their comments were an expression of their confusion and frustration over finding themselves on a nerdy website with a red-and-white color scheme instead of the familiar Facebook blue and white.

In our Skype rooms, we discussed whether this might be a giant prank, perhaps perpetrated by a Digg or Reddit sub-community. But then we looked more closely at the source of all the traffic: it was coming from Google and via the search phrase *Facebook login*. We investigated more and discovered that a Google search result for that phrase put our article near the top (there were a couple of results above us, but neither was in English). The actual Facebook login page was further down the Google results page, below our article! People had gone to Google search, typed in *Facebook login*, and clicked the first English-language result they saw. We decided to add a message to our article, to let people know about the mix-up: "Dear visitors from Google. This site is not Facebook. This is a website called ReadWriteWeb that reports on news about Facebook and other Internet services. You can however click here and become a Fan of ReadWriteWeb on Facebook, to receive our updates and learn more about the Internet. To access Facebook right now, click here. For future reference, type 'facebook.com' into your browser address bar or enter 'facebook' into Google and click on the first result. We recommend that you then save Facebook as a bookmark in your browser."

While this situation was funny and even become a social media meme that week, it was also a reminder that the web was now very much mainstream—and that platforms like Facebook and Google needed to do better in their user experience design. Anyone could've made the same mistake that the thousands of commenters on our site had done. "Laugh all you want about ReadWriteWeb, but two weeks ago I watched a 35 year-old friend with a PhD go to Facebook by googling 'facebook login,'" wrote MetaFilter founder Matt Haughey on Twitter.

This was the web in a nutshell in 2010: still controlled by Silicon Valley geeks, but increasingly the scene of a vast cultural shift. It wasn't just bloggers writing to the web now—it was everybody.

The ReadWriteWeb Mobile Summit was held that Friday, once more at the beautiful Computer History Museum in Mountain View. I would be giving the keynote presentation for the event and had built a presentation around five key mobile trends for 2010, based on a three-part series of posts I'd written in April. I even used RWW's own iPhone app—admittedly, a very basic one that we'd commissioned from an independent developer and launched in January—and the mobile version of our website (m.readwriteweb.com) to demonstrate some of these trends.

One of the interesting things about that time on the internet was that most people still thought the mobile web—websites optimized for mobile browsers—would ultimately win out over iOS or Android native apps. I cited some statistics showing that there were 185,000 iPhone apps in the App Store and 27,000 apps in the Android store, but 326,000 "mobile touch web sites" worldwide. The trend seemed clear: mobile websites were the future. Facebook certainly believed this, as it was focusing most of its mobile development at this time on HTML5, a mobile-friendly version of the staple web-markup language. Even Apple CEO Steve Jobs was a big proponent of HTML5—the previous month he'd published a now-famous open letter declaring that Apple would stop supporting Flash on its mobile devices going forward and support HTML5 instead. (That letter effectively spelled the end of Flash.)

In my summit presentation, the example I chose to illustrate the benefits of browser-based mobile apps would turn out to be deeply ironic. It was an application called Burbn, which I noted was an "HTML5 location-based social network." The slide I'd made of Burbn was a last-minute addition to my presentation. Earlier that week, a mutual friend had connected Sean with one of Burbn's founders, Kevin Systrom. Sean invited Kevin to demo the product at our event, during our "speed-geeking session" after lunch. "I'd love to have you show Burbn off," Sean wrote, "especially given the number of people who have mentioned they are interested in discussing browser based versus native apps." Kevin enthusiastically agreed.

I had joined Burbn that very day, less than forty-eight hours before our event. I befriended a couple of familiar names in the social-web scene, Brady Forrest and Chris Messina, and began poking around. I liked the ability to add a photo to the location you were checking into (this wasn't possible at the time on the Foursquare iOS app), but otherwise Burbn didn't seem that remarkable. Still, it was a nice example of an HTML5 application, and so I duly added it to my presentation.

Within five months, Kevin and his partner, Mike Krieger, had turned that minor photo feature into its own product: Instagram. They ended up ditching the HTML5 Burbn product and instead released Instagram as an iOS-only smartphone app. By the end of 2010, Instagram had a million users—it was a textbook example of a well-executed startup pivot.

Of course, native apps won out over mobile browser apps in the end.

My presentation went smoothly, and indeed, the whole event was a success. I was busy the entire day with people coming up to tell me about their mobile projects, and it seemed like everyone else had been immersed in stimulating conversations too. In addition, we exceeded 100,000 views on Justin.tv, which had livestreamed the event.

It didn't all go to plan. We felt we were perhaps fifty people short of a full house, there had been some communication issues (I was particularly annoyed by a few glaring typos in the housekeeping email to attendees the night before—"Do not hesitate to come joint us"), and we could've done a better job before the event identifying specific experts to invite. These were things to work on before our next unconference, which was set for New York in just five weeks' time.

Ideally, we needed a community manager to focus on getting our readers to the NY event, but we hadn't filled Jolie's position yet. Elyssa was responsible for marketing, which included our events, and so it was technically part of her purview. Regardless, it was my job to make sure we pulled together as a management team to make New York a success.

This, of course, was complicated by my romantic relationship with Elyssa, which was becoming increasingly frayed. She was back in New Zealand, so we had a Skype conversation on Friday night, after the Mobile Summit and the post-event drinks at the Tied House. It had been a long day and I was exhausted, but still Elyssa wanted to talk about the same old personal issues between us—she wanted me to commit to her, make plans for moving in, and so on. We were going in circles on the call and I just wasn't in the mood for it, so eventually I hung up. The next morning I apologized, but I was not feeling good about how things were going between us.

I tried to refocus on business. I had another busy week ahead of me in New York. Sean and I would be scoping out the venue for our June event as well as attending Creative Week, which I knew little about, even though we'd committed to be a media partner.

On Saturday, May 8, I took a midafternoon flight from San Francisco to New York. The flight was due to arrive at JFK near midnight, so I'd booked an airport hotel—thinking I'd make the journey into Manhattan the following morning, when I was more refreshed.

However, my travel got off to a bad start with a delay at SFO. By the time we got to JFK, it was the early hours of Sunday morning. I had to wait around for a while for the hotel shuttle, along with several other travelers—the shuttles didn't come along as regularly at this hour. Eventually we got to the hotel, only to be told it was full. I protested that I'd booked and prepaid for a room (and it seemed others had done the same), but these pleas fell on deaf ears. I suspected the hotel had sold our rooms again when we hadn't arrived on time. Perhaps this was just how things were done in New York, but even so, it was a shitty thing for them to do.

We were all told to wait while they tried to find us alternative accommodation. My brain was fried beyond tiredness by this point. We stood to the side with our luggage and glumly watched the person at reception phoning around to other hotels. After a while, we were told to get back on the shuttle again; it deposited us at another faceless airport hotel, and I collapsed into a bed.

Throughout all of this, I had been messaging Elyssa about my travel woes. It was early evening NZ time, but she hadn't replied to any of my messages. This wasn't a good sign, but I didn't give it any more thought— I was too busy feeling sorry for myself about the hotel debacle.

The next morning, feeling not at all refreshed, I took a Yellow Cab into the suburb of Williamsburg in Brooklyn. Sean had booked an apartment via a new web service I hadn't yet heard of, Airbnb. We'd be paying $150 per night plus a service fee for a five-night stay, which was a bargain in New York.

The apartment we'd be staying at was one of a number in Brooklyn being advertised on Airbnb under the brand name Hotel Toshi Toshi. After arriving and picking up the key at an office around the corner, I discovered that we'd be staying in an old five-story redbrick building at 188 South Eighth Street. Sean had booked one of the two-bedroom units in the middle of this complex, which turned out to be a serviceable but run-down apartment. Since Sean wasn't turning up till the following day, I got to choose which bedroom I wanted. I took the one nearest the door and duly unpacked.

I didn't realize it at the time, but Hotel Toshi Toshi was rather controversial among the residents of Williamsburg—just the week before I arrived, there was a report in Brooklyn Paper (a local media website) with the headline "Neighbors Say Hotel Toshi Is a Horrorshow Hostel." The article didn't seem to be about the specific apartment building we were in, but it warned of "transient guests" throwing "rowdy late-night parties." Questions were also being raised in the media about the legality of the operation, which was a common theme with Airbnb in its early years. I wasn't aware of any of this, but on the first night I discovered that noise would indeed be a problem for the next five nights. I could hear people coming and going in the building all night, and I got hardly a wink of sleep for the second straight night.

When Sean arrived the next evening and saw my haggard face, he offered to swap rooms—perhaps the room farthest from the door would be slightly quieter, he suggested. But by then I'd worked out that all the walls throughout the apartment were paper-thin, so I doubted that. I told him I'd stick with my current room. "Well at least this place is saving RWW a lot of money," Sean said, giving me a concerned look. I could see that he was worried he'd let me down by hiring a dubious apartment in Brooklyn, but I assured him that it was fine and we'd survive for the next four nights.

One positive about the location was that it was an easy subway ride from Williamsburg into Manhattan. Over Sunday and Monday, which were days I had mostly to myself, I toured all the main art museums: the Met, MOMA, the Guggenheim. On Monday evening I attended New York University's annual Interactive Telecommunications Program (ITP) Spring Show. I'm not sure how I'd heard about this, since it wasn't part of Creative Week, but ITP was a graduate program at NYU and the show was a chance for students to showcase their interactive projects. I saw everything from *Matrix*-like interactive squiddies to a woman on stilts powered by an iPhone app to a paintbrush that made music. My favorite project of the evening, however, was called Current, which I described in my writeup as "a prototype meme tracker using data visualization."

Current was a classic Web 2.0 mashup: the data came from a combination of Google Trends and Google News. The mashup's creator was a young woman named Zoe Fraade-Blanar, and I invited her to participate in our real-time web event in June—I figured Current would be perfect for the speed-geeking session. This was the type of creative technology solution that I hoped to see more of in the wider culture, and that I wanted RWW to advocate for. Its reliance on Google to supply the data wasn't so much a concern back then. But, in hindsight, it should've been.

I think Sean was more excited to meet Fred Wilson than I was. As a wannabe VC himself, he was in awe of Fred and had tried (unsuccessfully) to interview him for the *ReadWriteTalk* podcast. I certainly knew about Fred and subscribed to his blog in Google Reader, but it felt like we lived in different neighborhoods of the blogosphere. We only rarely ran into each other, virtually speaking—one of us would comment on the other's blog occasionally, but that was it.

If I'd been one of the first professional tech bloggers, Fred had pioneered the art of VC blogging. He religiously blogged every day on AVC .com and had a loyal, business-focused audience who hung on his every word. He'd been an investor in Feedburner before it was sold to Google, but ironically he didn't use an RSS reader. In that respect, he was an unusual ambassador for the Read/WriteWeb, since he published to the web but didn't subscribe to other bloggers. I knew that RWW was on his blogroll, however, along with the likes of TechCrunch and Business Insider—so I guessed he probably visited our website every now and then to check the news. But I didn't get the sense that Fred knew much about me personally, as a fellow blogger.

I'd been introduced to Fred over email by (who else?) Alex Iskold, and we'd arranged to meet him in his Union Square Ventures office at 915 Broadway, between Twentieth and Twenty-First. By coincidence, Sean and I had bumped into him earlier that day in a Manhattan café. So when we entered his fourteenth-floor office at 3:00 p.m. on Tuesday, it was our second encounter.

Fred was about my height and had short dark brown hair, styled almost in a bowl cut. Despite the boyish hair, he was exactly ten years older than me and so was forty-eight when we met. He wore a sky-blue-striped shirt and black blazer over a pair of designer jeans. But the thing I remember most about him that day were his eyes, which were pale blue but had a penetrating look that I found psychologically intimidating. This effect was enhanced by the deep rings under his eyes, which suggested a businessman who worked long hours and didn't have time to suffer fools.

After we'd sat down, he immediately peppered me with questions about RWW. One reason for our meeting was to discuss the possibility of getting funded, but he quickly nixed that—he wasn't interested in investing in media, he said, as it wouldn't scale enough. I'd already heard that line from other investors, so it wasn't a surprise. Still, I was beginning to feel uncomfortable at all the questions about RWW and how we did business. It wasn't the usual, easy conversation I had with other bloggers—it felt more like I was interviewing for a job (and what's more, a job I couldn't get). My face was getting flushed under Fred's relentless gaze and rapid-fire questions, so I was grateful when Sean took over the explanation of our revenue model.

It was good to meet Fred, but I didn't come away from that meeting thinking I'd made a new friend. Most of the time when I met other bloggers, we'd make a lasting connection. But I doubted that Fred would even remember my name the next time we met.

Later that day, Sean and I had a somewhat more relaxing meeting with Kaliya Hamlin to discuss our upcoming unconference. We met at the Heartland Brewery in Union Square and had a good discussion about event logistics. Since this was our third event with Kaliya, there weren't any surprises and we trusted that she had everything covered.

As we talked about how our event would unfold, I supped my beer and gazed up at the brewhouse that was a part of the pub building. It was encased behind glass and apparently wasn't currently active, but you could see all the old brewing equipment. Suddenly, something caught my eye on one of the horizontal pipes near the top of the brewhouse. As I looked closer, I realized it was a massive brown rat. It scurried along the pipe and then disappeared again into the darkness. I looked at Sean, whose eyes were now the size of plates—he too had spotted the rat! Kaliya was unaware and was still talking about the unconference, so we had to interrupt her to tell her about our sighting. Just as well we didn't order food here, I joked.

By this point in the day, I was feeling tired and a bit homesick. I was also wondering if I still had a relationship with Elyssa. That morning, I'd bought her an iPad at the Manhattan Apple Store. The first iPad had only just been released in the States the month before, so it wasn't yet available in New Zealand. I forwarded her the email receipt, along with a winky message: "Does this mean you'll start talking to me again?" I wasn't holding out much hope for a positive response.

I eventually read her reply when I got back to our Airbnb. Her email made it clear that she was breaking up with me. In truth, I was somewhat relieved to be free of all the personal drama. But I was also sad that this had happened while I was traveling. I told Sean about the breakup, adding that I was sorry for the extra pressure the relationship had put on him—my mixing business with pleasure. He commiserated with me and said that he understood why Elyssa and I had connected in the first place. It must've been nice to find someone who understood what you do for a living, he suggested. I just nodded.

After another near-sleepless night in Brooklyn, Sean and I made our way back into Manhattan to attend Creative Week. The venue was a fourth-floor gallery called the Metropolitan Pavilion, which was located on 123 West Eighteenth Street. This building would be the headquarters of Internet Week in June, a New York tech festival that we'd timed our event to coincide with. Internet Week had only begun in 2008, but I'd been assured it was already popular.

Our event would be held in that same gallery, so today was a good chance for Sean and me to scope it out. What immediately stood out to me was how white and shiny everything was. The room itself was rectangular and L-shaped, so it didn't feel as spacious as the large-in-all-directions Computer History Museum room we'd had for our first two events. Multiple large pillars throughout seemed to further constrain the space. But, overall, it had a modern commercial feel, with its high-gloss epoxy resin floor, high ceilings, and exposed HVAC ducts. All of this was painted white—even the chairs.

The day seemed to fly by, despite the content not being to my taste—it was much more focused on marketing than on the arts. Sean and I helped moderate one of the sessions, about messaging etiquette for online marketers on social networks. In the other sessions, I sat back and took notes on how marketers were using the social-web tools that we wrote about every day on RWW. I learned that many of them followed blogs like ours in order to track trends; this was useful knowledge as we continued to broaden our audience beyond developers and entrepreneurs.

By this time—May 2010—the social web was well and truly entrenched in the culture. A recent Pew Research report had found that, for the first time, more than half of Americans now used a social network. There were also signs that Facebook and other platforms were starting to wield a bit too much power. Later in the month, Marshall posted that Facebook was rolling back some of the controversial changes it had been making to the site's privacy settings. Facebook had made public posting the default in December, but some of its users objected to certain bits of information no longer being private. So, in May, Facebook had been forced to backtrack a little. "Users are now allowed to hide their friends list and their list of interest pages from the public at large,"[67] Marshall reported. Privacy issues would continue to be a problem for Facebook in the coming years.

Despite these teething problems, at Creative Week I was interested to learn about how the social web was increasingly being used by marketers. Apparently they liked to "follow the thought leaders in various tools," so that they could get in on new trends at the "embryo of ideas." Another phrase I jotted down was "footprint of influence."

Looking back on it, this was a time when influencer culture was just beginning to blossom on the internet. What would turn out to be the key influencer platform, Instagram, had yet to be launched. But by that May, some bloggers and YouTube users were using these platforms to market products and starting to cross-pollinate their content across social media services like Facebook and Twitter. But blogs were still at the center of the social web at this time—even on YouTube, the emerging influencers were known as "vloggers." Nobody back then knew that social media would completely take over during the rest of the 2010s.

If I'd unknowingly gotten a taste of the *new* new media on Wednesday, the following day we got to visit the apex of old media: the headquarters of the *New York Times*. I'd arranged a meeting with Vindu Goel, the person mainly responsible for syndicating our blog on the technology section of the *New York Times* website. Vindu had invited several other *Times* employees to sit down with Sean and me, including the current deputy technology editors, Suzanne Spector and Kevin McKenna.

I still couldn't quite believe that the RWW logo was on display every day on the technology front page of the *New York Times* website. What's more, it was currently "above the fold"—the first of the three tech-blog logos to show, above both GigaOm and VentureBeat (you had to scroll down to see those two). The *Times* had its own technology "blog," Bits, and it was ably led by Nick Bilton, but it was still mostly business focused. You'd see stories about IBM earnings reports, smartphone patent lawsuits, Facebook privacy, iPad sales updates, and so on. They needed RWW and the other tech blogs for our focus on cutting-edge internet technology.

Also, this was about ten months before the *Times* instituted its paywall, so everything on its website—including the tech front page—was freely available to all web users. We were getting maximum exposure on the hallowed digital pages of the *New York Times*, not to mention the continued bragging rights of telling non-tech people, including my family and real-world friends, that my blog was syndicated on the *New York* Fucking *Times*!

The New York Times Building was relatively new, having only opened in November 2007. It was a fifty-two-story skyscraper at 620 Eighth Avenue, between Fortieth and Forty-First Streets, and was then the fourth-tallest building in New York , behind the Empire State Building, Bank of America Tower, and Chrysler Building. The building certainly was impressive on the outside, with a curtain wall consisting of 186,000 ceramic rods and a giant *New York Times* logo stenciled in black over the top. Inside, the structure had an "inner wall" of floor-to-ceiling glass and a large lobby looking out onto an unlikely garden of fifty-foot-tall birch trees.

The *Times* occupied the first twenty-eight floors of the building. After Vindu came down to meet us in the lobby, he took us on a quick tour of the newsroom on the bottom three floors. This large, open-plan, multifloor room was surprisingly quiet. It was around noon, and what few staff were on the main floor were either tapping away silently on their computers or having hushed conversations in small groupings. The immense hubbub usually depicted in newsrooms on television shows or in the movies was not evident here. In fact, many of the staff I observed seemed oblivious to their coworkers.

We then took the elevator up to one of the anonymous floors above, and this felt more like a typical office area—rows of cubicles amid a bland decor dominated by greys, whites, and browns. We met the others in a small, windowless meeting room and we began talking about what types of stories they preferred from RWW. They liked smart analysis posts, the deputy editors told me (check!), but they were particularly looking for enterprise and business topics (er, okay). I was a little disappointed to hear that, since the Bits blog seemed to cover business topics sufficiently well. The value of syndicating RWW, I thought, was that we gave a glimpse into the next big thing on the consumer internet.

As the meeting went on, it became clear that I was from a different world to these well-mannered, grey-haired editors. They weren't necessarily interested in the next hot startup; instead they wanted "smart, advice-y" articles on topics like "what Windows 7 means for the enterprise." Stifling a yawn, I promised to send more posts from our ReadWriteEnterprise channel.

I realized then that this is why blogs like mine had broken through in the mainstream-media ecosystem—we were at the cutting edge of emerging internet culture, getting our hands dirty on the streets of the open web. Traditional mainstream media were still stuck in their skyscraper offices, apparently not even venturing down to their newsroom that much anymore. We were the leaders in internet culture; they were the followers. The only thing that gave me pause in this admittedly self-serving analysis was the gleaming curtain-wall exterior of the building. It proved that this company had the resources to throw at tech news—if it wanted to. I wondered how long it would be before they stopped syndicating small upstart blogs like ours and did everything in-house instead.

The following day I began the long journey back to New Zealand. I would be back in New York in less than a month, so I didn't have a lot of time to settle into my newly single life. But I already had a plan that I wanted to implement: buy a house and reestablish a home base for myself. I was still renting my small, shabby townhouse ("the hovel"), but I'd flagged to Sean that I would soon be making a capital withdrawal from the company bank accounts, which would allow me to put a deposit down on a proper house. It would become RWW's new international headquarters, I joked.

CHAPTER 16

SERENDIPITY

■ ■ ■ ■ ■

IT WAS ANOTHER LATE ARRIVAL coming into New York—near midnight on Sunday, June 6—but this time I had booked a hotel in Manhattan. It was a fifteen-minute walk from the Metropolitan Pavilion, our Real-Time Web Summit venue. That would be on Friday, but I'd arrived early to participate in events attached to New York's Internet Week.

The first event I planned to go to was the CM Summit, run by our advertising partners FM Publishing. The *CM* stood for "conversational marketing," which wasn't a subject of great interest to me. But both Sean and I would be attending as a favor to FM—and who knows, maybe we'd make some good contacts. Sean was due to arrive in New York at dawn on Monday and would be going straight to the event, but due to my late arrival I'd told him not to expect me until the afternoon.

In the end, I got only a few hours of restless sleep and woke up at 5:00 a.m. I had low blood sugar, which was a regular problem when traveling because of my type 1 diabetes. This was another thing I kept putting off due to work—finding a better way to manage the condition. I would eventually discover and commit to the low-carb diet, but that revelation was still a few years away. For now, severely jet-lagged and not wanting to get up to find a breakfast diner that was open early, I solved the low blood sugar with a muesli bar and a mini Toblerone.

Then I opened an F. Scott Fitzgerald book I'd brought with me—*Tender Is the Night*—and read for a while, hoping I'd eventually fall back asleep. But there was too much buzzing through my mind.

My personal life was going through another transformation—for the first time in my life, I was dating. I'd never done that as a teenager, due to my crippling shyness, and I'd had limited dating experience prior to my marriage. So it was a novel and often enjoyable experience. The only problem was, I was having trouble finding women I connected with in New Zealand—none of the people I met showed any interest in my business. So, despite arranging various first and second dates, I constantly felt lonely. It was something of a conundrum: I was a loner by nature, but I also didn't trust myself to be happy when alone.

When I arrived at the CM Summit, I ran into Dick Costolo, the Feedburner founder who was now COO at Twitter (within a few months, he'd be appointed CEO). I had always enjoyed talking to Dick, and from day one at Feedburner, he'd gone above and beyond trying to keep early adopters like me happy. When my blog was still relatively young, during the first half of 2005, he would email me back on support queries even when it was late at night his time. I hoped he would bring the same passion for customer satisfaction to Twitter. RWW was writing a lot of stories about Twitter, and there were ominous rumblings in the tech industry about the restrictions Twitter was starting to put on its developer platform. But if anyone would listen to the needs of early adopters and developers, I reasoned, it was Dick.

My first few days in New York were full of interesting one-on-one conversations like that. However, while I was enjoying the Internet Week events and schmoozing in the evenings, I was really struggling to get to sleep at night. I bought a bottle of NyQuil on Wednesday, which finally brought me some relief. You couldn't buy over-the-counter drugs like that in New Zealand.

Early afternoon on Thursday, I took a cab to the studio of ABC News Radio, up on West End Avenue, between Sixty-Fifth and Sixty-Sixth. A young journalist named Dan Patterson had reached out to me via Twitter and then email, requesting an interview. The plan was for Dan to record our radio interview on video and then upload to Vimeo, so that it could be integrated into the ABC News Radio website. This was years before podcasters began doing video as par for the course. But podcasting itself wasn't much of a thing in 2010—radio was still king, when it came to audio content. So I was intrigued by what Dan was doing.

I found myself surprisingly relaxed during the interview. Perhaps it was watching Dan do his radio voice in person, which both amused and impressed me, but I was confident and happy throughout the conversation. In his intro, Dan said that we'd be "talking the Semantic Web, real-time analysis, and the inevitable zombie apocalypse." I smiled and joked that I certainly felt like a zombie, after my long trip from New Zealand.

After I explained why the real-time web was an important trend, Dan perceptively brought up some of its issues. "Isn't there the danger that we become isolated in bubbles and in only what's interesting to us?"

What Dan was touching on was starting to be a regular talking point among the tech intelligentsia. The term *filter bubble* would eventually be coined for this, by the activist and author Eli Pariser, but that was still a year away.

Social media was still a relatively new phenomenon in the mainstream, so I felt the need to defend it that day. Also, *bubble* was a loaded word in the tech world—it also referred to markets, especially when it came to internet companies. So after Dan mentioned that word, it became lodged in my jet-lagged brain and I unwittingly used it twice in my extended answer. I noted that relevant information "bubbles up in your stream" on Facebook, thanks to your friends, adding that your location at any one time can provide you with real-time information that is useful to you.

"I travel quite a lot at the moment," I said, "and everywhere I go, there are new types of information that I wouldn't have found out if it weren't for Twitter or Facebook, or some of these other real-time streams of information. Wherever I am at one particular time, I find out about certain things that I wouldn't have found out about before, but they're actually relevant to me because I'm at that place at that time. So I think there's a lot of serendipity to the real-time web."

In conclusion, I said, "It all bubbles together."

Perhaps it was the success of RWW at that time as a niche media business, but I did feel like a lot of serendipity came my way online. I only wished I had more of it in my offline life, which was increasingly feeling like the opposite of a market bubble. But there was still time on this trip to meet new people—I'd also be visiting San Francisco and, for the first time, Portland.

For now, though, I was nervous and excited for tomorrow's RWW event.

We'd been a bit worried about ticket numbers in the days leading up to the RWW Real-Time Web Summit. The venue was relatively small, so we'd be able to fit 150 to 175 people in. But as of Tuesday we'd only registered 121 people—and the majority of those were freebies. It was looking like we'd make a loss on the event, but I was more concerned with having enough people there on Friday to make it a vibrant, busy day. After all, there was less incentive for people to turn up if they hadn't paid for their tickets.

However, as we kicked off proceedings on Friday morning, the large, rectangular room felt full and there was an excited buzz in the air. I gave a sigh of relief. As at our first unconference, Marshall was doing the keynote. This was his main topic of interest, and he also wanted to show off some of the real-time news-gathering tools that he and our news team used every day. So I was able to sit back and relax while he delivered his presentation.

Afterward, Kaliya facilitated the discussion that set the agenda for the day, and once again, the paper schedule quickly filled out. Everyone in the room chatted enthusiastically about the topics they'd jotted down with colored markers: "enterprise micro-blogging," "real-time curation," "real time where" (location), "privacy and identity," and so on. The topics ranged from broad ("collective knowledge") to specifically technical ("HTML5 WebSocket").

The morning sessions whizzed by, and the speed-geeking session after lunch was popular. Attendance dropped in the afternoon, but we were running our event on a sunny summer Friday, at the end of a long

Internet Week for many. However, we kept plenty of bums on seats until the final wrap-up session—no doubt helped by the fact that one of our sponsors, Alcatel-Lucent, was giving away six iPads. Redg Snodgrass and Mike Maney were the two Alcatel-Lucent reps (the company was a long-running sponsor and we knew both guys well), and they'd come up with a fun concept to give away the last two iPads: a rap contest.

To my surprise, one of the raps was a serenade to me. A tall, bearded guy with slicked-back dark hair got up and delivered his rap: "Richard's a real-time junkie / He swings through the web like a monkey / Never missing a beat / Of the word on the street / That's what makes him the blogger most hunky."

Not everyone liked the rap contest—one attendee compared it to a sleepaway camp activity—but most attendees appreciated the light touch at the end, and it was a nice segue into the post-event reception.

Everyone I talked to seemed to enjoy the event. One of our regular readers, Liz Pullen, later wrote a comment on our wrap-up post: "Coming at the end of a long, tiring Internet Week NY, I thought about skipping it but am so glad I came. It reenergized me and the meaningful conversations I had over the day made it well worth my time."[68] It was comments like that made the day worthwhile, overall, and it had been another boost for our brand.

However, I also knew that ticket sales had been lower than expected. Just how low, I wouldn't discover until after the weekend.

On Monday morning, at a New York café, Sean delivered the bad news to Marshall and me: we'd lost $25,000 on the event, a figure that surprised and disappointed me. A big reason for the loss was that we'd only sold $8,000 in tickets, which was 50 percent down on the previous event (and a further 50 percent down on the first event).

In addition to lack of event revenue, we were also struggling to sell our premium reports that year. So we'd have to make some tough decisions about reprioritizing RWW business for the rest of 2010. We first decided to put aside events for the time being and refocus on core RWW editorial in Q3. We also decided to only do further premium reports if we had a presigned sponsor (in other words, guaranteed revenue).

Finally, we made the decision to let go our marketing person, Elyssa, whose quarterly goals had been primarily tied to event ticket sales and report sales.

This, needless to say, was awkward for me. But the following day, I delivered a carefully worded email to Elyssa back in New Zealand. She took it well and, in the ensuing back-and-forth, I agreed to a four-week notice. I felt bad about the situation, but I knew that as a business we had to knuckle down on what we did best: writing blog posts and selling CPM adverts and sponsorships.

As a management team, we understood that we'd need to get momentum at some point, in either events or reports, in order to keep expanding the business. So we hadn't entirely dismissed the possibility of another event, perhaps even as soon as Q4. But for now, it was back to basics.

After the management meeting, I was ready to start winding down for a day or two on the business side. Mentally, I began preparing for the next day's trip to Portland. It'd be my first time in a city where almost half of our staff lived, so I was looking forward to experiencing the famous "keep it weird" vibe of that town. I'd also be meeting a few RWWers in person for the first time. But I still had a couple of informal meetings here in New York, with the web designer Jeffrey Zeldman today and paidContent founder Rafat Ali tomorrow. Plus, there was a social event that evening that I thought might give me a taste of New York's famed social life.

Serendipity NYC was a regular meetup run by Jen Nedeau, a twenty-something PR woman who worked for *Time* magazine's digital division. The RWW team often received pitches from Jen in our email inboxes, and I'd gotten to know her better during my previous trip to New York. On that occasion we'd met up for drinks at the Bowery Poetry Club in Manhattan's East Village. It was an eventful evening because I ended up leaving my laptop behind at the Bowery and only realizing it a couple of hours later, as a taxi was about to drop me off at my Airbnb in Brooklyn. So I'd had to ask the taxi driver to turn round, go back over the Brooklyn bridge and eventually back to the Bowery Poetry Club, where—miracu-lously—my laptop bag was sitting right where I'd left it!

Jen's Serendipity NYC event was being held at Bunny Chow, a South African restaurant and bar in the Lower East Side. The 2010 World Cup was happening in South Africa, so a match would be playing in the background on TV. I didn't know much about the type of people who would attend, but I assumed they'd be young professionals like Jen. She'd told me it had a business networking focus and, as the name *Serendipity* suggested, was promoted as a chance to meet folks outside your normal work context. I'd not experienced this type of social event in New Zealand, so I was looking forward to it—in my usual anxious way when it came to socializing.

The Lower East Side turned out to be a hipster area of Manhat-tan—a lot of young, trendy-looking people walking about—so it felt both alien and intriguing to me. After I gave my name at the entrance of Bunny Chow, I was directed to choose from several sheets of little circle stickers on the welcome desk. On the stickers were printed vari-ous occupations and people descriptors—I chose *geek* and *writer*, along with a sticker with *Serendipity NYC* written in a curlicue font.

The bar itself was small and very hot inside. After some awkward and humid schmoozing with people I didn't know and didn't seem to have much in common with, I met one of Jen's colleagues in the tech PR industry, a young woman who worked for a local startup. At first, I was just grateful to be talking tech again with someone, but I soon realized we had other interests in common too—music, literature, and more.

Given the muggy heat inside the bar, the woman and I ended up sit-ting on the curb outside and chatting. I told her about my tumblelog, Velvets Fan, where I posted cultural content—what I was listening to or reading, artworks I came across in my travels, and so on. She also blogged, it turned out, and so we talked about that, along with her business ambitions in the tech industry. She told me a little about her lifestyle as a twentysomething single woman in New York City. I was suitably envious—not of her, but of the lifestyle. She wasn't complimen-tary about the single men in the city, so it probably wasn't as glamorous a life as I thought. Nevertheless, I told her I wanted to live in America one day and that meeting people over here seemed so much easier than in New Zealand.

As the Serendipity event began wrapping up, I swapped emails with my new friend and said I hoped to keep in touch. I then took a taxi back to my hotel.

All too soon, I began to feel lonely and mopey. I browsed my emails, checked the RWW Skype rooms, and cast my eye over RWW's pageview stats for the day. Then I looked up the blog of the woman I'd met that night. I decided to email her, on the pretext that I wanted to give her the address of my tumblelog. There were several posts about F. Scott Fitzgerald on there at the time, and in her reply about twenty-five minutes later, she mentioned that she was a big Fitzgerald fan. Her favorite novel of his was *Tender Is the Night*, the one I was currently reading. What serendipity! I wrote back immediately and said I was currently reading through all his novels. Well, we know where to start the conversation if you ever came back to NYC, she replied.

I didn't know when that might be, though, given that RWW wouldn't be holding any further events out here in the foreseeable future, and I wasn't shopping RWW to an East Coast publisher. I was also leaving New York the next day, so I wouldn't have a chance to meet up with her again on this trip.

I sighed deeply, closed my laptop and took a gulp of NyQuil. Before I nodded off, I opened my red Moleskine journal and stuck in the three stickers I'd collected earlier that night: geek, writer, Serendipity NYC. At least I accepted who I was at this stage in my life—a geek writer. As for any further serendipity, I could only leave that up to chance.

For my stay in Portland, I had chosen the boutique Hotel Monaco. It was around the same price as the midrange hotels I typically chose on or near Geary Street in San Francisco, but in Portland you could get more class for your money. I arrived on Tuesday evening and didn't emerge outdoors again until the following morning.

I met up with Marshall and a couple of other RWWers on Wednesday afternoon, in order to plan my itinerary. Thursday was my chance to meet our production editor, Abraham Hyatt, for the first time. Marshall would be there too, so essentially it would be an editorial management meeting. Then, on Friday, we'd invite the whole Portland-based team to do a full coworking day at a local café chain called Urban Grind.

Later in the evening, after dinner with Marshall and his wife, Mikalina, at an Ethiopian restaurant in Richmond, I went back into town and wandered the famous Portland bookstore, Powell's. This was heaven to me—browsing a bookstore was one time when I was more than happy being alone. There was something beautifully distracting about walking around shelves of books, especially in a huge place like Powell's, where you could almost get lost. I snapped a photo of a book entitled *The Price Was High: Fifty Uncollected Stories by F. Scott Fitzgerald*. It obviously made me think of a couple of nights ago in New York.

The next day, I met up with Abraham at a café called Clyde Common. Marshall was running late, so it was just the two of us for a bit. Abraham turned out to be a tall guy with close-cropped dark hair, small round earrings in both ears, and a kind but inscrutable face. His right arm had a prominent dark blue tattoo from the sleeve down, but it had no design—it was as if half his arm had been painted over. He was wearing a plain white T-shirt and blue jeans, and I got the impression this was his daily uniform. The overall effect was of someone who'd had an interesting past but didn't particularly want to tell you about it.

Abraham was a friendly and attentive guy, though, so we quickly gelled. Which was good because we had some staffing issues to discuss that day. A couple of our writers were underperforming, and we'd need to decide what to do about that. But a more pressing issue had come up earlier that day regarding Curt Hopkins, a relatively new, older writer based in nearby Eugene.

We'd hired Curt at the end of March, but it had soon become obvious he was better at writing what I labeled "cultural" posts. For instance, he had an ongoing series called "Online Week in Tyranny" that discussed how the social web was being used cynically by certain countries. The content was compelling, although it wasn't the tech news I'd hired him to write. Nevertheless, I appreciated that Curt gave a more critical perspective about technology than our usual consumer-internet fare.

With this in mind, I'd emailed Curt that morning to suggest that we move him away from the news beat and onto a new "cultural" beat—with the same quantity of posts per day and same pay, so there would be no changes there. We'd be hiring another freelancer to take over the news role, I told him. He responded positively to my suggested role change, but added, "Why hire additional people when there are people who would like to go full-time?" I replied that this is something I'd address in the Friday team meetup.

We were already negotiating with Frederic to bring him on full-time, but we were waiting on him to tell us his decision. Frederic was based in Portland but was out of town that week, so unfortunately, I wouldn't get to see him. In any case, I was planning on telling our Portland crew that we were open to bringing on more writers full-time, but that it would be a slow process for a variety of reasons—including our budget after the event loss and the low premium report sales.

Soon after this brief email exchange with Curt about the role change, he sent me a much longer Google Doc that outlined his thoughts on RWW's direction. I hadn't asked for this document, so it came as a surprise. I hadn't had time to fully absorb it before my meeting with Abraham and Marshall, but I noticed that it listed a number of grievances. Among other things, Curt claimed there was "little in the way of reference material relating to policy and process" in the company and an "absence of clear guidance and expectations" from leadership. He complained about the coeditor role that Marshall and I shared, as an example of leadership issues, and said that the writers were not paid enough. There were also some odd strategic suggestions, such as "rethink the channels—fold them into the main page."

When Marshall arrived at the café, we began discussing Curt's screed. As I reread it with them, I found my anger rising. This was a highly presumptuous document from someone who had worked for us for less than three months, and I vehemently disagreed with a lot of his points. I knew that our writing and editorial guidelines were better than those of many of our blog competitors (we'd been told this by some of our own writers who had previously worked for other blogs).

The coeditor concept was something I'd borrowed from TechCrunch, since Mike Arrington had appointed Erick Schonfeld his coeditor in 2007 and I later thought a similar setup made sense for RWW. The pay criticism was fair, but what we paid our writers was the same as all the other leading tech blogs—and higher than rates at many pro blogs. Of course, there were things we could be doing better, but we were a small, fast-growing, international and *virtual* media company—not a local town newspaper with an office downtown and decades-old policies and procedures.

I'd already run Curt's document past Sean, who had told me it lacked context. He wondered if this was a roundabout way to ask for a full-time job with benefits. Back at the café, Marshall, Abraham, and I agreed that I should talk to Curt separately tomorrow. He would be coming to our coworking meetup, which would include an editorial meeting.

By the evening, however, I was pretty worked up about Curt's document. I didn't want to be told how to run my business, just as I didn't want people telling me how to run my life—which had been, at core, my issue with Elyssa. Perhaps equating this situation to a recent personal relationship breakup was overly sensitive. Nevertheless, I couldn't resist continuing the back-and-forth with Curt by email. I wrote, rather unkindly, that his document had made me question if he was suitable for the professional blogging business. "Hopefully tomorrow we can give you the guidance and expectations that you're looking for, but if you're still unhappy after tomorrow I suggest we part ways ASAP."

He replied just as angrily, and the situation was in danger of spiraling out of control. But thanks to some sage counseling from Marshall and Sean, I de-escalated matters by promising Curt we'd talk about it in person tomorrow. Perhaps Marshall had also reached out privately to Curt (he'd known him for longer than I had), because Curt quickly calmed down too. "I am mortified by the 'drama,'" he wrote, several emails in. "I was merely trying to contribute, however pear-shaped the results were." He offered to not come to the team gathering tomorrow, but I assured him I wanted him there. "Let's you and I discuss, just the two of us," I wrote. "I like your writing and I want you to continue, so I'm sure we can work it out."

Team RWW's coworking day had been scheduled at the Urban Grind café in northeast Portland. It was a chain with multiple locations, but Abraham had specified it was "not the one downtown" and that the "eastside location will be quieter." He'd arranged a private room for us, which was located down the hall to the left of the cashier.

The room was spacious, with mostly cinnamon-brown walls (one wall was bright red) and high windows that you couldn't look out of. The brown walls were dotted with abstract paintings, while the red one had a single large painting depicting a giant red mushroom set against an azure-blue sky. The weirdest thing about the room though was the table: a thick, silver, oval-shaped surface that hung from the ceiling by four hefty silver chains. As we all sat down and took out our laptops, the table gently swayed. A few of us looked warily up at the high ceiling, afraid the whole thing would crash down on us.

Soon we had a quorum of RWWers around the table. I sat next to Alex Williams, and on the other side of Alex was Deane Rimerman, a freelance researcher. On my left was Justin Houk, a government agency worker who was interning with us, and on the other side of the table were Marshall, Abraham, and Audrey Watters. Like Curt, Audrey had started toward the end of March. She was probably about my age but had spent almost her entire career so far in the academic field—most recently studying toward a comparative literature PhD. She was similar to Frederic in that regard, and like him, Audrey had quickly adapted to the blogging world.

Tyler Gillies, our "in-house hacker" as Abraham dubbed him, arrived soon after. My antagonist, Curt, was the last to arrive. He'd had to make a two-hour bus trip from Eugene, so he got in around lunchtime. It was awkward at first. He was a thickset guy in his mid-forties, with a greying goatee, thinning hair, and a pair of large tortoiseshell glasses. He had an aggrieved look in his eyes, but I suspected that was the case most of the time. I could sense we were both on edge, so I suggested we go to the main café and have a chat. Marshall gave me a wry smile and an encouraging pat on the back as Curt and I exited the room.

Over coffee, I began to see a different side to Curt. He was a poet, I discovered, and like me was an English literature graduate. I soon realized that his gruff exterior hid a sensitive soul, and so my attitude toward him began to soften. I told him I appreciated the type of writing he did for us, which analyzed the impact of web technology from an ethical and societal point of view—Marshall did some of that type of writing too, but Curt had doubled down on it. I also explained the situation with our budget and the many practical issues I had running a virtual company from New Zealand. So eventually we understood each other better.

The Curt drama and resolution was a valuable lesson for me. It was only when I sat down with him that we began to grok each other's perspective. It proved the value of regularly seeing your colleagues "in real life," so I resolved to make the effort to meet with RWWers in person as much as possible going forward. It was hard running a business virtually, especially from a tiny country across the world, so it also reinforced that having a US base for the business would be best long-term. I still didn't know how I'd achieve that—would I raise money here in the States or try to sell the business again? Once more, I filed away that question.

Later in the afternoon, the team made our way to the Green Dragon bar for Beer & Blog, a weekly meetup for the Portland startup community. The turnout was excellent, and I enjoyed meeting a variety of Portland bloggers and techies. One of them was Rick Turoczy, who ran a local tech blog called Silicon Florist, a reference to Rick's focus on covering startups from the "Silicon Forest"—Portland and the surrounding Oregon area. Rick had written for RWW for several months at the end of 2008, so he was a familiar name to me, but this was our first in-person meeting.

I also met Amber Case, a rising star in the Web 2.0 ecosystem. She was in her early twenties at this time and fashioned herself as a "cyborg anthropologist." Like me, she had been invited to O'Reilly Media's Foo Camp in Sebastopol, California, the following Friday—an annual schmooze fest I'd wanted to attend for a while but had never quite made it. I hadn't worked out how I'd get to Sebastopol, though, which was about an hour's drive from San Francisco. Amber said she'd been offered a lift by local entrepreneur Nate DiNiro, who was also at Beer & Blog that night. She introduced me to Nate, who said he was happy to drive us both. It was this type of in-person connection that made traveling in the States so worthwhile.

As my Portland visit neared an end, Marshall and Mikalina hosted a Team RWW dinner at their house on Saturday. I told everyone that I'd enjoyed my time in Portland and had found it to be an easygoing, cool city. I half-jokingly said it was a bit too hippie for me to want to live there, but I wanted to visit again soon.

Over the course of my week in San Francisco, I had a few dinners or drinks with women I knew in the industry. This was the good part of being single while traveling in the United States! On the work front, I attended the SemTech conference for the second year running. However, the most interesting event I went to that week was at Singularity University (SU), located at the NASA Ames Research Park near Mountain View.

I was taken to SU by a Canadian woman named Shawna Pandya, whom I'd had coffee with earlier that week. She worked for a startup called CiviGuard and was a recent graduate of SU. Shawna was a classic overachiever, well on her way to becoming both a doctor and an astronaut. So I was curious to know what SU was all about and what attracted people like her to it.

SU had begun in 2009 as a nonprofit organization; it was the brainchild of Ray Kurzweil and Peter Diamandis, both scientists and authors who had developed reputations in the tech industry as forward-looking but slightly wacky proponents of artificial intelligence. Kurzweil was known for his belief that AI would overtake human intelligence by 2045 and that humans would eventually merge with machines and become immortal. His two most recent books reflected these views: *The Singularity Is Near* and *Transcend: Nine Steps to Living Well Forever*.

The stated goal of SU was to teach students to "think exponentially" in order to solve "humanity's grand challenges."[69] The fee for the graduate course Shawna had done was $25,000, for ten weeks of study. There was also a nine-day, $15,000 "executive" course. Overall, I was skeptical. The philosophy that Kurzweil and Diamandis were peddling was dubious, especially since AI at that time was very far from being a viable form of computer science. And the quest for immortality just seemed like a pipe dream for aging white men.

Then again, if Shawna was any indication of the quality of students coming through the graduate program, then perhaps my gut instinct was wrong. She told me she was going to be a teaching fellow at SU this year, in medicine and neuroscience. It was all part of her ultimate plan to travel into space, she added.

The speakers that day included Kurzweil, Diamandis, NASA astronaut Dan Barry, and the cartoonishly named Dr. Larry Brilliant, a former director of Google.org, the search company's philanthropic arm. Larry Page, the cofounder of Google (a key sponsor of SU), briefly came onto the stage as well. "If I was a student, this is where I'd want to be," he remarked.

As the day wore on, I had to admit that I was impressed by the sheer wattage of intelligence onstage and sitting around me. I also, somewhat enviously, noted on Twitter that Kurzweil "got mobbed by a group of beautiful, smart women" after his speech.

It was an interesting day out, but years later I discovered that my initial instinct about SU had been correct. A 2018 investigation by Bloomberg News reported on alleged sexual and financial indiscretions. By that point, SU was a for-profit corporation—focused less on the graduate program and more on moneymaking conferences and executive education.

On the other hand, the state of AI technology is now vastly better than it was in 2010—so perhaps Kurzweil and Diamandis will get the last laugh. It's too early to say as I write this, although it's notable that the key advancements in AI over the past decade have come from graduates of traditional computer science universities—Stanford, Berkeley, and MIT—rather than from SU.

It had been a fun week of socializing in San Francisco, but I had one more event to look forward to before getting on a plane back home: Foo Camp.

Nate picked me up from my downtown hotel on Friday afternoon. We then picked up Amber at her friend's place somewhere in the suburbs of San Francisco and began the one-hour drive north to Sebastopol on the 101.

If SU was a new Silicon Valley institution that wanted a fast-track to legendary status in 2010, then Foo Camp was already an industry legend. *Foo* stood for "Friends of O'Reilly," and it was the ultimate insider gathering; you only went if you got an invitation from the man himself. It was an unconference, but also—as it said on the tin—it would be a camping trip, too. Nate was bringing along a tent that was big enough for him, me, and one other person. Amber would find some female bunkmates and do the same thing.

I wasn't entirely sure about the camping part—I'd never been an outdoor person, despite living in New Zealand—but I had wanted to attend a Foo Camp for several years. The first Foo Camp took place in 2003, and I had received my first invitation in 2006, but I hadn't been able to attend until this year.

We arrived at the O'Reilly campus around 5:30 p.m. The day was still hot and the sky blue and clear, so it felt like we were arriving for summer camp. The main O'Reilly office was a large, nondescript brown building, which we all filed into. In the emails leading up to the event, we'd been told there were some vacant office rooms available for bunking down—"on a carpeted floor"—but that most of us would have to pitch tents in the field out back. Nate and I soon made our way out to the field, which apparently used to be an apple orchard, and set up the tent on the rocky, uneven ground.

We then went back to the gathering area in the backyard of the office building. By this time most of the 250 or so attendees had arrived and were milling around, chatting and drinking beer from plastic cups. I saw a bunch of people I knew—Mike Arrington (who told me he wasn't camping and instead had booked a nearby hotel), Robert Scoble, Scott Beale, Brady Forrest, Tom Coates, Kevin Marks, Dave McClure, and others. As usual with tech events at that time, most of the attendees were men, and most were white, too.

To my surprise, there were also a bunch of kiwis at the event. One was, of course, Nat Torkington, the O'Reilly employee from New Zealand I'd met on my first trip to the States in 2005. He also ran a kiwi Foo

Camp, which I hadn't yet been to. Also present were Courtney Johnston (a Wellington blogger in her early thirties who worked in the cultural industries), Roger Dennis (a likable tech consultant from Christchurch), and Rowan Simpson (cofounder of New Zealand's eBay, Trade Me). And those were just the ones I knew!

Unlike me, my kiwi compatriots weren't shy about contributing to the group conversations that were a big part of Foo Camp. In truth, it was jarring to constantly hear the kiwi twang throughout the weekend—I was used to being the only New Zealander at these US events, other than occasionally running into Nat.

I enjoyed the first evening and got to meet some fascinating new people. I was most thrilled to meet Kevin Kelly for the first time. Kelly was in his late fifties and was one of the founding editors of *Wired* magazine. He'd written several books that I admired, although my current favorite wouldn't be released until a few months later. Entitled *What Technology Wants*, its theme was that technology is a force of nature—Kelly called it "the technium." I came away from our discussion filled with an almost spiritual sense of optimism about technological progress. Then I filled up my beer cup again and went to a session called "Why Minecraft is the new Lego & making some guy in Sweden $300,000/day."

Later that evening, a bunch of the campers organized a game called *Werewolf*. I'd not heard of it before, but most of the others were very enthusiastic about it, so I hung out on the periphery of the group to learn more. It was a card game that also went by the name *Mafia* and involved "lynching" and "villagers." Since I'd never been a fan of roleplaying games, I just couldn't wrap my head around it and so didn't participate. Also, by this point I was already experiencing what Scott Berkun (another attendee) later called "social fatigue."

Although I enjoyed unconference events, I was always grateful for the chance to unwind at the end of the day. After eight or so hours of nonstop socializing, I needed alone time to recharge my batteries— a classic introvert pattern of behavior. The problem with Foo Camp, though, was that the socializing continued into the night. I realized now why Mike had booked a hotel room (he'd once told me that he, too, was an introvert).

While the incomprehensible game roared on, I slipped away into the night and headed back to the tent. It was nearly midnight by this time, so I was tired. But I already knew I wouldn't be getting any sleep in the hubbub surrounding me, a feeling that was only exacerbated by the backbreakingly uneven turf beneath the tent. I tossed and turned for what seemed like hours.

By the end of Foo Camp on Sunday, I was wiped out from lack of sleep and completely drained introvert batteries. Another attendee that year, Michael Nelson, wrote after the event that "getting an invitation to Foo Camp is a pretty big deal, and you're reminded several times throughout the weekend that a return invitation depends on the quality of your contribution to Foo Camp."[70] As I traveled back to San Francisco that day with Nate and Amber, I realized that I probably wouldn't get invited back. I had spoken only rarely during the unconference sessions, and the socializing in between was almost excruciating to me by the end of the event.

My flight back to New Zealand was at 9:00 p.m. that Sunday. It had been a long trip—New York and our third conference, Portland and hanging out with the RWW team, a whirl of dinners and drinks in San Francisco, and the geek camping that had finally exhausted me. I was looking forward to getting back home, even though I'd be returning to winter and my small, rented hovel. My plan was to begin my search for a proper house to buy in Wellington and spend some much-needed time with my daughter.

CHAPTER 17

SPEARMINT GREEN

■ ■ ■ ■ ■

IN JULY WE FINALLY BEGAN the process of advertising the community manager role. We wanted someone who was an active user of social media tools and who had experience managing online communities. Ideally, we were looking for someone based in Silicon Valley, but since we'd had trouble getting writers who met that criterion, we figured that might be the case for the CM role too.

I wrote a post on RWW stating that we were looking for a new community manager. This got a great response, garnering more than a hundred applicants. I narrowed it down to ten and then to a shortlist of four. A couple of them were based in the Seattle area, one in Chicago, and the other in New Jersey—we went none for four on the Silicon Valley ask. Nevertheless, I proceeded to the interview stage confident we'd be able to hire someone decent.

The applicant from New Jersey, Seamus Condron, was our early favorite—purely based on his résumé and email pitch. He'd been community manager at the media publication Mediabistro for over three years and was currently consulting for Hearst Digital Media. By comparison, the three other shortlisted applicants either lacked experience in a CM role or hadn't worked in media. Seamus seemed to cover both bases.

Our main concern was his salary expectation, which was reasonable but still beyond what we'd budgeted for. Sean noted, "Our budget is razor thin at the moment" and suggested that if we chose Seamus, we might have to start him half-time in the role.

Part of the reason for our tight budget was that we'd had money set aside for the past two months for Frederic to come on as a full-time writer. However, we still hadn't gotten a decision from him about it. I'd first made the offer to Frederic in the last week of May. Initially he wanted to discuss it with his wife, who was traveling at the time, and he promised to give me an answer by the end of the month. But that date came and went without a decision. I followed up in early June, but this time Frederic said he was busy with his PhD dissertation. I didn't want to push further, as for some reason he seemed to be getting stressed out by my emails, so I put the matter to one side.

But it was now late July and we still didn't have an answer from Frederic. So I made the decision to use the portion of the budget we'd set aside for him to make the CM role a full-time one. "We still want to bring you on full-time," I assured Frederic, "but we understand that getting over those final hurdles for your PhD is your top priority at this stage. Likewise, we have to prioritize what is best for the business and right now we need to allocate budget to the new CM role."

Sean, Marshall, and I did a video call with Seamus over Skype. He appeared to be in his late twenties and was a heavyset guy with glasses. He'd obviously done his homework, because he gave us all the right answers. In my notes from the call, I jotted down that he was "passionate about media in general" and "big on human interaction and engagement when it comes to community management." The only thing we could nitpick was that he didn't use Digg, which was one of the social networks that drove the most traffic to RWW. But compared to the other candidates around his age or younger, and given our budget, Seamus seemed like the best bet. So we offered him the job and he accepted.

When Seamus started with us, in August 2010, social media was already an integral part of a professional blog business. It was also approaching a tipping point in mainstream culture. Facebook had just passed five hundred million active users in July, so it was already incredibly popular (my mum joined Facebook that very month, and Dad followed in August). Also, although we didn't know it then, Mark Zuckerberg and Facebook were about to be immortalized in the culture with the Hollywood film *The Social Network*, which would be released in September.

The mainstreaming of Twitter was more complicated. In September I wrote about Twitter's redesign of its home page. I noted that the new Twitter.com was designed to make it easier for non-tech people to consume content on Twitter. "You don't have to tweet," then Twitter CEO Evan Williams said at a press gathering, "any more than you have to make a webpage to use the Web."[71] A fair statement, but my mum and dad would not be visiting Twitter any time soon (as far as I know, they still haven't).

It wasn't just normal people who were struggling to understand Twitter, though. How to separate the professional from the personal on Twitter was a big topic of discussion among the tech community that year. One line of thinking was that Twitter would follow the same pattern as blogs, going from personal to professional. After all, that's what happened with RWW, TechCrunch, Mashable, GigaOm, and all the other top tech blogs. But others thought Twitter should always be personal, since it was a conversational medium.

Part of the confusion was that Twitter was fast encroaching onto blogger territory; it was becoming a viable publishing medium in its own right. I did an interview in January with Darren Rowse of ProBlogger in which we discussed this phenomenon. Darren said he'd noticed "a change in the environment," whereby people were increasingly sharing links on Twitter rather than on blogs. I concurred, saying that I'd noticed more people linking to our stories using Twitter rather than by providing a trackback link from their blogs—a big change from when I'd first started blogging in 2003. But I also said it had widened our audience, too. "It has brought a lot more people into the 'write' aspect of the Read/WriteWeb," I noted, "because they're able to contribute to the web without having their own blogs."

How to use Twitter was a hot topic internally, as well. Some of my team thought the @rww Twitter account should be more "professional," while others wanted me to keep it personal. Early in the year, one of our readers had written in to complain about my photo being used as the avatar for @rww. I admitted that I had been thinking about reverting to the RWW yin-yang logo, which I'd used when I first joined Twitter in 2007. One RWWer pointed out that people liked faces and that "logos are not personal." Marshall, who was probably the most effective Twitter user of all of us, thought that RWW was a "news brand" now and so it would look more professional to use our logo. "Faces are good for marketing or customer service, but I think people are subscribing to a news publisher in @rww," he said.

One of the team suggested I use a separate Twitter account for personal stuff. In fact, I had already started a new account (@ricmacnz) in January with that in mind, but I hadn't fully committed to the idea of running two separate accounts. It almost felt schizophrenic—RWW was such a big part of my identity now, so why would I want to divide my online persona into two?

The decision on how our company should use Twitter was complicated by the fact that I had a huge audience on @rww. According to the *NZ Herald*, I passed the one million mark in Twitter followers on Sunday, January 3, 2010. This apparently made me the 207th most popular person on Twitter, "with more followers than Kevin Rudd, Ben Stiller, Snoop Dogg and Yoko Ono, to name a few."[72] I was far and away the top kiwi on Twitter—our prime minister at the time, John Key, only had 7,522 followers. I'd been interviewed for this piece but had tried to downplay the milestone because I knew that most of those followers were via Twitter's SUL.

The hiring of our new community manager in August 2010 finally forced my hand—I decided then to turn over the @rww account to Seamus. The name of the account changed accordingly, from my own to "ReadWriteWeb."

It was, in retrospect, a terrible decision. Over the coming decade, social media would explode in popularity. Other tech bloggers of my vintage used their large Twitter followings to boost their public profiles over the twenty-teens. I was the odd one out, having given up my SUL privileges in 2010. It also meant that several of my writers ended up with accounts more popular than mine—Marshall, Sarah, Frederic, and others. I completely failed to foresee how important Twitter—and indeed, all social media—would become to personal branding.

But that was all in the future. In August 2010 all I was concerned about was how to increase page views to RWW via social channels. That month, we went over 5 million page views for the first time—over 2.5 million of which were unique visitors. This was helped by a big month on Digg. Both Google search and our Feedburner RSS feeds dwarfed social referrers at this time, but generally our best traffic months were dictated by the swings and spikes in social referrers.

Traffic from Digg, in particular, was wildly inconsistent. We'd gotten over 133,000 page views from it in August, but just 20,000 the month before. As it turned out, August was as good as it would ever get again from Digg—it had launched a controversial redesign at the end of August that saw its power users revolt and its popularity as a tech-news aggregator plummet. By the end of the year we were getting more traffic from Digg's competitors, Reddit and Hacker News.

Digg's troubles were exacerbated by the increasing power of Facebook and Twitter as social platforms for publishers like RWW. For the rest of the year, both social networks drove more monthly traffic to RWW than Digg. Indeed, by the end of 2010, Twitter was our top social referrer overall, followed closely by Facebook.

The underrated social referrer for us was StumbleUpon, the rather mysterious app that mimicked the "I'm Feeling Lucky" button on Google's search front page. Most commonly used as a browser extension on computers, StumbleUpon let you enter a topic and then took you to random related websites. The algorithm was a complete black box to publishers, so there was no gaming of StumbleUpon (unlike Digg). We never knew which of our articles would strike it lucky, but enough of them did that StumbleUpon was one of our top social referrers. However, it too was inconsistent, and there was a noticeable drop in the second half of 2010, especially compared to Facebook, Twitter, and other new forms of social media.

When Seamus took over the @rww Twitter account in August, he also assumed control of our Facebook Page, which had been mostly automated up till that point. We had just under 25,000 Page likes at the end of August, which grew to around 32,000 by the end of the year. Our main competitors were now GigaOm, VentureBeat, and a relatively new European site called The Next Web. We had more Facebook fans than each of them, but we were all a tier below Mashable (370,000) and TechCrunch (120,000) on the social media front.

In December, RWW named Facebook our Best BigCo of 2010. By then, most of my own family used it daily and it was an ever-more-important method for RWW to communicate with our fans via our Page. Facebook was also now the default method for sharing web articles. According to the link-sharing service AddThis, Facebook was selected 44 percent of the time by its users when sharing an article (up from 33 percent the year before). Email was a distant second.

For all these reasons, social media was increasingly important to us—it drove page views, and it increasingly drove online community too.

Throughout 2010 we released a few more channels: ReadWriteCloud to cover cloud computing, ReadWriteBiz for small-medium business owners, and ReadWriteHack for developers. ReadWriteEnterprise (for large business) and ReadWriteStart (for entrepreneurs) continued as well. The channels were my domain as coeditor, while Marshall looked after the news operation.

We had a solid roster of writers and editors for the channels. Alex Williams managed Enterprise and Cloud, Audrey Watters was doing Start, John Paul Titlow was on Biz (we'd hired him in June, when that channel began), and Klint Finley was covering the Hack channel, which had launched at the end of August.

Our sixth channel would be ReadWriteMobile. With the Apple App Store an increasingly popular part of the internet ecosystem, and Android beginning to make inroads too, there was a lot of demand for mobile content. While we covered this anyway as part of our consumer-focused content on the main site, we'd been discussing a specialist mobile channel with FM Publishing since February. FM had relationships with several major US mobile-phone vendors, so they were confident of providing a well-paying sponsor.

The initial sponsor FM had in mind didn't come through, but by July they were dangling Alcatel-Lucent as a potential exclusive sponsor. We were pleased to hear this, as Alcatel-Lucent had been a sponsor of our recent New York event and we had a good relationship with their point man, Mike Maney.

We pitched ReadWriteMobile as a channel "dedicated to helping its community understand the strategic business and technical implications of developing mobile applications." This template had been successful on some of our other channels: being a resource and guide for a specific audience, rather than covering news or product reviews. By the end of August we had the sign-off to launch Mobile. It would require seven posts per week, one of which had to be a poll.

Now my attention turned to finding a writer for it. There was one obvious candidate: our current star performer for the main site, Sarah Perez. In her Twitter bio she'd written that she was "obsessed with mobile"—the proof of that, I thought, was that she was just as passionate about covering the up-and-coming Android as she was writing about the more mainstream iPhone. Sarah was writing ten posts per week on RWW, so the additional seven for the new channel would allow us to bring her on full-time. At this point she was still doing blogging work for Microsoft as well.

I emailed Sarah near the end of August to make the proposal. She was enthusiastic in her reply but wanted a bit more money than we'd offered—and she also requested a small equity stake in RWW. Sarah wasn't the first to broach equity; Frederic had also asked about it when we were discussing his coming on board full-time earlier in the year. It wasn't as if we couldn't come up with an equity structure for the writers, even though we were an NZ company. After all, both Sean and Marshall had small equity stakes already. But this would mean diluting the equity stakes of the current shareholders.

I discussed it with Sean over email. He suggested that we could set up an option pool and allocate options to key staff members from that pool. However, he also hinted that he didn't want his own equity stake to be diluted. "I took a significant pay cut to take this job and have not entertained any incoming emails from recruiters over the last six months," he wrote. "This is primarily because I really enjoy this job and place a high value on honoring commitments, but also because I hope the equity makes the salary closer to competitive in the long term."

The implication was clear. If I was to give Sarah and our other full-timers an equity stake—because it would be unfair to offer it to Sarah and not to our five other full-time people—it would have to come from my own personal stake. Unfortunately, I was still trying to negotiate a financial settlement with my ex-wife (and had been for well over a year). I was reluctant to dilute the equity from my stake because I would almost certainly have to bear the cost of it by myself—my ex-wife's lawyer would see to that. I wasn't willing to entertain the thought of my ex ending up with a larger stake in RWW than I held.

This was all part of a larger issue I'd been grappling with for some time now: how to incentivize our full-time staff, given the restrictions inherent in our company structure. The problem remained that RWW was an NZ company and not a US one. Due to double taxation and other legal complications, we couldn't hire our people as full-time employees, which meant we couldn't offer health insurance and all the other benefits that our US-based competitors could. Over the past several years, I had spent a lot of money on lawyers and accountants—from both New Zealand and America—trying to come up with a legal structure that would fix this. But the answer was always the same: since I didn't live in the States, I couldn't create a Delaware corporation like most startups did. We were stuck in a no-man's-land of having all our full-time people on a rolling independent-contractor deal. It was deeply unsatisfactory, to both me and my staff, but I couldn't seem to find a way out of this muddle.

I went back to Sarah with an increased pay offer but told her we couldn't give her equity at this time. She was happy about the pay raise, though, and promptly accepted our offer. We were thrilled to bring her on board full-time, as she had consistently been our highest-performing writer all year—she was even getting higher page views than myself and Marshall.

We launched ReadWriteMobile near the end of September. With that sorted, I was able to turn my attention back to the Frederic situation. He was posting regularly on RWW again, although he wasn't among our top performers by page views. But I'd recently noticed he had launched his own tech blog, NewsGrange. This site included a section called Aggregator with the words "our competitors" listed beneath it on the menu. Sure enough, at the top of that page was our RSS feed. So he'd started a tech blog to compete with RWW? I was confused about this, but Marshall thought it was just another side blog project—which I agreed was common in our industry (I often had a side blog on the go myself).

Of course, since Frederic wasn't yet full-time with RWW, he could do what he wanted from a side-project point of view. I wasn't concerned about that. What did bug me, though, was that he wasn't replying to my emails—including when I once again reached out about a full-time role in November. We now had budget for two more full-time hires, and I still wanted to offer one of these roles to Frederic, given how long he'd been with us and his obvious talent as a tech blogger.

After November 19, things got even stranger. Frederic abruptly stopped posting on RWW, and I didn't know why. I found out later that he had taken some holiday time and traveled to the Le Web conference in Paris, which ran December 8 to 9 that year. He posted a few articles from there but still wasn't communicating with me. He didn't post again after Le Web and ignored all our emails about a year-end post he'd been assigned (we reassigned it to Sarah).

As all this was going on, Marshall floated the idea of hiring Mike Melanson for one of the available full-time roles. "Frederic has long been drifting slowly away," he wrote to me in early December, "and Mike has been working hard to be a full-time member of the team."

So we ended up hiring Mike and Audrey Watters to full-time writer roles. Eventually, Frederic sent the email he'd probably been sitting on for a month or two, subject line: "time to say goodbye." It was a polite email, and we all understood that he wanted to move on to new adventures. However, he did bring up the lack of equity for full-time people as one of his reasons for leaving.

Marshall informed the team, noting, "Frederic has been with us longer than anyone but Richard (obviously), myself and Sarah." It was true: he had been with us for two and a half years, so it was sad to lose him. I also didn't like seeing a writer we had developed in-house walk out the door, possibly into the arms of one of our competitors, rather than take the next step with us.

Naturally, I wondered if things would've turned out different with Frederic had RWW been a US company. I was now starting to worry about our ability to hang on to key writing talent.

In July, as I was trying to make progress on a number of troublesome fronts—including filling in paperwork for a US working visa and filing court papers for my divorce—I received an invitation out of the blue from Gary Shapiro, the leader of the Consumer Electronics Association (CEA). He was inviting me to serve as a judge at their third annual i-stage competition, which would be held on October 18 at the Fairmont Hotel in San Francisco.

I'd not heard of i-stage before, and I also hadn't been to the CEA's better-known Consumer Electronics Show convention, which ran every January in Las Vegas. As far as I could tell, i-stage was a clone of the DEMO conference or (more recently) TechCrunch Disrupt. "Finalists receive three minutes to pitch an audience of technology leaders, investors, press, and you, the judges, all eager to help them break out as the next big thing," Shapiro said in his email.

I decided to accept the invitation, as it would be something a bit different from usual. I-stage was scheduled just a month before the Web 2.0 Summit; initially I planned to attend both events, but soon I decided to skip the summit. I had a long history with the conference, but the Web 2.0 Expo earlier that year had left me a bit cold. Also, I was in discussions with a Chinese event called Global Internet of Things Technology Conference. If I really wanted a change of scene, a trip to Beijing in late November, followed by another IoT event in Japan the week after, would certainly achieve it.

However, by the time I flew out for the i-stage event, the Asia excursion wasn't happening anymore. Partly this was because I didn't want to add a Chinese visa application to my long list of paperwork, but also I had good reason to spend the last couple of months of 2010 at home. I'd been putting off house-hunting for months now, due to a mixture of travel and trying to sort out my messy personal life. But it was time to finally focus on buying a house, so that no matter what 2011 would throw at me, I'd at least have a secure home base for myself and my daughter.

The Fairmont Hotel turned out to be a grand old-fashioned hotel at the top of San Francisco's Nob Hill. But right from the start, my trip felt off. Partly it was the location—I was used to being near Union Square or Market Street, where I always enjoyed walking in the evenings. I quickly discovered that I preferred my usual rickety hotels on or near Geary Street, for the comfort of being able to freely wander. But also, the event itself didn't feel quite right. The CEA attracted a different crowd than the Web 2.0 conferences—it was more formal and businesslike and less developer-focused.

I knew one of the other judges, Frank Gruber—a blogger from Chicago who I usually saw at the Web 2.0 events. He was about my age and ran a series of small mixer events called Tech Cocktail. It was good to catch up, but apart from Frank I didn't see many other people I knew at i-stage.

As for the competing startups, they were all peddling consumer electronic devices—as you'd expect, I suppose, from a CES-related startup contest. The runner-up was something called the nPower PEG, described as "a small, lightweight device that recharges your hand-held electronic devices from the kinetic energy you generate while walking, running, or biking." The winner was a car appliance called AutoBot, which allowed you to control aspects of your car with your smartphone; "It's encouraging to see advanced Web technology starting to be deployed in cars" was all the enthusiasm I could summon in my RWW writeup dated October 27, 2010.

In truth, none of what I saw at i-stage inspired me as much as some of the Web 2.0 events I'd been to—and there was certainly no "next big thing." Perhaps I should've just gone to the Web 2.0 Summit after all, I reflected.

The highlight of my latest Silicon Valley trip was a journey down the 101 to Palo Alto to visit PARC—the Palo Alto Research Center, formerly known as Xerox PARC. The visit had been organized by Sonal Chokshi, who had originally emailed me in late August about attending PARC's fortieth anniversary celebration event in September. While I couldn't attend that, I was grateful to her for organizing this tour of PARC—to take in the history of the place—and a few meetings to see what the present-day PARC was working on.

In 2002 PARC had been turned from a division of Xerox into a wholly owned subsidiary company. It was basically a research-for-hire firm, trading on its illustrious reputation from the 1970s. It had become famous in its first decade for inventing a host of technologies that led to the internet age—including the Alto personal computer, the graphical user interface (GUI, famously appropriated by Apple and Microsoft in the early eighties), object-oriented programming (via the Smalltalk programming language), Ethernet, and laser printing.

I took the Caltrain to the California Avenue station and then a taxi to the PARC complex. It was a low, largely concrete complex with green shrubs growing all around its roof ledges. It was mid-autumn, so the greenery was tinged with red and yellow. The colors meshed nicely with the interior decor, which was the usual brown-and-beige color scheme you expected from a 1970s office complex.

Sonal came down to greet me at reception. A friendly and smart Indian American woman, a couple of years younger than me, she had been in charge of content and community at PARC for nearly six years now. We had lunch in the PARC cafeteria and then she took me on a personal tour of PARC's in-house museum. As I wandered the exhibits, Sonal encouraged me to take some photos. I self-consciously posed in front of the first Ethernet cable and then the ParcPad—an early nineties forerunner of the iPad—while Sonal snapped a few tourist pics with my iPhone.

Sonal had organized a few meetings with current PARC projects to fill out my visit. One was with Bo Begole, a computer scientist in his forties who managed the "ubiquitous computing" division—when anything and everything is connected to a computer network. "Ubicomp" was a close cousin of IoT, a concept I'd been writing a lot about over the past year. Begole excitedly showed me a location-based mobile app his team had developed, Magitti, which he said was currently in commercial trials in Japan. Before I could ask, he quickly added that it went further than popular Web 2.0 apps like Foursquare and Gowalla. As well as using GPS data to figure out where you are, he explained, Magitti computes a user's preferences and context, then makes recommendations of nearby places to go based on your personal data.

There was no doubt that what Begole showed me was ahead of the curve. "At PARC, we have a natural language parsing technology and we've got image content analysis," he said, a full decade and more before such technology was commercialized in the form of ChatGPT, Stable Diffusion, and other modern AI apps. However, Magitti was destined to fade into obscurity after its brief flurry of fortieth-anniversary-related write-ups in such publications as *Fortune* and *The Register*. Instead of Magitti taking over the world, Foursquare adopted the same ideas and commercialized them. History may not repeat exactly, but it certainly rhymes in Silicon Valley.

Foursquare was just starting to ramp up—earlier that very month, I'd called it "one of the trendiest apps of 2010."[73] Within a few years it became the dominant Silicon Valley location tool. I don't know if Foursquare took any direct inspiration from Magitti, but nowadays it is better known as an AI-powered data platform for apps like Uber. In other words, it does what PARC demoed to me back in 2010—but on a much grander scale. It took me several more years to fully absorb this lesson about Silicon Valley: that ultimately, it didn't matter where innovation was born, what mattered was which VC-backed startup commercialized it to a mainstream user base.

As I walked out of the PARC complex later that afternoon, I chatted with Sonal and thanked her for her hospitality. I could see the taxi I'd ordered waiting for me out front, but just as we were walking out into the sunshine again, it began to drive off. Perhaps it had been waiting there for a while, I don't know. In any case, I quickly excused myself and ran after the taxi, waving my hands frantically. The driver must've noticed me in his rearview mirror, because he stopped a hundred meters or so down the asphalt drive.

When I reached the car, huffing a little, I looked back at Sonal and gave her a wry smile. Clearly, ubiquitous computing hadn't yet reached the taxi industry. But we both knew it probably would eventually.

As soon as I got home, I focused my attention on house-hunting. In early November I found the house I wanted: a three-bedroom bay villa in Petone. It was a corner house and originally built in the 1890s, although of course it had been renovated multiple times since then. Still, it retained much of the charm of an old New Zealand villa. The house was near the Petone foreshore and a ten-minute walk from the local shops, which included a bunch of cafés—so the location was ideal, especially considering that my daughter went to a nearby school.

The exterior of the house was painted spearmint green with pink trim, which the real estate agent told me (after I'd bought it) was off-putting to other potential bidders. But I loved it—to me, the house felt vibrant and arty. The interior was an explosion of colors too: orange, mauve, royal blue, sea green, lemon yellow, and more. I discovered later that the color scheme was inspired by La Boca, a poor but brightly colored neighborhood of Buenos Aires.

The character of the house was further enhanced, to my mind, by an old stone fence that surrounded its front half. It had been painted in the 1980s by Tony Fomison, an "outsider artist" from New Zealand with whom I quickly identified after a bit of research. Much of his fence work was now faded after many years of salt air and sunshine, but embedded in the abstract yellow and red oval shapes he'd drawn were the faint words *many islands one sea, dancing,* and *music.* I didn't know the full story behind this, but I later read that Fomison had an interest in Māori rock drawings, which bore some resemblance to the curved shapes on the fence.

By the end of November I had confirmed the purchase—I'd be moving in early January! Since I was already renting in Petone, I'd come to love the area and was thrilled to have a permanent home base there. I was also looking forward to working from my new home office, which was at the front-right of the house, facing a wide street. It was a spacious, sunny room, so I hoped it would be a nice change of scene for me heading into 2011.

Things were looking sunny and optimistic on the business front too. In December RWW had its best-ever traffic month. We hit 5.6 million page views, with about 3 million of those being unique visitors. Despite losing Frederic at the end of that month, we had a talented and hardworking crew of writers. Five of them were now full-time with RWW: Sarah, Alex, Audrey, Klint, and Mike. So we were in a great place.

By the end of 2010 we'd also decided to unpause our events calendar. We began planning another New York event for Q2 2011, which would be our biggest yet. We already had a location; Sean had recently visited Columbia University, which had offered us an event space. With the location confirmed, along with the renewed confidence in our business from our December page-view numbers, we decided to get ambitious with the event format. Our goal was to create a hybrid event—a mix of unconference and traditional programmed conference. We would run it across two days, making it our first multiday event. To complete the grand vision, we made the theme of the event "The future of the Web."

As I usually did at this time of year, I created a Google Doc that outlined our business goals for the coming year. One of these goals was to sell the company by Q1 or Q2 of 2012. Both Sean and Marshall were on board with this. I knew that Sean, in particular, wanted to work toward an acquisition—having a successful exit for RWW would be a nice thing to add to his résumé, given his personal ambition to become a VC. I didn't know Marshall's true feelings on the subject, but he was as focused on growing our business as Sean and I were—and acquisitions in the tech-media business were commonly viewed as a logical end point.

As for me, I still thought scaling RWW would be easier under US ownership, given all the legal and accounting hassles I'd been dealing with in recent years. I also thought, perhaps naively, that selling RWW would finally put an end to the divorce saga and give me a form of freedom that I didn't yet have.

Before the year was out, there was one more surprise—but a much less pleasant one. In mid-December I went to see my doctor about a piercing pain on my left side, near my groin. It was a Thursday and I'd had a terrible night's sleep. I'd woken up in the early hours, clutching my side, then crawled to the toilet and fell unconscious next to it. My doctor informed me that it was a hernia and I'd need to go to the hospital straight away. I ended up being booked in for surgery on Monday.

So, rather than a triumphant end of the year, I spent Christmas week getting hernia surgery and recovering, very gingerly.

I had a quiet New Year's Eve, alone in my shabby rented cottage in Petone. I didn't have a girlfriend at this time, and anyway I'd always struggled with New Year's Eve—I'd had a couple of awful drunken experiences on it when I was young. So I was feeling pensive and still smarting a bit from my hernia wound.

For all that, I felt cautiously optimistic about what 2011 might bring. Sure, there might be more bumps along the road for me and for RWW, but I was up for continuing the ride.

CHAPTER 18

WRITER REVOLT

■ ■ ■ ■ ■

DURING THE FIRST COUPLE OF MONTHS OF 2011, Sean was busy renegotiating our revenue deal with FM Publishing. In early March he delivered the new contract to me for my signature.

Sean had done well. Although FM would continue to take a decent slab of the revenue they brought in, we still had leverage because FM had lost some of our main competitors in tech blogging over the past year. TechCrunch and GigaOm had struck out on their own, and there were rumblings that Mashable might soon follow suit. On the other hand, we had looked into FM's competitors and found them wanting—so FM was still in a strong position as well. Overall, I was happy with what Sean had negotiated. Our revenue had basically doubled over the last year, and we were now making a healthy profit every month. With the new FM deal, revenue looked like it would continue trending upward.

That said, the revenue targets in the agreement were contingent on continuing growth in traffic—and that was becoming a concern by March. Our page views dipped slightly after the stellar December, but even more worrying, there were signs of unrest among the writing staff. Ever since Frederic had walked at the end of last year, I'd been conscious that our inability to offer full-time employment (and all the benefits that accrued with it) was a major weakness in our business structure.

On March 9, just as I was about to board a flight to SXSW in Austin, Abraham emailed Marshall and me about his concerns about some of the writers. "Right now there are multiple writers actively looking for other jobs," he wrote. "I don't think I'm exaggerating when I say that we are in the middle of significant crisis, one that will lead to us losing some of our top page-view generators within the next couple of weeks." According to Abraham, some writers on the main site were feeling "disorganized and confused."

Although he didn't name names, I had a fair idea who Abraham was referring to. Recently Marshall had raised concerns to me about the attitudes of Klint and Mike—it was clear he was struggling to work with both. I'd also seen an email discussion between Marshall and Audrey that had turned fractious. An even bigger concern for me was how all this back-and-forth—some of which played out on the group chat in Skype—was impacting Sarah. She was the one I really didn't want to lose. Not only was she one of our top traffic drivers, but her articles were exactly what I wanted for RWW—cutting-edge, analytical, and passionate. I would see both Sarah and Mike at SXSW, so I made a mental note to talk to them one-on-one about the issues Abraham had raised.

Abraham had made some good suggestions to address the overriding issues, which basically amounted to putting more formal newsroom processes into our operation. He noted that he would be able to help implement this, as he'd had experience as a managing editor or section editor at other newsrooms.

Later that day, he and Marshall met up in Portland to discuss the situation, after which Marshall came back to me with some suggested editorial improvements that he wanted to implement immediately. I asked him to hold off for now, as I wanted to review the business operations with him and Sean while we were in Austin. I also wanted to talk to the writers first, to get their side of the story.

I arrived in Austin on Thursday, March 10. This year we had myself, Marshall, Sean, Sarah, Mike, Seamus, and Jared traveling to SXSW on the company dime (Alex and Tyler were also going, but they'd made separate arrangements). It would be my first time meeting both Sarah and Seamus, and I hoped to get to know them better during the trip. We arranged to all meet up at midday on Friday. Typically for a group email thread, we couldn't decide on a location, but we decided to use a group messaging app called Beluga to coordinate on the day.

Since the beginning of the year, group messaging had been lining up to be the breakout activity at SXSW, just as tweeting and "checking in" had been for previous SXSW events. Mike had profiled Beluga a few weeks ago, explaining that you create a "pod" of people (Beluga's name for a group), and each time one of you sends a message, everyone else gets it. Nowadays we associate this type of functionality with Whats-App, which was on the market then but was seen as less of an online product and more about SMS.

By the time we'd all arrived in Austin, however, Facebook had acquired Beluga. This put something of a dampener on the group messaging hype—Twitter (in 2007) and Foursquare (in 2009) had broken out at SXSW partly because they were scrappy underdogs. It was another sign that the big tech companies were starting to dominate the internet. Certainly it augured badly for startup innovation that small companies such as Beluga were being acquired and assimilated before they'd even had a breakout moment. In any case, the RWW team still used Beluga for that Friday meetup.

Sean's travel plans were disrupted, so the first chance for everyone to gather in one place was Friday evening, when we hosted a dinner at Stubb's Bar-B-Q for a small gathering of friends and sponsors.

Seamus had organized the dinner. When I met him that evening, I was a little surprised that he was shy and not that talkative. He was a heavyset guy with greasy black hair and thick glasses. He even seemed a bit morose. I didn't want to be too judgmental; it was just that his personality didn't match my idea of what a community manager in a social-web business should be. He was the opposite of our previous CM, the outgoing and vibrant character that was Jolie (although at least we actually saw Seamus at SXSW).

I'd met Sarah earlier in the day; it turned out she had a bubbly personality that matched her daily enthusiasm for tech. She was short, with shoulder-length straight blonde hair, and she seemed to be enjoying her first time at SXSW. She'd told me she had a full plate of interviews and parties on her calendar. "Welcome to the hustle and bustle of SXSW," I said, like an old hand—even though this was just my second event. We made a plan to catch up sometime when we both had a gap in our schedules (easier said than done), to discuss the editorial issues that Abraham had brought up.

As the sponsors began coming into Stubb's, Sean—who had arrived just in time for the dinner—led the way with glad-handing and small talk. Marshall and Mikalina arrived too, and then the rest of the team (other than Alex, who wouldn't arrive until the next day) joined us for a barbecue meal. It wasn't a big, loud party like the one Mashable was throwing, but our team, friends, and sponsors seemed to appreciate the chance to relax and chat about tech for a couple of hours before the chaos fully kicked in.

Sure enough, the first several days of SXSW were a whir of panels and parties (mostly the latter), but in between Sean, Marshall, and I made the effort to sit down a few times and discuss the business. First and foremost, we needed to address the editorial issues. I hadn't yet spoken to Sarah or Mike, but we all agreed there needed to be more structure in our fast-growing editorial team. We decided to enhance Abraham's role and have him facilitate the daily schedule and liaise directly with the writers. Curt would take over some of the copyediting role that Abraham had previously been doing. This would all free up Marshall to find stories for the team and, just as crucially, write more himself.

It wasn't just scaling our news operation that was a problem. I was having trouble juggling channels and feature content editing amid my CEO duties, so we made the decision to hire a dedicated channels editor—in particular, to further grow our business channels. Enterprise-focused content wasn't something I was passionate about, and we really needed a lift in the performance for those channels. We also wanted to move Alex Williams into a more community-focused role, as the sponsors loved him and he enjoyed networking with the enterprise IT community. So, to complement that, we figured we'd try and hire an old-school editor from one of the traditional IT publications—someone from ZDE or TechWeb circles.

Meanwhile, I would focus on what we called "evergreen" content—analysis posts that would stand the test of time, feature stories about long-term trends, and resource-style content (how-tos, and so on). I'd be working with Sarah to further that plan.

On the business operations side, we resolved to add a salesperson to the team to help Sean in his primary role of growing revenue. Seamus was managing our upcoming New York event, and Sean reiterated that it was especially important to make the event a financial success. We'd just announced it that very week on RWW, so it was too early to say how ticket sales would go. But we were a bit nervous, mainly because Seamus didn't strike us as being a dynamic salesman. Still, we had to give him a chance and support him in promoting the event.

Sometime after the management meetings, I met with Sarah to talk about the editorial issues. She was pleased to hear that Abraham would be moving into a more hands-on role in the news team, and she seemed enthused by her proposed role helping me with the evergreen content plan. While she had some critiques of both Marshall and me, especially regarding story allocation and daily communication, she offered them in a constructive manner. Overall, she was positive and promised to lend her support to the editorial changes.

My meeting with Mike Melanson wasn't quite so straightforward. We met up in the hallways of the main conference center on the afternoon of Tuesday, the day before I was to head out of Austin. In fact, it was my last scheduled meeting of the event. Mike was a talented writer and one of our best performers, but I'd also come to realize that he was an extremely sensitive character who often adopted a defensive posture in his online communications. He was a stocky guy with fair hair and a beard—and usually good-humored in person, in my limited experience seeing him. But on this afternoon, his face was red and he had a strange mix of anxiety and anger in his eyes. He clearly had something he wanted to tell me.

I asked him for his thoughts on our editorial systems and he immediately sounded off. He thought his story assignments from Marshall were inconsistent, and he questioned the content guidance the writers were being given by both Marshall and me. He seemed most perturbed, however, by the RSS system for covering news that Marshall had built. He complained that it felt like he was chained to his desk all day, watching RSS feeds roll by. He reminded me that he was currently living in San Francisco, the world's leading tech city, so he should be out doing original reporting and making contacts.

I told Mike about the proposed editorial staff changes and that I'd take his other concerns on board. I assured him he was a valued member of our writing team and that I personally enjoyed his stories—for example, he'd introduced us all to Beluga, which had been a useful tool through that SXSW. I said I'd do my best to make RWW a happy home for him.

After the meeting with Mike, I began to feel increasingly anxious about the situation with the writers. I was insecure about our ability to keep people like Mike, Audrey, and Klint happy. Part of me felt they all complained too much, and perhaps were more trouble than they were worth. But given our structural challenges in hiring full-time writers, we just didn't have the leverage of a TechCrunch or GigaOm in dealing with troublesome staff. So I had to try and keep them happy; I certainly didn't want another Frederic situation.

I also recognized that if RWW was to continue growing, we would need more structure in the editorial operations. Abraham's new role would help, but it was also on me to make sure our editorial strategy was consistent and clearly communicated.

To take my mind off the pressures of the business, I attended a Foo Fighters concert at Stubb's that evening. My Irish friend Lenny, who now worked for Automattic, had a couple of tickets and offered one to me. To everyone's surprise, the band debuted a brand-new album, *Wasting Light*, which was scheduled for release in April. Although none of the crowd knew the songs, they were so immediately catchy and hard rocking that everyone soon had their hands in the air and heads bobbing. The Foos followed the new album with an hour of greatest hits, culminating in one of my personal favorites from their first album, "This Is a Call."

The concert was just the tonic I needed to clear my head. For a moment I fancied that if I could lead a band of bloggers as effectively as the red-shirted Dave Grohl had just led his band, everything would work out fine. Hey, it was SXSW, it was okay to dream a little.

I'd missed my daughter and our new home in Petone, so at first I was grateful to be back in New Zealand. But I soon became overwhelmed again with work—and worse, I felt the depression I'd had in my youth starting to rear its ugly head again. My dating life was a contributing factor. Since breaking up with Elyssa the previous May, I'd met a bunch of women—mostly via online dating sites—but none of them had turned into a lasting relationship.

To try and kick myself back into gear, I resolved to start a clean slate with my social life. In the evenings I took long walks around the Petone foreshore to try and clear my head and find some peace within myself. I also began thinking about how to make more effective use of my work time.

Primarily, I was concerned that my dual role as CEO and coeditor meant that I wasn't focused enough on the editorial side of the business. I had discussed this a bit in Austin with Sean and Marshall, but now that I was back home, I realized it was still bothering me. Among my main tech-blog competitors, all the founders had stepped away from one side of their company—editorial or business. Mike Arrington now listed himself as "Founder & Co-Editor" (he had a CEO, Heather Harde), Pete Cashmore was "Founder & CEO" (he had at least three people running the editorial side of Mashable), and Om Malik had a CEO (he didn't even list himself as editor; he was simply "Founder and Senior Writer"). None of them were trying to straddle both sides of the business, as I was doing.

Sean had been RWW's COO for sixteen months now. He was around thirty or thirty-one at the time, so still young—but perhaps not so much in our industry, when you had millennials like Pete Cashmore and Mark Zuckerberg running companies. Regardless of his age, Sean was much better at financial and business planning than I was. Perhaps that's what RWW needed now, I reasoned: someone who was savvy with business strategy and execution to lead the company to the "exit" we all wanted. If Sean was CEO, I could focus on what I loved doing the most—leading editorial, writing, being a thought leader in our industry. I'd also be able to support Marshall more, to keep our editorial operations on track.

I had to admit, this was also a crisis of confidence on my part. I had enough of an ego to know that nobody else in our team could've created and grown a company like RWW—not Marshall, not Sean, and certainly not any of the writers who were complaining to me about how the company was currently being run! On the other hand, the problems we were having had shaken me. I was a lead-by-example type, but my writing and editorial involvement had necessarily dropped off due to my CEO duties. I needed to rectify that. Also, in order to scale the company, we would need more effective business management. That was a strength of Sean's. I felt that his communication skills were better than mine too—if anyone could rally our team behind the company's goals, it would be him. I decided to make the suggestion to Sean and see how he reacted. Since he was an ambitious guy, I didn't imagine he'd object to having *CEO* in his job title.

Sure enough, he was enthusiastic about the plan. In one email, I concluded with this line: "I feel like RWW is at a turning point now—and the company needs its people focused on what they do best in order to get the best outcome." It was a sentiment he thoroughly agreed with.

We quickly began drawing up a plan for the transition. We would need to beef up the sales and operations side of the company to take some of the load off Sean. Then it would be a matter of dividing up the leadership responsibilities. In a "First 100 Days Plan" document, we mapped out a plan of action. It included a visit to the West Coast by Sean during April. He would have a bunch of meetings in San Francisco, including with FM Publishing to tell them the news, and then visit Portland to hold an in-person company meeting (with me joining on Skype). Hopefully, by our next New York event in June, the new company structure would be well and truly bedded in.

In one of our emails in early April, Sean mentioned that we ought to check with our US lawyer, Camille Linson, about what might need adjusting in his contract. He pointed out that he would still technically be a contractor but would now be operating as a CEO contractor.

I hadn't considered that this might be an issue, but I told Sean to have a word with Camille about it.

Shortly after, Sean came back to me and said Camille's initial reaction was that we couldn't have a contractor with the title of CEO because it would likely cause tax issues. The problem was that the person running a company was pivotal in terms of assessing a company's tax residence. Sean suggested I set up a call between Camille and Jeremy (my NZ lawyer). I did so, but I had a feeling where this would lead. I'd already had a lot of experience with lawyers and accountants from New Zealand and the United States talking among themselves, at great expense to me, and it never failed to end up in the same place: no action because of double taxation issues.

Sure enough, after nearly seven weeks of back-and-forth, the conclusion was the one I had expected all along: we couldn't make the change because it was too risky from a legal and accounting perspective. Once again, international taxation laws had foiled our plans to put proper structure into the business.

Sean stoically accepted the situation, even though he'd been excited to take the reins of RWW. But I was exasperated. I felt like the company structure was hamstringing the business—not to mention my own career.

These constant company setbacks also seemed to mirror the situation with my long-running divorce settlement. I was effectively paying for two separate accounting firms—PWC for me, Deloitte for my ex-wife—to come up with a mutually agreed-on valuation for the company in order to settle on a divorce payout. But there were no signs of getting a satisfactory resolution there, either. To my growing frustration, our respective lawyers and accounting firms continued trading emails, squabbling over numbers, and trying to out-negotiate each other. It had now been over two years since we separated.

So I felt thoroughly stuck on both the company structure and the status of my personal life. But I didn't have time to sit and stew about it. It was nearly time to hop on a plane to New York City.

Before I left for New York in the first week of June, I reviewed our May traffic. It was dismal. We'd had our lowest monthly total page views since last November. Even worse, our unique visitors were the lowest they'd been since last July.

The issues with our writers were part of the problem, but I was also disappointed with our social media referral traffic. Twitter and Facebook referrals had plummeted in recent months, and we'd also dropped in our key tech communities (Reddit and Hacker News especially; Digg was no longer relevant in the industry). All our competitors were publicly boasting about huge growth in social channels during this time, so there was something deeply wrong with our performance in this area.

To make matters worse, even before I arrived in New York, we knew we'd be making a loss on the event. All throughout May, we'd used the term *train wreck* in our weekly management meeting agenda to describe the ticket sales. We'd even briefly considered canceling the event, but decided to soldier on.

Given the poor social media results and the even worse event ticket sales, it was clear we'd have to let Seamus go straight after the event. But the problems at RWW ran deeper than that. The low page views, I believed, reflected the poor quality of our content. We just weren't good enough, across the board. I sent out a message on Basecamp to the team about the May results, not hiding my disappointment. I probably should've held back and waited till I got to New York, so that I could discuss it in person with Sean and Marshall. But with all the other frustrations in my life at this time, my stress levels were bubbling over and I couldn't hold back.

Predictably, my Basecamp message further stoked resentment among the writing team. It was the final straw for Mike Melanson, who abruptly quit. Sarah also expressed her annoyance to me, in a private message via Skype. Coincidentally, Alex Williams announced his resignation the same week—he'd accepted a new position at a tech blog called Silicon Angle, so he'd already made plans to move on before the May stats bombshell.

It wasn't all bad news. In May we'd hired a new business channels editor: David Strom, an experienced IT reporter who'd had a long career with CMP, International Data Group, Ziff Davis, and other old-school IT media companies. David had already provided a boost to our enterprise channel in the couple of weeks he'd been at RWW (it was one of the few areas with increased page views). At the other end of the experience spectrum, we'd hired a young reporter from Boston named Dan Rowinski, whose initiative and enthusiasm had quickly impressed me.

The most significant move we made, though, was to promote Abraham Hyatt as our new managing editor. Abraham had been our production editor since the end of 2009, but we now needed him to introduce more structure into our daily newsroom. These changes in the team all augured well for the near future.

I was especially worried about Sarah's messages to me, so I tried my best to appease her. I assured her that I wasn't concerned about her own performance (quite the contrary, she was still our best-performing writer). But I was also honest about other writers in the team not performing as well. Some of the news writers had not even delivered their monthly quota after we had brought them on full-time, I noted. But ultimately, I accepted that it was my responsibility to find a solution to the current mess, so I promised I would implement changes after the event. I had a similar back-and-forth with Mike, whom I still hoped to convince to return to RWW. Despite all my problems dealing with Mike over the past few months, he'd been a good writer for us.

During my nearly thirty-hour flight from New Zealand to New York, I thought through the editorial issues and formulated a plan. I decided we needed to refocus RWW on analysis writing, to get back to the roots of the site. This would mean we'd stop trying to compete with TechCrunch and Mashable on news coverage, both of which had long surpassed us in measures such as Technorati and the Techmeme leaderboard (not to mention traffic!).

De-emphasizing news would have major implications for editorial operations, but especially for Marshall's role. Crucially, I decided I would resume the role of editor in chief and lead all editorial again. That would mean removing the coeditor title from Marshall, making him VP content development and lead writer (his previous role). He'd still be an executive of the company, and given the renewed analysis focus of the site, it'd be more important than ever to get his research tools right. But, of course, communicating this change to Marshall would be a delicate matter. I'd need to get Sean's feedback first.

On Monday morning I made my way to the location of our previous New York City event, the Metropolitan Pavilion. Once again it was head-quarters for Internet Week, so I spent the morning checking out the exhibits and talks. The highlight was a Digital Archaeology exhibit that charted the evolution of websites and web design over the past twenty years. It had thirty different web projects, from the first-ever website in 1991—the CERN website by the web's inventor, Tim Berners-Lee—to the highly interactive 2010 HTML5 music video for Arcade Fire created by Google. Each of these projects was displayed on a computer and soft-ware of its time. It was humbling to think that the roots of RWW were in the middle of this timeline; I'd started experimenting with blogging around 2001.

I chatted with the exhibit's curator, Jim Boulton, who suggested to me that "in a few years' time there won't be such a thing as a website." As the owner of a business based on a website, I raised my eyebrows in surprise. "With the rise of the social web, now online experiences are built around the individual rather than around the organization," Boul-ton explained.

While I didn't agree that social media would lead to the extinction of websites any time soon, Boulton had a point that more and more online conversation was gravitating to the likes of Facebook and Twitter. I'd recently seen evidence of this myself, with a post I wrote on May 3, 2011, entitled "Breaking Up With Your Favorite Apps." I had hoped it would generate an interesting discussion in our comments section ("Which web apps or services have you broken up with; and why?"). The RWW comments system currently ran on a third-party application called Dis-qus. At the end of the previous year, we'd switched from Movable Type's native commenting system to Disqus partly because the latter was itself a social media application—readers were able to track their comments across different blogs via their Disqus account.

Despite having the Disqus network to leverage, in the end we only got about ten comments on that post. However, we had many more comments about it on Twitter and Facebook. While it was encouraging to see all those comments across social media, this didn't necessarily correlate with referral traffic. Many people didn't click through to read the story—they simply commented based on the headline or teaser they saw in the tweet or Facebook post.

There was an old blogging truism that I'd learned very early on with RWW: an active comments section means higher page views. This was because readers often come back to a post later in the day to read the comments. If the comments continued for days after the post was published, it could translate into a lot of page views. However, thanks to social media, that truism no longer seemed to apply.

In addition to becoming the new nexus of daily internet conversation, Facebook and Twitter were becoming hugely influential in geopolitics. During the first quarter of 2011, activists in countries like Tunisia, Egypt, and Libya were using social media to organize protests against their governments—in some cases, even leading to the overthrow of rulers. This so-called Arab Spring would not have happened without the use of tools such as Facebook and Twitter to rally and mobilize citizens.

While I was happy to see the web being used as a tool of the people against oppressive regimes, selfishly I was much more concerned that social media was squeezing out blogs in the tech industry. The ever-growing popularity of Facebook and Twitter just added to my anxiety about the state of ReadWriteWeb.com in mid-2011.

Later that day, I had lunch with Sean. I told him about my plan to de-emphasize news and double down on analysis, and naturally he was concerned. If we were to do this "editorial pivot," as he put it, it would take time to implement and demonstrate success. It might push out the timeframe for finding an acquirer, he warned. We would also need to rethink our strategy of doubling revenue annually, since that was partly based on growing our news coverage. Finally, he asked about the future of Marshall's RSS system, which had been created to fuel our news coverage. I said that none of the writers were using the system—Mike had been especially vocal about his objections to it—so we couldn't very well claim it as a point of difference to a potential acquirer. But I hoped

Marshall would turn it into more of a research tool to help us with analysis posts.

While Sean's skepticism gave me pause, by the end of the day I was more convinced than ever that it needed to be done. That day, over on the West Coast, Apple had begun its annual Worldwide Developers Conference. Given that Apple was one of the key companies of this era of the internet, I expected us to be all over the event. But when I checked the site back at my hotel, I was dismayed at our coverage. I emailed both Marshall and Abraham about it. "We really need to organize for events like this in a much more systematic manner," I said to Marshall. I cited the news about iCloud, which Apple had launched that day and about which we'd had advance knowledge (under embargo). We should've had a post ready to go about it, I insisted. "I know we have a bunch of issues right now with editorial, but today's Apple event is precisely the kind of thing we need to organize and systematically assign stories on certain topics or angles," I wrote.

Marshall briefly acknowledged my email, admitting that the coverage of Apple's event wasn't up to par. The following day I followed up with another, much longer, email. "I think this is a good opportunity to bring up some other thoughts I've had recently on our editorial," I began. After explaining my analysis of RWW's performance and where I thought we fit compared to our competitors in the tech blogosphere, I told him about my plan to "take the reins of sole Editor again." I added that "the business has reached a crisis point in editorial and things cannot continue as they have been."

To his great credit, Marshall reacted to this calmly. "Lots to consider here but I'm certainly open to it all. I do love chasing and breaking news though. Will give this more thought but I think some radical changes are clearly needed."

I thanked him for being open-minded and said we'd discuss more after the event. Our 2WAY Summit was just a few days away, so we needed to focus on that for now.

CHAPTER 19

UNRAVELING

■ ■ ■ ■ ■

WE COULDN'T HAVE ASKED for a better venue. The Roone Arledge Auditorium at Columbia University had a full stage, sprung wooden floors, round tables decorated in elegant white cloth, and a huge digital screen onstage that said, "Welcome to The ReadWriteWeb 2WAY Summit NYC." The entrance was via Broadway, in uptown Manhattan, and outside the door was a sign that read *Experience the future of the Web 2 WAYS*. Inside, a group of young volunteers staffed the registration desk, decked out in red RWW T-shirts with our yin-yang logo on the front.

I couldn't help but smile seeing my company's brand so prominently displayed in this otherwise quintessential New York location. It gave me a surge of excitement as I placed the conference lanyard around my neck. But I was also nervous about how many people would attend—we had not sold anywhere near as many tickets as we'd hoped. It was also early on a Monday morning, and attendees at tech conferences didn't always turn up on time.

Sure enough, as the time for our opening remarks approached, I looked around the auditorium and saw that many of the tables—on the sides especially—were occupied by just one or two people. The middle tables were mostly full, so we had enough people in the room to make it look respectable, but the general impression was that our event was too small for this venue. Certainly, the vibe was more subdued than I would've liked. A full conference hall typically generates a kind of buzz, like the loud hum I once heard as I looked down on New York City from the top of the Empire State Building. But there weren't enough people at our event to generate that vibe.

Nobody could fault our lineup of speakers that first morning. First up was NPR senior journalist Andy Carvin, who spoke passionately about the Arab Spring. He said his Twitter feed of the uprisings that year was "as close to real-time war reporting as we've ever come." Then Fred Wilson, the well-known New York VC, did a keynote presentation on "content shifting." It was a commentary on the many different digital devices people were now using. Next up was danah boyd, a researcher who focused on how young people used internet technologies. She gave a talk about teen sexting and its impact on tech companies: "Your user-generated content dream can quickly turn into a nightmare." These three sessions were all intriguing, and, even better, the auditorium slowly filled up as the morning went on, although it never reached capacity.

To round out the morning sessions, we'd originally scheduled a debate between Mahalo's Jason Calacanis and Gawker Media's Nick Denton, two charismatic New York-based media entrepreneurs who often sniped at each other online but were rarely seen together onstage. Seamus had even organized a promotional poster of the pair in the style of an olden day's boxing match: *ReadWriteWeb Presents: A Battle of Epic Proportions.* Unfortunately, Denton had pulled out a couple of weeks before the event, so it was now a Q&A with Calacanis, with our managing editor Abraham lobbing the questions to him. Jason turned this into an entertaining session full of his off-the-cuff opinions—"There are a lot of stupid people out there … and stupid people shouldn't write"—but still, it was a shame the standoff with Denton never happened.

My interactions with both Seamus and Marshall were a little awkward that day. Marshall, of course, was polite and professional. He conducted an excellent interview with Chris Dixon, then CEO of a recommendation engine startup called Hunch (later that year it would be acquired by eBay). But given my email just days before the event about taking the coeditor title off him, he was understandably a bit standoffish with me. As for Seamus, I just didn't know what to say to him. The poor turnout at this event was disappointing, and the equally bad state of affairs with our social media channels continued to irk me. I had to give him credit for the event agenda, though, along with the signage and other aspects of the event. Still, I was dreading the inevitable conversation we'd be having later that week.

My time onstage that day was an interview with Flipboard founder Mike McCue, straight after Marshall's talk with Dixon. Again, the content was compelling. Flipboard was one of my favorite iPad apps, but I was surprised to hear from Mike that the app was designed pre-iPad (which came out in 2010). The goal had been to reimagine Web content, he said, and I certainly felt he'd succeeded in that.

Content shifting, Arab Spring, teen sexting, recommendation engines, new forms of web browsing—it had been a day full of big ideas and important discussions about the future of the web. Day two would be back to our usual "unconference" format, with the audience much more involved in proceedings, but I thought we'd put on a good show with the traditional conference format. It was just a shame the audience was not as big as we'd have liked.

The second day of the event went smoothly, and we had a good turnout for the speed-geeking session to end the morning. But as the afternoon wore on, the crowd thinned out and it was painfully obvious that our event hadn't been a success.

That Tuesday evening, I wandered around the East Village by myself to decompress. I went into several bookstores, which was a common way that I liked to relax while traveling. Sean, Marshall, and I would be having management meetings over the next couple of days, to review the state of the business and plan for the rest of the year. We were still doing well financially, but we'd stalled on the website growth in the first half of 2011. And now the event, our fourth, had been a disappointment and had lost money (exactly how much, I'd find out soon). We would have to come up with another way to grow the business in the second half of 2011.

The following day began with a breakfast meeting with our current web designers, a company called Copious. They were based in Portland but had made the trip out east for our event. Copious had designed the event website and the brand identity for the conference, both of which we'd been pleased with. We planned to have them create a new design for the RWW website, which was needed in part because we wanted to move off Movable Type and onto WordPress by the end of the year. It was also required to pivot the main site from news coverage to analysis. Copious promised to send us a plan and budget soon.

Next, Sean, Marshall, and I convened at a local café for our first day of management meetings. The agenda was to review the current state of the business and plan for the rest of 2011.

We began by talking through the editorial issues and my new vision for the site. I'd come up with a new mantra to define our renewed focus: "Smart news over breaking news." Consumer news would remain the primary focus of the main site, I said, as it was important our readers were kept abreast of web trends and product news. But our goal was no longer to be the first to cover the news—TechCrunch or Mashable were usually the first to a story anyway. Our new goal was to provide analysis and context around the news of the day, to help our readers understand it better. This would help reinforce RWW as a community that provides thoughtful discussion, I said.

In order to organize our writers in this new direction, I proposed to give each of them "beats." Each writer would be assigned a mix of beats, covering both the big companies (like Google and Apple) and topical beats that were important for RWW to cover but also complementary to the writers' own passions. For example, Audrey—whom I had sat down with on Tuesday afternoon in a one-on-one—was keen to cover the educational technology beat. Our unofficial tagline in recent years had been "What's next on the web," and I reiterated that this was still our guiding principle when deciding which beats to cover.

I would work with Abraham to come up with a daily process based on this new beats system. My initial thought was for the team to identify the main stories at the start of each day, perhaps via a Skype meeting, and Abraham would assign posts based on that. I suggested to Marshall that his RSS-based tool system would still be valuable as support for writers when writing their stories, although it probably wouldn't be as important now in finding stories. That would be up to the writers, who would be able to focus their attention more narrowly on their assigned beats.

Inevitably, we had to discuss removing the coeditor role from Marshall. He wasn't happy about this and questioned whether it would further impact the morale of our writers. He also pointed out that my time zone meant that I wouldn't be around in the mornings US time, so would the writers have enough direction from me each day? These were fair points, and I acknowledged that I would have to be more involved in editorial on a day-to-day basis—something that had slipped over the past year or two while I focused on business matters.

The following morning, Sean and I had scheduled a face-to-face meeting with Seamus. We'd already decided before the event that he had to go, and nothing that had transpired during the week had changed our minds about that. Still, it would be a difficult meeting—and the first time since Bernard that I'd had to sit down with an employee and give them this kind of news.

Seamus had suggested a restaurant called GustOrganics, on the Avenue of the Americas in lower Manhattan. We would be meeting him at 9:30 a.m., but Sean suggested he and I meet there forty-five minutes earlier to discuss a financial spreadsheet he'd prepared overnight.

It was a nice-looking restaurant, painted avocado green on the outside and with a spacious and colorful interior. We ordered breakfast, and I confirmed to Sean that I'd removed Seamus's access to our main publishing and social media accounts. Marshall had objected to my doing this, but since I wouldn't have access to the internet straight after the meeting, it felt like the sensible thing to do. As our community manager, Seamus had been in charge of our Twitter and Facebook accounts up till now, so I wanted to make sure nothing untoward happened after we gave him the bad news. I had no reason to believe he would do such a thing, so perhaps this was paranoia on my part.

As usual, Sean had prepared a thorough spreadsheet of his projections for the rest of the year. He was of course concerned about the stalled page views, which needed to start growing again if we were to meet our revenue goals. We also briefly discussed the event loss, which he estimated would be around $30,000. It was sobering to hear that, and it probably helped prepare me for what I had to tell Seamus.

Around 9:30 a.m., Seamus walked in. He looked glum and mumbled a greeting to us as he heavily plopped himself into a chair at our table. We'd finished our breakfast by this point, so I asked if he wanted to order anything. He shook his head and avoided eye contact. He likely knew where this meeting was headed, although I didn't know if he'd checked any of his logins that morning. I took a deep breath and proceeded to list out the issues in his performance over the past year: the poor ticket sales to the event that had resulted in us losing money, the decline in our social media referral traffic, the lack of progress in tech communities such as Reddit and Hacker News, and more.

I tried to couch all this with some positives, for example that we'd been impressed by the event programming and the quality of the speakers. Nevertheless, he took my criticisms poorly and tried to counter each one by deflecting the blame elsewhere. Sean interjected and pointed out that all the things I'd just said were a part of Seamus's KPIs, and so were in black and white as goals that Seamus had been set.

Things got quiet for a minute, and then Seamus asked what would happen now. I said that unfortunately this couldn't continue, and we were giving him his notice today. I told him we'd work out the details over email and that it was up to him if he wished to continue working for us during the notice period—we would pay him either way. He didn't say anything in reply and was still avoiding eye contact. Then he abruptly got up and walked out of the restaurant.

Sean's eyes were as wide as saucers, and I wiped some sweat off my brow. "Just as well I shut him out of the social media accounts," I said, only half-jokingly.

By the end of the week, I'd confirmed with Marshall that he was okay with me announcing the new editorial structure to the team. I was reluctant to announce it until he'd accepted the changes. He'd been noticeably unhappy during our management meetings—and a couple of times we had argued, with Sean trying hard to keep a neutral position between us. Marshall was normally such a laid-back guy and unfailingly polite in person (although in his articles he could be much more aggressive), so seeing him look at me with angry, flinty eyes had made me quite sad.

In my personal journal that week, I tried to reassure myself that I was making the right move. Running a business isn't about making friends, I wrote. I'd come a long way and the journey had taken its toll—I was still not taking enough time to manage my type 1 diabetes, and my family life was in tatters. Some of this was my own fault, but regardless, I felt like I had very little control over my life—the never-ending divorce settlement, the legal and tax restrictions on my company structure, not being able to move to the US, and more. I desperately wanted to be in control of something, and I'd decided that the editorial operations would be it.

Partly that was self-defensive bluster, though. I was worried I'd now alienated not only the writers, but Marshall too.

While I was still in New York, I sat down with Abraham to discuss the situation. If this new strategy was to work, he would be a key person going forward—my right-hand man on editorial operations. Abraham and I agreed that before I made a team announcement, I should communicate the changes one-on-one with the writers most at risk of leaving: Mike (who had already quit, but I still hoped to convince him to return), Audrey, and Sarah. I would also tell David Strom, our new enterprise channels manager, so that he was kept in the loop.

I did the personal outreach and then on Friday took a flight from New York to Seattle, where I'd be meeting with a number of companies about potential stories—including a visit to the Microsoft campus.

By the time I reached Seattle, Sarah had responded positively to the changes—which made me feel better. But, to my great frustration, Mike rejected the changes and confirmed he wouldn't be coming back. I was angry, but I had to take a deep breath and recognize that Mike wanted to implement his own life changes. I quickly moved to replace him with John Paul Titlow, our young Philly blogger on Biz, who was keen for a full-time role.

On Monday, Audrey emailed that she wanted to focus more on ed tech (her personal passion) and didn't think RWW would be the place for her to do that. She indicated that she'd be resigning, but thankfully Abraham got on the phone to her immediately and convinced her to stay. I breathed a sigh of relief, as losing both Mike and Audrey within a couple of days wouldn't have been a big vote of confidence for my new plan—even with Sarah getting behind it.

The five nights in Seattle and two in San Francisco went by in a blur. In truth, I was too distracted by the internal issues with my company to focus on these meetings. The following Friday, June 24, I was on a plane home to New Zealand. It had been a hectic and stressful trip. The pressure was unrelenting, and my blood-sugar levels had been erratic lately—it always seemed to be a problem when I traveled. Despite this, I tried to remind myself that I had a good life. I'd had fun visiting museums and art galleries in New York, Seattle, and San Francisco, having dinners and drinks with friends and new acquaintances, and taking in new sights and experiences across the three weeks. I recalled a quote from a book I was reading about Taoism: "The way you feel about life, people, and the world around you, the things you think, say, and do, fashion the response you get back from life, and shape your reality. So you get from the world what you give to the world."[74]

I had bought that book, *Every Day Tao*, the previous month during a visit to Christchurch. The city had been badly damaged by an earthquake in February 2011, and I'd attended a special TED event there in May to discuss solutions for rebuilding. It was sobering to see the destruction in the inner city—the havoc it had caused in people's lives, including for many of my extended relatives who lived there. The part of New Zealand where I lived, Wellington, was also prone to earthquakes, so it had made me think how easily it could've been my home that crumpled to the ground.

But I was lucky that my home was intact, and that my business was too. I had a lot to be grateful for, and a lot still to give—to my family and friends, and to my tech-blogging company.

Things continued to move fast in the tech industry. At the end of June, Google announced a new Facebook competitor called Google+. Other companies in our industry were also expanding: Microsoft had recently acquired Skype, Twitter had bought a popular tweet reader app called TweetDeck, and LinkedIn had done its IPO. Then, in July, Spotify announced its launch in the United States.

While our latest event had been a disappointment, the fact that Web 2.0 was still active and growing was encouraging to me. The continued sense of optimism gave RWW a boost, and by the beginning of July, we'd found our new community manager. Robyn Tippins had already held the role at Current TV, Yahoo Developer Network, and MyBlogLog—so she had plenty of relevant experience. She was a longtime reader of RWW, and when I spoke to her, she was clearly smart and passionate about the blogosphere. She also wanted a job where she could work at home, since she was moving to Savannah, Georgia, with her family at the end of the year. It seemed like the perfect fit all-round. I only wished we'd found Robyn a year ago, but better late than never.

Then, a few weeks into July, we hired another promising young writer. Jon Mitchell was based in Portland, so he'd be able to see Abraham and Marshall regularly. Jon reminded me a little of Marshall, as his recent work experience indicated a strong social consciousness. In any case, with him and Dan Rowinski now on board, we were starting to grow the second generation of RWW writers.

It seemed like RWW was finally gaining some momentum again. But then came the news I'd been dreading. On Friday, July 22, Sarah phoned me to give her notice. The main reason she was resigning was the lack of benefits in her RWW compensation. Naturally, her high performance as a tech blogger had not gone unnoticed by our competitors in the blogosphere, and she told me she'd had four or five offers from other companies—all of which were offering her a salary with benefits.

Of course, I immediately offered her a pay raise to try and put us on an equal footing with the other companies, but she wanted the job security above all else. "It's not about raising my base income, it's about having the stability of a corporate job and the benefits that provides," she said. She listed off health insurance, disability insurance, life insurance, dental, vision, and 401K, noting that those weren't things RWW could offer. Now that she had a child, she wasn't willing to forgo those benefits anymore—and I couldn't blame her one bit.

It was a big blow, as Sarah had recently told me she was happy with the new editorial structure. She thought Abraham's morning meetings were helping, and she'd been pleased about Robyn's hiring, too. But clearly, she had also been looking for other opportunities for at least several weeks. I wondered if the ructions within the writing team this year had influenced her decision.

The following week, Sarah confirmed my hunch. She told me that the complaints from other writers, along with the resentment they caused with other team members, had made her feel demoralized. She pointed to a very recent example of sniping between team members in a public comment on our blog, which I hadn't been aware of, and said she no longer wanted to deal with that kind of negativity. Once again, I couldn't blame her.

Pretty soon, I found out where Sarah was going to: TechCrunch. I wasn't surprised to hear it, especially since TechCrunch was now a part of a much larger company. AOL had acquired Mike Arrington's business at the end of September 2010 for a reported $25 million. Sarah confirmed to me that the package TechCrunch had offered her included basically the same corporate benefits that anyone at AOL gets. It made me feel a little better, I suppose, since there was no way a tiny NZ company could compete with an AOL salary and benefits. Still, I was bitterly disappointed that we'd lost one of our best writers in this way.

After Sarah's news came out, Audrey and Klint piled on the misery by handing in their resignations at the end of July. I was half-expecting it from Audrey, as it had been apparent for a while now that her heart wasn't in her RWW work. But Klint's announcement came as a surprise. It turned out he'd be joining Silicon Angle, the tech blog that Alex Williams had recently joined—he'd been poached by a competitor. Once again, it made me rueful that RWW couldn't offer a proper salary and benefits to our writers.

I didn't know what I could do to change this situation, other than try again to get acquired by a US company. In the meantime, I had to focus on replacing the defectors and developing a new crop of writers. Maybe Dan and Jon would become the new Sarah and Frederic, although that wouldn't happen overnight. I was also very worried about the short-term impact of losing multiple writers in such a short space of time.

To make matters worse, I was finding it difficult to write for RWW myself. The joy I'd long had in blogging had disappeared due to the pressures the business was under. I was about to turn forty in August, a milestone birthday that I should've been looking forward to. But, in truth, I was feeling depressed and wanted to get away from everything. If I'd been able to go live in a log cabin in the woods—just switch off for a while—then I would've jumped at the opportunity.

A few days before my birthday on the twenty-fifth, I had my annual diabetes check-up. My blood tests were fine, but I mentioned to my doctor that I was feeling anxious and depressed. He asked if I was struggling to get out of bed in the mornings, along with some other questions to determine how serious it was. I said the situation wasn't that bad, so he recommended I see a psychotherapist rather than take any medication. I took the business card he proffered and promised to contact this person. (Of course, I didn't do so for many months.)

I shrugged off my doctor's advice in part because I was convinced my current life and business situation were at fault. I compared the way I felt now to my late teenage years and early twenties—I would've answered yes to all my doctor's questions back then. I knew I didn't have clinical depression now, though, because my sense of self was much stronger than when I was young. I liked who I was now, and I loved life—it was just that everything around me seemed cluttered or stuck.

I was beginning to realize what I had to do to resolve the situation. I wrote in my journal, "I wonder if I should sell the biz now, so I can get both it and the divorce off my back."

An opportunity arose to discuss a possible sale when Sean got back from a trip out west at the end of August, during which he'd visited the FM Publishing office in San Francisco. I asked him how it went, and he replied that he'd had a positive discussion with FM about several ad campaigns. "The only sticky thing is that our traffic really is tough and we need it to start growing," he added.

The following day, September 2, I sent Sean the August statistics via

Google Analytics. It made for grim reading: our total page views had dropped 11 percent month over month, to 4.34 million. It was our worst month in well over a year. Obviously, this had been impacted by losing two of our highest page-view generators that year (Sarah and Klint), but I also had to admit to Sean that "both Marshall and I are struggling on the writing front." I said that I was feeling burned out and that I thought there was a big danger Marshall would quit, given his continued unhappiness with losing the coeditor role. I then made my rather weak pitch to him.

"I really hate to even suggest this, but I think we should at least consider it: should we start to look for an acquirer now? Obviously it's not good timing, but right now we still have a very strong brand, great audience demographics and lots of potential." I argued that the business would operate significantly better if it had a stable US entity behind it—particularly for the writing staff, but also our ops team. It would finally enable RWW to offer benefits to staff and have a corporate structure in place that would make our people feel more comfortable.

I said that the page views were struggling because we'd lost a bunch of senior and skilled writers, and we'd basically had to start over again with junior writers. But I thought we had a strong case for saying that the brand is still rock solid and we just needed a better corporate structure behind it to get page views going up again.

Sean was measured in his response. He said he could talk to four or five potential acquirers, but this wasn't an optimal time to sell. The site's shaky performance in this financial year would result in a business value well below what it would have been worth the previous December. "More importantly," he added, "if things turn around it will be worth much more then it is today. Obviously, conversely, if things don't, the sooner we sell this the better."

In my reply, I recognized that this year couldn't have gone worse from a growth point of view—which wasn't a good thing when trying to sell a company. But I explained that I was primarily worried about the structure of the company because there was no obvious fix given the tax and legal issues around hiring people.

"I still feel like there is a lot of untapped potential in RWW," I said.

"The brand is still unique and I know there is demand for the type of passionate, thoughtful web analysis that we do. Nobody else does that type of analysis well, plus is hip to new social media stuff, etc. But the staffing issues this past year have really hurt us; and I'm most concerned that we haven't plugged that hole. Marshall and to a lesser extent David could walk at any moment. But also someone like Dan, who we're building up slowly but surely—what's to stop him from jumping to Techcrunch when he's matured and become popular. We've developed a history of growing writers and then not being able to keep them (Frederic was an early warning, in hindsight)." I reiterated that I still believed in RWW's brand and our audience. "But I think if we got a good offer, I'd probably take it at this point," I said.

I told Sean I had already booked tickets to San Francisco (and Portland) in mid-October for the Web 2.0 Summit. He replied he would set up some initial conversations with potential acquirers during September so we could have more serious talks with interested parties in October if it came to that.

Of course, I had no idea if any company would even want to discuss an acquisition with us at this time. But I felt positive that I'd at least decided to explore this. It was better than sitting and waiting for the next writer to walk.

I arrived in California on Tuesday, October 11, after my usual twelve-hour flight from New Zealand. From SFO I took an Alaska Airlines flight to Portland, during which I spotted the musician Nick Lowe sitting in an aisle seat opposite me, but one row ahead. With his distinctive silver hair and big black glasses, he appeared to be absorbed in a crossword puzzle. But every so often he'd lean back, close his eyes, and mumble to himself. I wondered if he was creating a new song, since his lyrics were known for their clever wordplay. Perhaps he found inspiration in doing crossword puzzles.

I'd discovered Lowe's music over the past few years and was particularly enamored of an NPR recording that had just been released of his live solo show as the opening act for Wilco. I admired that Lowe had reinvented himself after the age of forty, from a rock musician into a solo balladeer. He was now in his early sixties, so his second career had lasted longer than his first one. In a way, I wanted to emulate that—in my journals I wrote about leaving my group blog behind and starting a new career as an independent author. I didn't know what types of books I wanted to write, but I would figure that out later. First, of course, I had to sell RWW.

By the time I got to Portland, we had six companies on our shortlist of potential acquirers: TechWeb, ZDE, O'Reilly Media, GigaOm, Federated Media, and SAY Media. We'd also had a conversation with Alan Meckler's WebMediaBrands, but he was already out. Sean would be traveling to San Francisco to join me for meetings with several of these companies.

Prior to my trip to Portland, I'd tried to arrange a meetup with Marshall and Abraham for Wednesday, but I hadn't heard back from Marshall before I left. He hadn't replied to a few of my emails recently and had been less responsive than usual over the past month or so. In the back of my mind, I was worried that he was about to leave. Then, while I was in the air, Marshall sent an email requesting that we meet up on Wednesday morning, just the two of us. It gave me a bad feeling.

We met up at a Peet's café in downtown Portland on Wednesday, around 10:30 a.m. It was Marshall's birthday, his thirty-fifth, so I started by wishing him a happy birthday. We talked for a little about life—he asked after my daughter, I asked how his wife, Mikalina, was doing. I sensed he had something he wanted to tell me; his face was harder than usual, though he was being his usual polite self. I already knew what he was going to say, so it wasn't a shock when he told me he was going to resign from his position as VP of content development at RWW. He was going to start up his own business, he said, adding that it wasn't going to be a tech blog. He said he'd continue to write for RWW if I wanted him to.

Of course, I asked him to reconsider, noting that we were in the middle of trying to sell the business, so he'd lose some of his stock options if he resigned now. But he was adamant he wanted to leave now. I saw the determination on his face—there would be no changing his mind. I agreed that he would stay on as a regular writer; we couldn't afford not to have his blog contributions at this time.

I discovered over the coming weeks that Marshall's business idea was an application called Plexus Engine—and it was further along than I had initially thought. The website had been live since at least February of that year, so clearly this had been months in the planning before he handed in his resignation. By the time Marshall announced it to the world, about a month after our meeting, it was in a private beta and was being described as "an app and data platform that discovers emerging topical information."[75] The following year, he raised money from Mark Cuban and others.

After my coffee with Marshall, I IM'd Sean about the news. Understandably, he wasn't happy—he'd just come out of a meeting with FM Publishing about a contentious ad campaign, so he told me this was the most frustrating day he'd ever had in business. I didn't know what to say to that, other than to internally reflect on what a terrible year this had turned into for RWW. How had it all gone so wrong? But I had a lunch meeting with Abraham that day, so I didn't have time to dwell on it.

That meeting cheered me up. Abraham had already shown over the past several months that he was an effective managing editor, and he'd recently taken the initiative to hire another new young writer, Alicia Eler, from Chicago. She had started with us at the end of September, and we were already impressed by her enthusiasm and writing. So we now had a promising cadre of young bloggers for our main site—John Paul, Dan, Jon, and Alicia. Poignantly, all had written excellent articles in memory of Steve Jobs, who had passed away at age fifty-six just a week before.

It wasn't just the young writers who gave me hope. We'd also shored up our enterprise channels in recent months with two experienced IT reporters, Joe Brockmeier and Scott Fulton, who were well managed by David Strom. We had Robyn, Curt, Jared, and others in the wider team, all performing well, so there was reason to be optimistic. Indeed, our statistics for September had jumped 14 percent to a shade under five million page views. Despite all the staffing setbacks, we still had a strong team at core.

However, the universe wasn't quite finished taking things away from RWW. On Thursday, our syndication partnership with the *New York Times* ended. We'd known about this for a month, when a *Times* executive emailed us to say they were ending the agreement—not just with RWW, but with GigaOm and VentureBeat too. "This is in no way a reflection on the quality of the content," we'd been told. They simply wanted to do everything in-house now. Frankly, I was amazed the *Times* had continued publishing external tech blogs on their growing online platform for so long. We never got paid a dime for it, and the traffic the *Times* sent us was minimal, so it wouldn't have a material impact on our business. But I was a little bummed that I would no longer be able to gloat to family and friends that we were published daily on the *New York Times*.

On Thursday evening we held a RWW meetup at the Green Dragon pub for the Portland tech community, which our community manager, Robyn, had organized. Marshall and I were able to have a friendly conversation—I didn't have any hard feelings toward him, and both of us were more relaxed by this point (no doubt helped by the beer). It was a relief not to have my defenses up talking to him, and I'm sure he felt a similar way. I wished him all the best in his new startup venture and told him I appreciated him staying on in the interim as our lead writer. He said he'd always have a soft spot for RWW and the four years he'd spent working with the team.

On Saturday morning I got on an Alaska Airlines plane back to San Francisco. I'd picked up a cold while in Portland, so I wasn't feeling 100 percent. But I knew I'd have to perk up before the business meetings Sean had organized for next week. I had no idea what to expect from these meetings, but at least I'd ridden in this M&A rodeo before. While it hadn't worked out with ZDE or TechWeb back in 2008, I was older and wiser now (well, certainly older).

I would also be attending the Web 2.0 Summit the next week. Had I known it would be the final Web 2.0 Summit or Expo, I might've summoned more enthusiasm. There had been no announcement to that effect yet, so as far as I knew, we were still in the midst of Web 2.0.

In hindsight, perhaps we were all burned out with the constant striving for growth. Whether any of us knew it or not, the end of an era was fast approaching.

CHAPTER 20

SAY WHAT

■ ■ ■ ■ ■

TO PREPARE FOR THE SAN FRANCISCO MEETINGS, I'd created a Read-WriteWeb Vision presentation and Sean had created a slide deck about our business growth. Mine was all about our brand and editorial vision, starting with the mission statement for RWW: "Where engaged technologists discover and discuss what's next on the Web." I noted that the editorial focused on "smart news and analysis," which had been our recent pivot after the writer revolt and Marshall stepping back from the editorial leadership. I left the growth goals open-ended, as I figured this would be something we'd discuss individually with each potential acquirer. Our overall goal was "to be the leading analysis site for web tech."

Sean's presentation focused heavily on the revenue, and in particular our strong financial year ending March 31, 2011. During that period, the business doubled in revenue while profits increased by almost a factor of five. We were still projecting to increase revenue for the March 2012 year, although it certainly wouldn't double. We'd also have a decent profit (but again, not five times the profit). So the financials were looking okay, albeit not quite what we'd hoped for.

For editorial statistics, Sean listed the monthly page views at about five million but didn't elaborate too much—we'd have to talk to the potential acquirers about that in the meetings. Instead, we emphasized our strong brand and community, and audience demographics.

The first meeting was on Monday morning with GigaOm CEO Paul Walborsky. This was the deal we were least optimistic about, since it would probably be stock based with only a little cash (perhaps even none). Sean also didn't think their stock would be worth much, given the number of funding rounds they'd had.

We met Paul at the GigaOm office on Second Street. I was disappointed to find that Om Malik himself wasn't in the office that day. Paul suggested I make a time to meet Om separately, so that the two of us could make sure we were aligned editorially. As for the meeting, it's fair to say that neither side learned much about the other. Paul and Sean danced around the key metrics of our respective businesses, each wary that we were competitors (albeit friendly ones). Paul did confirm, though, that any deal would have to involve stock.

Afterward, Sean and I agreed that it was unlikely anything would happen with GigaOm. I also questioned how serious they were, since Om hadn't been in the meeting. Still, we hoped they'd at least come to the table with an offer that we could play off against a better (read: mostly cash) deal.

The next meeting was with Laura Baldwin, the president of O'Reilly Media. She'd arranged to meet me at the Pied Piper bar at the Palace Hotel, the venue for the Web 2.0 Summit that would start tomorrow. She and Sean had already met earlier in the month in New York, when he'd briefed her on our business, so it would just be me meeting her today. The idea was for her to get to know me and my editorial vision for the site.

With the conference about to kick off, Laura was very busy, and I got the impression she was distracted by event business. Nonetheless, I thought we had a good chat. I told her I had a great deal of respect for Tim O'Reilly and would relish the chance to work alongside him. I then talked about the ways RWW would complement the O'Reilly Media business—primarily by bringing an active and passionate tech-blog community into their orbit. She said she'd discuss it with Tim and circle back to Sean soon.

Unfortunately, that was the last we heard from O'Reilly Media. Laura went radio silent after this meeting and didn't respond to follow-ups from Sean or me over the following weeks. For whatever reason, this wasn't a deal that O'Reilly Media wanted to make. (As far as I know, they have never acquired a blog business to this day.)

On Tuesday the Web 2.0 Summit kicked off. Since we had no business meetings scheduled, I figured I'd focus on the event for that day. Jon Mitchell was there, and it was great to spend some time with him. He was a young, bearded guy with dark hair and thin-framed glasses, and so even in person he reminded me of Marshall. Although as I got to know him better, I realized he had a creative streak and an interest in the arts—so, in hindsight, he was probably more similar to me.

One of the highlights of the Web 2.0 Summit every year was the Mary Meeker presentation, in which she did a rapid-fire delivery of a large set of data-heavy slides. This was her first year presenting it on behalf of her new employer, the VC firm Kleiner Perkins Caufield & Byers: she'd moved from Wall Street to Silicon Valley, a reflection of the growing influence of the tech industry in the economy. It didn't change her bullish outlook for the mobile internet, though. One of the more striking slides was that over half of Twitter's traffic now came from mobile devices.

What Meeker didn't cover, at least overtly, was the increasing power of the big-five tech companies. But I was noticing signs that Web 2.0 was becoming less about technology innovation from startups and more about a group of dominant platforms coalescing in the mainstream culture. The big five were increasingly competing with each other, rather than with startups. Amazon had just launched a low-cost tablet, the Kindle Fire, to compete with Apple's popular iPad. Meanwhile, Apple took on Amazon in cloud computing, with the release of iCloud in October.

The biggest mover, though, was Facebook. In October it released Timeline, a new version of the profile page designed to show highlights from a person's entire life rather than just recent posts. The goal was clear: to make Facebook much more attractive to "normal people" (the term I used at the time for non-geeks). Alongside the Timeline,

Facebook made an even bigger change—although it wasn't immediately obvious how it would impact society. It began phasing out its chronological News Feed with a new, algorithmic feed that curated what you saw. The company marketed this as "your own personal newspaper," since the algorithm would theoretically only give you the news you wanted to see. On the flip side, you would no longer get to see updates from everyone you followed.

Back then, nobody thought the algorithmic feed was a big deal. But suddenly, Facebook had great power over what you saw in your feed every day. Web 2.0 was supposed to be about giving users new powers—the power to "write" and not just "read" web content, the power to control your interactions with content through products like RSS readers. It was a subtle change that Facebook made, and the implication only became clear much later: you don't control what you see in your feed every day, Facebook does.

On Wednesday we had three more meetings with potential acquirers. The first was with FM Publishing CEO Deanna Brown. Since she was so busy that day, it had been scheduled for eight o'clock in the morning at FM's office, on Townsend Street in South Beach. It was so early, there were hardly any staff there when we arrived—certainly FM's founder John Battelle was nowhere to be seen. (I had to imagine he'd been partying the previous night with Web 2.0 Summit VIPs.) Deanna found a conference room for us to sit in, and we began talking through options.

Sean had warned me that FM didn't have the money to do a straight acquisition, so they would have to "get creative." I was skeptical, but since we were heavily reliant on FM for our ongoing revenue, it was at least worth a conversation. What Deanna suggested was a hefty advance in exchange for locking us into an exclusive three-year advertising deal. This offered a couple of advantages: one, I'd be able to pay out my ex-wife with the advance, and two, I'd continue to own RWW. However, the big downside was that it wouldn't solve any of my company's structural issues—I still wouldn't be able to hire US people as employees, for instance.

Afterward, I told Sean that the FM advance deal wasn't the solution I was looking for. He reminded me that we didn't currently have another offer on the table, so he advised to keep an open mind.

We also met TechWeb that day—including its CEO, Tony Uphoff, whom I'd gotten to know back in 2008. Tony had some enthusiasm for another bid, but I got a bad feeling when their numbers person began talking about all the steps and processes they'd have to go through with their parent company, UBM, before they'd be able to present an offer. This was what had sunk the deal with TechWeb back in 2008—constant delays with UBM and ultimately an offer that came up well short. I suspected it would be the same story this time round, so I didn't leave that meeting with much optimism.

As for the company I'd signed an LOI with in 2008, ZDE, Sean had not even gotten a response from them over the past month or so (I later heard that ZDE was laden with debt at this time, so acquisitions were probably off the table for them).

The other company we met that day was SAY Media, which I knew little about. Sean had told me it was an online advertising network, like FM Publishing, but that it also offered publishing services. As we walked to the meeting place, at the W Hotel just around the corner from the Web 2.0 Summit, Sean admitted he wasn't sure I'd like the fit as much as an O'Reilly or TechWeb. He was politely saying, don't expect too much from this meeting.

We met with two of their corporate development guys, Ken May and Kourosh Karimkhany. To my surprise, I liked the sound of what they were proposing. SAY already had a small portfolio of what they called "passion-based media properties." Currently these were niche blogs, including Remodelista, xoJane, Food52—none of which I'd heard of before. They had one tech blog, Pocket-lint, a UK gadget blog that I was vaguely familiar with. But they clearly wanted to expand their tech network. Kourosh said they were interested in acquiring RWW to become their flagship tech property.

I was intrigued, so Ken suggested we visit their office the next morning to meet their founder and CEO, Matt Sanchez.

It was Thursday, and I only had one meeting on my schedule: SAY Media at 9:00 a.m. The Web 2.0 Summit had ended yesterday, but with all the business meetings and M&A talk with Sean, I'd hardly noticed. I would be on a flight back to New Zealand that evening, so after the meeting, I planned to go back to my hotel and check out. Perhaps I'd browse some art galleries in the afternoon.

Overall, I'd been disappointed with how the face-to-face meetings had gone. Of the five companies we'd met, only SAY Media had seemed enthusiastic about acquiring RWW. I didn't know what to make of O'Reilly Media or TechWeb, but the signals hadn't been strong with either company. I didn't think GigaOm was serious about buying us, so I'd already dismissed them. As for FM, their advance-based proposal might help me pay out my ex-wife, but I didn't see much upside otherwise.

Like FM Publishing, SAY Media was located on Townsend Street— perhaps this street was where all the online ad networks worked, I mused. Ken met us outside the entrance and then led us downstairs to the SAY offices. We briefly shook hands with Kourosh before being led into Matt Sanchez's office. Matt was young looking (my guess was around thirty) and wore designer jeans and an expensive-looking checked shirt. He looked confident, but also somewhat reserved.

After a little prompting from Ken, Matt explained the history of SAY Media. Its origins were Matt's previous startup, a video-advertising network called VideoEgg, which had launched in 2005. That company had acquired the blogging network Six Apart in September last year (Mike Arrington broke the news), and the combined company was renamed SAY Media. I told Matt we were still on Movable Type, the publishing platform that Six Apart had created. He smiled and said that Ben Trott, the developer of Movable Type, now worked for SAY as its chief architect. Mena Trott, Ben's Six Apart cofounder (and his wife) was on the board of SAY.

Matt then explained that SAY was building a brand-new publishing platform called Tempest, which Ben oversaw. From the gleam in his eye, I could tell this was Matt's pet project. He said it was being built from the ground up for digital magazines. I didn't know exactly what he meant by "digital" magazines, but he said the platform would enable publishers to "create rich editorial experiences" that would in turn be attractive to advertisers. Tempest was still early in its development, but Matt said it would be easy to transfer RWW onto this platform, given that we were already using Movable Type.

I exchanged a quick glance with Sean at this point, since one of the big (and expensive) projects we'd originally slated for the end of 2011 was a migration from Movable Type onto WordPress. We'd put that project on hold while we explored an acquisition, but in one look with Sean we decided the WordPress migration was now canceled.

Matt reaffirmed what Ken and Kourosh had told us yesterday: that they viewed RWW as a potential flagship property. Since they were an advertising network, they would be able to replace FM Publishing's inventory on our pages. Although it was perhaps obvious already, this is when I fully realized that SAY Media was a direct competitor to FM Publishing. I'd been a partner with FM since 2006, and they had treated us well over the years. But if we went with SAY, it would be the end of that relationship. That would be a shame, but on the other hand, it would be a straightforward swap-out of FM's ads for SAY's.

By the end of the meeting I was enthused about potentially joining SAY Media, and it seemed like Matt was equally happy with what we brought to the table. As one of the leading tech blogs—still in the Technorati Top 100, albeit lower now at twenty-third overall—we would bring a level of prestige to SAY's blog network. We'd also become their largest blog property. As for us, I liked the sound of the new CMS, and I particularly loved the idea of not worrying about selling ads anymore. Certainly, it would solve my business-structure issues overnight if they decided to acquire us.

As Sean and I debriefed after, he noted that he hadn't discussed potential terms or deal structure yet with SAY. But he was pretty sure it'd be a cash deal, since SAY was a VC-backed startup. He was pleased I was happy with the SAY meetings and promised to follow up with Ken while I was on my way back to New Zealand.

I arrived home the day before the Rugby World Cup final at Eden Park in Auckland, between the All Blacks and France. It was a repeat of the final from the first World Cup in 1987, the last time the event had been held in New Zealand. I'd been fifteen years old back then, in my fifth-form year at school (the first year of exams), and had no idea what I wanted to do with my life. Now, I was forty and it was such a different world; the internet and the web only emerged after I'd left school. So I'd built a career—and a business—doing something that didn't even exist back in 1987. I was proud of this, even though 2011 had also been the toughest year of my life.

The All Blacks squeaked out their second World Cup win the following day, eight to seven, and the entire nation breathed a sigh of relief. I watched it by myself at home and drank too much wine. Over the next several days, I began to feel the weight of depression falling on me again—especially late at nights and in the mornings. I was lonely and not having much luck with dating (which had gone about as well as my business that year). To motivate myself, I read the Steve Jobs biography that had just come out. I admired that Jobs had followed his passions on his terms, regardless of what other people thought of him. I fancied there was a parallel in my own passion for tech blogging—a bit of a stretch, sure, but I was looking for ways to cheer myself up.

By the following weekend, Sean and I had a clearer idea of who was in and out of the RWW sweepstakes. SAY Media was definitely keen, and we were expecting them to make an offer very soon. FM Publishing was scrambling to come up with an advance structure that would keep us in their fold. Radio silence from O'Reilly Media continued, which was disappointing. GigaOm was either avoiding us or sending vague updates, so we didn't have high hopes there, either. The most frustrating, though, was TechWeb, with its usual slow process involving UBM. Sean wasn't getting much response from his contact, but we still hoped they would submit an offer.

On Wednesday morning my time, November 2, Sean and I had a video Skype meeting with SAY Media. It seemed like most of their executives were present on their side of the call, which took place in one of SAY's meeting rooms. It was Troy Young, SAY's president, who quickly took control and began outlining what their offer would be. Troy was in his mid to late forties, with entirely grey hair that was receding a bit at front. He had thick black glasses and a confident, sometimes brusque, way of talking. He'd worked with Matt Sanchez now for several years, going back to the VideoEgg days. But given Matt's reserved nature, I got the impression that Troy was the mouthpiece of the company in meetings like this.

Troy began by explaining that it would be a cash offer and there wouldn't be any earn-out clauses. This was music to my ears, since it was the earn-out fine print that had sunk my 2008 deal with ZDE. But then Troy segued into how much money SAY had available to spend on an acquisition like this, via its VCs. It was a number in the millions, but not what we'd been hoping for. "We know you value your business at more than this," he told us, "but this is all we have to spend." He noted again that it was a cash offer and that they wouldn't impose a revenue or profit target for earn-outs, since SAY would effectively be taking over the revenue side of the business. It was as clean an offer as we'd get. He finished by reiterating that they couldn't go any higher, so we should consider this their final offer.

The problem was that the number we were given was a low EBITDA multiple of our revenue, which Troy knew would be an issue for us. Even so, I was surprised he didn't try to massage the number some more—maybe tell us that this was the reality of what our business was valued at, given our stalled growth in page views and the current business climate.

The state of the economy was indeed delicately poised at this time. Although the US was no longer in the Great Recession of 2008 and 2009, growth in the economy had been sluggish throughout 2011 and the market was mostly downbeat. Just a few months before, Marc Andreessen had published his now-famous essay, "Why Software Is Eating the World." But despite his own bullish outlook for tech, Andreessen had admitted that he was out of step with how the public markets saw tech at this time. "Today's stock market actually hates technology, as shown by all-time low price/earnings ratios for major public technology companies,"[76] he'd written.

Troy didn't strike me as the kind of guy who sugarcoated things, and certainly there was a matter-of-factness about the offer he made. He knew as well as we did that 2011 had been a disappointing year for us and that this wasn't a good time for us to sell. Perhaps another company would come to the party and make an offer for RWW, but as a cash buyer for a small business that wasn't currently growing—and in a relatively down market—he knew that SAY held a strong hand.

We thanked the SAY team for the offer and promised we'd discuss it and get back to them as soon as possible. As soon as the meeting finished, Sean and I went to work trying to rustle up responses from the laggards in our acquirer list—ideally, we wanted a terms sheet from at least one of TechWeb, O'Reilly, or GigaOm, so that we had two offers on the table.

However, only FM came back to us, indicating that they would propose a deal based around revenue advances. FM didn't know that the other company was SAY Media, one of their primary competitors in the online ad market. I'm not sure it would've made a difference in FM's proposal had we mentioned it, but we also didn't want to upset FM— we'd been working with them for more than five years now, so it was important to keep that relationship positive.

While we tried to get more offers on the table, the following day Sean wrote back to SAY with our counter. We knew we couldn't push on the price (at least while we had no other offers), so we tried to improve our outcome in a couple of other ways. First, we wanted to keep the receivables and cash on hand (a not insignificant amount, in the several hundreds of thousands of dollars). Second, I asked for some stock in SAY Media as part of my employment agreement.

While we waited to hear back from SAY, our talks with FM Publishing progressed. They proposed two advance payments based on future revenue: the first would be in January 2012, the second in January 2013. It was two-year commitment and was highly dependent on page-view growth, since it would involve a certain number of ad impressions and content marketing campaigns. In other words, there was risk involved in accepting these advances. That aside, it was a decent proposal, and the total amount of the advances was more than what SAY Media was offering.

Other than the risks of not hitting our page-view goals, there were a few drawbacks with the FM deal. One was that I would have to pay a large amount of tax on the advances (since it was revenue), whereas I would pay no tax on the SAY payments (New Zealand didn't have a capital gains tax). Two, in my discussions with Sean, it quickly became clear that he wouldn't stick around if I inked a deal with FM—I knew he'd had his frustrations working with FM, but I discovered it was worse than I'd thought. I wasn't sure I'd be able to find someone as good as Sean to take over the FM relationship, and I sure as heck didn't want to do it myself. The third issue was that now years-long problem for my company: it would still be an NZ business, so I couldn't hire US staff full-time.

In addition to all that, I was mentally burned out by the tech-blogging business and I wanted a clean break. The FM proposal would lock me in for two more years of scrabbling for page-view growth. Did I want to sign up for that? No, I didn't.

We never did get a response from O'Reilly or GigaOm. TechWeb officially pulled out when we told them it was now or never for an offer—the UBM rep admitted they couldn't get a terms sheet prepared at short notice. So in the end the only real option was to sell to SAY Media or continue to go it alone; and I really would be alone, as Sean would most likely leave.

Even if the SAY offer wasn't as big as we'd have liked, it was clean, basically guaranteed (in that there were no financial or page-view goals to hit), and I was only required to do a one-year earn-out. Also, not having to pay capital gains tax in New Zealand was a rare win in terms of business structure. If we could squeeze out an extra several hundred thousand dollars via the receivables and cash on hand, then it would be an acceptable outcome for me—especially given everything going on in my life at this time.

In the end, it was an easy decision. SAY sent a revised terms sheet, and I signed it on Friday, November 11. Now I just had to hope the due-diligence process would be smoother than the disastrous ZDE due diligence in 2008.

When I arrived in San Francisco on Saturday, December 3, I was hoping to close the deal with SAY Media by the end of the week. Sean and I would be in meetings with them from Monday to Wednesday, and I would fly back to New Zealand on Friday (I'd added Thursday just in case it was needed).

The contract talks weren't as advanced as I'd have liked by this point. That said, I thought the SAY Media due-diligence team was much more efficient than what I'd experienced with ZDE a few years ago, and I was still hopeful the meetings would get us over the line. There were a few key points still to sort out: our request to keep receivables (to which they hadn't yet agreed), the termination clause on my employment contract being super-tight (since I needed to be working for SAY for at least a year to get the second half of the sale payment), and my own tax situation (as usual, I was paying accountants left, right, and center to figure this out for me).

Kourosh was put in charge of looking after me for the three days. He was relatively new to the company, having joined in August as its head of integration—his role was to help companies like ours settle into SAY. I soon discovered that part of his role was to devise editorial strategies for acquired companies, and it turned out that both he and Troy had opinions on RWW's editorial direction.

Kourosh was a good-looking guy in his forties who had a stylish dress sense. He usually wore skinny jeans with a brightly colored button-down and blue jacket, and his salt-and-pepper hair was slicked back. He looked exactly like how I imagined a Silicon Valley executive wanted to look; indeed, he'd worked at many of the usual tech media suspects throughout the years (*Wired* Digital, Yahoo, Condé Nast). I found that I got on well with him in person, although I felt underdressed compared to both him and Matt. Perhaps I'd have the budget to upgrade my wardrobe once this deal went through!

Despite the friendly welcome from Matt, Troy, Kourosh, and the rest of the SAY team, they did play hardball over the three days I was there. We didn't end up getting all the receivables—we eventually agreed that RWW would keep the direct-sales receivables (about $100,000 worth), but SAY would keep the FM receivables (over $300,000). This revenue had been earned before the date of acquisition, they said, and so it was needed to cover short-term staffing and other expenses. It was a fair point, but just one of a number of little things that SAY dug in about.

I also discovered they would not be giving all the writers full-time positions and in fact wanted to move most of them to a paid-per-post freelancer model instead of a set monthly sum. However, they did want a couple of writers based in San Francisco, so we discussed hiring Jon and Dan as full-time employees for those roles. We also discussed hiring Abraham and David full-time, and one or two of the channels team. Unfortunately, Robyn, Curt, Jared, and Tyler didn't fit into the structure SAY wanted. So while I was pleased for the people who would get hired as employees, I was disappointed for the others in the team.

Troy and Kourosh were keen to expand the scope of RWW's editorial vision. They wanted us to cover tech beyond just the web, so that we reached a wider range of tech consumers. They envisioned RWW covering hardware (like the gadget blogs) and even space technology. In one of our conversations, Kourosh mentioned that he was obsessed with nuclear energy—he sent me a Gizmodo article about Bill Gates funding a nuclear plant in China. "I'll make sure I study up on nuclear reactors," I replied, tongue in cheek. "Not sure I want them on my doorstep, personally, but agree those are the big tech challenges (energy in this case) that RWW can eventually tackle."

As part of this expanded scope, Kourosh wanted to change our domain name to ReadWrite.com. I said I'd inquired about buying that domain back in 2007 but had balked at the asking price of $75,000. I admitted I'd made the rookie error of telling the owner of the domain that I ran RWW, which probably accounted for the high cost. Kourosh asked me to forward him my email conversation and to leave this with him. (SAY bought it that very week by pretending to be a random person unconnected with RWW; they paid much less.)

During my week in San Francisco, our respective lawyers and accountants were working furiously behind the scenes to sort out the various legal and accounting issues with the sale. Of course, being an NZ company made everything more complicated (same old story!), but our US lawyer, Camille Linson, was doing an incredible job making sure we made progress. If it wasn't for her, I'm not sure I would've been in a position to sign on the dotted line by the end of 2011. But by the time I got back to New Zealand on Sunday, December 11, it did indeed seem like the sale would go through in the coming week.

I spent most of Wednesday, December 14, nervously waiting for my bank to confirm receipt of the first SAY payment. The announcement of the sale was scheduled for Thursday morning, and multiple news sites had been told under embargo. But I still didn't quite believe it was happening, so I wanted to see the money in my bank account to make sure I wasn't getting screwed. SAY's lawyer Jason Crain had confirmed to Camille earlier that day that he'd wired the money. However, the international banking system was prone to delays because of intermediary banks, so I was worried it would take a few days to show up.

I'd phoned the bank several times that day and had been checking my online account at regular intervals, but nothing had turned up. By 5:30 p.m., I'd resigned myself to not getting the confirmation before the embargo lifted. But I decided to check my bank account one last time. I logged back in, and then I saw it: a seven-figure deposit! I sat back in my chair, put my hands on my head, and exhaled. Needless to say, I'd never seen that much money before, and I was pleasantly shocked. It was real.

The next morning, I got up at 3:30 a.m. The plan was for the news announcement from SAY Media and a blog post on RWW to go up at 5:00 a.m. my time (it was a Thursday for me, but Wednesday in San Francisco). I would tell the editorial managers, Abraham and David, an hour before the embargo time, and then the entire RWW team a half hour before the news broke.

I stumbled into my home office, located directly opposite my bedroom, and switched on my iMac computer. While still rubbing the sleep from my eyes, I saw an email from January Machold, SAY's director of communications. She'd just discovered, via a Google Alerts notification, that a site called Adweek had broken the embargo. She said she'd called Adweek to try and get the story taken down but "wanted to give you a heads up ASAP so you can alert your staff."

That woke me up! I checked Skype and saw a panicked message from Sean. I flipped to Twitter and saw that the news was beginning to bubble up there as well. I was also getting DMs congratulating me on the sale. By 3:40 a.m. my time, TechCrunch had posted a story based entirely on Adweek's (the writer must not have gotten the embargoed news). This was problematic, since Adweek's story focused a little too much on SAY's hiring of Dan Frommer as a RWW "editor at large." So the messaging, at least from my side, was already out of whack. Dan was well-known in tech media as a former *Forbes* reporter and an early employee at Business Insider. I was pleased that SAY had hired him, but in my draft post I'd only briefly mentioned it. Now it was part of Adweek and TechCrunch's lede.

The breaking of embargoes was a known problem in the blogosphere at this time. The cynical goal was to get juice on social media before anyone else, as well as land the lead story on Techmeme. I found out later that it was an Adweek editor who had broken the embargo (the reporter profusely apologized to me). Regardless, I had a frantic back-and-forth on Skype with Sean and members of the SAY team. I hadn't even had time to get a coffee, but it didn't matter because I was running on adrenaline now.

Since members of the team were already pinging me individually about the news, I sent a group Skype message: "Guys, this wasn't how I wanted to tell you this, but someone broke the embargo on this story. It was due to go public at 8am PT. If you did see the Adweek story, the gist of it is true. RWW has been acquired. I will give you all the full details about this as planned at 7.30am."

By now it was time for my scheduled meeting with Abraham and David. I sheepishly confirmed the news to them and confirmed that both would become full-time employees of SAY Media. I promised we would have a proper talk later in the day, but I said I had to get our official blog post up ASAP. That I duly did, around 4:10 a.m. my time.

The meeting with the whole team went well. I apologized again that they'd found out about the sale via a broken embargo, but I don't think anyone minded too much. They were obviously more concerned about what this would mean for their jobs. I explained that SAY Media would be hiring some of the editorial staff as employees, and that everyone else would go on rolling contracts for now—the same as their current status.

Sean and I would have individual conversations with each person, I said.

The rest of the morning was a blur of emailing with reporters, talking to members of my team, and Skyping and DMing with people I'd not heard from in a while. I talked on the phone with my local newspaper, the *Dominion Post*, and arranged for them to come to my house at 1:00 p.m. for a sit-down interview.

By midday my time, the story of RWW's acquisition was at the top of Techmeme—and thankfully, my blog post had finally taken over Adweek and TechCrunch as the lead story. The *Dominion Post* crew arrived as scheduled and did a video interview of me standing in front of a built-in bookcase in my hallway. After I saw it later that week, I was taken aback at how exhausted and drained I looked.

The following morning, a Friday for me, I finally opened my paper journal to acknowledge the big change in my life. "A new chapter," I wrote, "I've sold RWW." Then, as had become my habit, I rolled a couple of dice across the pages of my journal to get an I Ching reading. How I interpreted these readings typically depended on what I had going on my life at the time—and, frankly, what I wanted the I Ching to tell me. For the reading I got that Friday morning, I chose to transcribe the following into my journal: "The sixth line, undivided, shows the overthrow (and removal of) the condition of distress and obstruction. Before this there was that condition. Hereafter there will be joy."

EPILOGUE

■ ■ ■ ■ ■

THE PRESSURE CERTAINLY CAME OFF me in 2012, but I still had a job to do as RWW's editor in chief. I traveled back to San Francisco for a week in February, during which I went to SAY's office every day like a normal employee, with Kourosh as my guide. I would also be relying on Abraham as my on-the-ground lieutenant—SAY had convinced him to move from Portland to San Francisco, and he began working at their office on the Monday after I'd gone home.

As for the others, David Strom had decided not to become a SAY employee, so his role as channels editor was taken by Fredric Paul (who'd spent about nine years at TechWeb). SAY also hired Ted Greenwald, another veteran of the eighties and nineties IT media era, as senior editor. But, to my disappointment, Kourosh decided not to immediately hire any of the writers as full-time employees. This was frustrating to me, since I wanted RWW to be the kind of place where a Sarah Perez or a Frederic Lardinois would want to work. (By mid-2012, both were full-time employees of TechCrunch—and are still there to this day!)

The two key writers I wanted to hire as employees were Jon and Dan. Fortunately for RWW and SAY, both were still young enough that they didn't mind continuing as contractors for now. But I objected to this decision because one of the main reasons I had sold RWW to SAY was to give the business more resources.

During my February trip, I did a "brown-bag" presentation to all of SAY's employees about RWW. This is when I unveiled our new editorial direction, which had been heavily influenced by Kourosh and Troy. The new mission of the site was as follows: "Cheap computerization, pervasive networks and the cloud will reshape the world. ReadWrite will be the most influential news source." The name change—we were dropping the *Web* part—was already firmly in the plans, primarily because we would be broadening our coverage area from web technology to technology in general. Our target audience would shift accordingly, from "engaged technologists" to consumer users of tech—"everyone from power users to people who just bought their first iPhone." The exception to all this were the channels, which would remain business focused (I wryly noted in the presentation that "they pay the bills").

To support the editorial changes, SAY Media had commissioned a redesign from their design team, led by Alex Schleifer. At the same time, the site would be moved from Movable Type to Orion, the beta version of Tempest.

I came back to the States in March, mainly for SXSW, and things seemed to be progressing well—other than the writer employment situation. I continued to bang the drum for both Jon and Dan, and in May I even reached out to Sarah Perez to try and poach her back. (She replied that the salary at TechCrunch was stellar and the AOL benefits were great, so she was happy where she was.) Jon got hired in June, but I didn't know what was happening with Dan. Indeed, I complained to Kourosh at this point that I was not being kept in the loop on daily operations—I hadn't known about Jon's hiring until he tweeted about it, and I didn't know what was happening with the redesign (its timeframes kept slipping).

Since this wasn't my business anymore, I didn't push too hard on being involved in the operational aspects of running RWW. I figured Kourosh would work with Abraham directly on the writer hires, and I didn't want to meddle on the redesign. I must admit, though, it bothered me to not be a part of the inner circle. It just felt odd, since I was the founder and RWW had been such a big part of my life for so long. But I accepted that this was part of the deal. Also, of course, my geographic location and time zone were factors.

To my great relief, I finally reached a settlement on my divorce in early July. Now it felt like the financial burden I'd been carrying over the past few years had been lifted. To celebrate, I took my first-ever extended tour of Europe that month—a solo trip including London, Barcelona, Rome, Florence, and Paris. It was a wonderful holiday, a real head-clearer, even though I got lonely by the end.

Before I headed home, I spent several days in the SAY office. But by then, things had begun to turn for both RWW and SAY Media.

Troy Young left SAY at the end of July. I hadn't had much contact with him in recent months, so I didn't think it would have much of an impact on me. However, when Kourosh left suddenly in mid-August—for the proverbial "personal reasons," we were told—I began to get worried. Not only had Kourosh been my main contact at SAY throughout 2012, but both he and Troy had (as I understood it) been the two main advocates for acquiring RWW in the first place. Now both were gone; what did this augur for RWW? Kourosh hadn't given me any warning of his departure, so it was left to SAY's CEO Matt Sanchez, with whom I'd had little personal contact, to tell me how it would affect my team. Matt emailed Abraham and me on the day Kourosh left: "Effective immediately, I am your point of contact for any support needs, budget approvals, etc.," he wrote.

Just over a month later, on Friday, September 21, Abraham abruptly resigned. This was a shock to me, as he'd moved to San Francisco for this job just seven months before. I phoned him as soon as I heard, and he told me he'd quit because he was disillusioned with SAY management. He sounded angry and frustrated, and also a little panicked for the rest of the team—including me. He said that SAY planned to significantly downsize RWW's budget and that they wanted to replace me as editor in chief before the ReadWrite.com relaunch next month.

I immediately emailed Sean, the only person other than Abraham who I was close to and still had a vested interest in RWW. I told him what had happened and that I was starting to get concerned about the second acquisition payment, due in December 2012. But after some back-and-forth with Sean, I said I'd hold off contacting Camille for now.

At the end of the month I had a call with Matt and SAY's lawyer, Jason Crain. I was given my notice. Matt told me they were replacing me with a US-based editor in chief. Jason assured me that the second payment in December would not be affected. But naturally, I was very concerned with this development. I immediately contacted Sean and Camille.

I had a trip to San Francisco booked in just a week's time, in early October for the Health 2.0 conference. I went ahead with that trip, but I did not visit the SAY office. While I was at the conference, we did a call with Matt and Jason to sort through the end of my contract. I found a quiet spot somewhere in the depths of the Hilton at Union Square, where the conference was being held. Sean and Camille were also on the call, and Camille did a lot of the talking on our behalf. I'd always been impressed with Camille, and I was so glad she was on my side that day.

In the end, the second acquisition payment was made in October and my contract ended with no fuss or acrimony on either side. To their credit, SAY Media didn't try to mess me around. On my part, I accepted that they wanted a local employee to manage operations from their US office. More importantly, this was clearly a sign that it was time for me to let go of RWW and move onto my next career adventure.

As it happened, the Health 2.0 conference inspired me to write my first book, about health technology, which I did over 2013. Even better, I finally got my act together about my own health. By early 2013 I had committed myself to the low-carb diet to help manage my type 1 diabetes (I still follow this diet today). The resulting book, *Trackers: How Technology Is Helping Us Monitor and Improve Our Health*, was published at the end of 2014.

The rebranding from ReadWriteWeb to ReadWrite, and the attendant switch in domain name, happened a week or so after I left the site. It was, in retrospect, a good way to mark the end of an era. My tech blog will forever be known to me as ReadWriteWeb. After that, it just wasn't the same anymore—literally, in terms of its name, but also in spirit.

Web 2.0 was well and truly over by the time I left RWW. There had been no Web 2.0 conferences in 2012, and by the end of the year, even O'Reilly Media—the company that had coined *Web 2.0*—had stopped using the term. It's no coincidence that during this time, there was an expectation in the public markets that the tech bubble was about to burst.

In a December front-cover profile in *Wired* magazine, Tim O'Reilly was asked if there was a disconnect between the tech world and the rest of the country. "Oh, absolutely," he replied. "I think people in Silicon Valley don't realize what a bubble they're living in. We saw that bubble get pricked in 2001, and it will get pricked again."

My guess is that by not promoting Web 2.0 anymore, O'Reilly Media was frontrunning the bursting of the bubble. The *Wired* writer, Steven Levy, then asked Tim about his latest credo, "Create more value than you capture."

"So many technologies start out with a burst of idealism, democratization, and opportunity, and over time they close down and become less friendly to entrepreneurship, to innovation, to new ideas," Tim had replied. "Over time the companies that become dominant take more out of the ecosystem than they put back in."[77]

Of course, he was describing what Web 2.0 had turned into: an ecosystem where several large companies dominated and the dream of democratization had turned sour. Just before I left RWW, Facebook reached the one-billion-user mark in early October. But the product was also riven with privacy issues; one of my last RWW posts, dated September 30, 2012, was an analysis of "yet another privacy controversy"[78] from Facebook, when old Wall posts from 2007 to 2009 were automatically converted into Timeline posts. The problem was that some of those old Wall posts were private in nature. Although a relatively minor controversy, especially compared to what happened to Facebook in the years to come, it was an indication that internet platforms held too much power over their users.

Developers were also starting to get screwed by Web 2.0. In September 2012, Twitter implemented restrictions on third-party use of its API. Suddenly, applications that had been built on top of Twitter's platform—including some that had turned into businesses—were not viable anymore.

While Tim O'Reilly was busy running away from the Web 2.0 bubble, another Silicon Valley insider, Marc Andreessen, was jockeying to position himself ahead of the *next* bubble. Andreessen, whose Web 2.0 company Ning had been a relative failure, had started a VC firm in 2009 called Andreessen Horowitz. By the end of 2012 he was arguably the most influential VC in Silicon Valley, with investments in the likes of Facebook (where he was a board member), Airbnb, Foursquare, Pinterest, and Twitter.

"The public right now hates technology, just hates technology," Andreessen claimed in December. "We're in a tech depression." He wasn't necessarily wrong about that: Apple stock was on a downward trajectory, and Facebook was trading below its May 2012 IPO price. But Andreessen was also heavily invested in tech as a private investor, and so he was motivated to talk his book. "Airbnb is gonna eat real estate," he said, referencing his influential essay from October 2011, "Why Software Is Eating the World." He added that "the smartphone revolution is really hitting its stride now"—and as a board member of Facebook, he'd placed a bet on that by approving Facebook's acquisition of Instagram in April.[79]

Many of Andreessen's market bets turned out to be true. The dominant companies of Web 2.0—Amazon, Apple, Facebook, Google, and Microsoft—not only entrenched their power over the 2010s but significantly expanded it. Meanwhile, startups like Airbnb and Uber "reshaped the world," to paraphrase the mission statement I'd helped create for the new ReadWrite in 2012.

So Andreessen was a winner from the tech bubble that emerged in the 2010s. I, on the other hand, had gotten out of the tech-blogging business before the new wave happened. ReadWrite also failed to ride the wave; the site was a shell of itself within just a year of my departure. I heard later that the domain-name change had been devastating to its all-important Google search ranking. But that didn't explain why ReadWrite disappeared entirely from the Technorati list of popular blogs—maybe that was because it simply wasn't popular anymore.

SAY Media quit the blog-network business altogether in 2015, when it sold off ReadWrite along with its other properties.

As the years passed, I grew increasingly concerned about the negative impacts of smartphones and social media on our culture. By the end of the 2010s, everyone (including children) had an iPhone or Android phone, and were constantly checking the likes of Facebook, Twitter, Instagram, and YouTube. The web was mainstream, and internet culture had taken over the world.

Most of the successful products and platforms of the 2010s had been launched during Web 2.0, and I'd helped chronicle their rise on my blog. But in later years, it became apparent that Web 2.0 blogs like mine hadn't written enough about the downsides of the democratization of media. I had always been a techno-optimist—no different from Tim O'Reilly and Marc Andreessen. So I'd perhaps been blinded by the shiny new consumer tools of the internet and didn't dig deep enough into what it was doing to society, especially the impact on my daughter's generation. She'd been born in 2001, so was part of the first generation to grow up a digital native. Looking back now, I wish I'd paid more attention to the internet's impact on her.

The irony, at least for me, is that nowadays blogs are passé in the culture. Social media usurped blogging early in the 2010s. That was hard for me to accept, since blogging had helped define not only my career but my entire identity. As the 2020s began, I no longer knew where I fit in the tech world. I'd tried to start up a new tech blog in 2018 (about blockchain, which would later have the term *Web3* foisted upon it), and I'd pivoted to email newsletters in 2019 (on Substack, a then-emerging platform in which Andreessen Horowitz invested). Neither of my projects gained traction. But that's okay: I'll continue to try different things as a blogger and a writer, and maybe I'll strike it lucky again one day.

Regardless, I'll always be nostalgic about Web 2.0 and the opportunities that blogging gave me back in the first years of the 2000s. Web 2.0 may've turned into a bubble over the course of that decade, and then turned darker in the following decade, but it had started out so innocently. It had been a way for me to become a creator on the web and not just a consumer, as I'd been in the dot-com era. What I created online, using blogging tools and web standards like RSS, eventually set me up for life.

Blogging also enabled me to find my community—although the camaraderie I'd felt with my fellow tech bloggers in those early years didn't last nearly long enough. By 2005 blogging had turned into a business, and we soon became competitors instead of friends. I even lost touch with the people who had worked for me at RWW. It probably says more about me than them, but I'm not in regular contact now with any former RWWer or blog buddy from that time. Once an outsider, always an outsider.

Regardless, I'm thankful that blogging, and my role in the emergence of Web 2.0, fundamentally changed me as a person. I'd been merely half a human before I started blogging—a young man with low self-esteem who didn't know his place in the world. Blogging was a lifeline, and I grabbed onto it. As I slowly grew my weblog into a thriving company, I also grew in self-confidence and began experiencing much more of the world around me. My online identity was developed through Read-WriteWeb, but it also helped shape—and indeed, complete—my offline identity.

The yin-yang was always more than a logo for me. I was a writer in Web 2.0, not just a reader. But that wasn't all. I was made whole by the web. Inside, I became the man I was destined to be.

ABOUT THE AUTHOR

RICHARD MACMANUS is the founder of technology blog ReadWriteWeb (RWW). Widely read globally, it was ranked among the top ten blogs in the world by Technorati and was syndicated by The New York Times from 2008–2011. In 2011, Richard sold ReadWriteWeb to San Francisco-based SAY Media and in 2012 left his job there as Editor-in-Chief to write books and pursue other media opportunities. As Read-WriteWeb's founder, he is widely recognized as a leader in articulating what's next in technology and what it means for society at large.

Bubble Blog, Richard's third book, was serialized during 2023–2024 at https://cybercultural.com, Richard's newsletter about internet history and its impact on our culture.

Richard's homepage is https://ricmac.org. He is active on social media and you can follow his ongoing thoughts about technology at https://mastodon.social/@ricmac. Richard is a New Zealander now living in the United Kingdom.

ACKNOWLEDGMENTS

I'm proud to be an independent author, but I couldn't have done it without support from some key people.

Kellie M. Hultgren edited the manuscript and provided valuable guidance during the publishing process.

The cover and design of the book was done by Kevin Barrett Kane, an award-winning book designer and typographer whose work I greatly admire.

Finally, thank you to the following premium subscribers of my newsletter at Cybercultural.com: Tobias Fank, Alex Iskold, John Musser, Susan Scrupski, Paolo Valdemarin. Your contributions helped cover the expenses for this project.

INDEX

NOTES

1   Sam Harris, "#290 - What Went Wrong? A Conversation with Marc Andreessen," July 21, 2022, Making Sense, podcast, https://www.samharris .org/podcasts/making-sense-episodes/290-what-went-wrong.

2   James Surowiecki, *The Wisdom of Crowds* (*New York: Anchor Books, 2005*).

3   Frederico Oliveira, "Ning!", October 4, 2005, https://web.archive.org /web/20051025080305/http://webreakstuff.com/blog/2005/10/ning.

4   "XSLT, 2004 goals, and general blather," Read/WriteWeb, November 30, 2003, https://web.archive.org/web/20040216103321/http://www .readwriteweb.com/2003/12/30.html#a177.

5   "It Is Not the Critic Who Counts," The Theodore Roosevelt Conservation Partnership, accessed February 5, 2024, https://www.trcp.org/2011/01/18 /it-is-not-the-critic-who-counts/.

6   "The Man Who Makes the Future: Wired Icon Marc Andreessen," Wired, April 24, 2012, https://www.wired.com/2012/04/ff-andreessen/.

7   "Random thoughts about Blogging Overload," Read/WriteWeb, January 31, 2004, https://web.archive.org/web/20050210171104/http://www .readwriteweb.com/archives/001795.php.

8   "Interview with Marc Canter," Read/WriteWeb, March 29, 2004, https:// web.archive.org/web/20040624214129/http://www.readwriteweb.com /archives/001818.php.

9   "I guess this makes me a journalist," Read/WriteWeb, April 19, 2004, https:// web.archive.org/web/20040701131714/http://www.readwriteweb.com /archives/001824.php.

10 Broadband Mechanics home page on June 19, 2004, via Wayback Machine, https://web.archive.org/web/20040619212911/http://www.broadbandmechanics.com/.

11 "Tim O'Reilly Official Bio," O'Reilly Media, accessed 5 February, 2024, https://www.oreilly.com/tim/bio.html.

12 Tim O'Reilly, "Inventing the Future," O'Reilly Media, 4 September, 2002, https://www.oreilly.com/pub/a/tim/articles/future.html.

13 Tim O'Reilly, keynote presentation at the Open Source Convention (OSCON) 2004, 28 July, 2004, audio recorded by IT Conversations, http://web.archive.org/web/20130729214320/http://itc.conversationsnetwork.org/shows/detail168.html.

14 John Battelle and Tim O'Reilly, opening keynote, Web 2.0 Conference 2004, 5 October, 2004, https://web.archive.org/web/20110630122407/http://itc.conversationsnetwork.org/shows/detail270.html.

15 "Lessons Learned, Future Predicted," panel at Web 2.0 Conference 2004, 6 October, 2004, https://web.archive.org/web/20050728121920/http://www.itconversations.com/shows/detail316.html.

16 "Lessons Learned, Future Predicted," panel at Web 2.0 Conference 2004, 6 October, 2004, https://web.archive.org/web/20050728121920/http://www.itconversations.com/shows/detail316.html.

17 "The Marqui Experiment," Read/WriteWeb, November 29, 2004, https://web.archive.org/web/20041208185508/http://www.readwriteweb.com/archives/002493.php.

18 "On story-feeding and lack of kick-ass post," Read/WriteWeb, January 01, 2005, https://web.archive.org/web/20050103033037/http://www.readwriteweb.com/archives/002610.php.

19 Michael Arrington, "Google Base Launched. Yuck.", TechCrunch, November 15, 2005, https://web.archive.org/web/20051124043349/https://techcrunch.com/2005/11/15/google-base-launched-yuck/

20 Jeremy Zawodny, "Blogs as the web evolves...", Jeremy Zawodny's blog, October 11, 2005, https://web.archive.org/web/20051107091446/http://jeremy.zawodny.com/blog/archives/005516.html

21 "Web 2.0 Workgroup," October 10, 2005, Read/WriteWeb, https://web.archive.org/web/20060115050008/http://www.readwriteweb.com/archives/web_20_workgrou.php

22 Dave Winer, "The Two-Way-Web," TheTwoWayWeb.com, accessed 7 February, 2024, https://web.archive.org/web/20010202130700/http://www.thetwowayweb.com/

23 Eran Globen, "There is no Bubble!", Supr.c.ilio.us, 19 November, 2005, https://web.archive.org/web/20060503160250/http://supr.c.ilio.us/blog/2005/11/19/there-is-no-bubble/

24 "Web 2.0 is Taking Over the Nation," Geek Entertainment TV, November 2005, accessed on YouTube, 7 February, 2024, https://www.youtube.com /watch?v=ObA-KB9Hjfc

25 Beth Kanter, "Joshua Schachter: Future of Tagging," Beth's Blog, November 13, 2005, https://web.archive.org/web/20060219085218/http://beth.typepad .com/beths_blog/2005/10/joshua_schachte.html

26 Robert Scoble, Transcript of interview with Steve Ballmer, Channel 9 Forums, July 8, 2005, https://web.archive.org/web/20051210104241/http:// channel9.msdn.com/ShowPost.aspx?PostID=85648#85648

27 John Musser, "Web 2.0 Principles and Best Practices," ProgrammableWeb, November 9, 2006, https://web.archive.org/web/20061121181437/http://blog .programmableweb.com/?p=467

28 John Battelle, "The Start of Something," FM Publishing blog, March 31, 2005, https://web.archive.org/web/20050404005722/http://fmpub.net/ archives/2005/03/the_start_of_so.php

29 Jason Calacanis, Propeller forum, June 2, 2006, https://web.archive.org/ web/20080704113701/http://tech.beta.netscape.com/story/2006/06/02/ hazards-of-the-new-online-collectivism/comment/253

30 "Netscape wears Digg's clothing - but underneath it's still a portal," Read/ WriteWeb, June 14, 2006, https://web.archive.org/web/20110830152230 /http://www.readwriteweb.com/archives/netscape_wears.php

31 "Episode 10: Digg 3.0 Launches – Interview With Founders Kevin Rose & Jay Adelson," TalkCrunch, June 22, 2006, https://web.archive.org /web/20111118055314/http://www.talkcrunch.com/2006/06/22/episode-10 -digg-30-launches-interview-with-founders-kevin-rose-jay-adelson/

32 "Digg stats analysis," Read/WriteWeb, July 18, 2006, https://web.archive .org/web/20060828081237/http://www.readwriteweb.com/archives/digg _stats.php

33 "about digg: frequently asked questions," digg, Wayback Machine copy dated June 2, 2006, https://web.archive.org/web/20060602153252/http://www .digg.com/faq

34 Kevin Rose, "Digg Friends," digg blog, September 2006, https://web.archive. org/web/20110718154904/http://diggtheblog.blogspot.com/2006/09/digg -friends.html

35 Bradley Horowitz, "Opening Up Yahoo!", Audio recording of Supernova presentation, IT Conversations, recorded June 23, 2006, http://web.archive .org/web/20130729204928/http://itc.conversationsnetwork.org/shows/ detail1636.html

36 Flickr Services API Documentation, Flickr, Wayback Machine copy dated 15 June, 2006, https://web.archive.org/web/20060615205834/http:// flickr.com/services/api/

37 BloggerCon IV audio recordings, Scripting News subsite, Wayback Machine
copy dated 10 January, 2012, https://web.archive.org/web/20120110041749
/http://bloggercon.scripting.com/

38 BloggerCon IV audio recordings, Scripting News subsite, Wayback Machine
copy dated 10 January, 2012, https://web.archive.org/web/20120110041749
/http://bloggercon.scripting.com/

39 PeopleAggregator home page, Wayback Machine copy dated 13 October,
2006, https://web.archive.org/web/20061013091120/http://www
.peopleaggregator.net/

40 "Google Office: a Micro Media bulletin," Read/WriteWeb, September 26,
2006, https://web.archive.org/web/20061017004346if_/http://www
.readwriteweb.com/archives/google_office_micro_media.php

41 Michael Arrington, "Odeo Releases Twttr," TechCrunch, July 16, 2006,
https://techcrunch.com/2006/07/15/is-twttr-interesting/

42 "Amazon Launches Elastic Compute Cloud," Read/WriteWeb, August 24,
2006, https://web.archive.org/web/20060903123804/http://www
.readwriteweb.com/archives/amazon_ec2.php

43 "New-look Google Reader Is Stunning!", Read/WriteWeb, September 28,
2006, https://web.archive.org/web/20070101025509/http://www
.readwriteweb.com/archives/google_reader_redesign.php

44 Alex Iskold, "Amazon Rolls Out its Visionary WebOS Strategy,"
Read/WriteWeb, November 03, 2006, https://web.archive.org/
web/20070103041621/http://www.readwriteweb.com/archives/amazon
_webos.php

45 "Web 2.0 Summit Wrap-up," Read/WriteWeb, November 10, 2006, https://
web.archive.org/web/20090916092142/http://www.readwriteweb.com
/archives/web_20_summit_wrap-up.php

46 Nicholas Carr, "Welcome Web 3.0!", Rough Type, November 11, 2006,
https://www.roughtype.com/?p=577

47 Michael Arrington, "TechCrunch Bashing Heats Up," CrunchNotes,
November 1, 2006, https://web.archive.org/web/20061111082533
/http://www.crunchnotes.com/?p=300

48 Steve Jobs, keynote presentation, Macworld, January 9, 2007, accessed
via YouTube, "iPhone 1 - Steve Jobs MacWorld keynote in 2007 - Full
Presentation, 80 mins," Protectstar Inc., https://www.youtube.com
/watch?v=VQKMoT-6XSg

49 "Announcing AltSearchEngines: Second Read/WriteWeb Network
Blog," Read/WriteWeb, June 4, 2007, https://web.archive.org
/web/20101021051834/http://www.readwriteweb.com/archives
/altsearchengines_launch.php

50 Alex Faaborg, "Microformats - Part 0: Introduction," Alex Faaborg's blog on mozilla.com, December 11, 2006, https://web.archive.org /web/20070105213628/http://blog.mozilla.com/faaborg/2006/12/11 /microformats-part-0-introduction

51 Brad Stone, "Facebook Expands Into MySpace's Territory," *The New York Times*, May 25, 2007, https://www.nytimes.com/2007/05/25 /technology/25social.html

52 Technorati "Popular Blogs" page, Wayback Machine copy dated June 24, 2007, https://web.archive.org/web/20070624124649/http://www.technorati .com:80/pop/blogs

53 "Beyond Blogs: Old & New Media Converge," Read/WriteWeb, October 1, 2007, https://web.archive.org/web/20071006163536/http://www .readwriteweb.com/archives/beyond_blogs_old_new_media_converge.php

54 O'Reilly Media, Web 2.0 Summit 2007 home page, Wayback Machine copy dated October 10, 2007, https://web.archive.org/web/20071010110410 /http://conferences.oreillynet.com/web2007/

55 Gary Vaynerchuk, "The Day I Decided to Become GaryVee," June 26, 2017, https://garyvaynerchuk.com/day-decided-become-garyvee/

56 Josh Catone, "Facebook Unveils Ad Strategy - Users Become Marketers," November 6, 2007, https://web.archive.org/web/20071209164831/http:// www.readwriteweb.com/archives/facebook_unveils_ad_strategy.php

57 "New Design For ReadWriteWeb," ReadWriteWeb, December 17, 2007, https://web.archive.org/web/20071218235609/http://www.readwriteweb .com/archives/readwriteweb_new_design.php

58 Marshall Kirkpatrick, tweet on April 22, 2008, https://twitter.com /marshallk/status/794526754

59 Bernard Lunn, "about me," Emergent Business Networks, accessed on 10 February, 2024, https://bernardlunn.wordpress.com/about/

60 Ken Fisher, "Ars Technica acquired by Condé Nast: the low-down," Ars Technica, May 19, 2008, https://web.archive.org/web/20080525201526 /http://arstechnica.com/news.ars/post/20080519-ars-technica-acquired-by -conde-nast-the-low-down.html

61 Kara Swisher, "Mary Meeker's Entire Bummer PowerPoint on Her Internet Outlook," All Things Digital, November 6, 2008, https://web.archive.org /web/20081109070211/http://kara.allthingsd.com/20081106/mary-meekers -entire-bummer-powerpoint-on-her-internet-outlook/

62 Marshall Kirkpatrick, "Introducing the ReadWriteWeb Guide to Online Community Management," ReadWriteWeb, May 14, 2009, https://web. archive.org/web/20090517013418/http://www.readwriteweb.com/archives /introducing_the_readwriteweb_guide_to_online_commu.php

63 EventBee, Quotes from ReadWriteWeb Real-Time Web Summit online ticketing, 2010, accessed 12 February, 2024, https://www.eventbee.com /view/readwritewebrtw#/tickets

64 Mary Meeker, "Economy + Internet Trends - Presentation from Web 2.0 Summit," Morgan Stanley, October 20, 2009, https://web.archive.org /web/20091023055300/http://www.morganstanley.com/institutional /techresearch/internet_ad_trends102009.html

65 David Ng, "Artist Ai Weiwei makes rare U.S. appearance to talk about digital activism," Los Angeles Times, March 15, 2010, https://www.latimes.com /archives/blogs/culture-monster-blog/story/2010-03-15/artist-ai-weiwei -makes-rare-u-s-appearance-to-talk-about-digital-activism

66 Jolie O'Dell, "Why SXSW Sucks," Jolie O'Dell's blog, March 16, 2010, https://web.archive.org/web/20100322231648/http://jolieodell.wordpress .com/2010/03/16/why-sxsw-sucks/

67 Marshall Kirkpatrick, "Facebook Rolls Back Some Key Privacy Changes," ReadWriteWeb, May 26, 2010, https://web.archive.org /web/20101225231933/http://www.readwriteweb.com/archives/facebook _rolls_back_some_key_privacy_changes.php

68 Liz Pullen, comment on "Real-Time Web Summit Photo Roundup," ReadWriteWeb, June 12, 2010, https://web.archive.org /web/20100724043752/http://www.readwriteweb.com/archives/real-time _web_summit_photo_roundup.php#comment-217427

69 Ashlee Vance, "Merely Human? That's So Yesterday," The New York Times, June 12, 2010, https://www.nytimes.com/2010/06/13/business/13sing.html

70 Michael L. Nelson, Web Science and Digital Libraries Research Group, July 5, 2010, https://ws-dl.blogspot.com/2010/07/2010-07-05-foo-camp-2010 .html

71 "Twitter Aims to Duplicate YouTube's Success," ReadWriteWeb, September 15, 2010, https://web.archive.org/web/20100918093035/http://www .readwriteweb.com/archives/twitter_aims_to_duplicate_youtube _success.php

72 Alice Neville, "Kiwi king of the tweets," NZ Herald, 3 January, 2010, https://www.nzherald.co.nz/nz/kiwi-king-of-the-tweets /RCJWSHD67D436YBSCRASKEWJNQ/?c_id=1&objectid=10618215

73 "5 Check-in Apps to Check Out," ReadWriteWeb, October 11, 2010, https:// web.archive.org/web/20101023003357/http://www.readwriteweb.com /archives/5_check-in_apps_to_check_out.php

74 Leonard Willoughby, "Every Day Tao: Self-Help in the Here and Now," published November 1, 2001 by Red Wheel / Weiser

75 Plexus Engine homepage, Wayback Machine copy dated November 13, 2011, https://web.archive.org/web/20111113162126/http://www.plexusengine.com:80/

76 Marc Andreessen, "Why Software Is Eating the World," Andreessen Horowitz blog, August 20, 2011, https://a16z.com/why-software-is-eating-the-world/

77 Steven Levy, "Tim O'Reilly's Key to Creating the Next Big Thing," Wired, December 21, 2012, https://web.archive.org/web/20121226041610/http://www.wired.com/business/2012/12/mf-tim-oreilly-qa/all/

78 "Sorry Facebook, This Was A Privacy Bungle! Here's What You Should've Done," ReadWriteWeb, September 30, 2012, https://web.archive.org/web/20121002205645/http://www.readwriteweb.com/archives/yes-facebook-this-was-a-privacy-bungle-heres-what-you-shouldve-done.php

79 Sarah McBride, "Andreessen denies Internet bubble, advises Times to stop printing," Reuters, December 12, 2012, https://www.reuters.com/article/us-venture-andreessen-dealbook-idUSBRE8BB1GZ20121212/

www.ingramcontent.com/pod-product-compliance
Lightning Source LLC
LaVergne TN
LVHW041208050326
832903LV00021B/522